W. H. I. (Wilhelm Heinrich Immanuel) Bleek

A comparative Grammar of South African Languages

W. H. I. (Wilhelm Heinrich Immanuel) Bleek
A comparative Grammar of South African Languages
ISBN/EAN: 9783337122317

Printed in Europe, USA, Canada, Australia, Japan

Cover: Foto ©ninafisch / pixelio.de

More available books at **www.hansebooks.com**

A COMPARATIVE GRAMMAR

OF

SOUTH AFRICAN LANGUAGES,

BY

W. H. I. BLEEK, Ph.D.

PART I.

PHONOLOGY.

LONDON:
TRÜBNER & Co., 60, PATERNOSTER ROW.
1862.

CONTENTS OF PART I.

	§	PAGE.
Preface		vii
INTRODUCTION	1–49	
I. Classification of South African languages	1–14	1
II. Short view of the literature of the dialects described	15–49	
1. Hottentot language	15–18	
a. Nama dialect	15	4
b. /Kora dialect	16	4
c. Cape dialect	17	4
d. Eastern dialects	18	4
2. South African Bâ-ntu languages	19–49	4
a. South-eastern Branch	22–32	5
aa. Kafir language	26	6
bb. Zulu language	27	6
cc. Se-tshuâna	28–31	6
dd. Tekeza dialects	32	7
b. Middle Branch	33–45	
aa. South-eastern, or Mosambique genus	33–34	7
bb. North-eastern, or Zangian genus	35–36	7
cc. South-western, or Bunda genus	37–42	8
dd. North-western, or Kongo genus	43–45	9
c. North-western Branch	46–48	9
d. Unknown Bâ-ntu languages	49	9
A. PHONOLOGY	50–397	
I. General characteristics	50–53	11
II. Consonants	54–240	
1. Clicks	54–73	11
2. Aspirated Linguals	74–80	15
3. Explosive consonants	81–119	
a. Faucal explosives	81–82	17
b. Guttural explosives	83–90	17
c. Dental explosives	91–107	19
d. Labial explosives	108–119	21
4. Fricative consonants	120–160	22
a. Faucal fricatives	122–131	23
b. Guttural fricatives	132–135	24
c. Labial fricatives	136–144	25
d. Dental fricatives, or sibilants	145–158	27
e. Semivowels	159–160	28

CONTENTS OF PART I.

		PAGE.
5. Liquid consonants ... ... §	161–165	29
6. Combined consonants, or consonant diphthongs	166–208	
a. in the Hottentot language	166	30
b. in the Kafir species	167–170	30
c. in the Se-tshuâna dialects	171–174	31
d. in the Tekeza species	175–181	31
e. in the Eastern Middle Branch ...	182–199	32
f. in the Western Middle Branch ...	200–206	34
g. in the North-western Branch ...	207	35
h. Combinations of lingual and guttural consonants	208	35
7. Nasal sounds	209–240	
a. Hottentot nasals	209–210	36
b. Bântu nasals	211	36
c. Nasalisation in Kafir	212–217	36
d. Nasalisation in Se-tshuâna and Tekeza	218–223	37
e. Nasalisation in the Middle Branch ...	224–233	39
f. Nasalisation in the North-western Branch	234–235	41
g. Nasalisation in the Hottentot language	236–240	42
III. Vowels	241–251	
a. in the Hottentot language	241–247	43
b. in the Bâ-ntu languages	248–251	43
IV. Syllables	252–260	
1. Simplicity of their structure	252–253	45
2. Nasal terminations	254–256	45
3. Consonantal terminations	257–260	
a. in Bâ-ntu languages	257	46
b. in the Hottentot language	258–260	46
V. Radical and servile letters	261–265	47
VI. Grammatical changes of sound	266–368	49
1. Phonetic influence of the Suffixes upon the Stem	268–304	
a. Suppression of the original terminal vowel	268–269	49
b. Assimilation of vowels	270–271	50
c. Transmutation of consonants ...	272–300	
aa. Palatalisation of labials ...	273–290	51
bb. Permutations of other consonants	291–300	56
d. Vowel Harmony	301–302	58
e. The Initial of the stem affected by the end	303–304	59

		PAGE.
2. Phonetic influence of the Stem upon the Suffixes ...	§ 305–319	
a. Assimilation of consonants ...	305–307	59
b. Vowel Harmony ...	308–316	60
c. Assimilation of vowels ...	317–319	62
3. Phonetic influence of the Stem upon the Prefixes ...	320–328	63
a. Adaptation of nasals ...	321	63
b. Depression of the vowel *a* ...	322–324	64
c. Coalescence of vowels ...	325–328	64
4. Phonetic influence of the Prefixes upon the Stem ...	329–368	67
a. Initial Vowels ...	330	67
b. Nasal Prefixes ...	331–364	68
aa. in Kafir ...	332–334	68
bb. in Se-tshuâna and Tekeza ...	335–344	69
cc. in the Middle Branch ...	345–353	72
dd. in the Kongo genus ...	354–364	74
c. Initial inflection in Mpongwe ...	365–368	77
VII. Intonation and Accentuation ...	369–378	
1. Intonation ...	369–373	79
2. Accent ...	374–378	80
VIII. Dialectical Transitions of Consonants ...	379–397	
1. in the Hottentot language ...	379	81
2. in the Bâ-ntu languages ...	380–397	81
a. Tables of transitions from the Kafir ...	381–387	
aa. to Se-tshuâna and Tekeza (South-eastern Branch) ...	381	82
bb. to the Mosambique genus (Tette, Sena and Makua) ...	382	83
cc. to the Zangian genus (Kisuáheli and Ki-nika) ...	383	84
dd. to the Bunda genus (Angola and oTyi-hereró) ...	384	85
ee. to the Kongo genus (Kongo and Mpongwe) ...	385	86
ff. to the North-eastern Branch (Benga, Isubu and Dualla) ...	386	87
b. Comparative Etymology ...	388–397	88
The name of God ...	389–397	88

PREFACE.

The history of South Africa, as far as it can be learnt from written records, does not extend beyond a few centuries back, and refers only to some small portions of the coast line of this continent. But there is another kind of historical research accessible to us, which embraces thousands of years of the bygone times of our race. From the facts brought to light by Comparative Philology and Ethnology, a knowledge can be gained—superior in its certainty to that of the historical record—of the descent and mixture of the different nations inhabiting South Africa, their consanguinity with and influence upon each other, their gradual breaking up into several tribes, or the confluence of different tribes into one powerful nation. We shall be able to learn by these means, whence and by what races South Africa was originally peopled, how they came into contact with each other, whether they peacefully commingled, or whether the stronger drove the weaker race victoriously before them. We may with some degree of certainty even ascertain at what periods and from what causes the different nations of each race were separated, and when and how their tribal subdivision took place,—each individual branch of a race fashioning in its own way what it had inherited from the common stock, with regard to language, habits and customs, religious ideas, and political institutions. Small in comparison with this grand history of South Africa, accessible to us by means of Comparative Philology and Ethnology, are the facts revealed by the traditions of the different tribes and nations, though they go in one instance at least (that of the Frontier Kafirs),* as far as eighteen generations back, and are all well worth recording.

There are some main facts established through the last twelve years' researches which stand in bold relief to the groping uncertainty till then existing with regard to African Ethnology.

---

* *Vide* Dr. Nicholson's notes at pp. 166-168 of Col. Maclean's "Compendium of Kafir Laws and Customs," No. 164a of Sir G. Grey's Library, Vol. I.

One is the North African origin of the Hottentots,* the other the extension of that class of languages and nations to which the Kafir belongs over all parts of South Africa known to us (with the exception of those inhabited by the Hottentot and Bushman tribes), and over the greater part of Western Africa as far as 13° northern latitude, extending in that region from the banks of the Senegal to those of the upper Nile.† This knowledge that the great mass of African languages is reducible to two families is mainly due to comparative researches which had taken as their basis the Hottentot and Kafir languages, as exhibiting in general the most primitive state of the two races, in speech, customs, &c.

Thus the two principal native races inhabiting the borders of this colony may be said to furnish us with a firm basis for the general history of the African races, as far as this can be gained by means of ethnological and philological comparisons. If, therefore, besides the practical advantage and political expediency of facilitating our intercourse with the different native races, a particular interest is attached to such philological and ethnological studies at the Cape, as forming our only extensive legitimate field of colonial historical researches,—the importance of the South African languages (and particularly of the Kafir and Hottentot) for Comparative Philology, or the so-called "Science of Language," cannot well be overvalued. Nay, it is perhaps not too much to say that similar results may at present be expected from a deeper study of such primitive forms of language as the Kafir and Hottentot exhibit, as followed at the beginning of this century

* The fact that the Hottentot language is nearer akin to North African languages than to those of the black nations of South Africa was ascertained independently and almost at the same time by different scholars,—for example by the Rev. Dr. J. C. Adamson (Journal of the American Oriental Society Vol. iv, No. 2, 1854, p. 448), by Mr. Logan (in the Journal of the Indian Archipelago, if I recollect rightly, about 1853), and by myself (De Nominum Generibus Linguarum Africæ Australis, &c., 1851, pp. 45-60).

† The late lamented first Bishop of Sierra Leone, O. E. Vidal, was the first who publicly stated that some of the languages of Sierra Leone (the Timneh and Bullom) belong to the Bâ-ntu family of languages (Introductory Remarks to Crowther's Yoruba Dictionary, 1852, p. 7). The same fact had independently about that time become clear also to other observers,—for example, to Mr. Norris (Prichard's Natural History of Man, 4th edition, edited by E. Norris, 1855, vol. ii, p. 421).

the discovery of Sanscrit and the comparative researches of Oriental scholars. The origin of the grammatical forms of gender and number, the etymology of pronouns, and many other questions of the highest interest to the philologist find their true solution in Southern Africa.

The forms of a language may be said to constitute in some degree the skeleton frame of the human mind whose thoughts they express. Sounds, too may be considered as forming the elements of language; and, the portion of my work relating to these has, therefore, some analogy to organic chemistry in its application to animal structures. Such phonological researches are of course necessary for any sound investigation into the nature of a language; but they have not that interest and practical importance which the exposition of the structure of the languages will present. The organic features of the languages, as they will be laid down in the following parts of this book, are in one respect especially attractive, since they afford the clue to the original mental tendencies of the two races, of which the Kafir and Hottentot are the most primitive representatives. For any one who has studied the subject, the dependence to a great extent of a nation's mode of thought on the forms of their language is a well-known fact. How dependent, for example, the highest products of the human mind, the religious ideas and conceptions of even highly civilized nations, may be upon their manner of speaking has been ingeniously shown by Max Müller, in his essay on Comparative Mythology (Oxford Essays, 1856). This will become still more evident from our African researches. The primary cause of the ancestor worship of the one race (Kafirs, Negroes, and Polynesians) and of the sidereal worship (or of those forms of religion which have sprung from the veneration of heavenly bodies) of the other (Hottentots, North African, Semitic and Aryan nations) is supplied by the very forms of their language.

The nations speaking Sex-denoting languages are distinguished by a higher poetical conception, by which human agency is transferred to other beings, and even to inanimate things, in consequence of which their personification takes place, forming the origin of almost all mythological legends. This faculty is not developed in the Kafir mind, because not suggested by the forms of their language, in which the nouns of persons are not (as in the Sex-denoting languages) thrown together with those of inanimate beings into the same classes or genders, but are in separate classes, without any grammatical distinction of sex. This can, of course, not be fully understood without entering into all the details of the grammatical classification of nouns and pronouns, and I must, therefore, refer for further explanation to the second part of this book, which will treat of the nouns, pronouns, adjectives, &c.

It seems here, however, important to point out the fact that not only the grammatical structure of the language in this regard was fixed, before the Hottentots separated from their North African cousins. The very tendency of the mind produced by the peculiar structure of the language, must to a certain extent have been settled before the period of separation. The lunar worship, which, according to Kolb, formed originally the main feature of the devotional practices of the Hottentots, renders it probable that their religious ideas already had a direct tendency in favour of sidereal worship before they were cut off from the more northern Sex-denoting nations.

The character of the Hottentot literature, as far as we are as yet acquainted with it, shows a singular agreement with the most primitive phases of our own literature. The personification of irrational beings, which is caused in the first instance by the structural peculiarities of the Sex-denoting languages, leads to that class of fictitious tales known as fables which form such a charming portion of our early literature. The Hottentot imagination seems to have been employed in the same direction; and many of the fables which have been collected from the mouth of the natives bear a great resemblance to parts of the poem of Reynard the Fox and other world-renowned fables. It is possible that one or more of these fables may have been derived from European sources, but the majority is certainly original; and the very facility with which those others have been adopted by the natives is a great proof of that congeniality of disposition in the Hottentot mind which we ascribe to common ancestry.

It is true, also, that in the legends of the black nations of South Africa animals are sometimes made to act and speak like men; but then, in general, this is less a real personification than a mere consequence of their religious belief in metempsychosis or migration of the soul, and intimately connected with their ancestor worship. The literature of the negro tribes has mainly an epical, historical or half historical character, relating the adventures of real men, varied sometimes by spectral phantoms or metamorphoses of men into lions or other animals. Witchcraft is, of course, here one of the principal moving agents.

I do not lay much stress here upon the fact that the law of composition in Hottentot poetry seems to be the same as that met with in the productions of the Semitic poets. The parallelism which in the Psalms and other poetical portions of the Old Testament takes the place of the rhyme, metre and alliteration of the Aryan languages, seems also to constitute the essential quality of Hottentot poetry. As a specimen I give the following song, furnished by Mr. Krönlein :*

THE ZEBRA.

Thou who art thrown at by the great (shepherd) boys,
Thou whose head the (kirrie's) throw misses!
Thou dappled fly,
Thou party-coloured one.
Thou who spiest for those
Who spy for thee.
Thou woman's thigh,
Thou thigh of jealousy!

Regarding the stage of civilization in which the Sex-denoting nations, (if this title is admissible) stood at the time of separation, it is probable (though by no means certain) that the use of domestic cattle had already been introduced. At all events it is singular that amongst the Hottentots as well as amongst the more Northern nations, the milking of the cows is woman's business, whilst amongst Kafirs and kindred tribes a woman generally is not allowed to touch the cattle, or enter the cattle fold.—(*Cape Monthly Magazine*, Vol. i, April, 1857, p. 207.)

It was my intention to say a few words regarding the nomenclature employed, and the principle of classification on which it is based. But as I foresee that this would lead me too far, I must defer it to an other opportunity, trusting that the terms which I have used are sufficiently clear in themselves to be understood without any particular explanation.

Extended introductory remarks were not required, as all the necessary information regarding the different languages,

---

* The Rev. G. Krönlein has already enriched Sir George Grey's Library with thirteen fables, thirty-two proverbs, five riddles, and five songs, all in Nama Hottentot, with German translation and notes. (§ 15.—Cape Monthly Magazine, Vol. xi. No. 65, May, 1862, p 316.)

and a detailed description of their respective literatures, has been given in the first volume of the catalogue of "Sir George Grey's Library." The literary treasures of this collection were, however, out of my reach, when I wrote this first part of my work. Amongst them there is perhaps not one work which I missed more than Livingstone's Analysis. (Vide § 30.)

I am aware that on this and many other accounts, the present work cannot but be in some degree deficient; but I thought it better, while I had the time and strength, to give those results of my labours which I considered would be useful to the student of these languages.

With regard to the selection of my sources of information, I am conscious that in general I have been sufficiently particular. Only in the case of the dialects of the Mosambique genus, I felt myself constrained to rely upon data furnished by a mere traveller; and here, therefore, my statements may be most liable to error. But this will not, I trust, be found materially to affect the rules laid down.

The reader will see that I have endeavoured to follow Lepsius's Standard Alphabet in general as much as possible. In some cases, however, the typographical difficulties were too great; and on this account, for example, *sh* and *tsh* had to represent his *s'* and *ts'*. In writing the aspirated linguals, I have ventured to add the χ (which sound is really heard in these letters) to the signs chosen by him.

For a comparative work of this nature, the adoption of a uniform system of transcription was almost a necessity. With reference to publications in the different native languages I may be allowed to say that a general agreement in their orthographies would indeed be very desirable; but I am afraid that under present circumstances an immediate change for this purpose would be connected with great practical inconveniences. Gradual alterations, however, with a view to ultimate uniformity, can easily be introduced with advantage.

Finally, I have thankfully to acknowledge the aid which has been afforded in the publication of this work by numerous subscriptions, among which I may especially mention those of the Cape of Good Hope, Natal, and Imperial Governments.

W. H. I. BLEEK.

Capetown, 18th June, 1862.

A COMPARATIVE GRAMMAR

OF

SOUTH AFRICAN LANGUAGES.

INTRODUCTION.

I. CLASSIFICATION OF SOUTH AFRICAN LANGUAGES.

1. It is the object of this work to give a comparative view of the structure of the languages spoken in *Africa to the South of the Equator*, as far as we are yet acquainted with them. These languages are, according to their structure and origin, divided into three classes. As representatives of these three classes we may name the languages of the Kafir, the Hottentot, and the Bushman.

2. The *Bushman* tongue is as yet too insufficiently known to allow us to assign to it its proper place in a general classification of languages; but it seems to be clear that its relationship to the Hottentot language is, at least, very remote. In fact, the probability is that it will be found to belong to what may be called the class of Genderless Languages. Members of this class seem to exist in almost all other parts of the world, and they interrupt particularly the contiguity of Sex-denoting languages, in Northern Africa (Bornu, Mandenga, &c.), Europe (Basque, Hungarian, Finnian, &c.), Asia (Tartaric, Mongolian, Dravidian, &c.) They occupy also some portions of America, and the whole Australian continent.

3. The *Hottentot* language is known to us in three or four different dialects, one of which (the Nama language) is represented by a large amount of missionary

literature. Its nearest relations are met with in Northern Africa, whilst its relationship to other South African Languages is, perhaps still more distant than to the Bushman Language.

4. The *Kafir* Language belongs to an extensive family of languages which occupy (as far as our knowledge goes) the whole remaining portion of the South African continent, extending on the Eastern side from the Keiskamma to the equator, and on the Western side from 32° southern to about 8° northern Latitude.

5. Members of this family of languages, which we call the *Bâ-ntu family* (§ 12 and 140), are also spread over portions of Western Africa, as far west as Sierra Leone, where the Bullom and Timneh languages are cousins of the Kafir. They are here interspersed particularly by members of the Gōr family of languages (Fulah, Wolof, Ga, &c.), which belongs to the same class of languages as the Bâ-ntu family, and forms together with it the African section of this class; whilst the Malay, Polynesian, and Papuan families are to be considered as members of the Oceanic section of the same class.

6. The chief characteristic of this class of intertropical languages is that the *pronouns* are originally borrowed from the *derivative prefixes of the nouns*, whilst in that class of languages to which the Hottentot, Egyptian, Semitic, and Aryan or Indo-European families belong, the *pronouns* are originally borrowed from the *derivative suffixes of the nouns*.

7. The former class is, on this account, called that of *Prefix-pronominal Languages*, and the latter the class of *Suffix-pronominal Languages;* both classes together are included in the group of *Pronominal Languages*.

8. Their main distinctive feature is a concord of the *pronouns* and of every part of speech, in the formation of which pronouns are employed (*e. g.* adjectives and verbs) *with the nouns* to which they respectively refer, and the

hereby caused *distribution of the nouns into classes or genders.*

9. This concord is evidently produced through the original identity of each pronoun with the respective derivative particle (prefix, or suffix) of the nouns which may be represented by it.

10. The different classes or gender of the nouns are, in the only family of Suffix-pronominal languages which has as yet been clearly made out, brought into some reference to the distinction of sex as seen in nature. They are, therefore, termed *Sex-denoting Languages.*

11. Among the classes or genders of the nouns in the Prefix-pronominal languages, only two have a decided reference to the distinctions observed in nature, being restricted to nouns denoting reasonable beings, the one in the singular the other in the plural.

12. That the derivative prefix and pronouns of this last gender (of personal nouns in the plural) are either actually *ba-*, or contracted, or in some other manner changed from it, is one of the characteristics of the *Bâ-ntu* family of languages, which have on this account been called *Ba-Languages* by Dr. H. Barth.

13. If we leave, therefore, the Bushman language, as too little known,[*] out of sight, we have here to do, on the one hand with a *South African species of the Sex-denoting languages*, and on the other with the *South African division of the Bâ-ntu family of languages.*

14. The former is represented merely by a few dialectical varieties of one and the same language (the Hottentot), whilst the latter is divided into three great branches, each branch comprising several languages which are as distinct from each other as, perhaps, English is from German, or French from Italian and Portuguese.

[*] A manuscript grammar of the Bushman language by the Rev. C. F. Wuras is in Sir G. Grey's Library.

II. SHORT VIEW OF THE DIALECTS DESCRIBED.

15. The most important *Hottentot dialect* is that of the *Nama-qua* (msc. plur. obj.) or *Nama-na* (comm. plur. obj.), which is still spoken by about 20,000 souls, and is the fullest in forms and the most original in structure. It is described in two grammars (Wallmann's in German, Tindall's in English, the latter being the best), and a large amount of missionary literature has been published in it. A few pieces of native literature are in manuscript in Sir G. Grey's Library; and also two grammatical documents, one by Mr. Josias C. Rivers, the other by the Rev. H. C. Knudsen.

16. The *!Kora Hottentot dialect*, which resembles most nearly the Nama dialect, is now nearly extinct. An extract of a grammar of this dialect by Mr. Wuras is published in Appleyard's Kafir grammar. A manuscript dictionary by the same author is in Sir G. Grey's Library, together with a manuscript revision of a catechism in this dialect, the published copies of which are defective.

17. The *Cape Hottentot dialect* has disappeared many years ago. Specimens of it are preserved in translations made previous to 1679, and published in Leibnitz's Collectanea Etymologica, and in Witsen's vocabularies (of 1691), published in Junckeri Vita Ludolfi. Both these texts and vocabularies were reprinted in the January and February numbers of the "Cape Monthly Magazine" of 1858.

18. In the *Eastern Hottentot dialects* only scanty vocabularies are now in existence; for Dr. van der Kemp's catechism (published in 1805 or 1806) which represented one of these dialects, has totally disappeared.

19. The *South African division of the Bâ-ntu family of languages* consists of one large middle body, occupying

almost the whole known territory between the tropic of Capricorn and the equator, and of two detached branches, one to the south-south-east and the other to the north-north-west.

20. In the *Middle Branch* the Eastern and Western languages offer distinct characteristics; and this branch is accordingly divided into two portions, each of which contains again at least two genera.

21. The Middle branch languages are, as a whole, distinguished by a greater softness of pronunciation, and by a tendency to mollification, which shows itself most strongly in the Western portion, and particularly in the South-western or Bunda genus. The members of the latter particularly offer, in comparison with those of the South-eastern branch, a strikingly opposite phonetical development.

Their main difference seems to be that in the languages of the South-eastern branch, the terminations of the words affect, almost exclusively, the preceding syllables, whilst in those of the Western portion of the Middle branch, the terminations are also varied in accordance with the preceding syllables. The prior tendency has particularly led to the palatalisation of consonants, and the latter to vowel-harmonic changes, and to an alliteration of consonants.

22. The *South-eastern Branch* consists of three distinct species, *Kafir*, *Se-tshuâna*, and *Tekeza*.

23. Of these three languages the *Kafir*, with its variety the *Zulu*, presents in general the fullest forms, and the most original features with regard to its structure, and the greatest melodiousness in its sounds.

24. The *Tekeza* is broader, and *Se-tshuâna* more guttural and less nasal, with darker vowels and less primitive consonants.

25. The *Kafir proper* differs from the *Zulu* less in the form of the words than in their idiomatic use.

26. Besides a great amount of missionary literature, there are three grammars of the *Kafir language* published by competent authors, Messrs. Boyce, Davis (who describes particularly the Ma-mpondo dialect), and Appleyard, and a neat little English-Kafir vocabulary by Ayliff. A Kafir-English dictionary is much wanted. A few pieces of native literature are in manuscript in Sir G. Grey's Library.

27. In *Zulu* a great portion of the native literature has been brought to light, particularly by the labours of J. W. Colenso, Bishop of Natal. Other pieces collected by the Rev. Dr. H. Callaway are in manuscript in Sir G. Grey's Library. Very useful grammars were also published by the Bishop of Natal, and by an American missionary, the Rev. L. Grout. Small Zulu-English and English-Zulu vocabularies by Mr. J. Perrin were published by the Bishop of Natal; and a large Zulu-English dictionary by Rev. J. L. Döhne was printed at Cape Town under the patronage of Sir G. Grey.*

28. The amount of dialectical variety is much greater in *Se-tshuâna* than in the Kafir species.

29. The *Eastern Se-tshuâna dialects* approach nearer to the Kafir and Zulu than those of the west.

30. Numerous missionary publications have been issued in one eastern Se-tshuâna dialect (the Se-suto), and in two western dialects, the *Se-roloṅ* and *Se-χlapi*. Into the latter the whole Bible has already been translated. The remarks in Casalis' Etudes give only scanty fragments of a Se-suto grammar, and Livingstone's Analysis (printed only in twenty-five copies) is of course not accessible to the general public. A manuscript dictionary by the same author, revised by Mr. Moffat, and a manuscript grammar by Mr. I. Hughes are in Sir G. Grey's Library.

31. The difference between the Se-χlapi and Se-roloṅ dialects is apparently not even so great as that between Kafir and Zulu.

---

* Its usefulness might be increased by the addition of an English-Zulu vocabulary.—A complete Zulu-English dictionary by the Bishop of Natal has just been published.

32. *Tékeza dialects* are known to us only through short vocabularies, the largest of which (referring to the dialect of *Lourenzo Marques* at the Delagoa Bay) is published in my edition of Dr. Peters' Mosambique vocabularies.

33. The *Southern Genus of the Eastern portion of the Middle branch*, extending over the Mosambique Coast and the Zambezi River system, is represented mainly by vocabularies, of which those collected by Dr. Peters, referring mainly to dialects spoken on or near the coast, are published, whilst those from the farther interior, collected by Dr. Livingstone, are still in manuscript in Sir G. Grey's Library, together with a few manuscript texts in the dialects of *Tette* and *Sena*, with grammatical tables of the latter dialect, and with specimens of conjugations in several Mosambique languages.

34. With regard to their phonetical characteristics, most of these Mosambique languages show only slight modifications (consisting mainly in contractions, abbreviations, mutation of more difficult consonants, &c.) in comparison with the structure of the Kafir language. Striking transitions of sound occur, however, in the *Makua* language.

35. In three of the languages of the *Northern Genus* of this Eastern portion of the Middle branch, extending along the Zanzibar Coast, books have been published, viz., in *Ki-suaheli*, *Ki-nika*, and *Ki-kamba*. The two former dialects have been described grammatically by Dr. L. Krapf, who has also published extensive vocabularies of these three dialects and of the *Ki-pokomo*.[*]

36. Also the *Hinzuan* spoken on Joana (one of the Comoro Islands) and described in Mr. Elliott's manuscript

---

[*] The *Ki-hiau* belongs more properly to the South-eastern or Mosambique genus. It is nearest akin to the Marawi, &c.

grammars and vocabulary, which are in Sir G. Grey's Library, belongs to this North-eastern or Zangian genus; and likewise the jargon spoken by the *Sidi* in Sindh, of which a short vocabulary is published by R. F. Burton.

37. The languages of the *Southern Genus of the Western portion of the Middle branch* are distinguished from the North-western or Zangian genus by a still farther extension and more striking application of vowel-harmonic influences affecting the terminating syllables.

38. Publications have been issued by missionaries in two languages of the South-western or Bunda genus, the *o Tyi-hereró*, spoken by the oVa-hereró, and the *Bunda* proper, or language of *Angola*.

39. The former, though now almost extinct, has only of late been made known through the labours of two Rhenish missionaries, one of whom (C. H. Hahn) has also published a grammar and dictionary of the language. Sir G. Grey's Library contains also valuable pieces of native literature in o Tyi-hereró, collected by the Rev. J. Rath.

40. The *Angola* (or *Bunda*) catechism, four editions of which have been published, represents the language as it was spoken two centuries ago. It was written by a Jesuit, F. Pacconio. Another Jesuit, P. Dias, has compiled a Bunda grammar, mostly with reference to this catechism. It is not known, whether more than one printed copy of this grammar is still in existence. A manuscript copy is in Sir G. Grey's Library.

41. Of the language of *Benguela*, which is quite distinct from that of Angola as well as from the Herero species, a vocabulary with a few songs, has been collected from the mouth of a liberated slave.

42. A *Londa* vocabulary compiled by Dr. Livingstone is in manuscript in Sir G. Grey's Library.

43. Among the languages of the *Northern Genus* of this Western portion of the Middle branch, the *Kongo* is the most important, and it seems to be well described in Brusciotto à Vetralla's grammar, printed more than two hundred years ago. A Kongo catechism, published in two editions before that time, is mentioned by Cannecattim.

44. A few grammatical remarks referring to the *Kakongo* language were published in Proyart's History of Loango, &c., nearly a hundred years ago.

45. The third known member of this North-western or Kongo genus, the *Mpongwe*, is accessible through a considerable amount of missionary literature, published by American missionaries, together with a grammar and vocabularies of the language, which in comparison with the more southern species of this genus, exhibits very broken and mutilated structural features.

46. The *North-western branch* extends along the coast from 1° to 4½° northern latitude, but in the interior it reaches several degrees south of the line and to at least 8° northern latitude.

47. The *Di-kele* is the only inland language of this branch, which is, as yet, represented by missionary publications, and described in a grammar and vocabulary.

48. The *Benga, Dualla,* and *Isubu* are three coast languages of this branch, regarding which grammatical works have been published, and portions of vocabularies of the latter two dialects have also been printed. A large amount of missionary literature exists in Dualla, and also, though less, in Isubu, which seems to differ only dialectically from the Dualla. In Benga a primer and catechism are the only texts known to us.

49. A vast amount of inland territory between 10° northern and 10° southern latitude, being wholly unknown, it may be supposed that numerous members of

the South African division of the Bâ-ntu family of languages will eventually be discovered here; and it is very possible that several new genera of this division, and perhaps even some new branches, of which, as yet, not a single dialect is recognized, are here still hidden from our view.

THE COMPARATIVE GRAMMAR.

A. PHONOLOGY.

I. GENERAL CHARACTERISTICS.

50. Regarding their primary elements the main difference between the *Hottentot* dialects and the languages of the Bâ-ntu family is that the structure of the former is *monosyllabic* and that of the *Bâ-ntu* languages *polysyllabic*.

51. This means to say merely that most words in the Hottentot language which are not monosyllabic are at once recognized as derivatives and composites; whilst in the Bâ-ntu languages such a reduction is, in general, even beyond the reach of deeper analytical researches.

52. This is in a great measure due to the fact that the syllables of a compounded or derived word in *Hottentot* do not cohere so closely together, nor do they influence and affect each other to such an extent as in the Bâ-ntu languages. In fact, the syllables of a Hottentot word stand more in juxtaposition, each having its own peculiar accent, than form a continuous whole, bound together by an overruling accent, as is the case in the *Bâ-ntu* words, in which almost every syllable of a word is more or less affected in sound by the syllables surrounding it, and has been brought into some accordance with it.

53. The tendency towards an easier pronunciation of the words which is visible herein is also shown by the abandonment in the *Bâ-ntu* languages of such syllabic elements as are more difficult of pronunciation.

II. CONSONANTS.

1. CLICKS.

54. In the Hottentot language, three fourths of the syllabic elements of the language begin with *clicks*.

55. Among the Bâ-ntu languages known to us, clicks appear only in languages adjoining the Hottentots, namely, in the varieties of the Kafirs species, and in the dialect of the Ba-yeye. It is probable that in both cases they are due to Hottentot influence, though none of the Se-tshuâna dialects (except the Se-suto, *vide* § 61) have been tinged with this phonetical feature, nor has the oTyi-hereró, another neighbour of the Hottentots. This may, perhaps, arise from the circumstance that these languages seem not to have encroached so much upon former Hottentot territory as the Kafir has, or they may only in later periods have come in contact with clicking tongues.

56. The two easiest Hottentot clicks, the dental and cerebral, have, without any remarkable modification, been adopted by the Kafirs.

57. The dental click | (∧ of Le Vaillant, $t^{\prime\prime}$ of Lichtenstein, — of Schmelen, · of Knudsen, ⟨ of Schreuder, *c* in Kafir and Zulu books, *q* in Se-suto) is in Kafir, as in Hottentot, "sounded by pressing the tip of the tongue against the front teeth of the upper jaw, and then suddenly and forcibly withdrawing it." (Tindall.) It resembles our interjection of annoyance.

58. The cerebral click ! (| of Schmelen, ' of Knudsen, ⋛ of Schreuder, *q* of Kafir and Zulu books, + of the Rhenish Missionaries,) is "sounded by curling up the tip of the tongue against the roof of the palate, and withdrawing it suddenly and forcibly." (Tindall.)

59. A third click, generally called lateral ‖ (V of Le Vaillant, $t^{\prime 2}$ of Lichtenstein, ' of Schmelen and Knudsen, ⋛ of Schreuder) is, according to Tindall, in Nama Hottentot generally articulated by covering with the tongue the whole of the palate, and producing the sound as far back as possible, either at what Lepsius calls the faucal or the guttural point of the palate. European

learners, however, imitate the sound by placing the tongue against the side teeth and then withdrawing it. This latter articulation, harsh and foreign as it is to the Hottentot ear, is, however, also that of the corresponding Kafir and Zulu click, which is in most books expressed by the letter x. A similar sound is often made use of in urging forward a horse.

60. The palatal click ≠ (Δ of Le Vaillant, t'^3 of Lichtenstein, ∩ of Schmelen, : of Knudsen, ǀ of Lepsius) is in Nama Hottentot sounded by pressing the tip of the tongue with as flat a surface as possible against the termination of the palate at the gums, and removing it in the same manner as during the articulation of the other clicks. This difficult click is rarely, if ever, employed in Kafir and Zulu words. (*Vide* Boyce-Davis, p. 4, where the *qc* is probably intended to indicate this sound.)

61. The occurrence of clicks in the Kafir dialects decreases, almost in proportion to their distance from the Hottentot border. Yet the most southern Tekeza dialects and the Se-suto have also (probably through Kafir influence) become to a slight extent, possessed of this remarkable phonetical element.

62. There is, further this distinction between the Hottentot and Kafir clicks, namely, that the latter are only found in the place of other consonants, and are used like consonants at the beginning of syllables, whilst in Hottentot a guttural explosive consonant (k, kh, or g), the faucal spirant h and the nasal n, can be immediately preceded by a click, and form together with it the initial element of the syllables.

63. The so-called harder or guttural modification of the Kafir clicks, which is generally indicated by a prefixed g, seems to be rather a guttural pronunciation of the click than a full guttural sound added to it.

64. In the *Bushman language*, even labial (and probably also dental) consonants are pronounced together with clicks, and *e. g.*, the Bushman word for " to sleep" seems

to be ǀphkoīnyé, beginning with a combination of dental click, aspirated labial, and guttural tenuis, in which three letters are sounded together. (Compare also the Bushman words for "louse," "food," &c.)

65. According to Wuras, however, the Bushman language has, what he calls, a labial click ⊗ to articulate which the tongue moves very quickly, like that of the performer on a flute.

66. He distinguishes also, a dental click peculiar to the Bushman tongue, > which is produced by pressing the air through the upper and lower teeth, which stand slightly apart.

67. Clicks are, besides, as far as we know, only found in one other African language, the *Galla**, a member of the Semitic family of Sex-denoting languages, and, therefore, nearer akin to the Hottentot than to the Kafir. The Galla language agrees, however, in its whole phonetical system, as also in the mode of employing clicks, far more with the Kafir than with the Hottentot dialects.

68. Clicks occur, according to v. Klaproth, also in the *Circassian* tongue; and two clicks are distinguished in the ǀiχe (⨶, *iche*) language, spoken in Guatemala, of which an old Spanish grammar is in manuscript in Sir G. Grey's Library.

69. Here the click expressed by the letter ⨶ is produced with the middle of the tongue, by withdrawing the breath within, and giving a little snap (castanetilla) in the beginning of the palate with the centre of the tongue, in such a manner that a sound is formed in the interior of the throat like as a guttural, if not something more in addition.

---

* I write this, subject to correction, for I have not one of Tutschek's publications with me, and see from Lepsius's Standard Alphabet that he has not noted any clicks in Galla. As I am, however, not the only one who believes that according to Tutschek's description, two of his letters indicate clicks, I think it right to draw attention to this point.

70. An other click is marked by 4, and pronounced with force by beating (slamming) the tip of the tongue, which is for that purpose drawn back sufficiently, against the upper teeth to their highest point. It is somewhat retarded or detained in its pronunciation.

71. One cannot say that these ǀiχe clicks are exactly identical with any of the Hottentot clicks; but the second 4, resembles mostly, the Hottentot dental click ǀ, and the first 4 the palatal ≠ combined with some guttural.

72. The drawing in of the breath appears to me to be a distinguishing feature in the pronunciation of ǀiχe clicks, though by Lepsius it is also ascribed to African clicks.

73. Whether some other sounds in ǀiχe are meant for clicks is doubtful; *e. g.* the *tq* which is to be pronounced with the tip of the tongue beginning to pronounce *t*, and ending in *z*, and by bringing quickly the tip of the tongue to the upper teeth. If this is a click, it is of course, one of the dental order.

---

2. ASPIRATED LINGUALS.

74. Next to the clicks, the sounds most difficult in pronunciation are the *aspirated linguals*. They are, however, found only in the languages of the South-Eastern Branch of the Bâ-ntu family.

75. In Kafir proper three letters of this class are distinguished, in Zulu and Se-suto two, in the Western Se-tshuâna one, and in the Tekeza of Lourenzo Marques, again, three, which seem, however, to differ somewhat from the Kafir aspirated linguals in pronunciation.

76. The first aspirated lingual $\hat{\chi}l$ (hl in Kafir books, ⸝ of Schreuder, tl of the Se-tshuana, tlh of a Lourenzo Marques manuscript, ^cl of Lepsius,) sounds in Kafir as if the sounds of the guttural fricative χ (like the German ch in "suchen") was pronounced in combination and at the same time with the lingual l.

77. The second aspirated lingual $\xi\chi l$ (kl in Kafir, clh of the Lourenzo Marques manuscript) appears, in Kafir at least, to be merely a stronger, or sharper, pronunciation of the first, in the place of which it always stands after a nasal, nor is it found otherwise. In fact, Appleyard is probably right when he says that it ought to be written khl (or $k\overset{c}{\chi}l$), the intermediate k between the n and χl facilitating in the same manner the pronunciation, as, $e.g$ the p does between m and t in the medieval Latin words "$assumpta$," "$redemptio$," or the t between n and s in Kafir words, as $intsapo$, children (plural of $usapo$, child). In Delagoa Bay this aspirated lingual occurs, indeed, without a preceding nasal; but we have already remarked that the pronunciation of the Tekeza aspirated linguals is different from that of the corresponding Kafir letters. The Se-tshuâna tl is, in fact, rather this harder $\xi\chi l$ than the first aspirated lingual.

78. The third aspirated lingual $\dot{\chi}l$ (ghl, jl, and dhl in Kafir books, ⸝ of Schreuder, thl of the Sesuto, dlh or lh of the Lourenzo Marques manuscript, 'l of Lepsius,) sounds in Kafir as if the aspirated palatal fricative $\dot{\chi}$ (like the ch in German ich) was pronounced simultaneously with the lingual l.

79. The aspirated linguals of the South-eastern Branch languages are, in other Bâ-ntu languages, changed into guttural, dental, or palatal consonants, and also into sibilants, pure, aspirated, or lisping.

80. Regarding the probable later origin of aspirated linguals by means of a gutturalisation of pure linguals, or in some other way, $vide$ § 208.

3. EXPLOSIVE CONSONANTS.

a. FAUCAL EXPLOSIVES.

81. The ǃKora dialect has, probably, the faucal explosive ȝ (the Semitic y, ȝaïn), if we are right in assigning this pronunciation to the sound indicated by Wuras (in Appleyard's grammar) by the letter *x*. In the corresponding Nama words this letter has generally been changed into the "spiritus lenis."

82. None of the South African Bâ-ntu dialects as yet known to us, seem to possess a faucal explosive, except, perhaps, the Kafir and Zulu, where we find "a peculiar hard, rough sound, which seems to be made by contracting the throat, and giving the breath a forcible expulsion, at the same time modifying the sound with a tremulous motion of the epiglottis," as Grout says, who marks it by *x́*, certainly, not in accordance with Lepsius' system, as he intended to do. The Bishop of Natal expresses it by x, and says that " it may be pronounced either as a guttural from the bottom of the throat, or as a click in a peculiar way."* We must acknowledge to be, as yet, at a loss regarding the sound of this letter which occurs only in very few words.

b. GUTTURAL EXPLOSIVES.

83. Among the explosives, those of the guttural class are the most common in the Hottentot language. They are three in number, *k*, *kh*† and *g*. Of these the *g* is least frequently used, though different observers vary considerably, some writing *g*, where others employ *k*.

84. Also in Kafir *g* is much less frequent than *k*, except after a nasal.

---

* He distinguishes it from the lateral click (§ 59) by using an Italic *x* for the faucal among Roman letters, or a Roman x among Italics.

† Krönlein assures me (in a letter) that this consonant (which he writes k^c) is merely a sharply aspirated guttural, and not the consonantal dipthong $k\chi$.

85. The aspiration of the latter letter is so slight in Kafir and, perhaps, even more in Zulu, that it has very rarely been distinguished in writing. If we are not mistaken, it is, in fact, rather a stronger aspirated pronunciation of the *g*, which brings it near in sound to the *k*, than really an aspiration of the *k*.

86. In Zulu the *g* is more frequent, but in most cases it is not exactly a *g*, but a floating sound between *g* and *k*.

87. In Se-tshuâna the *g* does not exist at all. The *k* of this language corresponds to the Kafir *ṅg* (§ 219); and the *kh'* of the Se-suto, k_χ of the Western Se-tshuâna (§ 174), to the Kafir *ṅk*; whilst the Kafir *k* has in the Western Se-tshuâna been mollified into the fricative guttural χ, and in the Eastern Se-suto dialect, into the faucal *h'* (both χ and h^c written *g* in Se-tshuâna books.) Kafir *g* has probably in Se-tshuâna been dissolved into the "spiritus lenis."

88. In the Northern Tekeza the existence of the not-nasalized *g* is very doubtful; *ṅg* is found here in place of the same Kafir letter; but Tekeza *k* corresponds, not only to the *k*, but also to the *sh* of the Kafir language. If an aspirated form of the *k* is distinguished in the pronunciation of the Tekeza, it has at least, not been indicated in writing.

89. The Kafir *ṅk* is entirely dropped in the Tekeza, and also in the dialect of Inhambane, the spiritus lenis taking its place; but in almost all languages of the Middle Branch, it becomes *ṅg*, which letter stands here also generally for Kafir *ṅg*, whilst *ṅk* is scarcely ever found,* except in the languages of the North-western Genus, Kongo and Mpongwe, where it is found occasionally. Also in Isubu and Dualla it is seldom met with, and in Benga it seems not to occur at all.

---

* In oTyi-hereró one missionary (J. Rath) writes in a few cases *ṅk*, whilst the other (C. H. Hahn) has constantly *ṅg*.

90. *G* is rare in the Middle Branch languages, and also in the North-western Branch dialects, except as a mollification of *k* and of *ng*, and even then generally only at the beginning of a word.

c. DENTAL EXPLOSIVES.

91. Next to the guttural explosives, those of the dental order are most frequent in the Hottentot language, and here the stronger *t* is well distinguished from the softer *d*; though there are a number of cases, in which some observers have heard a *d*, and others a *t*.

92. Also the Kafir language has both these dental explosives; but the Se-tshuâna has no *d*, and its *t* corresponds to the Kafir *nd*, whilst an aspirated modification of the tenuis *th* (*not* the lisping English *th*), takes the place of the Kafir *nt*.

93. In the Northern Tekeza the *d* is only found before *i* as a demipalatalized sound; otherwise, as in Se-tshuâna, the liquids *r* and *l* correspond to the Kafir explosives *t* and *d*, whilst the Tekeza *t* stands in the place of a Kafir *z* and Se-tshuâna *ts*.

94. Kafir *nd*, however, is not altered in the Tekeza; but of Kafir *nt* only the nasal *n* remains in the Tekeza.

95. In Inhambane, *d*, *nd*, and *t* are found, the *t* standing for Kafir *t*, *nt*, *χl*, *z*, and *nz*, though sometimes also *d* is found instead of Kafir *t* and *z*.

96. In Sofala, Sena and Tette, *d*, *nd*, *t*, *nt*, and also *tt* and *ntt* (stronger explosives) are met with, generally corresponding in use to the identical Kafir letters.

97. The same is the case in the Makua language, though here particularly the *t*, not unfrequently, represents the sibilant of other dialects.

98. In this, it agrees with the Coast language of the North-eastern or Zangian Genus, the Kisuáheli, where *t* and *nt* (and even sometimes *nd*) stand frequently for *z* and *ns* of the Kiníka and Kipokómo.

99. On the other hand, the *t* of the Kisuáheli, Kikámba and other dialects is changed, in Kiníka and Kipokómo, into *h*.

100. The original *nt* of the Kafir is generally only preserved in Kipokómo, whilst in Kiníka and Kisuáheli (as well as in the Makua language) it becomes *t*, and in Kikámba (and Kihiáu) *nd*.

101. The *nd* is more constant in the Zangian dialects, whilst the *d* occurs in Kisuáheli and Kiníka mostly in Arabic words; but it is, frequently indigenous in Kikámba and Kihiáu, which two languages seem, however, to have no *nt*.

102. The latter letter is also very rarely, if ever, found in the languages of the South-western, or Bunda Genus, being changed in o'Tyihereró (as in Kikámba and Kihiau) into *nd*, in Benguela (as in the Tekeza) into *n*, and in Angola (as in the Se-tshuâna) into *t*.

103. But in the North-western, or Kongo Genus the *nt* is retained, and corresponds in Kongo at least to the same Kafir sound.

104. The simple *t* and the nasalized *nd* are in all the languages of the Western portion as frequent as in the other members of the Middle branch.

105. But the unnasalized *d*, which is very rare in the languages of the South-western or Bunda Genus, whilst in the Kongo language it seems to be only found as a modification of the *r* of other dialects, is here written *d*, and has probably, a peculiar pronunciation (§ 165). In Mpongwe, however, the *d* is not unfrequent.

106. In the North-western Branch languages (Benga, Dualla, and Isubu), the *nt* is again discarded and becomes here (as in the Angola and Se-tshuâna) *t*, besides which *nd* is here very frequently met with.

107. Simple *d* is in these dialects (of the North-western branch) generally interchangeable with the liquids *l* and *r*, and corresponds, not rarely, to an original *z*.

d. LABIAL EXPLOSIVES.

108. The Hottentot language possesses both labial explosives *p* and *b*; but the former (*p*) seems to be found only in one case at the beginning of a syllable, namely in *pirip* goat, and its derivatives, as *Piriku* (obj. *Pirikwa* in the /Kora, *Pirika* in the Nama Dialect), the Be-tshuâna and Kafir tribes.

109. In Kafir both labials are found in their simple as well as in their nasalized forms.

110. The Kafir *p* is in Sesuto changed into the corresponding fricative *f*, and in the Western Se-tshuâna into the spirant *h*, whilst in Tekeza it generally disappears altogether.

111. The dialects of the Tekeza species seem to be entirely destitute of this labial tenuis (*p*); but in Se-tshuâna the *p* stands in the place of Kafir *mb* and *mv*, and of Tekeza *mb* and *mf*.

112. An aspirated *ph* corresponds, in Se-tshuâna, to the Kafir *mp*, which sound becomes *m* in the Tekeza.

113. On the other hand, in such cases where Kafir *mb-* is contracted from *mub-*, and corresponds, therefore, to Tekeza *mob-*, the explosive has prevailed over the nasal in the Se-tshuâna, which has retained here a simple *m*. For example, Kafir *si-m-buza* we ask him = Tekeza *tu-mo-botisa* = Se-tshuâna *re-motsa* (from χo-*botsa* to ask, *re-botsa* we ask) = oTyi-hereró *tu-mu-pura*.

114. The unnasalized *b* of the Kafir, generally retained in Se-tshuâna, keeps also its place in the Tekeza as the initial of the stem of a word; but in other cases it has, in the Northern Tekeza, been softened into *v*.

115. This is most generally the case in the Middle Branch languages, in which the *b* is either softened into the corresponding fricative *v* (rarely *f*), or the semivowel *w*, or it is dropped altogether. Where a *b* is here found, it does not in general correspond to the *b*, but to the *p* or

mb of the Kafir, or it is of foreign origin, as in many Ki-suáheli words.

116. Thus *b* is not unfrequent in the Angola, *b* and *bh* in the Kongo language. For example, Bunda *fuba* (meal flour) is the Kafir *impupu*, Tekeza *mûpu*, Maravi *ûpfa*; and Kongo *bhobha* (to speak, talk) is Hereró *pópa* (to warn, persuade).

117. In fact in the Kongo language simple *p* is rare, whilst in other Middle Branch languages it is generally more tenacious, except in the Ki-níka, where we see it sometimes changed into *v*, and in Ki-kámba into *w*.

118. Nasalized *mp* is most generally commuted in the Middle Branch languages into *mb*, which corresponds, therefore, both to the *mp* and *mb* of the Kafir. Yet in Sena and Tette we find occasionally *mp*, and also in Kongo. In oTyi-hereró, whilst one missionary (Hahn) writes always *mb*, another (Rath) has here and there *mp*, though in cases, where it does not correspond to the Kafir *mp*, as for example, in *ompura* or *ombura* (rain), Kafir *imvula*, Se-tshuâna *pula*, Tekeza *infula*, Inhambane *nvula*, Tette *vûra*, Mosambique *ipulla*, Ki-hiáu and Ki-níka *mfúla*, Ki-kámba *mbúa*, Ki-suáheli *mfúa*, Ki-pokomo *mfúiya*, Benguela *ombela*, Angola and Kongo *nvúla*, Dualla and Isubu *'mbua*.

119. The Mpongwe language, again, shares with the members of the North-western Branch the possession of all these labial sounds *p, mp, b, mb*.

4. FRICATIVE CONSONANTS.

120. Of fricative sounds, the Hottentot language possesses only the faucal spirant *h*, the guttural χ (Schmelen's *g*, Knudsen's *ch*, Tindall's *gh*, said to be pronounced like Dutch *g* in "gaan" and German *ch* in "lachen,") the sibilant *s*, and perhaps the semivowel *w*. But it has

neither a palatal semivowel (*y*), nor the labial spirants *f* and *v*.* In this poverty of fricative sounds it approaches very near to the condition of the Australian languages which are entirely destitute of fricatives, except the semivowels.

121. Among the Bân-tu languages, the Kafir exhibits, perhaps, on the whole the greatest number of fricative consonants.

a. FAUCAL FRICATIVES.

122. The faucal spirant *h* is found in few Kafir words, part of which are of foreign extraction. In others it seems to be a mollification from some other consonant, for example for *hamba* (walk) the dialects of Sena, Sofala, Inhambane, and the Northern Tekeza (Lourenzo Marques) have the form *famba*, and the Southern Tekeza (Ma-n!olosi) *kamba*.

123. In Zulu the *h* has, except in a few cases, a more aspirated pronunciation, like *h'*, or almost like χ.

124. In the Eastern Se-tshuâna (Se-suto) *h* rarely occurs, and seems then derived from a Kafir *k* (Western Se-tshuâna χ, *vide* § 135), whilst in the Western Se-tshuâna the labial spirant *f* of the Se-suto (corresponding to the *p* and *f* of the Kafir and Zulu) has been changed into *h*.

125. The *h* of the Northern Tekeza is similarly descended either from *nk* or *p*, and seems frequently to have been further softened into the "spiritus lenis." In the words of the Southern Tekeza which are known to us, this letter does not occur at all.

126. In the dialect of Inhambane the spirant *h* seems usually to represent a sibilant (*s*) and sometimes a *k*; whilst in that of Sofala it stands generally for *k*, and occasionally for a sibilant.

* Except in the pronunciation of the Orlams, who have softened the explosive *b* frequently to the fricative *v*, written *w* by the Rhenish missionaries.

127. In the Makua language the *h* has also come from a sibilant *s*, (*z*), *nz*, or the dental *t*; and this dental tenuis is in the Ki-níka and Ki-pokómo most frequently softened to *h*, and sometimes this is also the case in these dialects with regard to the labial tenuis *p*.

128. The *h* of the Ki-hiáu language is generally descended from a labial consonant, *f*, *v*, *p*, or *mb*.

129. In Ki-suáheli the *h* is of frequent occurrence, but mostly in foreign (particularly Arabic) words which have been introduced into this, and, in a less degree, into the Ki-níka and Ki-pokómo dialects.

130. In Ki-kámba and in the dialects of the Maravi, Tette, and Sena, the spirant *h* does not occur at all; and it seems to be entirely foreign to the Western languages of the Middle Branch (certainly to the Mpongwe, Kakongo, Kongo, and probably to the language of Angola), with the exception of the oTyi-hereró, where it is a sort of floating sound between *sh* and *h* (*vide* § 156) corresponding to the *s* (or *ss*) of the Bunda, Kongo, and Kafir.

131. In the same manner the Benga *h* is derived from an original *s*, as still preserved not only in the abovementioned languages, but also in other dialects of the North-western Branch, as in the Isubu and Dualla, which latter dialects are again destitute of the spirant *h*.

b. GUTTURAL FRICATIVES.

132. The Kafir guttural χ (*r* of missionary orthography), is found again in the Western Se-tshuâna (where it is written *g*), in the Tekeza (for certain in the Southern dialect of the Ma-nǃolosi), and also in at least some of the Eastern languages of the Middle Branch (for example, in the dialects of Sena, Tette, the Maravi and Ki-suáheli, where Krapf writes it *c*), and in the dialects of the A-lui, of Benguela and Angola (Cannecattim's *gʿ*, and perhaps also *hʿ*, represented by *hʿ* in the Bunda Catechism.)

133. But neither the oTyi-hereró, nor the Kongo and Mpongwe languages seem to have a guttural fricative, nor is it found in the North-western Branch dialects, the Benga, Dualla, and Isubu.

134. In those Bâ-ntu languages, in which this consonant is found, it is everywhere of rare occurrence, except in the Western Se-tshuâna, where it takes throughout the place of the explosive *k* of the Kafir and most other Bâ-ntu languages.

135. In the Eastern Se-tshuâna dialect (the Se-suto) this guttural has been changed into the aspirated faucal spirant *h'* (written also *g* in Sesuto books), which has occasionally been converted into the pure spirant *h* (vide § 124). This aspirated faucal is, perhaps, also indicated by Cannecattim's h^c (the *h* of the Bunda Catechism.)

c. LABIAL FRICATIVES.

136. The labial fricatives *f* and *v* of the Kafir, are very common among the Middle branch languages, whilst the more northern of the North-western Branch dialects, namely, the Isubu and Dualla, have no *v*, and very rarely use *f*. The Benga, however, has a *v* which is generally derived from an original *p*; but the *f* seems in Benga not to occur except in foreign words, as for example in *fato* stocking, probably derived from the Portuguese *fato*.

137. Among the Se-tshuâna dialects, the Eastern (Se-suto) has lost the *v*, but retained the *f*, which latter letter is, in the South-western Se-rolon and Se-χlapi, constantly changed into *h*, whilst the North-western Se-tshuâna dialects have a *v* instead of it.

138. In Tegeza, the *f* stands, not only for the same letter of the Kafir, but also for the *v* of this language; whilst the Northern Tekeza dialects have mollified the *b*, in the grammatical parts of the language and in some other cases, into *v*.

139. It may be said that the Tekeza in this regard, and in some others, has been influenced by the Middle Branch languages, where the same mollification is most general.

140. For example, the Kafir word *a-bâ-ntu* (people), Se-tshuâna *bathu*, Isubu and Dualla *batu*, Benga *bato*, Southern Tekeza (Ma-n¹olosi) *bânu*, becomes in the Northern Tekeza *vanu*, in Sofala, Sena, Tette *vánttu*, oTyihereró *o-vandu*, Nano *omano* (by assimilation from *ovano*, formed like *ova-lome* men).

141. This *v* has then further been softened down into the semivowel *w*, in the Maravi and Ki-pokómo form *wántu*, Ki-hiáu *wá-ndu*, Ki-suáheli *wátu*, Cape Delgado *wánu*; and it has been entirely dropped in the Makua form *attu*, Quellimane *antu*, Ki-kámba *andu*, Kiníka *atu*, and among the Western Middle Branch languages, in Angola *o-atu*, Kongo *o-antu*, Mpongwe *anwana* (children = Zulu *abantuana*, diminutive of *abantu*.)

142. If we may trust to Krapf's orthography, the Ki-biáu language has no *v* at all, and the Ki-kámba neither *v* nor *f*.

143. The latter letter (*f*) has also disappeared in oTyihereró* and Nano, but the more Northern languages of the Western side have it, as for example, the Bunda and Kongo. The latter language seems, however, to be without the *v*; but both labial spirants are again found in the Mpongwe.

144. The orthography of Portuguese and German writers, from whom most of our information regarding the Middle Branch languages is derived, renders it extremely difficult to know in all cases, whether the spirant *v*, or the semivowel *w*, is intended to be expressed; and it is, therefore, possible that, in this regard, the above remarks may be open to correction.

---

* Where it is commuted into S͡ʻ.—(*Vide* § 150.)

d. DENTAL FRICATIVES, OR SIBILANTS.

145. In a similar predicament we are with regard to the geographical distribution of the sibilants *s* and *z*.

146. Both letters *s* and *z* seem to be found in the dialects of Sena and Tette, but we have no evidence that they are distinguished in any other of the Eastern dialects of the Middle Branch, and the presumption is that only *s* is known to most of them.

147. Among the Western languages both letters (*s* and *z*) are found in Mpongwe, and, probably, also in Kongo and Angola.

148. The Nano language (of Benguela) seems to possess only *s*, whilst the oTyihereró has lost these sibilants altogether.

149. It has, however, two lisping sibilants ϑ^c (similar to the English *th* in "think"), and $\vartheta^{\prime}$ (similar to the English *th* in "this" and "that"), which in the missionary orthography are expressed by *s* and *z* (*s̰* and *z̰* in Hahn's last publications).

150. The softer $\vartheta^{\prime}$ which is also found in the Nano language, sounds sometimes much like *l*, and corresponds to the *z* of the Kafir and other kindred languages, whilst the sharper ϑ^c is descended from an *f*, as found in corresponding words of the Bunda, Kafir, and other Bâ-ntu languages.

151. The North-western branch seems also to have only the sharper sibilant *s*, as far, at least, as we are able to judge from the Benga, Dualla, and Isubu.

152. Among the languages of the South-eastern Branch the Kafir and Zulu alone have both *s* and *z*, but the Tekeza and Se-tshuâna dialects do without the latter softer letter, which is converted into *t* in the Tekeza (and also in the aMa-swazi dialect), and into *ts*, or *l*, and *r* in the Se-tshuâna.

153. The Hottentot dialects have only one sibilant *s*, being also destitute of the aspirated sibilant *sh*, the *s̃* of

Lepsius Standard Alphabet which I should have followed also in this instance, if not prevented by typographical difficulties.

154. This aspirated sibilant (*sh*) is found in Kafir, Se-tshuâna, and Tekeza. In the latter it represents Kafir ҳ*l* (*hl*) and *s*, whilst instead of Kafir *sh* we find in the Tekeza generally a *k*.

155. The *sh* is also found in most languages of the Eastern Coast, except in the Ki-kámba and Ki-pokómo, in which it seems not to exist.

156. Among the Western languages of the Middle Branch, the absence of *sh* is apparent in the Nano and in the Kongo language. It is doubtful in the Bunda, but certain in Mpongwe, whilst in oTyi-hereró (as in some New Zealand and other Polynesian dialects) an intermediate, or floating sound between *s* and *h*, takes its place (written *h* in the missionary orthography), derived in most words, from the sharper unaspirated sibilant of other languages (Kafir *s*, Angola *ss*, &c.)

157. In the dialects of the North-western Branch again, in the Benga, Dualla, and Isubu, no aspirated sibilant is in use.

158. I do not, however, include here such cases where an aspirated sibilant joined to a dental (or guttural, or labial) explosive, forms a palatalised consonant; as I shall treat of all such palatal sounds under the head of consonantal diphthongs.

e. SEMIVOWELS.

159. Regarding the semivowels *y* and *w* (particularly the latter), it is frequently very uncertain, whether they may be said to belong to a language, or not; for they are very liable to be expressed by the vowels *i* and *u*.

160. For example, Tindall enumerates them among the sounds of the Hottentot language; but in his vocabulary we find only one word with *y* (*yáp*, a rebok,) and two or three with *w* (*wa* all, *owa* return, and *swas* water barrel,

written by Knudsen *hoa, oa*, and *soas*, and by Schmelen *howa, oowaa*.) In fact, Schmelen's *w* seems frequently meant, not for the *v* sound, which it generally represents, but for the semivowel.

5. LIQUID CONSONANTS.

161. The Hottentot, as well as the Kafir, dialects are restricted to one liquid consonant for each language; but this is *r* in Hottentot and *l* in Kafir, Zulu, and the Southern Tekeza (aMa-n|olosi.)

162. The Se-tshuâna and the Northern Tekeza (Lourenzo Marques) have both letters *l* and *r* (the latter sound being most frequently descended from a Kafir *t*).

163. Among the Middle Branch languages, the Kikámba, Mbiza, and Kakongo agree with the Kafir in possessing only the *l*, and the dialects of Tette and Sofala, and likewise the oTyi-hereró, have only *r*. But both letters *l* and *r* are again found in all the other languages of this branch known to us; for example, on the Eastern side, in those of the Maravi, Sena, Inhambane, Quellimane, Mosambique, Cape Delgado, Kiníka, Kipokómo, and Kisuáheli (where *r* is however chiefly, or perhaps exclusively, used in words of Arabic origin); and on the Western, in those of Angola, the Kongo, and Mpongwe.

164. Among the dialects of the North-western Branch the Benga has only the *l*, but the Isubu and Dualla have again both letters, *l* and *r*.

165. With regard to the *r*, it is to be remarked that it is never guttural, but always dental (sometimes perhaps lingual), and approaches frequently in sound the *l* and *d* very nearly, as, for example, in the Se-tshuâna. In Kongo it is then written *d*; e. g. Kongo *sambuadi* (seven) corresponds to Bunda *sambuári*, oTyi-hereró *hambombari*.

6. COMBINED CONSONANTS.

a. HOTTENTOT COMBINATIONS OF CONSONANTS.

166. Of so called consonantal diphthongs, the Hottentot language possesses only *ts* (usually written *z*), if we do not comprise under this head the combinations of click with guttural, faucal, or nasal consonant (§ 62.) The so called palatal class of explosives is entirely missing here.*

b. KAFIR COMBINATIONS OF CONSONANTS.

167. In Kafir, on the contrary, the palatal sounds *ty*, *tsh*, and *dsh* (*j*) are of frequent occurrence.

168. In Zulu books, the *tsh* is frequently written *ty*, and etymologically this is perhaps, not wrong, though it does not always express the exact pronunciation.

169. We shall see afterwards, how in certain cases in the Kafir (and Zulu) language, a *p* and *mp* is, in the middle of a word, changed into *tsh* and *ntsh*, and a *b* and *mb* into *ty* or *dsh* and *ndsh* (§ 280). Also in other Kafir words palatal sounds can, by comparison with other dialects, be traced to a palatalisation of original labial explosives (§ 277), and it is doubtful whether, in any case, a Kafir palatal sound can be considered as primitive.

170. Also the combination *ts* is found, though it occurs not frequently without a preceding nasal in the proper Kafir language, and never in Zulu. The nasalized form *nts* seems to be derived from *ns*, the *t* being a mere help to the pronunciation. (§ 77.) That the simple *ts* is rather a foreign introduction, we are also led to assume from the fact of its prevalency in the Kafir female Xlonipa words, where it stands for common *d*.

---

* In the ǃKora dialect Wuras distinguishes a *ky* (written by him *kj*), which is found in a few cases corresponding to the simple *k* of the Nama dialect.

c. Se-tshuâna Combinations of Consonants.

171. In Se-tshuâna the *ts* is very common, and it corresponds here, usually, to Kafir *z*, and Tekeza *t*; but there is a general tendency towards this sound in the Western Se-tshuâna dialects, by which also other consonants (as aspirated linguals, or the simple lingual *l*, or hard guttural or labial explosives) may be commuted into *ts*. It can also stand merely for Kafir *ns* and *nts*, though the Se-tshuâna has also the nasalized *nts*.

172. Besides this, the Se-tshuâna has the *tsh* (*ch* of Se-suto, *c* of Se-χlapi books), which stands, usually, instead of the same Kafir sound. It also occurs, as a modification of the *ts*, in certain inflections (*vide* § 281), and in some cases it is used even where the Kafir has a labial sound; for example *tshuâna* (be alike) is the Kafir and Ki-suahéli *fana*, oTyi-hereró $ɡ^c ana$, Bunda *fángana*, Kongo *fanana*.

173. The other palatals *ty* and *dsh* do not exist in the Se-tshuâna; but when *b* is palatalised, it disappears altogether, before the inserted *y*, which therefore, corresponds in these cases, to Kafir *ty* and *dsh*.

174. Another consonantal diphthong peculiar to the Se-tshuâna, is the kh^c of the Sesuto, $k\chi$ of the Western dialects (both sounds expressed alike by *kh* in the missionary orthography, *kg* in some native manuscripts), which corresponds to Kafir *ṅh*, and seems to be originally a mere aspiration of the guttural explosive, intended to compensate for the loss of the suppressed nasal.

d. Tekeza Combinations of Consonants.

175. Though in the Northern Tekeza (Lourenzo Marques), the process of palatalisation is not carried so far as in Kafir, yet we have a greater variety of palatal sounds, the intermediate changes of palatalisation showing here very prominently its origin.

176. Thus we find in Lourenzo Marques *bdsh* corresponding to Kafir *ty*, and *mbdsh* to Kafir *ndsh*; e.g. *ribdshu*

(stone), Kafir *ilitye*, Seƛlapi *leintshue* (pl. *maye*); and *imbdshana* (little dog), Kafir *indshana*, Sesuto *ntshana*; and also *nambdshana* (little river), Kafir *umlandshana*, Se-tshuâna *molatshana*, from *nambo* (river), Kafir *umlambo*, Se-tshuâna *molapo*.

177. Then we find in Lourenzo Marques *mps* instead of Kafir *tsh*, as *ma-mpsa* 6. (new), Kafir *(a)ma-tsha*, 6. Se-ƛlapi *(a)ma-sha* ,Inhambane and Ki-suáheli *-pia*, Makua *-psia*, Sena and Tette *-psa*, Sofala *-psha*, Kiníka and Ki-pokómo *-fia*, Ki-kamba *-nsao*, oTyi-hereró *-pe*, Bunda *-be*. This shows evidently a descent of the *tsh* from a palatalised labial.

178. In the same manner, *ps* of the Lourenzo Marques, corresponding to a *z* in Kafir, indicates the latter's origin from an original *p*, as found still in Middle Branch dialects.

179. Also *tsh* is not unfrequent in the Lourenzo Marques. It does not, however, correspond to Kafir *tsh*, but to Kafir *s*; and it is (as from comparison can easily be seen) derived from an original *k*.

180. A *dsh* is once or twice found in the Lourenzo Marques, corresponding to a Kafir *k*.

181. *Ts* corresponds in Lourenzo Marques almost constantly to Kafir *t* (particularly before *i* and *e*) and *d* (particularly before *u* and *o*); whilst the *dz* of Lourenzo Marques is descended from a Kafir and Se-tshuâna *l*, when followed by *i*, or *e*.

e. EASTERN MIDDLE BRANCH COMBINATIONS CONSONANTS.

182. In the most Southern languages of the Southeastern or Mosambique genus of the Middle Branch, consonantal diphthongs are, in general, less usual.

183. In the dialect of Inhambane *tsh* occurs, not unfrequently, instead of Kafir *s*, sometimes also instead of x̌*l* (*hl*) and | (dental click) of the Kafir, corresponding, in the latter case, to a *t* of the Tekeza.

184. The softer palatals *dsh* and *ndsh* occur less frequently in Inhambane, where they are found corresponding to Kafir *nxl (ndhl)*, the *ndsh* also to Kafir *nz*, as *inyandshe* (fish), Kafir *inxlanzi*, Lourenzo Marques *nxlamfe*, Se-tshuâna *xlapi*.

185. In Sofala the *tsh* is of much rarer use, though also corresponding to Kafir *s*; but *dsh* is not unfrequent in the place of Kafir *z* (particularly before *i*), and *ndsh* in the place of Kafir *nz* and *nxl (ndhl)*. Once at least Sofala *ndsh* corresponds to an *ng* of the Western languages, namely in *vandshi* (elder brother), Bunda *pangi*, Kongo *mpangi*, Mpongwe *omwăngwe*.

186. In one solitary instance, *ty* is found in Sofala, namely in *batya moriro* (light a fire), Kafir *basa umlilo*.

187. A greater variety of consonantal diphthongs is again found in the dialects of the interior (Sena, Tette, Maravi), in which, again, combinations of labial sound with sibilant are found, though in these cases the sibilant is not aspirated.

188. Thus we find *ps* in Tette instead of Kafir *z* in cases where the dialect of Sena has retained the primitive *p*. In an other case, where both dialects (Sena and Tette) have *ps*, the Kafir has merely *sh*, whilst other dialects show the primitive simple *p* (vide § 177.)

189. The *bz* of Tette, when corresponding to Kafir *z* (and Sena *dz*), seems to be merely a mollification of the *ps*. In other cases it corresponds to Kafir *s*, whilst the Sena has the unpalatalised *bv*. In several instances Tette and Sena *bz* is found in the place of Kafir *ty*. In one word the dialect of Sena has *bz* for Kafir *zw*, namely *ribze* (voice, word), Kafir *ilizwi*, Sesuto *leintsue*, Lourenzo Marques *rito*, Inhambane *lito*, Mosambique *inzú* (pl. *mazu*), Angola *risui* (pl. *masui*).

190. The combinations *ts* and *dz* occur in Sena, Tette and Maravi, corresponding to Kafir *nts*, *nz* and *z*.

191. The aspirated *tsh* is found in Tette and Sena (which has also *dsh*) instead of Kafir *s* (before *i*) and the

more primitive *k* of some other Middle Branch languages, whilst the Maravi has, in these instances, either the intermediate *ksh*, or the more palatal sounds *ty* and *dy*.

192. Also labial combinations occur in these dialects, as *bf* (or *pf*) in Sena and Tette in the place of Kafir *f*, and *bv** in Sena and Maravi instead of Kafir *v* and Zulu *zw*.

193. A gutturalised labial occurs in the Maravi word *mpχanga*, brother.

194. The combination *ps* occurs in the Mosambique Makua word for "new" (§ 177), and *bz* in one other word of this language.

195. The Cape Delgado dialect of the Kisuáheli offers one instance of the use of *mps*, and a few cases of words with *bv*.

196. Otherwise the languages of the North-eastern or Zangian genus known to us, do not offer any instance of a combination of labials with palatals or sibilants.

197. The palatal *tsh* (mostly derived from *k*, and corresponding to Kafir *s*) occurs in the Makua dialects of Quellimane and Mosambique, in the Kisuáheli dialects of Cape Delgado and Mombas, and in the Ki-hiáu, where Krapf writes it *tj*.

198. The softer *dsh* (*j*) is not only found in these dialects, but also in the Kiníka, Kikámba and Kipokómo. It is found here also nasalised.

199. The Kisuáheli and Kiníka dialects distinguish besides also the *dy* (written *j̣* by Krapf) and *ndy*.

f. WESTERN MIDDLE BRANCH COMBINATIONS OF CONSONANTS.

200. On the Western coast, the palatal sounds, or consonantal diphthongs are comparatively few.

201. The oTyihereró has, indeed, even the labial palatals *py* and *mby*, but they occur extremely seldom.

---

* I am not quite certain, whether the *v* does not here indicate the semivowel *w*. (*Vide* § 144.)

202. Frequent are, however, in this language, palatal sounds descended from gutturals, namely *ty* and *ndy* (Hahn's *k'* and *ng'*) which, like the Zulu *ty*, have a tendency to be pronounced as *tsh* and *ndsh*.*

203. Also in Nano (Benguela) *ty* and *ndy* are found; but whether the language of Angola possesses similar palatal sounds is doubtful.

204. The old Kongo language keeps entirely clear from palatal sounds, or any other consonantal diphthongs.

205. The modernised state of the Mpongwe language is sufficiently shewn in its possessing, not only, the palatals *dsh*, *ndsh* and *nty*, but also the palatalised soft sibilant *zy*.

206. The Mpongwe has also a labial sound, intermediate between *f*, *v* and *w*, usually written *fw* or *vw*, which is probably similar in pronunciation to the *bv* noted above (§ 192).

g. NORTH-WESTERN BRANCH COMBINATIONS OF CONSONANTS.

207. In the North-western Branch, the palatal *dsh* (*j*), with *ndsh* (*nj*), occurs in Benga, Dualla, and Isubu, which latter dialect has also the intermediate forms *gy* and *dy*, whilst in the Benga again the labial combination *bw* is found.

h. COMBINATIONS OF LINGUAL AND GUTTURAL CONSONANTS.

208. It is possible that the so-called aspirated linguals may also not improperly be considered as consonantal diphthongs. Very frequently their origin seems indeed to be that of a lingualised guttural, or of a gutturalised lingual. For example, Kafir *ҳlala* (sit) seems derived from Inhambane and Mosambique *kala*, Sofala *gara*, Tette, Sena, and Maravi *kára*, Cape Delgado *ikála*, Ki-suáheli *ká*, Ki-níka *sagala*, Ki-kámba *ikala*, Ki-pokómo

---

* In his last publications Hahn distinguishes also the semipalatised letters *t* and *d*, as he writes them, and the nasalised *nd*. The latter represents here also the *ndɜ'* (*ndz*) of his grammar. (*Vide* § 230.)

kaa, oTyi-hereró *kara*, Angola *kàla*, Kongo *ikala*, Dualla *ga* or *dsha*, Isubu *gya* or *dsha*. The Kongo and Kikamba form seems here the most primitive, and from it (by a change produced by assimilation, the initial guttural becoming an aspirated lingual) the Kafir form may have descended.

7. NASAL SOUNDS.

a. HOTTENTOT NASALS.

209. A distinguishing trait of the Hottentot language is also its small variety of clear nasal consonants.

210. The Hottentot language is mainly restricted to the dental nasal *n* and to the labial *m*; and these nasals are not found before other consonants at the beginning of a syllable, but they either immediately precede a vowel, or follow it, closing the syllable. In the latter position, also, the guttural nasal *ṅ* is met with, though exceedingly rarely. At the beginning of a syllable, however, the dental nasal *n* can (like the guttural explosives and the faucal spirant) have a click before it. (§ 62.)

b. BÂ-NTU NASALS.

211. The Bântu languages have at once a greater variety of nasal consonants, and they are here made to precede most other consonants at the beginning of a syllable.

c. NASALISATION IN KAFIR.

212. This is particularly the case in the most primitive types of these languages; for example, in the Kafir.

213. Here we find not only the simple *n* and *m*, and the palatalised *ny* beginning syllables, but all other consonants (except *h*, *χ*, *sh*, and *l*) can be preceded by a nasal.

214. This initial nasal is the guttural *ṅ* (which is, however, in Kafir and Zulu books always written *n*) before the guttural consonants (as *ṅk* and *ṅg*), the aspi-

rated lingual (as n'x̯l), and of course also before the guttural pronunciation of the clicks (as ṅ|, ṅ‖, ṅ!, vide § 63); whilst the labial m is constantly found before labial consonants, (as mp, mb, mv, mf); and whenever, in the course of grammatical formation, the dental nasal is put before a guttural or labial consonant, it is changed, respectively into the guttural or labial nasal.

215. The dental nasal n is, therefore, only found before dental explosives (as nt and nd) and fricatives (as ns and nz), pure palatals as (nty, ntsh, ndsh, nx̯l,)* and clicks (as n,| n‖, n/).

216. When n comes to stand before s and sh, a t is inserted, so as to produce the combinations nts and ntsh. (§ 170.) Before h and l, the nasal is usually dropped.

217. This nasalisation of consonants is a very ancient characteristic of the Kafir language, which has frequently been lost in more modernised Bâ-ntu languages; whilst the employment of an initial labial nasal m before all consonants, of whatever order, is a recent feature, and has evidently arisen from the suppression of some vowel (most generally u) which is still visible in most cognate dialects. In fact, a sort of indistinct vowel sound may still be said to be heard with this initial m, separating it to such an extent, from the following consonant, as to prevent its influencing or being influenced by the latter.

d. NASALISATION IN SE-TSHUÂNA AND TEKEZA.

218. Whilst the Se-tshuâna and Tekeza have in the lastmentioned cases, by the retention of the vowel (which

---

* It is a misprint in Hahn's Hereró Grammar, p. 3, when in the system of consonants given there according to my arrangement, the palatal nasal is ma 'e to precede the palatal media. It ought to be nǵ (i.e. ndy) instead of n'y' (i.e. nydy). Besides the n m, n̈ and n' (ny), Hahn distinguishes in his latest Hereró publications also an n̰, a nicety of pronunciation which is observed by him alone. This n̰ seems to be lingual, as it is said to be pronounced broadly, the tongue being pressed flat against the palate.

is in Kafir here suppressed or made indistinct) after *m*, avoided even the semblance of an indiscriminate labial nasalisation of initial consonants;—the Se-tshuâna has, on the other hand, almost entirely suppressed the ancient initial nasalisation of consonants. Only in few cases (and these mostly monosyllables) it has retained such initial nasals preceding other consonants; but in general, the nasal has disappeared, leaving however, traces of its influence upon the consonant which was preceded by it, and which has generally assumed a somewhat altered form.

219. Thus we find as a general rule that a transition take place in the South-eastern Branch from

Kafir nasalised tenuis..	*ṅk*	*mp mf*	*nt*
to Se-tshuâna aspirated tenuis................................	*kχ*, or *kh^c (kh)*	*ph*	*th*
from Kafir nasalised media....................................	*ṅg*	*mb mv*	*nd*
to Se-tshuâna simple tenuis...................................	*k*	*p*	*t*
from Kafir nasalised aspirated lingual, or palatal........	*ṅx̱l (ṅkl)*	*nx̱l (ṅdhl)*	*ntsh ndsh (nj)*
to Se-tshuâna simple aspirated lingual, or palatal.......	*x̱l (tl)*	*x̱l (thl)*	*tsh (c or ch)*
from Kafir nasalised sibilant, or palatal aspirated lingual.........	*ns (nts)*	*nz*	*nx̱l (ndhl)*
to Se-tshuâna simple explosive sibilant		*ts*	
from Kafir nasalized palatal semivowel, or soft explosive........	*ny*		*ndsh (nj)*
to Se-tshuâna simple palatal semivowel....................		*y*	

220. In fact, in Se-tshuâna a consonant following immediately a nasal sound, may be said to become, almost throughout, more explosive, and on account of the greater stress laid upon the explosive pronunciation, the nasalisation dwindles almost entirely away.

221. The Tekeza has, on the contrary, nearly throughout, retained the nasal, and before a tenuis the nasal has even prevailed entirely, and has made the tenuis disappear after it, so that Kafir *nt* becomes *n* in Tekeza, Kafir *mp* becomes *m* in Tekeza; and the guttural nasal entirely disappearing, Kafir *nk* is in Tekeza dissolved into the " spiritus lenis."

222. In other cases, before a soft explosive (media), or before an aspirated lingual, the nasalisation remains, in general, in the same cases as in Kafir, with slight changes of course in the pronunciation, such as the relation in which both languages stand to each other may require. For example, Kafir *mv* is in Tekeza changed into *mf*.

223. Whether the Se-tshuâna *ṅ* (*ng* of Sesuto, *ñ* of Seχlapi books) is exactly like the Kafir and Tekeza *ng* is uncertain. It certainly is, to such a degree, peculiar in its use, as it occurs most usually at the end of a syllable, and particularly of a word, and is here generally descended by contraction from the Kafir syllables *-ni* and *-nga*.

c. NASALISATION IN THE MIDDLE BRANCH LANGUAGES.

224. Among the Middle Branch languages, few have preserved the initial nasals in such integrity as we find them in Kafir; but none have gone quite so far in discarding them as the Se-tshuâna.

225. The Middle Branch languages agree with the Tekeza in retaining, generally, the nasal media, whilst the nasal tenuis is rarely met with, except in the Northwestern genus (Kongo, Mpongwe). In other Middle Branch languages, the nasal tenuis is either converted into the nasal media, or it is changed in some other way.

226. Thus the dialect of Inhambane agrees with its neighbour, the Tekeza, in the elision of the *nk* (particularly at the beginning of words). For example, Kafir *inkosi* (chief) becomes in Se-tshuâna *kχosi* or *khᶜosi*, in Lourenzo Marques *a-hose*, and at Inhambane *osi*. Farther, Kafir *inkomo* (cow, ox) is in Se-tshuâna *kχomu*, or *khᶜomo*, Lourenzo Marques *omo*, Inhambane *ombé*, Makua *inyope*, and in all other Eastern Middle Branch languages *ngombe*, and in the South-western or Bunda genus *ongombe*.*

227. The *nt* offers a far greater variety in its treatment. It is retained in Sofala, Sena, Tette, Kipokómo, and in the languages of the North-western genus (Kongo, &c.) It is softened into *nd* in the Kikámba, Ki-hiâu and the oTyi-hereró. It loses (as in the Se-tshuâna) the nasal and becomes *t* in the Eastern Coast dialects of Inhambane, Quellimane, Mosambique, Ki-suáheli and in the language of Angola. Finally, the *t* disappears and the nasal *n* alone is retained (as in the Tekeza) in the language of Benguela.

228. The *mp* stands only in Sena, Tette, and in the North-western or Kongo genus. Otherwise a mollification of this sound to *mb* takes place, most generally, throughout the Middle Branch.

229. The North-western or Kongo genus of the Middle Branch has retained the nasal not only (as many

---

* Is this perhaps the same word with the Nama Hottentot word *gumap* (of Tindall, Le Vaillant and others, *komap* of Schmelen, *kamab* of Knudsen) masc. sng. ox, with the plur. *gumaku* oxen, fem. sng. *gumas* cow, plur. *gumati* cows, common plur. *guman* cattle, &c.? Or is the similarity merely accidental? In the North-western branch of the South African division of the Bá-ntu languages, other words for cattle are found, and this is also the case in Mpongwe. In the latter language a cow is called *nyare*, which word corresponds exactly to the Kafir noun *innyati* (buffalo), Lourenzo Marques *inyarre*, Inhambane *nyarri*, Sofala, Sena, Tette and Kisuñheli *nyáti*, Makua *náre*, Ki-nika and Ki pokóma *nyáki*, oTyi-hereró *o-nyati*. On the other hand, Madagascar has borrowed the first word from the Continent of Africa, the Malagasy form *umbi* (written *omby*) coinciding most nearly with that of the dialect of Inhambane.

other Middle Branch languages) before *v* and *z*, but also before *f* and *s*.

230. The *nz* is also found in the language of Angola, and corresponds here to the *ndϑ'* (*ndz*) of the oTyi-hereró. (§ 202 note.) In the latter language the nasal is always dropped before *ϑ'* (*s*) and *h*.

231. It is curious to remark that in Brusciotto de Vetralla's Kongo Grammar, the nasal before a labial consonant (*p*, *bh*, *f*, *v*), is always written *n*. Whether this is merely an orthographical habit, or whether, indeed the dental (and not the labial) nasal was here heard, is not quite clear. In some Mosambique languages, a similar orthography is not unfrequently observed.

232. The so-called false labial nasalisation of the Kafir (§ 217) occurs only in very few Middle Branch languages, as in Ki-suáheli and Ki-nika, and is here quite evidently (as in Kafir) a mere modern contraction.

233. In Mpongwe a few cases are mentioned in which a nasal precedes a liquida, as *nl*. Here, however, the *n* is said not to belong to the consonant, but to indicate the nasal pronunciation of the preceding vowel. We suppose, therefore, that in the monosyllables which begin with this sound, the *n* has a similar power.[*] A nasal pronunciation is also ascribed to other syllables. (Mpongwe Grammar, p. 9.)

f. NASALISATION IN THE NORTH-WESTERN BRANCH LANGUAGES.

234. In the North-western Branch (Benga, Dualla, &c.,) the nasalised guttural and labial tenues are indeed found, but they occur very rarely, and are perhaps even then not original. The nasal *nt* is here (as in the Setshuâna, &c., § 227) changed into *t*.

235. In Isubu, in one instance at least, a guttural nasal is found before a labial media, namely in *'ngbwa* or

---

[*] Comparative philology seems to render it probable that the Mpongwe sound *nl* (more frequent in modern publications in that language) is intended to indicate an intermediate sound between the liquid and the nasal, or an *l* which is in the course of transformation into *n*.

mbwa (dog), Dualla *mbo̱*, in Mpongwe and in the North-eastern or Zangian genus *mboa*, in the South-western or Bunda genus *o-mbua*, in the South-eastern or Mosambique genus and in the Tekeza *imbua*, (whence the Malagasy *ambua*, written *amboa*), but in the other South-eastern branch languages palatalised to Sesuto *mptsha*, Sex̌lapi *entsha*, Kafir *indsha*. If this were more than a solitary instance of such a combination of sounds in the Isubu, it would invite a comparison with the sounds *kp* and *gb*, which are so frequently met with in West African languages.

g. NASALISATION IN THE HOTTENTOT LANGUAGE.

236. We mentioned above that in the Hottentot language (in distinction from the Bâ-ntu languages) a nasal cannot precede another consonant, or, at least, form the beginning of a syllable in combination with it. But notwithstanding the hereby limited use of clear nasal sounds, the Hottentot language sounds much more nasal than the Bâ-ntu languages. This is produced by an unclear nasal pronunciation, which affects very many syllables, and though it extends over the whole length of a syllable, is perhaps, most strongly felt in its vowel.

237. This unclear nasalisation of Hottentot syllables has been marked by different writers in a very different manner. Schmelen's method in this regard is not quite clear, but a *g* at the end of a syllable seems frequently intended for this purpose, and sometimes an *n*. Knudsen marks it in his spelling-book by a star prefixed to the syllable, and in his Luke by a prefixed dot at the bottom of the line. Wallmann in his vocabulary, Tindall and, recently, the Rhenish missionaries indicate it by a French circumflex ∧ over the vowel; but in his grammar Wallmann has, in accordance with Lepsius's standard alphabet, commuted the latter mark into the Greek circumflex .

238. For example, Schmelen's *siig* (and) is Knudsen's *°zi* (of the spelling book) and *.zi* (of the Gospels), Tindall's *zĭ*, Wallmann's *zī* (to be pronounced *tsi*); and Schmelen's *káin* (good) is Knudsen's ⁾⁾*°gai* (of the spelling book) and *.ᶜgai* of the gospels), Wallmann's (vocabulary) *ʽgâi*, Tindall's *qkâi*, and Wallmann's (grammar) *!gāi*.

239. In the /Kora Dialect, Wuras distinguishes even a slight nasal pronunciation (which he expresses by a prefixed ㄱ) from a broad nasal sound, marked by a Greek circumflex over the vowel. (*Vide* Sir G. Grey's Library, vol. i, p. 20.)

240. This unclear nasalisation of the Hottentot language seems, in some cases at least, to have been caused by an ending nasal, which has at present disappeared, but is still felt in the nasal pronunciation of the syllable which it once followed.

III. VOWELS.

a. IN THE HOTTENTOT LANGUAGE.

241. The Hottentot differs further, most decidedly, from the Bâ-ntu languages by the possession of diphthongs. Whilst the latter languages are almost entirely restricted to clear simple vowels, the Hottentot language has besides them at least half a dozen different diphthongs, by which very nice distinctions of pronunciation are marked.

242. Thus we find in Nama Hottentot distinguished *ei* (Knudsen's *œi*, Schmelen's *y*) and *ai* (Schmelen's *ay*). The difference between both diphthongs is probably nearly the same as that between Dutch *ij* and *ei*. Tindall says that *ai* is like English *y* in "my," and *ei* like English *ey* in "they." The latter comparison is, indeed, only approximate.

243. The Nama Hottentot diphthongs *au* and *ou* may be supposed to be identical with the same Dutch sounds.

Tindall assigns to *au* the sound of English *ou* in "house," and to *ou* that of English *ow* in "sow." Wallmann writes the latter diphthong o̱u.

244. Finally, the Nama Hottentot has *oi* (like English *oy* in "boy") and *ui* (like Dutch *ui* in "tuin.")

245. The *ae* of Tindall (like English *ay* in "bay") seems not to be exactly a diphthong, but merely the broader pronunciation of the *e*, (Lepsius's e̱ German *ä* or *ae*.)

246. Wallmann distinguishes also a more indistinct pronunciation of the vowels noted by a circle written under the letter, namely, ḁ, e̥, i̥, o̥, u̥, &c. He states also that in the pure Nama dialect an intermediate vowel between *u* and *o* is met with, which he writes *o*, but which would better be represented by *ŭ*. The Orlams pronounce an almost clear *o* instead of it.

247. In the orthography of a great number of Nama words, different observers are found to vary greatly, particularly with regard to the exact vowel sounds to be ascribed to them.

b. VOWELS IN THE Bâ-NTU LANGUAGES.

248. The Bâ-ntu languages may be said to have no diphthongs at all; yet some vowels, as *ai* and particularly *au*, are frequently—(for example, in Kafir and oTyi-hereró) pronounced so rapidly, as almost to approach the sound of a diphthong (like English *i* in "mine," and *ou* in "house").

249. Though in general, in the systems of writing adopted for the different South African Bâ-ntu languages, only the five clear vowels *a*, *e*, *i*, *o*, *u* (with German or Italian pronunciation,) are distinguished, it cannot, however, be denied that in many of them also nicer shades of pronunciation can easily be marked, besides those necessarily arising from difference of quantity and accentuation.

250. In Zulu, for example, and in Se-suto a sound intermediate between *u* and *o* is found, which properly ought to be written $\overset{o}{u}$, but which is generally in the former language merely expressed by *u*, and in the latter by $\overset{u}{o}$. The sons of Moshesh denoted it by $\overset{u}{o}$ (*o* with a *u* over it, instead of our *u* with an *o* over it.)

251. The broad vowel o̲ (having the sound of English *a* in " water" or " all," and of Danish *aa*) is met with in Mosambique languages, and also in the Mpongwe. In the missionary orthography of the latter language it is expressed by *â*.

IV. SYLLABLES.

1. SIMPLICITY OF THEIR STRUCTURE.

252. The Bâ-ntu languages and the Hottentot dialects agree, in general, with regard to the simplicity of the composition of their syllables. In both these families of South African languages, a syllable can begin with only one of the above described consonants (consonantal diphthongs, nasalised consonants, and combinations of clicks with other consonants reckoned for this purpose as substantially simple consonants). The semivowel *w* may, however, intervene between a consonant and a following vowel.

253. A South African syllable, as a general rule, ends always either in a vowel, or in a nasal sound, but never in any other consonant. (Exceptions *vide* § 257—260.)

2. NASAL TERMINATIONS.

254. In the Hottentot language, syllables and words end frequently with nasals (*m*, *n*, and once or twice *ṅ*.)

255. But in the Kafir and Zulu and most Bâ-ntu languages originally no word is found to end in a nasal; and nasals in the middle of a word generally may more

properly be said to belong to the initial consonant of the following, than to the termination of the preceding syllable.

256. In Se-tshuâna, however, the ringing ṅ (*ng* of the Se-suto and ñ of the Seχlapi) is very frequent at the end of words, being here mostly descended from the terminations -*ni* and -*nga* as found in Kafir.

---

3. CONSONANTAL TERMINATIONS.

a. IN BÂ-NTU LANGUAGES.

257. By the falling off of the generally extremely short and almost indistinct terminal vowel of a word, there are sometimes, in Bâ-ntu languages, instances produced of consonantal endings of words. (*Vide* Hahn's Hereró grammar § 3.*) These cases are, however, so exceptional that they do not affect the character of the language, or the general constancy of the above rule.

b. IN THE HOTTENTOT LANGUAGE.

258. In the Hottentot language, on the contrary, this rule of non-consonantal terminations of syllables applies, in strictness, only to the roots of the words, but in the grammatical portions of the language, consonants are frequently made to close syllables.

259. Thus, as derivative suffixes of the nouns and as suffixed pronouns, we find most extensively used in Hottentot the sex-denoting and personal endings -*p* (masc. sng.), -*s* (fem. sng., and *II.* sng. fem.), -*ts* (*II.* sng. masc.) and in the /Kora dialect also -*r* (*I.* sng.)

260. There is no doubt that these consonantal endings were produced by a mere throwing off of a following

---

* The interjection *iḣ!* (pronounced *iṡh!* or *sh!*) given by Hahn may more properly be said to consist merely of the aspirated sibilant, used here like a vowel,—in the same manner as also a click sound is used in the Kafir and Zulu interjection ‖ (*x*). Also in European languages clicks and spirants are in this way employed as interjections.

vowel, and what this vowel was can, in some instances at least, still be clearly shown.

V. RADICAL AND SERVILE LETTERS.

261. The last paragraphs afford a very clear exemplification of the observation, that the more frequent use to which, generally, the grammatical elements of a language are subject has the tendency to more rapidly wear them off, and by such modifications to bring them, as a general rule, into a more advanced stage of phonetical development.

262. It is on this account that, in the grammatical elements of the Hottentot language, clicks and diphthongs have entirely disappeared;* and though three-fourths of the words of this language may be said to contain clicks, yet it is as possible to speak whole sentences without a click as it is to write a page in English without using any but words of Anglo-Saxon origin.

263. For example among the phrases given by Tindall in his Grammar, the following are quite clickless:

Taro ho-tsi hā?	What is the matter with you?
Hui-ī hā-ba-tsi-dama hā.	There is no help for you.
Nep ke amaba-ra mi, noup ke-ra kara.	This one tells the truth, the other deceives.
Tariba dāusa soriī?	What a burning sun?
Hamo ni soua?	When will it be fine weather?
Tsī ni hamo uwa?	And when will it return?
Ho-n-ta kmi.	Just as they find.
Hē-ē, arin u-si-hā.	No, the dogs have her.
Buruχa khoi-ts ke satsa.	You are a strange person.
Turi konkon-tsi hā?	What has disturbed you?

* There are, indeed, several directives and emphatical pronouns which begin with clicks; but as almost all these are also found used as other parts of speech, and their etymology as such is very clear, they cannot be called mere grammatical elements with any more right than, for example, the English "on account of" may be called a mere preposition, or "His Honour" a pronoun.

Mabu-ta huiba ni ho?	Where shall I find help?
Tē-ti-ts-ka, o-ta ha mi-ba-tsika hā.	If you had asked me, I would have told you.
O-ta kmo ni owa.	Then I will return.
Anip ta a.	The cock crows.
Ti sisinsa ta ko di twa.	I have finished my work.

In some Nama fables collected by Mr. Krönlein, the following clickless sentences occur:

I. In the fable of the elephant:

Os gere mī:	And she said:
"*Hem! ti õab geib χaiñi go huga mī-hetamanara mīheo.*"	"Umph! By the wife of my eldest son things are said which she never had said (before)."
"*O! huga ta hī titeē ta hīa.*"	"Oh! what I always should not do, I do."
"*Huga mī-hetamanara mīē χuige dībaχare!*"	"As she says things which she never said (before), do it then!"

II. In the fable of the flying lion:

χami ge goma hana hana ge toē.	The lion, it is said, used once to fly.
Tsīb gege mī: "Hāb garao, o-mī-babi.	And he said: "When he comes, so say to him:"
Tsī sībge, obge ge tē: "Hamtiro dī-hā?" ti mi, &c.	And when he came, he asked: "How have you made it?" saying, &c.
"*Neba ge aue go hā.*"	"Here came a man."
"*Ne χūi ge khom ta titeē.*"	"Of that matter nothing is to be said."

III. In the fable of the giraffe and the tortoise:

"*Hugas ta dī gamte, os nī dī gamte?*"	"Have you not always sprinkled me (with boochoo) that you will sprinkle me now?"

IV. In the fable of the white man and the snake:

"*Ta ukhāi eibi!*"	"Do not lift him up."

V. In the fable of the ostriches hunted by tortoises:

Tsī gu ge māgu hā iage hana tegu: "Hātsa?" ti mī.	And standing they asked each other: "Art thou there?" so saying.

264. In the same manner Appleyard, distinguishes in Kafir the clicks, the deep guttural, and the spirants (*v*,

f, h) as "radical letters, as they are only found in the roots of words," and proposes to call the remaining letters "serviles, as they are used in the formation and inflection of words, as well as in their roots."

265. This rule allows of much nicer distinctions, and similar natural distinctions of sounds can be observed in many other languages besides those of South Africa.

VI. GRAMMATICAL CHANGES OF SOUND.

266. In the grammatical portions of the Hottentot language, also, the rigidity of the non-interference principle of its syllables with each other (§ 52) is most signally broken through, particularly with regard to the derivative suffixes of nouns, the pronouns derived from them, and the personal particles. Here we find the different elements affecting each other to a considerable extent, and several coalescing into indivisible unities, the single component parts of which are not discernible, except to the most searching comparative analysis. As, however, these cases are too few in number to allow us to deduct from them any constant rules of euphony, we leave the deduction of what can be made out in this regard to the chapters regarding the analysis of the different parts of speech.

267. In the Bâ-ntu languages, on the contrary, such phonetical changes do not only affect the grammatical portions of the language, but the very stems of the words are commuted, not unfrequently, in accordance with the grammatical elements (suffixes or prefixes), and the different syllables of a stem can affect each other.

1. PHONETICAL INFLUENCE OF THE SUFFIXES UPON THE STEM.

a. SUPPRESSION OF THE ORIGINAL TERMINAL VOWEL.

268. In this manner, the ending vowel of the stem of almost all verbs has been entirely lost; for, in all verbal

forms grammatical suffixes are found, and before these the ending syllable of the stem has been constantly suppressed.

269. For example, in Zulu *uku-tand-a* is "to love" and *ngi-tand-ile* "I have loved." This would give the stem TAND; but as (according to § 253) a consonantal ending is incompatible with the original principles of structure in the Bâ-ntu languages, a vowel must be supposed to have been suppressed before the -*a*, which is the grammatical ending of the positive infect in the infinitive, indicative, &c., and before the -*ile* of the perfect, as well as before other grammatical terminations. As, however, the verb is always found with such grammatical terminations, it is scarcely possible, in the case of any verb, to say what was the original ending vowel of its stem; but for the purpose of analysis of the forms of the verbs, we shall indicate this obliterated vowel by the sign of the Hebrew א (aleph); and we can, therefore, say that *tanda* is contracted from TANDא-A.

b. ASSIMILATION OF VOWELS.

270. If we reduce in this manner any of the derivative forms of the verb, for example the causative *tandisa* to TANDא-IS-A, the causative suffix seems to have the form IS, which is again impossible in the Bâ-ntu languages. But by analogy, we are led to conclude that the original form of this causative particle was SI, and that its ending vowel generally disappeared, after having influenced the preceding end vowel of the stem, in which it is, therefore, still preserved. Thus TANDא-SI-A became by assimilation of vowels first TANDISIA, then by contraction *tandisa*.

271. Similarly, in most verbal terminations, a vowel does not originally belong to the syllable in which it is found, but is derived from the syllable following it. For example, *bonakalisela* (be manifest to) is probably to be dissolved into BONא-KALA-SI-LE-A.

c. Transmutation of Consonants.

272. But not only the ending vowel of the stem is affected by the grammatical terminations following it, but also in certain cases the last consonant, and sometimes the consonant of even distantly preceding syllables (very rarely, however, that beginning the stem) is changed through the influence of a grammatical suffix.

aa. Palatalisation of Labials.

273. This is regularly, under certain conditions, the case in the languages of the South-eastern branch, being effected by means of a palatalisation of labials. The rule by which this sort of palatalisation has been originated is that, when a labial explosive (*p, mp, b, mb,* or *m*) is followed by a labial vowel (*u, o*) or semivowel (*w*) which is by a succeeding vowel or syllable pressed against it,—then, for the purpose of facilitating the pronunciation, which seems rather impeded by the immediate contact of two labial sounds, the palatal semivowel *y* is produced as separating them from each other.

274. Through this insertion of *y*, there are in the first instance such palatal labial sounds produced as *py, mpy, by, mby, my*. From these primitive labial palatals, all those palatal sounds which are descended from labials, are to be derived, the labial rarely remaining such, but being generally converted into a more dental sound, which, together with the following *y*, forms then a true palatal consonant. The *y* may then also, through the influence of the preceding dental, go over into an aspirated sibilant, and thus:

ty, nty, dy, and *ndy* can become
tsh, ntsh, dsh, and *ndsh*.

275. The true explanation is indeed that the dental has, in these cases, originally been first inserted between the labial and palatal, and has then most generally got the better of the labial, so as to make it entirely disappear before it.

276. In the same manner, even the palatal semivowel *y* may completely swallow up the labial consonant before it, on account of which it was at first originated, and it may, therefore, at present appear as if the labial had been immediately commuted into this semivowel.

277. How in such a manner a Kafir and Se-tshuâna palatal may have descended from an original labial, as still preserved in the more Northern languages, can be seen from the example of the Kafir and Zulu ord *indsha* (dog), Seχlapi *entsha*, Sesuto *'mptsha*, if compared with the form of the Tekeza and of the Mosambique Genus *imbua* &c. (§ 235). That we find here in a Tekeza dialect (the most southern one, spoken by the Man!olosi) the same form as in its neighbours of the Middle branch, may probably to some extent be due to the influence of the latter; for, otherwise the Tekeza shows generally intermediate forms (§ 175—177.) One Northern Tekeza dialect (that of the Ma-tonga) has, however, the form *imbiya*. What may be the exact Lourenzo Marques form of this word cannot be clearly made out from the diminutive *imbdshana* (§ 176).

278. But what concerns us here much more, and is of far greater importance from a grammatical point of view, is the constant phonetical change from labial to palatal sound which takes place within the same language, when in the course of inflection those circumstances are produced under which such a palatalisation is effected.

279. This is most regularly the case in the formation of passive forms of verbs in Kafir and Se-tshuâna. Whether also in Tekeza, we do not know, since no specimens of passive forms are given in our scanty vocabularies of Tekeza dialects.

280. The passive voice being formed by the apparent insertion of a labial vowel (*u* in Kafir and Zulu, *o* in Se-tshuâna) before the terminal vowel of the inflection of the verb, a preceding labial explosive is, in these

languages, always palatalised in consequence; and in this manner in Kafir and Zulu

    p   *mp*   *b*   *mb* and *m* of active verbs become
tsh ntsh ty, or *dsh ndsh* and *ny* of the passive;

whilst in Se-tshuâna, where the nasal pronunciation has generally been converted into a stronger explosive one, with similar regularity in passive forms

    p   *b* and *m* become

tsh, or *pi y* and *ṅ*, the latter being a further change from *ny*, which palatal nasal, even when found in the active form of Se-tshuâna verbs is always, in the passive, converted into the above guttural nasal *ṅ* (*ng* or *ŋ*.)

281. The Se-tshuâna offers indeed a number of semi-palatal changes of other consonants, besides labials, in the passive formation. For example, the insertion of an *i* before the *o* takes place after *u*, *s*, *ts*, and *nts*; and this is accompanied by a liquidisation of *ts* to *r*, when the *ts* is contracted from LIS (§ 296.) But when the *ts* is derived from an L which followed the syllable -*si*- (§ 306), it is merely commuted into *tsh* before the passive -*o*-, without an intervening *i*.

282. These changes, however,—though they may either be explained by assuming that the passive inflection itself contained originally the vowel *i* besides its characteristic labial sound, or that the labial vowel is (as the English *u*) even without a preceding labial, apt to call into existence an *i* or *y* before itself,—do not affect the indubitable rule of the palatalisation of labials, a rule not only apparent in these passive forms, but also in other inflections, as in diminutive nouns, and in the suffix locative case.

283. But before we proceed to a contemplation of the further illustrations of this rule, it is necessary to mention that this palatalisation of labial sounds never affects the first consonant of the stem of the verb; though, if the passive ending stands immediately after it, the first

step towards palatalisation, namely the insertion of the *i* before the *u*, takes place. This change does not, however, depend upon the precedence of a labial, but is general with such verbal stems with one consonant. Thus we have in Kafir

pa (give) pass. *piwa*, but *kupa* (turn out) pass. *kutshwa*;

bha (steal) pass. *bhiwa*, *aba* (judge) pass. *abiwa*, but *!huba* (drive) pass. *!hutywa*;

and likewise

aka (build) pass. *akiwa*, but *faka* (put in) pass. *fakwa*;

ya (go) pass. *yiwa*, but *fuya* (possess) pass. *fuywa*;

ta (pour) pass. *tiwa*, but *puta* (touch) pass. *patwa*;

and in Se-tshuâna *ya* (eat) pass. *yeoa*.

284. The palatalisation of a labial consonant, according to the above rule, seems only then ascribable to merely phonetical influences, when labial and labial come immediately in contact with each other, *i.e.*, when the commutable consonant stands immediately before the passive termination. Yet in Kafir and Zulu also labials separated by one or more syllables from the passive *u*, are changed into palatals. In this manner, sibilants (as *s* and *z*), liquids (*l*), or nasals (*n*), and in fact any inflectional elements (or servile letters, § 264) may intervene between the two labial sounds, without apparently interrupting the mutual influence which they have upon each other in the above described manner. It may be, however, that these cases of apparently far-working phonetical influence are rather to be explained as formations caused by analogy, or as grammatical inferences of the natives. I mean to say that any one who was accustomed to the form *botshwa* (be bound) as passive of *bopa* (bind), would by analogy form from *bopela* (bind for) the passive *botshelwa*; or from *bambelela* (hold on) *bandshelelwa*, as from *bamba* (hold) came the passive *bandshwa*. Similarly,

of *bubisa* (destroy) the passive is *budshiswa*, of *kumsha* (KUMUSHA, translate) *kunyushwa*, of *gubungela* (cover) *gudshungelwa*, &c. &c.

285. This indirect palatalisation of labials, in consequence of which this process has from a mere euphonic change, become in Kafir and Zulu quite a characteristic of the passive voice, has not made its appearance in the Se-tshuâna, nor does it extend to the other cases of regular inflectional palatalisation of labials, which occur in the languages of the South-eastern Branch.

286. Among these cases, one at least which is also restricted to the Kafir and Zulu, is produced by the same causes as the direct labial palatalisation before the passive termination. This palatalisation takes place before the only case termination of nouns, existing in the Bâ-ntu languages, that of the locative case, which is formed in Kafir and Zulu by the suffix *-ini* or *-eni*. When, therefore, the end vowel of the noun is a labial (*u* or *o*), preceded by a labial consonant, those circumstances arise which require the palatalisation of the latter consonant (§ 273). The palatalisation is, however, here accompanied by the disappearance of the ending vowel which primarily by its presence caused the palatalisation. The changes of sound effected hereby are the same as in the passive formations. But it is to be remarked that the palatalisation in the locative case is by no means so universal as in the passive,—there being not few cases, in which the labial consonant here remains unaltered.

287. This case termination having in Se-tshuâna dwindled down into a mere ringing nasal sound at the end of the syllable, the circumstances which would produce a palatalisation of a labial sound did not arise (§273); and, therefore, such commutations are not found in this instance in the Se-tshuâna language.

288. The third case of inflectional palatalisation of labials, that of diminutives of nouns, is common to all

three species of the South-eastern Branch. It is produced by the addition of the diminutive suffixes *-ana*, *-anyana*, &c. Here, however, the palatalisation of the labial explosives is not merely restricted to such cases, where an original ending labial vowel (*o* or *u*) has been suppressed before this termination, but in Kafir and Zulu at least, the change takes also place in numerous nouns ending in other vowels (as *a*, *e*, *i*). For example:

indaba news, *iṅdatyana* little news,
iṅkabi ox, *iṅkatyana* a little ox,
mxlope white, *mxlotshana* a little white,
fupi near, *futshane* rather near.

289. We find corresponding to these last words in the Western Se-tshuâna: χ*a-uhe* near, and χ*a-utshuanyana* rather near, where the change from the original *p* to *h*, peculiar to this dialect (§ 110 and 124), produces the appearance of a change of the spirant to palatal sound.

290. In Tekeza one instance of a palatalised labial in a case of this inflection is on record, namely, *nambo* (river, Kafir *umlambo*, Se-tshuâna *molapo*) has as diminutive form *nambdshana* (little river, Kafir *umlandshana*, Se-tshuâna *molatshana*).

bb. *Permutations of other Consonants.*

291. In Se-tshuâna, some other changes at the end of the stems, or in the terminations, take place, arising also out of the incompatibility of some consonant with a following vowel. In this manner the vowel *o* cannot stand immediately after the sibilants *s* and *ts*.

292. It is shown above (§ 281) how this is obviated in the case of passive verbs, by the insertion of the vowel *i*, accompanied in the case of *ts* by the latter's commutation into *r*.

293. But in the case of verbal nouns formed by the suffix *o*, an aspiration of a preceding sibilant takes place, and *s* and *ts*, therefore, become in this case in the Se-tshuâna, *sh* and *tsh* (*ch* or *c*.)

294. Even of more extensive influence in Se-tshuâna is perhaps the incompatability of the sharp vowel *i* with a preceding *l*.*

295. If such a combination happens to take place in the formation of verbal nouns, then the *l* is always commuted into *r*, and in this case the rule extends also to such instances, in which the labial vowel *o*, indicative of the passive voice, intervenes between the liquid and the *i*,—e.g., *moaberoi* a partaker, from *abeloa* partake.

296. But when in the Se-tshuâna, the *i* (after L) is followed by the *s* of causative verbs, or by the *-le* of the perfect form, then the preceding *l* is either also merely changed into *r* (in which case the following termination remains without alteration), or into *ts*. In the latter case, the vowel and consonant following (that is the *-is-* of the causative and *-il-* of the perfect) become contracted with this sibilant explosive. Thus from verbs terminating in *-ola*, causative verbs are formed ending in *-orisa* (-N-LO-SI-A); and from those in *-ala* and *-ela*, causatives in *-atsa* (-N-LA-SI-A) and *-etsa* (-N-LE-SI-A).† Likewise of verbs ending in *-ila*, *-ula*, and *-ala*, the perfect termination is *-irile*, *-urile*, and *-arile*, and from others in *-ela* and *-ola*, it is *-etse* and *-otse*.

297. Other cases where the *l* of a suffix is influenced by the preceding syllable will be treated afterwards (§ 306 and 307.)

298. When in the Angola language, the end consonant, is an *l*, *t*, *nd*, or *z*, it is changed into *r*, *tsh*(*ch*), *ndsh*(*ng*), or *dsh*(*g*), if the perfect termination immediately following it is *-ile*; and this is always the case, when the vowel preceding it is sharp (*i* or *u*, § 311), Dias p. 26.

---

* Also in Kongo and Bunda, the *l* before *i* is changed into *r*; but of course not in Kakongo, this language having no *r* (§ 163).

† The Kafir goes in this instance quite with the Se-tshuâna, forming from primitive verbs in *-ala* and *-ela*, causatives in *-aza* and *-eza*, the *z* corresponding to Se-tshuâna *ts*, (§ 171)

299. In the case of the perfect of inversive verbs, however, generally a contraction takes place, the first liquid (or nasal, *vide* § 305) being omitted; and the initial vowel of the perfect termination by coming into immediate contact with the vowel characteristic of the inversive verbs, retains its sharp nature, whilst it transforms in its turn a preceding flat vowel into a sharp one (§ 302). For example, *sukula* (wash,) perf. *sukuile, sokola* (gather) perf. *sokuile, samuna* (comb) perf. *samuine*.

300. The Kongo has in this case similar contractions, preserving however, the vowel harmonic law in letting the quality of the preceding vowel preponderate over the following (§ 310), as in *zimuna* (speak ironically) perf. *zimuini, funguna* (confess) perf. *fungini, ebhola* perf. *bhoele*, and *mona* (see) perf. *muene*, the *u* of which is probably intended for the semivowel *w*.

d. VOWEL HARMONY.

301. An influence of the beginning vowel of the suffixes of the verbs upon the last syllable of the stem is also sometimes remarked. For example, the Kafir perfect of the verb *ambat-a* (dress, Se-tshuâna *apara*) is *ambete* (Se-tshuâna *apere*) which is contracted from AMBATᴎLE; and in the same manner we have the perfects *pete* from *pata* (touch, handle), *twele* from *twala* (carry), *lele* from *lala* (sleep), *bulele* from *bulala* (kill). The case of the change of the termination of reciprocal verbs in *-ana*, passive *-anwa* in the perfect into *-ene*, passive *-enwe* as contracted from -ANᴎLE or (-ᴎNALI) and -ANᴎLWE (or -ᴎNALWI), comes more under the head of § 271.

302. But the alteration of the ending *u* of the stem into *o* before the termination *-e* of the subjunctive, which is visible in the Se-tshuâna verb *utshua* (steal), subj.

utshoe, betrays a tendency for accommodating the stem to the suffixes. For a similar case in the Angola language *vide* § 299 (*sokuile*).

e. THE INITIAL OF THE STEM AFFECTED BY THE END.

303. The same is the case even with regard to the initial consonant of the stem, in the perfect form of *lula* (sit) which is *rutse*, instead of LULℵLE, the influence of the *i* which has now actually disappeared, having extended so far back as to touch even the more distant liquid, which forms the initial of the stem of this verb.

304. An analogous action of the posterior consonants of a stem upon its initial is observable in the South-western or Bunda genus of the Middle Branch, in which the nasals are apt to overrule the other consonants, and to attract them in such a manner that they are themselves transformed into nasals. Thus the verb *bona* (see) of the South-eastern branch (*vona* of Sofala, *pona* of the Mpongwe) becomes by this process *muna* in oTyi-hereró, *mona* in Bunda and Kongo, whilst in the other Middle Branch languages, the initial spirant *v* has been entirely dropped in the form *ona*. And in another language of this South-western genus, the Nano (of Benguela), the noun *omano* (men, sing. *omuno*) is in like manner descended from *ovano* (oTyi-hereró *ovandu*) corresponding to the Kafir *abantu* (sng. *umuntu*), Northern Tekeza *vanü* (sing. *munü*) § 140.

2. PHONETIC INFLUENCE OF THE STEM UPON THE SUFFIXES.

a. ASSIMILATION OF CONSONANTS.

305. This process of nasal alliteration is, however, of considerably more importance, as affecting some verbal terminations in the Western languages of the Middle Branch; and in this case, the suffixes, instead of influencing the stem, are influenced by it, or rather in this case

by its last consonant. It is here again the liquid (*l* or *r* of the Kongo and Angola languages, and *r* of the oTyi-hereró) which, when in the termination of respective verbs and perfect forms, it happens to follow a preceding nasal *m* or *n* (be this radical or inflectional), is itself transformed into a nasal. Thus for the Kafir *tumela* (send to) and *tumile* (have sent), Se-tshuâna *roméla* and *romile*, the Bunda genus (*i. e.*, the oTyi-hereró, and the Angola language) has the forms *tumina* and *tumine*, the latter of which sounds in Kongo *tumini*; and instead of the Kafir perfect of the respective forms of verbs *tumele* (contracted from *tumelile*, have sent for), Se-tshuâna *rometse*, the oTyi-hereró, has the form *tuminine*, and the Angola language *tuminene*. This rule applies also to some extent to the terminations of inversive verbs.

306. In Se-tshuâna, the liquid *l* is in the perfect suffix also sometimes influenced by the preceding consonant; namely, when this is a sibilant *s* or *ts*, after which the above liquid becomes itself the sibilant explosive *ts*. To avoid, however, the close approach of two such identical consonants, the preceding consonant when *ts*, is then in its turn liquidised (to *r*), and, therefore, the Se-tshuâna verbs ending in -*sa* and -*tsa* are in the perfect commuted in -*sitse* and -*ritse*, instead of -SILE and -TSILE, the latter of which is itself most frequently a contraction from -LISILE (§ 296).

307. In case of verbs with the sibilant explosive *ts* as end consonant, this change extends also to the respective forms of verbs, which end, therefore, in -*letsa* instead of -TSELA, or -LISELA (§ 296).

b. VOWEL HARMONY.

308. But the most general instance of a modification of the inflectional terminations in accordance with the stem of the word, takes place in consequence of the law of vowel harmony. According to this law, the vowel of the suffix is in so far brought into accordance with that

preceding it that, after a flat vowel (*a, e, o*), one of the same class is to follow, and likewise after a sharp vowel (*i, u*) only a sharp vowel.

309. This rule, in the Kafir and Tekeza species, affects only the locative termination, which is regulated in this manner, according to the quality of the terminating vowel of the noun to which it is suffixed. The latter disappears before the vowel of the suffix, or in case it is a labial vowel (*o, u*), it may also remain, being in that case in Kafir commuted into the semivowel *w*. Thus Kafir nouns ending in *-a* or *-e*, form their locative in *-eni* (Se-tshuâna *-eṅ*), and those ending in *-o* either in *-eni* or *-weni* (Lourenzo Marques *-oeni,* Se-tshuâna *-oṅ*), whilst the nouns ending in *-i* change this in the locative into *-ini* (at Lourenzo Marques also *-ini,* Se-tshuâna *-iṅ*), and those in *-u* have *-ini* or *-wini* (Se-tshuâna *-uṅ*.)

310. The immediate contact of the vowels may be said to have had here this harmonizing influence; but in the Bunda Genus and in the Kongo language, we meet, besides similar cases (§ 300), also regularly with such applications of this rule, in which its force is not interrupted by an intervening consonant. On the contrary it is the vowel preceding the last consonant of the stem, which here exerts its power over the vowel following it and belonging to the flectional termination (*vide* § 270).

311. In this manner the ending of respective verbs is in Kongo and Angola *-ela* (oTyi-hereró *-era*) or *-ena* after flat, and *-ila* (oTyi-hereró *-ira*) after sharp vowels. The ending of the perfect form is in Kongo and Angola *-ele* (oTyi-hereró *-ere*), or *-ene* after flat vowels, and in Angola *-ile* (oTyi-hereró *-ire*) after sharp vowels. The Kongo, in exhibiting in this latter instance the endings *-iri* or or *-ini,*—has carried the principle of vowel harmony also to the last syllable; wherewith the commutation of the *l* into *r* follows as matter of course (*vide* § 294 note.)

312. Whether the application of this rule to the ending of subjective causative verbs, which is in oTyi-hereró

-eka after flat, and *-ika* after sharp vowels, extends also to other Western Middle Branch languages, is uncertain.

313. In oTyi-hereró the rule has certainly no reference to the almost identical ending of subjective intransitives, *-ika* which retains its *i* also after flat vowels; and the same is the case with the causative termination *-isa* in oTyi-hereró, though in Kongo the latter is after *e* and *o* (but not after *a*) converted into *-esa*.

314. In oTyi-hereró we find also that the characteristic vowel of the passive termination varies in this manner, being *u* after sharp, and *o* after flat vowels. The Kongo passive forms appear not to be affected in this manner.

315. This rule of vowel harmony is in a very restricted manner carried out in the termination of inversive verbs, *-ura* or *-una*, which becomes *-ora* or *-ona* after a preceding *o*, but retains its sharp vowel after all other vowels, even after the flat *a* and *e*.

316. The law of vowel harmony in its full application is not restricted to these South African languages; but almost the same law is found in many other languages, particularly Tataric; and, in fact, it has here been considered by some comparative grammarians as a distinguishing characteristic of this family or class of languages. A detailed comparison, however, of the Asiatic and South African modifications of this grammatical feature cannot at present be given.

C. ASSIMILATION OF VOWELS.

317. More striking even than the vowel harmonic changes are those of the assimilation of vowels. They apply, as far as we know, only to the terminative *-a* of verbs, which is, in the Bunda Genus, in certain cases commuted into the vowel of the preceding syllable, whatever this may be. Thus in oTyi-hereró *suta* (pay), *tona* (beat), *pita* (go out), *teka* (dip), and *taka* (turn, swing), are respectively commuted into *sutu*, *tono*, *piti*,

teke, and *taka**, and in the Angola language *tunda* (go out), *zola* (love), *dshiba* (kill), *enda* (walk), *banga* (make), become *tundu, zolo, dshibi, ende,* and *bange*

318. That in the Angola language (as in the last verb) the *a* is also after another *a*, in this case, commuted into *e*, shows that the whole originated in a depression or shortening of the pronunciation of the end vowel, the quality of which being laid less stress upon, it became sufficiently indistinct or undefined to be attracted by the preceding vowel so as to be assimilated to it.

319. This assimilation has in the Angola language as yet only been recognised in one tense; but in oTyi-hereró in several positive infect tenses of the indicative active, and in one negative imperative active form. Where, however, the imperative, infinitive, and participial forms have originally the termination *a*, this is also retained unaltered in oTyi-hereró.

3. PHONETIC INFLUENCE OF THE STEM UPON THE PREFIXES.

320. Though the stem of a word very frequently quite overwhelms the prefixes which are thus contracted, suppressed and wholly absorbed by it, yet there are only few cases of regular inflectional changes on this account.

a. ADAPTATION OF NASALS.

321. The nasal *n*, of course, when forming a prefix or ending it, is accommodated to the consonant which it precedes, and is therefore, changed before a labial

---

* Hahn is wrong in considering the assimilated as the radical forms of such verbs. Even if *sutu* and *tono* were not derived from *suta* and *tona*, the end vowel can only have been produced by assimilation from SUTN and TONN; or if the end vowel were here really preserved, then the preceding vowel must have been assimilated with it, and the above forms have descended from SNTU and TNNO; so that in neither case we are able to get at the full form of the stem of the verb. It is, however, in the highest degree probable that the explanation given above in the text, is the right one.

consonant into *m*,* and before a guttural into *ṅ* which latter letter is, however, in most orthographies written *n* (§ 214).

b. DEPRESSION OF THE VOWEL a.

322. A depression of the vowel *a* to *e* in prefixes is frequently caused, not through the influence of the stem, but through the pressure of other prefixes following it and intervening between the commutable vowel and the stem. Thus when in oTyi-hereró the objective (pronominal and personal) prefixes are immediately preceded by prefixes ending in *a*, this vowel is depressed to *e*.

323. Similarly in Kafir the negative prefix particle *nga-* becomes *nge-* when standing before the verbal prefix particle *ka-* (yet), or when placed before any simple or demonstrative pronoun, or personal particle, in such a conjunction as that thereby the substantive verb is implied.

324. But whether the change of the *a* to *e*, observable not unfrequently in pronoun prefixes (for example in the objective pronouns of the oTyi-hereró, and the participial subjective pronouns of the Kafir), is also due to mere pressure, or other various causes, is not quite clear.

c. COALESCENCE OF VOWELS.

325. The change of the *a* of prefixes which takes place immediately before the stem of certain verbs in oTyi-hereró as well as in Kafir and Se-tshuâna, seems not so much caused by depression as by a coalescence with a vowel *i* or *e*, which formed originally the initial of the

---

* The *n* of the derivative prefixes of the nouns of the 9th (n-) and 10th (Zin-) classes seems indeed in Kafir and Zulu also before the "spiritus lenis" to be changed into *m* (Appleyard p. 100, Colenso § 63, Grout § 96). One of the few nouns exemplifying this rule is, however, evidently contracted, namely Kafir *imazi* 9. (cow) from Zulu *inkomazi*, which is probably itself derived from I-N-KOMO-KAZI. Others are of foreign origin, for example *imali* (money) which is most likely of Arabic origin, and the *m* belongs here to the stem. In other cases, as in that of the Kafir noun *imalato* 9. (forefinger) from *alata* (point out), we cannot know whether an initial labial formerly appertaining to this stem, did not influence the nasal, as in some Tekeza nouns, in which the *m* is now found immediately before a vowel (§ 340).

stem, but has now in most cases been entirely suppressed, and is only visible, when in the above manner it has coalesced with the *u* of prefixes. For example, from the oTyi-hereró verb *ku-ya* to come, Kafir *u-ku-za*, Se-tshuâna χo-χ́la (*go tla*) we have the irregular forms *u-e-ya* he came, Kafir *w-e-za*,* and the Se-tshuâna χe-χ́la (*gé tla* Luke xxii, 7 &c.) there came (besides which we find indeed also χa-χ́la in Moffat's books as Mark x, 35, &c.) The original initial *i* of this stem is still apparent in the Angola form *iza*, and the Ki-hiáu *issa*. In other verbs the original initial vowel *i* is still more generally found, though in the Kafir language it is now only visible in the alteration of the *u* of prefixes. For example, the Kafir *w-e-bha* he stole, from *u-ku-bha* to steal (but *w-a-ba* he was, from *u-ku-ba* to be) can be easily explained by comparison with the Quellimane infinitive *w-iba* to steal, Mosambique *w-iya*, Cape Delgado *ku-iwa*, the Ki-suáheli and Ki-hiáu imperatives *iba* steal, Ki-pokómo *iwáa*, Ki-níka *ia*, Angola *iya*, Dualla and Isubu *iba*, and with the Mosambique noun *muiyi* 1. thief, Cape Delgado *muivi*, Ki-suáheli, Ki-níka and Ki-pokómo *muifi* (pl. *waifi* 2.), Ki-hiáu *múihi*, Kongo *múivi* (*evi* 2.), Mpongwe *ofe*.†

326. The last paragraph shows in the Kongo plural form *evi* 2. thieves (whilst Ki-pokómo *wa-ifi* remains

* Whilst the regular form *w-a-za* meaning "then he was," or "then he did" is peculiar to the idiomatic use of this verb, as a sort of auxiliary verb. (Appleyard, § 568.)

† If the Mpongwe verb *dshufu* "steal" and the corresponding Se-tshuâna word *utshua* are really identical with the above verb *iba*, then it becomes probable that the original form of this verb was IBUA, or some similar word, the *u* of which has now everywhere been lost except in the Se-tshuâna, in which language it has produced the necessary palatalisation of labial consonants, whilst at the same time it has caused the assimilation of the *i* into *u*. The same process of assimilation seems also to have caused the form of the Se-tshuâna verb χo-uχ́lua (*go utlua*) "to hear," if we compare it with Kafir *u-ku-va*, Zulu *u-ku-zwa* (from which is derived *w-e-va* or *w-e-zwa* he heard), Inhambane *ku-púa*, Sofala *ku-zuu*, Tette and Sena *ku-bva*, Quellimane *u-iwoa*, Mosambique *w-iwa*, Maravi *ku-mvá*, Ki-kamba *hu-twa*, oTyi-hereró *ku-ϑ'uva* (*ku-zuvu*), Angola *ku-uva*. The primitive form of this verb is, however, not yet quite clear.

uncontracted) an instance of a coalescence of the initial *i* of the stem with the *a* of the derivative prefix of the noun. This initial vowel of the stem may then also entirely disappear, its former presence being only visible in such cases of coalescence or in kindred dialects. In the latter then sometimes this initial vowel is found to be even preceded by a consonant which has in the other dialects entirely vanished. For example, the Kafir noun *i-zinyo* 5. (Tekeza *tinyo*) "tooth" has as plural either *a-ma-zinyo* 6. (Tekeza *ma-tinyo*) teeth, or with elision of the *z*, the contracted form *a-menyo*. The corresponding Se-tshuâna forms are *le-ino* 5. and *meno* 6. The Mosambique dialects have correspondingly, Sofala *zino* 5. and *meno* 6., Tette and Sena *zino* 5. and *mânu* 6., Quellimane *zino* 5. and *mênu* 6., Mosambique *n-ino* 5. *meno* 6.; and the Zangian dialects, Cape Delgado *rínu* 5. and *menu* 6., Ki-suáheli *dshino* 5. and *meno* 6., Ki-níka *zino* 5. and *meno* 6., Ki-kámba *ĩo* 5. and *máyo* 6. The Ki-kámba forms are, with the exception of the accent, almost identical with oTyi-hereró *e-yó* 5. tooth, *o-ma-yó* 6. teeth. Cannecattim gives as the Angola forms *rí-shu* (*ríchu*) 5. and *má-shu* (*máchu*) 6., and as Kongo plural *ménu* 6. In Mpongwe the corresponding forms are *i-no̱* 5. tooth, and *a-no̱* 6. teeth.

327. A similar instance of contraction by which apparent flectional irregularities are produced, is met with in the plural of the South African Bâ-ntu word for "eyes", namely Kafir *a-me̍xlo* 6. (sng. *i-li-so* 5. an eye), Tekeza *a-ma-'x-lo* 6. (sng. *tíxlo* 5.), Se-suto *ma-'xlo* 6., Se-xlapi *maíxlo* 6. (*le-íxlo* 5.), Sofala *messo* 6. (*dshisso* 5.), Tette and Sena *maso* 6. (*dziso*, or *diso* 5.), Quellimane *méto* 6. (*ni-to* 5.), Cape Delgado *masho* 6. (*rísho* 5.), Ki-suáheli *má-to* 6. (*dshito* 5.), Ki-níka *ma-tso* 6. (*dzitso* 5.), Ki-kamba *medo* 6. (*ido* 5.), oTyi-hereró *o-me-ho* 6. (*e-ho* 5.), Angola *o-me-sso* 6. (with the singular *rissu* 5. according to Cannecattim who also gives the Kongo form *dissu* 5.), Mpongwe *antyo̱* 6. (*intyo̱* 5.), Benga *miho̱* 6. (*diho̱* 5.),

Dualla and Isubu *miso* 6. (*diso* 5.) Whilst the forms of the Kafir, Sofala, Makua and Ki-kamba languages and of the Bunda genus have here been produced by a coalescence of the *a* with the initial *i* to *e*,—most other South African languages have allowed the *a* to prevail over the *i*. But in this instance the North-western branch has, before the *i*, suppressed the vowel *a* of the prefix, which has hereby in form become identical with the *mi*- prefix of the fourth class of nouns. An analogy to this case is found in the Se-tshuâna plural *mixlua* thorns (Se-suto *meuxlua*, Mosambique *miwa*), if we compare it with the corresponding Kafir word *a-meva* 6. (sng. *i-li-va* 5. a thorn). But this Se-tshuâna word *mixlua* has not only in form, but now also in use been transferred to the fourth class of nouns, and is found constructed with pronouns and adjectives of this fourth class.

328. In Kafir the *a* of prefixed particles coalesces as a general rule with the initial vowel of the derivative prefixes of nouns (which vowel forms really a sort of prefixed article,) and in this manner:

a with *a* coalesces to *a*
a ,, *i* ,, *e*
a ,, *u* ,, *o*

In other South African Bântu languages (few of which have retained any traces of this old article,) these cases of coalescence have not yet been observed.

---

4. PHONETIC INFLUENCE OF THE PREFIXES UPON THE STEM.

329. With regard to the beginning of the stem of a word, it is to be remarked that it is, in the course of inflection, usually much less affected by the prefixes, than the end of the stem by the suffixes.

a. INITIAL VOWELS.

330. Regarding stems beginning with vowels, it is indeed true that a contraction of the later with a pre-

ceding vowel, or even their entire elision, is a circumstance of so very general occurrence, that in many instances such an initial vowel is only in very rare cases visible, or has indeed in many languages been entirely lost,—its former existence being recognised merely by comparison of kindred dialects or languages.

b. NASAL PREFIXES.

331. But if the first letter of the stem is a consonant, it generally remains immutable, except when it comes in immediate contact with a preceding consonant. As this, however, according to the phonetic principles of the Bâ-ntu languages (§ 253), can only be a nasal, it is but in cases where the prefix either ends in, or consists entirely of, a nasal, that such initial changes of the stems of words are generally visible.

aa. *Nasal Prefixes in Kafir.*

332. In the Kafir species such a nasal occurs purely only in the derivative prefix of the 9th (*N-*) and 10th (*Zin-*) classes of nouns and adjectives, and impurely in the derivative prefixes of the 1st (*M-* personal) and 3rd (*M-* impersonal) classes of nouns and adjectives, and in the objective pronouns of the 1st (*M-* personal) class.

333. In the latter cases the stem remains, in the Kafir species, always unaltered, and in the first case (of pure nasalisation) the only alteration which takes place, occurs in the stronger pronunciation of a few consonants, when as initials of the stem they are preceded by the nasal. (§ 77, 170, and 216).

334. In this manner in the Kafir language

initial *s* after prefixed nasal becomes *ts*
„ *sh* „ „ „ „ *tsh*
„ *ƶl(hl)* „ „ „ „ *ꝗl(kl)*
„ |(c) „ „ „ „ ·|(gc)
„ ‖(x) „ „ „ „ ·‖(gx)
„ !(q) „ „ „ „ ·!(gq)

Inflectional Changes of Initial Consonants. 69

bb. *Nasal Prefixes in Se-tshuâna and Tekeza.*

335. In Se-tshuâna this stronger explosive pronunciation of consonants after pure nasalisation is of far more general extent, and takes place, not only where the nasal is still visible, as in the derivative prefixes of a few nouns of the 9th (*N-*) and 10th (*Lin-*) classes, and (before active verbs) in the objective prefix of the first person singular '*n-* or '*m-*, but also where it has now vanished, leaving as trace of its former presence an increase of the explosive force of the initial consonant. This disappearance of the nasal, combined with retention of the commutation of the initial of the stem effected by it, is met with in most of the nouns and adjectives of the 9th (*N-*) and 10th (*Lin-*) classes, and in the reflective verbs, which are formed at present by the prefix *i-*. That the latter has the influence of commuting the following initial consonant (if changeable) in the same manner as if a nasal preceded it, or had been suppressed, renders it probable that really this prefix once contained a nasal, though none at present is visible here, either in Se-tshuâna, or in any of the kindred Bâ-ntu languages known to us.

336. Including, therefore, the latter case in this our rule, we may say that in the Western Se-tshuâna initial ℵ* after prefixed or suppressed nasal becomes *k*

,,	$\chi(g)$	,,	,,	,,	$k\chi(kh)$
,,	*h*	,,	,,	,,	$k\chi(kh)$ or *ph*
,,	*b*	,,	,,	,,	*p*
,,	*l*	,,	,,	,,	*t*
,,	*r* (before sharp vowels)	,,	,,	,,	*t*
,,	*r* (before flat vowels)	,,	,,	,,	*th*
,,	*s*	,,	,,	,,	*ts*
,,	*sh*	,,	,,		*tsh* (*c*, or *ch*)

The harder consonants *k*, $k\chi$ (*kh*), *p*, *t*, *th*, *ts* and also *x̌l* (*tl*), *m*, *n*, *ny*, being of course incapable of any further

---

* The Hebrew Aleph serves us to indicate the "spiritus lenis."

hardening, remain unaltered after a nasal sound; and cannot, therefore, by themselves afford any indication of the former presence of nasalisation of the stems which begin with them.

337. If we compare with the preceding table that of the correspondence of Kafir nasalised to Se-tshuâna unnasalised consonants (§ 219), the origin of most of the above changes becomes clear, particularly if we bear in mind that Se-tshuâna *l* and *r* are frequently descended from *d*, and likewise *r* from *t*, as still preserved in the corresponding Kafir words (§ 162, 165), that Se-tshuâna *h* is derived from Kafir *p* and *f* (§ 124), and χ (*g*) corresponds to Kafir *k* (§ 87 and 134).

338. Whilst in this manner the initial of the stem is in the Se-tshuâna strengthened through the influence of a preceding nasal (even when the latter has now entirely disappeared),—in the Tekeza, on the contrary, a prefixed nasal has a tendency to make away with the beginning consonant of the stem, before which it stands. The changes hereby produced are, however, of such a nature that they can only be explained by comparison with the more primitive Kafir forms. For example, *mararo*, as numeral adjective of the 6th (*Ma-*) and *tinaro* of the 10th class (*Tin-*) class, both meaning "three," correspond to Kafir *amatatu* 6. and *ezintatu* 10. (three); and the rule deducible from this comparison is that in Delagoa Bay the initial *r* of a stem is suppressed after a nasal preceding it (§ 221).

339. In the case of an initial *k*, the disappearance of this consonant is, in the Tekeza, accompanied by that of the preceding nasal, and thus the "spiritus lenis" of the Tekeza corresponds here to Kafir *nk* (§ 221). For example, *e-ulo* (great) 9. is the Kafir *e-n-kulu* 9., Se-tshuâna *e-kχolu* (*e kholu*) from the stem *-kulo*, Kafir *-kulu*, Se-tshuâna *-χolu* (*-golu*).

340. As the Kafir *p* also disappears in the Tekeza, and Kafir *mp* in Tekeza becomes *m*, such words, in which an

original initial *p* was nasalised, appear in the Tekeza as if the initial א required by itself the labial nasal before it, whilst the labial quality of this nasal is, of course, only due to the omitted labial explosive. For example, *liondo* is the Lourenzo Marques word for Kafir and Zulu *upondo* 11. (horn). We do not know the exact plural of the word in this dialect; but in another Northern Tekeza dialect, we find *timondo ta teomo* 10. for Kafir *impondo zenkomo* (ZI-ZIM-PONDO ZI-A-ZI-ZIN-KOMO) the horns of the cattle.

341. No other cases of pure nasalisation of the initial consonant have been observed (in the few specimens of the Tekeza language as yet collected) besides those of the prefixes of nouns (and adjectives) of the 9th (*N-*) and 10th (*Tin-*) classes. It is, however, not improbable that these are the only instances existing in this language.

342. Although the Tekeza and Se-tshuâna avoid even the appearance of an impure indiscriminate labial nasalisation by retaining the vowel of the derivative prefix (of the nouns and adjectives) or objective pronoun, the disappearance of which gives rise to this feature of the Kafir language (§ 217 and 218),—yet each of the two former languages has, before one particular initial consonant of the stem, not only omitted the vowel of this prefix (*mo-* of the Se-tshuâna, *mu-* of the Tekeza and Zulu), but also the initial consonant of the stem.

343. In Se-tshuâna this omission takes place when the prefix of the 1st and 3rd classes comes to stand before an initial *b* (§ 113), and in Tekeza before an initial *l*. In the latter case also the *m-* of the prefix undergoes a change, being converted into the dental nasal *n-*. Thus in Lourenzo Marques,

nanda 1. slave, follower (MULANDA) is derived from *e-ko-landa* 15. (Kafir *uku-landa*) to follow;

nomo 3. mouth (Kafir *umlomo*, Se-tshuâna *molomo*) from *e-ko-luma* 15. (Kafir *u-ku-luma*, Se-tshuâna χo-*loma*) to bite;

nambo 3. river (Kafir *umlambo*, Se-tshuâna *molapo*);

nege 3. leg (Kafir *umlenze*), plur. *milenge* 4. legs (Kafir *imilenze*);

a-noi 1. sorcerer, (Sofala *muroi*, Se-tshuâna *moloi*, from Xo-*loa*, 15. to bewitch).

344. This *n-* seems, however, not to have immediately descended from MUL-, or ML-, but the liquid *l* seems in the first instance to have been commuted into the dental explosive *d* which then disappeared after having effected the commutation of the labial *m-* before it, into the dental nasal *n-*. The intermediate stage of *nd* is even preserved in the Lourenzo Marques word *a-ndolo-ene* in the fire (Kafir *e-m-lilw-eni*, from *u-m-lilo* fire, Se-tshuâna *mu-lelo*, Southern Tekeza *unilo*), the first *o* of which is evidently due to the principle of assimilation of vowels (*vide* §§ 270 and 271). In fact the Matonga dialect supplies, as an intermediate link, the form *undilo* fire.

cc. Nasal Prefixes in the Middle Branch.

345. Contractions of these labial nasal prefixes of nouns of the 1st and 2nd classes with the initial of the stem, occur indeed also in the Middle Branch languages, but no certain rules on this head can as yet be laid down.

346. With regard to the pure nasalisation by means of a prefix of the 9th and 10th classes of nouns and adjectives, it is to be remarked that, where in the languages of the Middle Branch, the nasalisation is here not altogether thrown off, it has a similar tendency as in the Tekeza, viz., of softening the initial of the stem, without, however, (as in that South-eastern species) entirely suppressing it.

347. This is connected with the tendency which this Branch (excepting always the Kongo genus) has for the combination of a media explosive with a preceding nasal (§ 225), whereby generally not only tenues, but also fricative and liquid consonants, are after pure nasalisation changed into mediæ.

348. Thus we find in Kikámba *ukú* 11. firewood (Kafir and Kisuáheli *ukúni*, Western Se-tshuana *loχoñ*, Mpongwe

okoni) with the plural *ńgu* 10. (Kafir *inkuni*, Kisuáheli *kúni*, Southern Tekeza *tuni* [*i.e.* TIN-KUNI], Western Se-tshuana *likχoṅ*, oTyi-hereró *oṅgune*.)

349. In this language (the Kikámba), an initial *ts* disappears even altogether, after nasalisation, as

utsiégi 11. straw, plural *niegi* 10.;
utsigi 11. mule, plural *nigi* 10.

350. The same is the case, in at least one noun in Kiníka: *lutsérre* 11. hair (Kafir *unwele*, Zulu *unweli*, Kisuaheli *unuelle*), plur. *niérre* 10. (Kafir *innwele*, Zulu *izinnwele*, Kisuáheli *nuelle*).

351. In Kisuáheli we have instances of a change of a liquid consonant, and also of a labial spirant (or semi-vowel? *vide* § 144) into the corresponding media; for example, *ulimi* 11. tongue (Kafir *ulwimi*, Seχlapi *loleme** Sofala *rurimi*, Kibiau *lulimi*, Cape Delgado *lurimi*, Kiníka *urimi*, Kikamba *uimi*, Kipokómo *dshuimi*, Kongo *ludimi*, Mpongwe *oleme*) has as plural *ndimi* 10. (Kafir *izilwimi*, Seᶜₓlapi *liteme*); *uwingo* 11. heaven, plur. *mbingo* 10.

352. In oTyi-hereró the commutation of the initial of the stem of nouns after the nasal of these prefixes into a media is most general. In this manner:

k   y   ty   p   v   ʒˀ   t   r become

ṅg ṅg ndy ndy mb mb ndʒˀ nd nd, which changes are in their tendency almost exactly opposite to those observable in the Se-tshuâna under the same circumstances (§ 335 and 336.)

353. By nasalisation the liquid *l* becomes indeed *d* in the Angola language, but then the nasal before it is dropped. This disappearance of the prefixed nasal seems

* The Se-suto which, by commuting the *lo-* prefix of the 11th class into *le-*, has combined the 11th with the 5th (*Le-*) class of nouns, shows here of course the form *leleme* 5. tongue. Also in other South African Bâ-ntu languages, this noun seems to belong to the 5th class, as in Lourenzo Marques *redime*, Inhambane and Quellimane *lilime*, Mosambique *inlimi*, Sena and Tette *ririmi*, Maravi *lerúme*, Angola *ririmi*. The Duałła form *eyemi* (tongue), however, seems to belong to the 7th class, plur. *beyemi* 8. (tongues,)

also to take place before tenues, which here are not converted into medias; nor is this the case with the fricatives. But the fricative media retains the nasal of the prefix before it. For example,

nvunda 9. quarrel (oTyi-hereró *ombunda*), plur. (*d*)*shinvunda* 10. (oTyi-hereró *oϑ'ombunda*);

nvula 9. rain (Kafir *imvula*, oTyi-hereró *ombura*, §118);

fuba 9. flour, (Kafir *impupu*, § 116), plur. (*d*)*shifuba* 10.;

pango 9. plan, design (oTyi-hereró *ombango* will, intention,) plur. (*d*)*shipango* 10.

dd. *Nasal Prefixes in the Kongo Genus.*

354. In the Kongo language we find, as a case of change of *l* into *d* after the prefixes of the nouns of the 9th and 10th classes, the word *ndongi* 9. and 10. teacher (Angola *dongishi*) from *longa* (teach, oTyi-hereró *ronga*), from which also the Angola words *mulongi* 1. teacher, and *mulonga* 3. doctrine, plur. *milonga* 4. are derived.

355. But the Kongo Genus is particularly distinguished by certain changes of the initial consonants of the verbs. These changes are, in the Kongo language, restricted to the case when the prefix pronoun of the first person singular (subjective or objective) which is here abbreviated to *n-* or *m-* (from $^n gi$-, as still preserved in the Zulu and Bunda) comes to be placed immediately before the stem of verbs commencing with *l* and *bh*. These initial letters are under such circumstances converted respectively into *d* and *p* or *ph*. For example, we find:

ku-lakama 15. to persecute, *n-dakama* (I.s.) persecute me, *n-dukamini* I.s. I persecute or have persecuted;

ku-bhinga 15. to pray, *n-pingiri* I.s. I have prayed;

ku-bhingila 15. to pray for, *u-m-pingila* 1. (I.s.) he prays for me;

ku-bhobha 15. to speak, *n-pobhele* I.s. I have spoken;

ku-bhobhesiana 15. to speak with one another, *n-pobheseanini* I.s. I have spoken together with;

ku-bhobhabhobha 15. to be talkative, *n-pobhabhobhele* I.s. I have been talkative;

ku-bhanga 15. to make, *n-pangiri* I.s. I have made, but *a-bhangiri* 2. they have made.

356. It is to be remarked that an initial *r* remains unaltered after this nasal, at least in the one case which came under observation, *ku-ria* 15., perfect *n-riri* I.s., pass. *ku-riua* 15., perfect pass. *nrilu* I.s. This word occurs in the idiom *kuria mukúri* esse dominum mortis, and *kuriua mukúri* esse captivum mortis. It means probably "eat" corresponding to the Kafir *ǩla* (*dhla*) and *tya*, Se-tshuâna *ya*, Lourenzo Marques, Sena, Tette, Maravi, Mudshau *dïa*, Sofala, Cape Delgado, Kihiáu, Kiníka, o'Tyi-hereró, Angola *ria*, Quellimane *dsha*, Mosambique, Benguela, Kakongo *lïa*, Anjuane and Isubu *la*, Mpongwe *nya* or *nye*, Dualla *da*.

357. In the contraction of the objective prefix of the first person singular to *n-* and *m-*, and the hereby caused affection of the initial of the stem, the Kongo agrees with the Se-tshuâna (§ 335 and 336). But whilst in the latter language a total distinction between the objective and subjective forms of this personal prefix has been effected by assigning to the form *ki-* (also descended from Kafir *ṅgi-*) the latter (subjective) meaning,—in the Kongo language, on the contrary, the form with the mere nasal is used with both, subjective and objective meanings. There is, however, also another abbreviation from NGI, namely *i* or *y*, used in Kongo as subjective verbal prefix of the first person.

358. Of the Loango or Kakongo verbs we read that verbs commencing with *l* and *v* change these letters in certain tenses respectively into *d* and *p*. Whether this takes place only in the first person singular, as in Kongo, or whether it agrees more with the Mpongwe practice, I am, from want of examples, unable to say. I am, however, more inclined to the latter opinion.

359. The modernised state of the Mpongwe language has given rise to numerous contractions and abbreviations, and in this manner new instances have arisen in which the prefixes press immediately upon the begining of the stem of nouns or verbs, and either are amalgamated with it (whereby they are not unfrequently entirely lost in it), or the initial consonant of the stem is affected by them.

360. For example, by elision of the end vowel of the prefix *ma-* or *a-ma-* of Mpongwe nouns and adjectives of the 6th class, the labial nasal (*m-*) comes to stand immediately before the initial of the stem, and when this is a *v*, this fricative labial is converted after this *m* into a corresponding explosive, either *p* or *b*, as *i-vava* 5. wing, plur. *a-m-pava* 6. (Lourenzo Marques *li-papa* 5., Inhambane *ma-papi* 6., Sena and Tette *papidwe* 5. plur. *ma-papidwe* 6., Quellimane *papiko* 5., Kafir *i-piko* 5. plur. *ma-piko* 6.), with which one may also compare Kafir *u-pape* 11. quill, feather, plur. *i-m-pape* 10. (Mombas Suáheli *u-báwa* 11. plur. *m-báwa* 10., Cape Delgado *lw-awa* 11. plur. *báwa* 10.)

361. The same is the case in Mpongwe (at least in adjectives) not only (as in Kafir) with the prefixes of the 1st (*Mo-* personal) and 3rd (*Mo-* impersonal) classes, but also with that of the 4th (*Mi-*) class. When these Mpongwe prefixes preserve their nasal, they lose the vowel following it, and bring, therefore, the nasal into immediate contact with the initial of the stem. The latter, when a *v*, is then after them, as also after the prefixes of the 9th (*N-*) and 10th (*Sin-*) classes (which show of course here also a labial nasal, as *m-* 9. and *sim-* 10.), changed either into *p* or *b*. For example, the Mpongwe adjective "large" sounds in the 2nd class *a-volu*, in the 5th *i-volu*, in the 7th *e-volu*, and in the 8th *volu*; but in the 1st and 3rd classes *o-m-polu*, in the 4th *i-m-polu*, in the 9th *m-polu*, and in the 10th *i-m-polu* or *sim-polu*. In the same manner "bad" is in Mpongwe *o-m-be* 1., *a-ve* 2., *o-m-be* 3., *i-m-be* 4., *i-ve* 5., *a-m-be* 6., *e-ve* 7, *ve* 8., *m-be* 9., *i-m-be* or *sim-be*

10. (Kafir *o-mu-bi* 1., *a-ba-bi* 2., *o-mu-bi* 3., *e-mi-bi* 4., *e-li-bi* 5., *a-ma-bi* 6., *e-si-bi* 7., *e-zi-bi* 8., *e-m-bi* 9., *e-zim-bi* 10., &c.) And "two" in Mpongwe: *a-vani* 2., *i-m-bani* 4., *a-m-bani* 6., *vani* 8., *m-bani* 10., (Kafir *a-ba-bini* 2., *e-mi-bini* 4., *a-ma-bini* 6., *ezi-bini* 8., *e-zim-bini* 10); the Mpongwe, together with most other Western Bâ-ntu languages, being here probably more original as far as concerns the preservation of the first vowel of the stem, which has been assimilated to the second in Kafir and other Eastern languages, whilst both the Kafir proper and the Mpongwe have substituted a nasal for the primary liquid of Zulu *-bili*, Se-tshuâna *-beri*, Lourenzo Marques *-bire*, &c., &c. The ground form of the stem of this numeral is evidently BALI.

362. It is, however, only after the original nasal prefixes of the 9th (*N-*) and 10th (*Sin-*) classes that in Mpongwe *l* becomes *d*, and *r* and *t* become *ty*. For example, "long" is in Mpongwe *o-la* 1., *a-la* 2., *o-la* 3., *i-la* 4., *i-la* 5., *a-la* 6., *e-la* 7., *la* 8., *n-da* 9., *i-n-da* 10. (Kafir *o-m-de* 1., *a-ba-de* 2., *o-m-de* 3., *e-mi-de* 4., *e-li-de* 5., *a-ma-de* 6., *i-si-de* 7., *e-zi-de* 8., *e-n-de* 9., *e-zin-de* 10).

363. In case of the *r* and *t* being changed into *ty*, the original nasal, on account of which this change took place, is now lost in Mpongwe; for example, in the third numeral *a-raro* 2., *i-raro* 4., *a-raro* 6., *raro* 8., *tyaro* 10. (Kafir *a-ba-tatu* 2. *i-mi-tatu* 4., *a-ma-tatu* 6., *e-zi-tatu* 8., *e-zin-tatu* 10.), and in the fifth *a-tani* 2., *i-tani*, 4., *a-tani* 6., *tani* 8., *tyani* 10. (Kafir *a-ba-xlanu* 2., *i-mi-xlanu* 4., *a-ma-xlanu* 6., *e-zi-xlanu* 8., *e-zin-xlanu* 10.)

364. We see that it may in general be said that the more original form of the initial has, in Mpongwe, been preserved after the nasal, or in such forms which began formerly with a nasal, whilst the unnasalised forms are generally softened or liquidised.

c. INITIAL INFLECTION IN MPONGWE.

365. But the most remarkable change of letters in Mpongwe is that affecting the initial consonant of almost

all the verbs. They begin in the imperative and in one historical tense, with a soft or liquid letter, which is in all other moods and tenses and even in the negative of the above mentioned historical tense, commuted into a harder or more explosive consonant. Thus

g r l v w y zy z become
k t d p, or f f, or b dsh (j) sh s

and only the nasals *m* and *n* remain unaltered.

366. In the Mpongwe Grammar this is described as a change from the harder to the softer consonant, and according to its real origin the harder sound was probably more original with most beginnings than the softer. But for the grammatical and lexical purposes of the Mpongwe language, the form with the soft initial is to be considered as the ground form; for, from it most derivations take place. For example, from *gamba* speak, infinitive *go-kamba* (Bunda *o-ku-amba*), comes *gambagamba* speak at random, infinitive *go-kambagamba*, and also *i-gamba* 5. word, pl. *a-gamba* 6. (perhaps Kafir *i-gama* 5. name, plur. *a-ma-gama* 6.);

from *roma* send (Kongo, Bunda, Kisuáheli, Kikámba, Tette, Sena, Sofala and Kafir *tuma*, Kiníka *huma*, Mosambique *ruma*, Se-tshuûna *roma*), infinitive *go-toma* to send, comes *eromi* 7. messenger;

from *lingilia* mark, infinitive *go-dingilia*, comes *e-lingilio* 7. mark;

from *genda* go, walk (Kongo and Kafir *enda*), infinitive *go-kenda*, comes *o-genda* 1. visitor, stranger, &c., &c.

367. Regarding the origin of this change of initials, it seems probable that in its tendency for shortening the pronunciation, the Mpongwe pressed all such prefixes of the verbs (be they subjective or objective pronouns, or verbal particles) which consisted only of a nasal or of a short vowel, with or without preceding consonant, hard towards the beginning of the stem, thereby either raising the explosive character of the initial consonant of the

verb, or retaining its primitive harder pronunciation, which otherwise where this pressure did not take place, has generally been softened down. The softer pronunciation has thus been attached to the imperative form which is generally destitute of prefixes, and after the open *a-* of the historical tense and of the optative *ga-* and *a-* (first person of the imperative, and negative imperative). By the strong tendency to contraction which makes the Mpongwe quite a modern language, the original verbal prefixes have mostly been suppressed before the harder form of the initial; and with their disappearance, the reason for this hardening of the initial has also disappeared. This harder pronunciation must then have been so frequent in certain tenses and moods, that from a mere phonetic process it has become quite a characteristic of these tenses and moods; and so it came to pass that, also with such verbs, which had originally the harder initial, the change into the softer was by analogy enforced for those tenses and moods, which in the other verbs claimed a softer consonant.

368. This explanation is of course partly hypothetical; and it is very possible that a stricter investigation of the Mpongwe language, and a comparison with those dialects and languages which are most nearly related to it,—as, for example, those of Kakongo and Loango,—will enable us to understand more clearly and with greater certainty the development of the verbal formations in Mpongwe.

VII. INTONATION AND ACCENTUATION.

1. INTONATION.

369. A striking feature of the Mpongwe is also the use which has been made of the different modes of intonation for the distinction of the negative form. Probably this was originally indicated by one or more prefixed particles, and a prefixed *n-* is still used for the indication of the negative of the past tenses, and an *a-* in the imperative.

But even in these cases the intonation or prolongation of the penultimate seems to be more characteristic of the negative form than those prefixed letters.

370. We have evidently here again to do with a case, in which what was at first an external distinction has been commuted into an internal inflection,—that form which was originally longer, in its present contraction being distinguished by this intonation or prolongation from an originally shorter form, with which the former had otherwise, in its phonetic elements, become identical.

371. The exact nature of this intonation is not quite clear; it seems, however, that it consists rather in a prolongation of the accented syllable than in anything else; so that *mi kámba* means "I speak," and *mi kâmba* "I do not speak." In Mpongwe books the latter is indicated by an italic letter for the distinguishing vowel, as "mi ka*m*ba," or "*mi kamba*."

372. Such cases of intonation used for the distinction of homophonous words occur also in other Bâ-ntu languages,—for example, in Kafir and Zulu. Thus Kafir *intánga* 9. is "the house of the second wife," &c., and *intânga* 9. "seed of pumpkin," *úmkómbe* 3. rhinoceros, and *umkômbe* 3. ship. (Appleyard § 68, Colenso § 28.)

373. The Hottentot language seems, however, to avail itself much more extensively of the difference of intonation for the distinction of different words, the sounds of which are otherwise the same. Wuras distinguishes in this manner three keys (as he calls them), in which words which have otherwise the same sound may be spoken. (*Vide* Sir G. Grey's Library, Vol. I. p. 20).

2. ACCENT.

374. On what principles the accentuation in the Hottentot Language may be based, is not clear to me.

375. In the Bâ-ntu languages the accent lies, most generally, on the penultimate—(may this form a part of the stem of the word, or be merely an inflectional syl-

lable)—and it is shifted with a terminal increase of a word. For example, in Kafir *ímvu* is "a sheep," *imváŋa* " a lamb," *imvukázi* "an ewe," *imvukazána* "a little ewe," &c.; *u-ku-bóna* "to see," *u-ku-bonakaliséla* "to manifest to," &c., &c.

376. Of the Eastern Middle Branch languages, the Kikámba forms an exception by throwing the accent as close as possible to the beginning of the word, whilst its nearest neighbours, the Kiníka and Kisuáheli, agree, as regards accentuation, with the Kafir.

377. Of the Western Middle Branch languages, the oTyi-hereró, for certain, has the accent generally on the last syllable of the word, although there are also a large number of oTyi-hereró words which have the accent on the penultimate.

378. How the shifting of the accent affects the structure of the language, and influences the phonetic formation of the words, is still to be ascertained.

VIII. DIALECTICAL TRANSITIONS OF CONSONANTS.

379. The comparative study of the Hottentot dialects has not yet been carried to such an extent as to enable us to state what changes of sound take place between them; and still less is this the case with regard to the relations obtaining between the Hottentot and the kindred Sex-denoting languages. Yet, we may state that in the flectional or grammatical parts of speech, a Nama-Hottentot *t* (before *i* or *e*) is liable to be converted into *r* in the /Kora and Cape dialects, and that an ancient *t* has in Hottentot an inclination to be converted into the sibilant *s*.

380. The transitions of consonants in the various Bû-ntu languages are so multifarious that it is impossible

to note them all here. I give, however, a few tables of changes obtaining between the Kafir and other languages of the South African Division. It need not be remarked that the Kafir by no means always exhibits a more original form of consonant, but not rarely a more modern one, effected by palatalisation or other phonetic influences. For example, a *k* before *i* is palatalised, in most Bântu languages, to *tyi* or *tshi*; and this palatal sound has, in Kafir, sunk down to the mere sibilant *s*. On the other hand, the Kafir *l* is, in perhaps the greater number of kindred South African languages, changed into *r*; in a few it is commuted into *n* (as in Makua and Mpongwe), or into *y* (as in the Tefula dialect of the Zulu language), and in others, it has entirely disappeared.

381. The changes of sound obtaining between the different species of the South Eastern Branch have been at first noted at p. 40 of Sir G. Grey's Library, Vol. I., and are given here with a slightly altered arrangement:

KAFIR.	TEKÉZA.	SE-TSHUÂNA.
(Kafir and Zulu.)	(Lourenzo Marques.)	(Se-Xlapi and Se-suto.)
The *k* corresponds to *k*	and to	χ or h^c (*g*)
,, *ṅk* ,, ,, ℵ or *h*	,, ,,	k_χ or kh^c (*kh*)
,, *ṅg* ,, ,, *ṅg*	,, ,,	*k*
,, *t* ,, ,, *r*	,, ,,	*r*
,, *nt* ,, ,, *n*	,, ,,	*th*
,, *d* ,, ,, *l*	,, ,,	*l*
,, *nd* ,, ,, *nd*	,, ,,	*t*
,, *p* ,, ,, ℵ or *h*	,, ,,	*f* or *h*
,, *p* ,, ,, *bz*	,, ,,	*p*
,, *mp* ,, ,, *m*	,, ,,	*ph*
,, *b* ,, ,, *b* or *v*	,, ,,	*b*
,, *mb* ,, ,, *mb*	,, ,,	*p*
,, *mb-* ,, ,, *mob-*	,, ,,	*m-*
,, *f* ,, ,, *f*	,, ,,	*f* or *h*
,, *v* ,, ,, *f*	,, ,,	*b* or *r*
,, *v* ,, ,, *f*	,, ,,	*ku* or *tshu* (*chu*)

Dialectical Transitions of Consonants. 83

KAFIR. (Kafir and Zulu.)	TEKÉZA. (Lourenzo Marques.)	SE-TSHUÂNA. (Se-Xlapi and Se-suto.)
The *mv* corresponds to	*nf* and to	*p*
,, *s* ,,	,, *s* ,, ,,	*s*
,, *s* ,,	,, *tsh* ,, ,,	*ts*
,, *z* ,,	,, *t* ,, ,,	*ts* or *xl* (*tl*)
,, *zi* ,,	,, *te* ,, ,,	*li* or *ri*
,, *nz* ,,	,, *t* ,, ,,	*ts*
,, *nz* ,,	,, *mf* ,, ,,	*p*
,, *sh* ,,	,, *k* ,, ,,	*sh*
,, *ty* ,,	,, *bdsh* ,, ,,	*y*
,, *l* ,,	,, *l* ,, ,,	*l*
,, *li* ,,	,, *li* or *dzi* ,, ,,	*le*
,, *ml-* ,,	,, *n-* ,, ,,	*mol-*
,, *n* ,,	,, *n* or *ny* ,, ,,	*n*
,, *ny* ,,	,, *ny* ,, ,,	*n*
,, *-ni* ,,	,, *-ne* ,, ,,	*-ñ* (*ñ* or *ng*)
,, *m* ,,	,, *m* ,, ,,	*m*

382. Comparing the Eastern portion of the Middle Branch, we have observed in the Mosambique Genus mainly the following changes:

KAFIR.	TETTE AND SENA.	MAKUA.
The *k* corresponds to	*k* and to	*y*
,, *ṅk* ,,	,, *ṅg* ,, ,,	*k* or *g*
,, *ṅg* ,,	,, *ṅg* ,, ,,	*ṅg*
,, *t* ,,	,, *t* ,, ,,	*r*
,, *nt* ,,	,, *ntt* ,, ,,	*tt*
,, *d* ,,	,, *t* ,, ,,	
,, *p* ,,	,, *p* ,, ,,	*v*
,, *mp* ,,	,, *p* ,, ,,	*p*
,, *b* ,,	,, *ℵ* ,, ,,	*ℵ*
	mb	,, ,, *p*
,, *f* ,,	,, *p* ,, ,,	*v*
,, *f* ,,	,, *v* ,, ,,	*l* or *r*
,, *fu* ,,	,, *fu* ,, ,,	*ku* or *tu*

KAFIR.	TETTE AND SENA.	MAKUA.
The *fu* corresponds to	*ku*	and to *u*
,, *x̣l (hl)* or *s*	,, *s*	,, ,, *t*
,, *s*	,, ,,	,, *s*	,, ,, *h* or ℵ
,, *z*	,, ,,	,, *dz (?)*	,, ,, *d* or *r*
,, *l*	,, ,,	,, *r*	,, ,, *l*
,, *li*	,, ,,	,, *ri*	,, ,, *ni*

383. In the Zangian Genus the following transitions have been observed:

KAFIR.	KI-SUAHELI. (Mombas.)	KI-NIKA. (Rabbai.)
The *k* corresponds to	*k*	and to *k*
,, *k*	,, *g*	,, ,, *g*
,, *ṅk*	,, *ṅg*	,, ,, *ṅg*
,, *ṅg*	,, *ṅg*	,, ,, *ṅg*
,, *t*	,, *t*	,, ,, *h*
,, *nt*	,, *t*	,, ,, *t*
,, *nd*	,, *nd*	,, ,, *nd*
,,	,, *nd*	,, ,, *t*
,, *nx̣l (ndhl)*	,, *nd*	,, ,, *ns, nts (nz)*
,, *x̣l (hl)*	,, *t*	,, ,, *ts (z)*
,, *p*	,, *p*	,, ,, *h* or *v*
,, *b*	,, *w*	,, ,, ℵ
,, *ba*	,, *ba*	,, ,, *ba*
,, *mb*	,, *mb*	,, ,, *mb*
,, *f*	,, *f*	,, ,, *f*
,, *v*	,, *f*	,, ,, *f*
,, *s*	,, *s (ss)*	,, ,, *s (ss)*
,, *si*	,, *ki*	,, ,, *dshi*
,, *ns*	,, *nt*	,, ,, *ts (z)*
,, *z*	,, *dsh*	,, ,, *ts (z)*
,, *z*	,, *z (?s)*	,, ,, *z (?s)*
,, *nz*	,, *dy*	,, ,, *ts*
,, *l*	,, *l* or *ll*	,, ,, *r* or *rr*
,, *la*	,, *la*	,, ,, *la*
,, *l*	,, ℵ	,, ,, *l*
,, *n*	,, *n*	,, ,, *n*
,, *m*	,, *m*	,, ,, *m*

Dialectical Transitions of Consonants. 85

384. The transitions of consonants observed, in the South-Western or Bunda Genus are as follows:

KAFIR.	OTYI-HERERÓ. (Damara Language.)	ANGOLA. (Bunda Language.)
The k corresponds to	k and to	k
,, ṅk ,,	,, ṅg	,, ,, ṅg
,, ṅg ,,	,, ṅg	,, ,, ṅg
,, t ,,	,, t or s	,, ,, t
,, ti ,,	,, ti	,, ,, tshi (chi)
,, nt ,,	,, nd	,, ,, t
,, d (?) ,,	,, t	,, ,, nd or l
,, nd ,,	,, nd	,, ,, nd
,, p ,,	,, p	,, ,, b
,, b ,,	,, p	,, ,, b
,, b ,,	,, v	,, ,, א
,, mb ,,	,, mb	,, ,, mb
,, f ,,	,, ϑ͑ (s)	,, ,, f (ff)
,, fu ,,	,, t	,, ,, fu
,, v ,,	,, ϑ͑ (s)	,, ,, f
,, mv ,,	,, mb	,, ,, nf
,, mvu ,,	,, nd or ndϑ͑	,, ,,
,, s ,,	,, t	,, ,, s
,, s ,,	,, ty	,, ,, k
,, s or x̌l ,,	,, k	,, ,,
,, s or x̌l ,,	,, h	,, ,, s (ss)
,, z ,,	,, ϑ͑ (z)	,, ,, sh (x or g)
,, z ,,	,, h	,, ,, sh (x)
,, z ,,	,, y	,, ,, א
,, z (?) ,,	,, r	,, ,, l
,, tsh ,,	,, pi	,, ,, be
,, ndsh ,,	,, mbu	,, ,, mbu
,, nx̌l ,,	,, ndy	,, ,, nz
,, nx̌le ,,	,, ndyi	,, ,, ndshi (ngi)
,, l ,,	,, r	,, ,, l
,, li ,,	,, ri	,, ,, ri
,, y ,,	,, y	,, ,,
,, ny ,,	,, ny	,, ,, ny (nh)
,, n ,,	,, n	,, ,, n
,, m ,,	,, m	,, ,, m

84   *Phonology.*

	KAFIR.	TETTE AND SENA.	MAKUA.
The	*fu* corresponds to	*ku*	and to *u*
,,	*x̂l (hl)* or *s*	,, *s*	,, ,, *t*
,,	*s*	,, *s*	,, ,, *h* or א
,,	*z*	,, *dz (?)*	,, ,, *d* or *r*
,,	*l*	,, *r*	,, ,, *l*
,,	*li*	,, *ri*	,, ,, *ni*

383. In the Zangian Genus the following transitions have been observed:

	KAFIR.	KI-SUAHELI. (Mombas.)	KI-NIKA. (Rabbai.)
The	*k* corresponds to	*k*	and to *k*
,,	*k*	,, *g*	,, ,, *g*
,,	*ṅk*	,, *ṅg*	,, ,, *ṅg*
,,	*ṅg*	,, *ṅg*	,, ,, *ṅg*
,,	*t*	,, *t*	,, ,, *h*
,,	*nt*	,, *t*	,, ,, *t*
,,	*nd*	,, *nd*	,, ,, *nd*
,,		,, *nd*	,, ,, *t*
,,	*nx̂l (ndhl)*	,, *nd*	,, ,, *ns, nts (nz)*
,,	*x̂l (hl)* ,,	,, *t*	,, ,, *ts (z)*
,,	*p* ,,	,, *p*	,, ,, *h* or *v*
,,	*b* ,,	,, *w*	,, ,, א
,,	*ba* ,,	,, *ba*	,, ,, *ba*
,,	*mb* ,,	,, *mb*	,, ,, *mb*
,,	*f* ,,	,, *f*	,, ,, *f*
,,	*v* ,,	,, *f*	,, ,, *f*
,,	*s* ,,	,, *s (ss)*	,, ,, *s (ss)*
,,	*si* ,,	,, *ki*	,, ,, *dshi*
,,	*ns* ,,	,, *nt*	,, ,, *ts (z)*
,,	*z* ,,	,, *dsh*	,, ,, *ts (z)*
,,	*z* ,,	,, *z (?s)*	,, ,, *z (?s)*
,,	*nz* ,,	,, *dy*	,, ,, *ts*
,,	*l* ,,	,, *l* or *ll*	,, ,, *r* or *rr*
,,	*la* ,,	,, *la*	,, ,, *la*
,,	*l* ,,	,, א	,, ,, *l*
,,	*n* ,,	,, *n*	,, ,, *n*
,,	*m* ,,	,, *m*	,, ,, *m*

Dialectical Transitions of Consonants.

384. The transitions of consonants observed, in the South-Western or Bunda Genus are as follows:

KAFIR.		oTYI-HERERÓ. (Damara Language.)			ANGOLA. (Bunda Language.)
The *k* corresponds to	*k*	and to	*k*
,, *ṅk*	,,	,, *ṅg*	,,	,,	*ṅg*
,, *ṅg*	,,	,, *ṅg*	,,	,,	*ṅg*
,, *t*	,,	,, *t* or *s*	,,	,,	*t*
,, *ti*	,,	,, *ti*	,,	,,	*tshi (chi)*
,, *nt*	,,	,, *nd*	,,	,,	*t*
,, *d* (?)	,,	,, *t*	,,	,,	*nd* or *l*
,, *nd*	,,	,, *nd*	,,	,,	*nd*
,, *p*	,,	,, *p*	,,	,,	*b*
,, *b*	,,	,, *p*	,,	,,	*b*
,, *b*	,,	,, *v*	,,	,,	א
,, *mb*	,,	,, *mb*	,,	,,	*mb*
,, *f*	,,	,, ϑʿ (*s*)	,,	,,	*f (ff)*
,, *fu*	,,	,, *t*	,,	,,	*fu*
,, *v*	,,	,, ϑʿ (*s*)	,,	,,	*f*
,, *mv*	,,	,, *mb*	,,	,,	*nf*
,, *mvu*	,,	,, *nd* or *ndɜ'*	,,	,,	
,, *s*	,,	,, *t*	,,	,,	*s*
,, *s*	,,	,, *ty*	,,	,,	*k*
,, *s* or *x̌l*	,,	,, *k*	,,	,,	
,, *s* or *x̌l*	,,	,, *h*	,,	,,	*s (ss)*
,, *z*	,,	,, ϑ' (*z*)	,,	,,	*sh (x* or *g)*
,, *z*	,,	,, *h*	,,	,,	*sh (x)*
,, *z*	,,	,, *y*	,,	,,	א
,, *z* (?)	,,	,, *r*	,,	,,	*l*
,, *tsh*	,,	,, *pi*	,,	,,	*be*
,, *ndsh*	,,	,, *mbu*	,,	,,	*mbu*
,, *nx̌l*	,,	,, *ndy*	,,	,,	*nz*
,, *nʿx̌le*	,,	,, *ndyi*	,,	,,	*ndshi (ngi)*
,, *l*	,,	,, *r*	,,	,,	*l*
,, *li*	,,	,, *ri*	,,	,,	*ri*
,, *y*	,,	,, *y*	,,	,,	
,, *ny*	,,	,, *ny*	,,	,,	*ny (nh)*
,, *n*	,,	,, *n*	,,	,,	*n*
,, *m*	,,	,, *m*	,,	,,	*m*

385. In the North Western or Kongo Genus the following transitions of consonants have been noted:

KAFIR.		KONGO.			MPONGWE.
The *k* corresponds to	*k*		and to	*g*
,, *ṅk*	,,	,,		,, ,,	*k*
,, *ṅk* (Se-tshuâna *x̣l*)	*nz*		,, ,,	*d*
,, ℵ	,,	,,		,, ,,	*g*
,, *ṅg*	,,	,,	*ṅg*	,, ,,	*ṅg*
,, *t*	,,	,,	*t*	,, ,,	*r*
,, *nt*	,,	,,	*nt*	,, ,,	
,, *nt*	,,	,,	*t*	,, ,,	*ty*
,, *d*	,,	,,		,, ,,	*l*
,, *nd*	,,	,,		,, ,,	*nd*
,, *p*	,,	,,		,, ,,	*v*
,, *b*	,,	,,	ℵ	,, ,,	*v*
,, *bh*	,,	,,	*w*	,, ,,	*f*
			bh	,, ,,	*p*
,, *mb*	,,	,,		,, ,,	*mb*
,, *f*	,,	,,	*f*	,, ,,	*w*
,, *mv*	,,	,,	*nv*	,, ,,	
,, *s*	,,	,,		,, ,,	*zy* or *nty*
,, *s* (?)	,,	,,		,, ,,	ℵ or *k*
,, *s*	,,	,,	*k*	,, ,,	*z*
,, *s* or *x̣l* (*hl*)	,,	,,	*ss*	,, ,,	
,, *su*	,,	,,	*fu*	,, ,,	
,, *ns* (?)	,,	,,	*nz*	,, ,,	*nty*
,, *z*	,,	,,	*z*	,, ,,	*g* or *s*
,, *z*	,,	,,		,, ,,	*dsh* (*j*)
,, *nz*	,,	,,	*nz*	,, ,,	
,, *nz*	,,	,,		,, ,,	*ndsh* (*nj*)
,, *sh*	,,	,,	*k*	,, ,,	*g*
,, *x̣l* (*hl*)	,,	,,	*t*	,, ,,	*t*
,, *nx̣l* (*nkl*)	,,	,,	*t*	,, ,,	*ty*
,, *nx̣l* (*ndhl*)	,,	,,	*nz*	,, ,,	
,, *nx̣l* (*ndhl*)	,,	,,		,, ,,	*ndsh* (*nj*)
,, *l*	,,	,,	*l*	,, ,,	*n* or *nl*
,, *l*	,,	,,		,, ,,	*ny*
,, *ml*	,,	,,		,, ,,	*n*
,, *n*	,,	,,	*n*	,, ,,	*n*
,, *m*	,,	,,	*m*	,, ,,	*m*

386. In the North-Western Branch the transitions of consonants which have been observed are:

KAFIR.	BENGA.	ISUBU (Dualla.)
The *k* corresponds to		and to *k*
,, *t*	,, ,, *l*	,, ,, *l*
,, *nt*	,, ,, *t*	,, ,, *t*
,, *nd*	,, ,,	,, ,, *n*
,, *p*	,, ,,	,, ,, *w*
,, *b*	,, ,, *b*	,, ,, *b*
,, *mb*	,, ,, *mb*	,, ,, *mb*
,, *f*	,, ,, *v*	,, ,,
,, *mvu*	,, ,,	,, ,, *ngu*
,, *s*	,, ,, *h*	,, ,, *s*
,, *ns*	,, ,,	,, ,, *s*
,, *z*	,, ,, *d*	,, ,, *r*
,, *nz*	,, ,, א	,, ,, *d*
,, *ndsh (nj)*	,, ,,	,, ,, *ngb*
,, *nxl (ndhl)*	,, ,, *ndsh (nj)*	,, ,, *ndsh (nj)*
,, *l*	,, ,, *d*	,, ,, *d*
,, *l*	,, ,,	,, ,, *l*
,, *l*	,, ,, א	,, ,, א
,, *n*	,, ,, *n*	,, ,, *n*
,, *ny*	,, ,, *n*	,, ,, *n*
,, *ny*	,, ,,	,, ,, *ny*
,, *m*	,, ,, *m*	,, ,, *m*
,, *m*	,, ,,	,, ,, *mb*

387. It does not appear to be as yet practicable to bring these different tables of transitions of consonants into one large table, showing the correspondence of consonants throughout the South African Division of the Bâ-ntu languages. For, though some of these transitions are very general, others are only partial, *i. e.*, restricted to certain cases of the occurrence of such consonants; and they take perhaps place only under peculiar circumstances. The same Kafir letter can, therefore, in different cases, correspond to different consonants of one and the same other language; and as the conditions under which these variations in the transition of consonants are met with, have not been fully ascertained, or stated here,—it is impossible to assign to all these instances of mutual correspondence, their right place in a general table. Some further researches will, however, it is hoped, soon render it feasible to construct at least an outline table of the most general transitions of sound noticed throughout the different members of the Bâ-ntu family of languages.

388. It must be evident to any one who looks through these tables how futile any attempt at etymology on a larger scale must be from the narrow point of view of one particular language, even if this were the Kafir or Zulu, which languages have in general best preserved the ancient forms. But as they have not done so in every regard, and as there are many instances in which the kindred languages are more original, it follows that only on the basis of a comprehensive comparison, any sound and satisfactory etymology of the South African Bâ-ntu languages can be instituted. The limited space does not allow me to give here more than one specimen of etymological comparison, in illustration of these rules of phonology.

THE NAME OF GOD.

389. The word by which "God" is translated in Zulu by the best authorities is *Uṅkuluṅkulu* 1. It is derived by reduplication of a (nasalised) form of the 9th (*N-*) class from the adjective stem *-kulu* (great, large, old, *u-ku-kula* 15, to grow, &c.), and seems to mean originally "a great-great-grand father," or the first ancestor of a family or tribe, though perhaps the unnasalised form *u-kulukulu* 1. (Se-suto *mo-hʿoluhʿolu*) is at present more usual in this signification. Then it was applied by metaphor to that being from whom everything was derived, who according to the Zulu tradition has created all men,

animals and other things to whom life and death is due, &c.*

390. Regarding the form *U-ṅkuluṅkulu*, it is to be remarked that like many proper names and nouns expressing relationship it seems to have been transferred from the 9th (*N-*) class, to which originally, according to its prefix (*ṅ-*) it must have belonged, to the 1st (*Mu-* personal class) to which it is referred by the prefixed article *u*. (Bleek, De Nominum Generibus, &c., cap. ix, p. 45.) As the latter is derived from the prefix *Mu-*, the full form of the word may be concluded once to have been MU-N-KULU-N-KULU. From this, there descended then, with suppression of the first *ṅk*, and commutation of the second *ṅk* into the corresponding nasalised media *ṅg* (§§ 89 and 226), the Inhambane word for "God" *Muluṅgúlu* 1. In this inconstancy with regard to the transition of the *ṅk*, the dialect of Inhambane shows its character as an intermediate link between the Tekeza dialects (which almost constantly suppress the *ṅk*†) and the Middle Branch languages which are generally inclined to the nasalised media. Of course, the position of the first *ṅk* close to the unaccentuated beginning of the word had also something to do with its disappearance.

391. The language of Inhambane is, however, the only Middle Branch dialect in which the two liquids (*l*) of this word are preserved; for, in all other languages of the Mosambique as well as of the Zangian genus, the second *l* (that immediately following the accentuated syllable, and, therefore, for contrast's sake, least intoned) has been elided. Thus we find in Ki-hiáu, Ki-kámba and Ki-nika

---

* I have treated this subject at greater length in a paper which probably soon will be published.

† For example in Lourenzo Marques *le-ulo* (Kafir *e-ṅ-kulu*, Se-suto *e-hh͡ᶜolu*, Se-x̌lapi *e-kχolu*, Sena and Tette *i-húru*) as adjective form of the 9th (*N-*) class from the stem *-kulo* great (Kafir, Cape Delgado and Kinika *-kulu*, Se-suto *-h°olu*, Se-x̌lapi *-χolu*, Sofala *-guru*, Sena and Tette *-kuru*, Ki-suáheli and Ki-pokómo *-ku*).

the form *Mulúngu** (the accent retrograding according to § 375), and with suppression of the vowel of the prefix (§ 232) in the Ki-suáheli dialect of Cape Delgado *Mlúngu*.

392. From the form *Mulungu*, as general primitive type of this word in the Eastern Middle Branch languages, there are also derived, on the one hand, by transition of the *ng* (as derived from an original *nk*) into *k* or *g* (§ 382), the Makua form *Mulúgo* or *Mulúko* (Quellimane and Mosambique); and on the other hand, with commutation of the *l* into *r*, in those dialects which have no *l* (§ 163), the Sofala word *Murungu*, Tette *Murungo* or *Morungo*. The Tette form is also employed in the dialect of Sena, which has otherwise the *l*. Lastly, the Ki-suáheli dialect of Mombas, which retains an original *l* only in such cases where the Ki-nika has an *r* instead of it (§ 383), has the further contraction *Múngu*, and the Ki-pokómo *Mungo*.

393. Of course it is surprising at first to find that two apparently so different words as this *Mungo* and the Zulu *Unkulunkulu* are really identical, but we can follow the gradual mutilation of the word in this instance so closely that no doubt can remain. It deserves to be remarked that, notwithstanding its otherwise strongly contracted form, the Ki-pokómo has yet preserved one letter which the full Zulu form has already lost,—namely, the initial labial nasal.

394. Among the Western Middle Branch languages, only the oTyi-hereró has derived its name for the deity, from the same stem; but here neither a reduplication of the stem, nor a derivation from the nasalised form has taken place; and thus we have *oMukuru*,† which, however, in

---

* This is not to be confounded with the Kafir and Zulu word *u-m-lungu* 1. white man, European (plur. *a-be-lungu* 2.), to which corresponds the Ki-nika noun *mu-zungu*, Ki-suáheli *m-zungu* 1. (plur. *wa-zungu*, 2)

† It is not improbable that the Timneh (§ 5) word for God, *Kuruh* 1., is also to be compared herewith; but the laws of transitions of sounds obtaining between this West African and the South African Bâ-ntu languages must of course be first ascertained before such a comparison can be considered as in any way reliable.

almost every detail of its signification, seems exactly to correspond to the Zulu *Uṅkululuṅkulu*. The oTyi-hereró adjective stem *-kuru* (*o-ṅ-guru* 9.) means, as the corresponding Kongo stem *-kulu*, "old," and the idea of age is also generally implied in the meaning of the identical East African adjective (§§ 389 and 390, note).

395. In other South African languages, different words are found indicating the idea of a supreme being; but in Se-tshuâna at least the word for "God" has a similar reference to their ancestor-worship, as the Zulu *Uṅkuluṅkulu* (§ 389). Thus in Se-suto *Mo-limo** 3. means God, and *me-limo* 4. gods, but *molimo* 1. ancestral spirit, plur. *ba-limo* 2. The corresponding Se-x̱lapi words are: *Mo-rimo* 3., *me-rimo* 4., *morimo* 1., *barimo* 2. In Zulu the Bishop of Natal's Dictionary furnishes us the almost obsolete word *u.M-zimu* "apparently a collective name for *a-ma-tongo*" (6. dream-ghosts *a-ma-x̱lozi* 6., Kafir *i-mi-shologu* 4., Se-suto *liriti* 8., *i. e.* shadows of the dead, oTyi-hereró *o-vi-ruru* 8. spectres), "used only in the phrase *e-z-o-m-zimu* (*iziṅkomo* 10.) *e-z-e-mi-lwane*, the cattle killed in honour of the ancestral spirits." The word for "spirit, soul" in Sena and Quellimane is *muzimo* 1., plur. *azimo* 2. The Maravi word for "God," *'nsimmo*, is probably of the same origin. Except in these languages of the Mosambique genus, no traces of this word have as yet been discovered in any other Middle Branch dialects; but it occurs again in the North-western Branch in Dualla *modimo* 1. demon, Isubu *modimo* 1. ghost, spirit of a dead, plur. *badimo* 2., besides the synonymous Isubu nouns *edimo* 7., plur. *bedimo* 8.

---

* A derivation of *Molimo* from *Moh'olimo*, as "one who is in heaven," has been proposed by Mr. Casalis ("Les Bassoutos," p. 262); but this is the more improbable as the spiritual world, for the ancestor-worshipping nations, is beneath, as Mr. Casalis has himself remarked (p. 261). Whatever may be the origin of the words *h'olimo* (Se-x̱lapi *x̌orimo*) above, and *leh'olimo* 5. heaven, plur. *mah'olimo* 6. (Se-x̱lapi *lex̌orimo* 5. *max̌orimo* 6.), their similarity with *Molimo* seems to be almost accidental.

396. In these North-western Branch languages, however, "God" is indicated by other words, as *Obasi* in Isubu, *Loba* in Dualla, and *Anyambi* in Benga. The latter word belongs properly to the Kongo genus, where we find in Mpongwe *Anyambia*, and in Kongo *Nzambi-a-npungu*, which, according to W. D. Cooley (Inner Africa laid open, 1852, p. 6), means "the spirit above, or on high." Also the language of Angola uses *oNzambi* 9. God, and *o-u-nzambi* 14. divinity.

397. For completeness' sake, I add here the Hottentot name for God, which is *Tsui ‖ hwap* (Schmelen's *Tsoeikwap*) or *Tsŭi ‖ goap* (Wallmann's *Zŭi ‖ goab*) in the Nama and *Tshu ‖ koap* in the /Kora dialect, *Thui ‖ kwe* (Van der Kemp's *Thuickwe*) amongst the Eastern Hottentots, and *Ti ‖ k(w)oa* (Kolb's *Tikq̄uoá*, or *touq̄uoa*) near the Cape. The Kafir word for "God" borrowed from the Hottentot, *uTi‖o* (*uTixo*), agrees best with the form of the Cape dialect. Whilst this word is in Zululand comparatively unknown, it occurs again in the Tekeza dialect of Lourenzo Marques, in which the word *Tillo* 1: (God) betrays at once its late foreign introduction, by not observing the regular transition of consonants from Kafir to Tekeza (*t* to *r*, or *z* to *t*, § 381). The origin and true etymology of this Hottentot name of "God" is not yet established with any amount of certainty. It would perhaps be bold to assert that the word did not exist two hundred years ago, because in the texts sent by Witsen at the end of the seventeenth century to Leibnitz (§ 17), God is called *Thoró*. Or, is perhaps this last word really identical with *Theu ‖ kwap* (msc. sng.), as I have heard a Hottentot woman at Robben Island name God, and with the *Theu ‖ ge* or *Tui ‖ ko* of two Bushmen from the same place? Kolb's *Tou ‖ kwoa* (if that is not a misprint at p. 414 of the German original edition) leads us also on this trace.

A COMPARATIVE GRAMMAR

OF

SOUTH AFRICAN LANGUAGES,

BY

W. H. I. BLEEK, Ph. D.

PART II.

THE CONCORD.

SECTION I.

THE NOUN.

LONDON:

TRÜBNER & Co., 60, PATERNOSTER ROW.

1869.

CONTENTS OF PART II.—SECTION I.

Preface ... . PAGE. xix

B. THE CONCORD.

I. The Nature of the Concord ... ... § 398—425
   1. In general ... ... 398—404   93
   2. In the Bâ-ntu Languages ... ... 405—420   96
   3. In the Hottentot Language ... ... 421—425   112
II. Etymology of the concord-indicating Derivative Particles of the Nouns ... 426—447
   1. Etymology of the Bâ-ntu Derivative Prefixes ... ... 426—443   123
   2. Etymology of the Hottentot Derivative Suffixes ... ... 444 & 445   133
   3. Analogies ... ... 446 & 447   137
III. The Genders (or Classes) and Numbers of Nouns ... ... 448—558
   1. The Classes and Numbers of Nouns in the Bâ-ntu Languages ... ... 448—540
     a. Numerical value and correspondence of the Derivative Prefixes of the Nouns   448—454   139
     b. Disappearance of Classes or Genders   455—457   146
     c. Nomenclature ... ... 458—460   148
     d. The Prefixes of the Nouns in their different forms and in their numerical correspondence ... ... 461—514
        A. In the South-eastern Branch ... 461—471
           The Kafir Species (Kafir and Zulu)... 461—468   150
           The Setshuâna Species (Seχlapi and Sesuto) ... ... 469 & 470   162
           The Tekeza Species (Lourenzo Marques) 471   167
        B. In the Middle Branch ... ... 472—501
          aa. *The Mosambique Genus* ... 472—475
            Dialects of Tette and Sena ... 472 & 473   169

		§	PAGE.
The Makua Language	...	474	174
Kihiau (Tshiyao &c)	...	475	176
bb. *The Zangian Genus* ...	...	476—484	178
Kikámba	...	481	184
Kiníka and Kisuáheli	...	482 & 483	186
Kisambala (Shambala)	...	484	190
cc. *Languages of the Interior*	...	485 & 486	192
Bayeiye or Bakχoba ...	...	486	193
dd. *The Bunda Genus* ...	...	487—497	196
Otyihereró (Damara language)		490—494	197
Sindonga (Ovambo) ...	...	495	212
Nano (Benguela) ...	...	496	216
The Angola Language (Bunda)		497	220
ee. *The Kongo Genus* ...	...	498—501	223
The Kongo Language	...	499	224
The Mpongwe Language	...	500 & 501	227
C. In the North-western Branch	...	502—514	231
Dikele	...	507	234
Benga	...	508	237
Dualla and Isubu	...	509—512	240
Fernandian	...	513 & 514	248
e. Review of the Derivative Prefixes of the Nouns (Occurrence, Forms, Etymology, Range of Meaning, and Correspondence)		515—533	251
First Prefix (**MU-**) ...	...	516	251
Table of Forms of the First Prefix	...		252
Second Prefix (**BA-**) ...	...	517	254
Table of Forms of the Second Prefix	...		254
Third Prefix (**MU-**) ...	...	518	255
Table of Forms of the Third Prefix	...		256
Fourth Prefix (**MI-**) ...	...	519	258
Table of Forms of the Fourth Prefix	...		258
Fifth Prefix (**DI-** or **LI-**)	...	520	259
Table of Forms of the Fifth and Sixth Prefixes			260
Sixth Prefix (**MA-**) ...	...	521	261
Seventh Prefix (**KI-**) ...	...	522	262
Table of Forms of the Seventh and Eighth Prefixes			264
Eighth Prefix (**PI-**) ...	..	523	264
Ninth Prefix (**N-**) ...	...	524	265
Table of Forms of the Ninth Prefix	...		266
Tenth Prefix (**THIN-**) ...	...	525	267
Table of Forms of the Tenth Prefix	...		268

		§	PAGE.
Eleventh Prefix (**LU-**) ...	..	§ 526	269
Table of Forms of the Eleventh, Twelfth, and Thirteenth Prefixes ...			270
Twelfth Prefix (**TU-**)		527	271
Thirteenth Prefix (**KA-**)... ...		528	272
Fourteenth Prefix (**BU-**)... ...		529	273
Table of Forms of the Fourteenth and Fifteenth Prefixes			274
Fifteenth Prefix (**KU-**)		530	275
Sixteenth Prefix (**PA-**)		531	276
Table of Forms of the Sixteenth, Seventeenth, and Eighteenth Prefixes ...			276
Seventeenth Prefix (**KO-**) ...		532	277
Eighteenth Prefix (**MO-**)... ...		533	277
f. The different Systems of Classification		534	280
Synoptical Table			278
g. The Ancient Forms of the Derivative Prefixes of the Nouns		535 & 536	281
Table of the Fullest and most Primitive Forms			282
h. The Mutual Correspondence of the Classes of Nouns as Singular and Plural		537—540	287
Table shewing the Distribution of the Correspondences			288
2. The Genders and Numbers of Nouns in the Hottentot Language ...		541—558	292
The Nama Dialect		546—552	299
The !Kora Dialect		553—555	310
The Cape Dialect		556 & 557	315
Review of the Concord-indicating Derivative Suffixes of Hottentot Nouns ..		558	320
Table of Forms of the Hottentot Suffixes			321

PREFACE.

In presenting, after seven years interval, another portion of this Comparative Grammar to the public, I am grateful that I have been permitted to proceed, at least so far, with my work. Yet I feel truly sorry that I have not been able to publish, at the same time with this, the remaining portion of the Second Part. For, in giving only the Noun, and not all the other forms of Concord, I have only afforded half a view of a subject which, in order to be rightly understood, almost requires to be presented in its entirety. For my own part, I should gladly have delayed the publication of this first section until the completion of the whole of the Second Part; but as it may be years before such is the case, I think that I have no right to defer the publication of that which is now ready.

The more I study the subject, the more I become convinced of the great dependence of human thought upon language, and the more examples I meet with of human errors that are mere consequences of the forms of language. The sources of popular error in every nation have to be mainly looked for in the impressions produced by the spoken idiom upon the national mind. Language frequently sets before our eyes images which are more or less distorted, which deceive us, and lead us to erroneous conceptions. The forms of a language, especially, are continually moulding our thoughts, keeping them in certain grooves, and confining them within certain limits. On this account, an intelligent study of the structure of different languages gives us the leading outlines of the history of human conceptions and misconceptions; and the gradual development of mind can only be traced upon the basis of comparative researches into the forms of human speech. Those classifications of the nouns, particularly, which are based upon the different forms of concord, exert a powerful influence upon the mind, and impress upon it different associations of ideas. The Bântu languages, for example, with their sixteen distinct pronouns, which indicate as many separate classes of nouns, not one of which has any reference to sex,—must naturally cause the mind to view the world very differently from the Hottentot language, in which the pronouns, although eight in number, have each a certain sex-denoting, as well as numerical, meaning connected with them. For these reasons, the apparently dry study and exact comparison of the forms of the concord in the different South African languages, and the inquiry into the causes and origin of this concord, possess an interest extending far beyond that of facilitating the study of the individual languages.

The principle of representing the whole of a compound noun by one of its parts (which has led to the concord, and to the classification of the nouns as we find it regularly developed in the South African languages) may possibly be identical in the main with the so-called mode of "incorporation" peculiar to many American languages. I say this, however, with hesitation; for, upon the whole, this region is still a *terra incognita*,—no trained philologist having yet been found to devote himself to the comparative study of these languages. If even as much were done for America, as has been already accomplished for the African languages, general philology would be in a very different position, and we should be able to obtain, at least, some glimpses of the general history of human conceptions. However, it is not as if much had been done for Africa. On the contrary, the field of inquiry is very large, and promises a wealth of important results and new discoveries. Yet, excepting those who are practically engaged with one or another of these languages, scarcely any one has occupied himself with this branch of philology.

It is to be regretted that the greater number of comparative philologists appear to be still in a sort of rudimentary stage, corresponding to that in which zoologists would be if they refused to study any animals excepting those directly useful to man, and their nearest kindred species. In fact, the so-called Indo-European Comparative Philology now occupies the same place that Classical Philology did fifty or sixty years ago. It will not go beyond itself, and, as it were, shuts its eyes to the possibility that any other circle of languages can be akin to the Aryan. Yet it is clear that the complex phenomena which characterise the Aryan circle of languages cannot be rightly understood without a careful comparative examination of other languages of simpler organisation, which shew more of the ancient structure. Some of that energy, now so frequently wasted upon the discussion of questions to which the Indo-European circle of languages alone can never afford the clue, might well be given to the systematic comparative study of the more primitive Sex-denoting languages. To direct the attention of comparative philologists to these lower forms of language, and to prove the relations in which they stand with regard to the more highly developed Sex-denoting tongues, is one of the chief aims of this work. On this account, I particularly regret that the present volume only elucidates one part of that grand system of Concord which is the fundamental principle of the Pronominal languages. To have shown how the pronominal elements pervade the whole life of these languages, and how the concord is everywhere originally due to the presence of such representative elements, would have removed many difficulties, and would have given the student a fuller insight into the relations which the different Pronominal languages occupy towards each other, and especially that in which Hottentot stands with respect to some of the more northern Sex-denoting languages,—such as the Egyptian, the Semitic, and the Aryan or Indo-European.

I desire gratefully to acknowledge the assistance I have received in my labours from many who are special authorities in different departments of these languages, among whom I may particularly mention,—for Kafir, the Revds. J. W. APPLEYARD and TIYO SOGA,—for Zulu, the Rev. H. CALLAWAY, M.D., and the Right Rev. J. W. COLENSO, D.D., Bishop of Natal, —for Setshuâna, the Rev. I. HUGHES and the late Rev. J. FRÉDOUX,—for Setshuâna and other languages of the Interior, Dr. LIVINGSTONE,—for the Zangian languages, the Rev. Dr. STEERE,—for those of the Bunda Genus, the Revds. C. H. HAHN and J. RATH,—for Hottentot, the Revds. G. KRÖNLEIN, H. TINDALL, and the late Rev. F. H. VOLLMER.

I need not say how much I am in every way indebted to Sir GEORGE GREY, to whom it is mainly due that I could undertake this grammatical work, helped by so unique a philological collection referring to South African languages, as that in the Grey Library.

To the present Governor of the Cape of Good Hope, Sir PHILIP WODEHOUSE, to the Executive, and to the Legislature of the Colony especial thanks are due for having enabled me to complete this portion of my Comparative Grammar.

W. H. I. BLEEK.

Cape Town, 2nd April, 1869.

B. THE CONCORD.

I. THE NATURE OF THE CONCORD.

1. GENERAL REMARKS.

398. As we indicated already, in the first part of this Grammar (§§ 6—9), the common characteristic of the so-called Pronominal Languages is that a concord exists between nouns and certain other parts of speech, which are thereby referred to their respective nouns. Through this, a distribution of the nouns into classes (or genders)* takes place, which does not exhibit a strict analogy with any natural distinction, except in some of the most advanced of these languages,—particularly in English, and with modifications in Danish. But in all the more primitive types of the Pronominal Languages, the classes of nouns do not correspond exactly to the distinctions observed in nature, though they may have a certain reference to them. English *he*, Danish *han*, refers only to male beings, and English *she*, Danish *hun*, similarly to the opposite sex; whilst every noun denoting a being in which such distinctions of sex are not discernible is referred to in English by *it*, and in Danish, in some nouns, by *den*, in others by *det*.

---

* This use of the term *gender* has been objected to. In explanation I beg to state that in investigating the origin of the grammatical gender of nouns it will be found that the further we go back, the more it loses the apparent identity which it has at present in the English language, with the distinctions of sex. It is, therefore, necessary to divest one-self of the idea that gender must imply sex, and to treat the genders of nouns as that which they originally were,—namely, classes ; thus giving to the term *gender* a wider meaning, having no necessary reference to sex.

399. In German, however (though this language is nearly akin to both English and Danish), the pronoun *er* is not only, like the English *he* and Danish *han*, referred to nouns expressing male beings, but also to a great number of inanimate things, which are in English referred to by *it*, and in Danish by *den;* and in the same manner the German *sie* corresponds frequently in the extent of its meaning not only to the English *she*, Danish *hun*, but also to the English *it*, Danish *den*. It follows thence that the German *es*, though etymologically identical with the English *it*, is by no means so extensively used as the latter word; for the *es* does not refer by any means to all nouns expressing inanimate things, but only to a certain portion of them,—mainly to those to which also the Danish *det* refers.

400. We all know that a comparison of the kindred languages,—nay, a mere retracing of the English to its Anglo-Saxon parent—shows that the German has in this case preserved the more original conditions of the language, and that the more logical arrangements of the English and Danish tongues are of modern origin.

401. But it is not only with regard to the more logical arrangement of the classes (or genders) of nouns that the English differs from German and other kindred languages; but also with regard to the more limited extent of the concord between nouns and other parts of speech. Thus, if we compare the English sentences, *This handsome man appears, we love him*, and *This handsome woman appears, we love her*, we see that the only words in which the distinction of the nouns into classes (or genders) is visible, are the end words *him* and *her*. But if we translate the same sentence into German, we have *Dieser schöne mann erscheint, wir lieben ihn*, and *Diese schöne frau erscheint, wir lieben sie*, in which sentences a concord is apparent, not only in the last words (*ihn* and *sie*), but also in the first ones, *dieser* and *diese*. And if we go back to Latin, and render the above sentences literally, *Hic pulcher vir*

apparet, amamus eum, and *Hæc pulchra mulier apparet, amamus eam*, we meet with various forms for the different genders, not only in the first and last words (*hic* and *hæc, eum* and *eam*), but also in the second word (*pulcher, pulchra*).

402. On the whole, a comparison of the different Aryan languages, and a study of their various development, tend to show that, in general, those languages in which the division of the nouns into classes (or genders) is rendered visible through the concord of the greatest number of other parts of speech with the nouns to which they refer, may *primâ facie* be expected to exhibit the most primitive structural features. Further we may consider it as in the highest degree probable that the less the classes (or genders) of nouns in a language agree with natural distinctions, the more original will be found to be the state of that language. In both these regards the South African languages claim a prominent, if not the most prominent, position among all the languages as yet known to us. The Ba-ntu languages particularly extend the concord with the noun to almost all other parts of speech, and make it strongly visible in the various forms which these parts assume, when referred to different classes (or genders) of nouns. The number of classes (or genders) into which the nouns are here distributed, is far greater than in any other known language, amounting in most of the South African languages to more than a dozen classes (or genders), and in one, at least, to sixteen (if not eighteen); and of this large number of classes (or genders) in the Bâ-ntu languages only two agree with any natural distinctions, being restricted to nouns indicating personal beings (though not, however, including all of them), one class (or gender) to them in the singular, the other in the plural.

403. If, therefore, it should be ascertained that the distribution of the nouns into classes (or genders), as we find it in our (European and other Aryan) languages, is based

upon the same principle as in the South African languages, —it seems highly probable that the cause of this curious structural arrangement will be more easily discernible in the latter languages (the South African) than in the former (the Aryan).

404. Our plan is now, first to inquire into the cause of the distribution of the nouns into classes (or genders), in the BA-NTU languages, as well as in the HOTTENTOT language, this South African member of the Sex-denoting Family; then, to show how this affects the different parts of speech in the various South African languages; and, lastly, to see whether the distribution of the nouns into classes (or genders) in the other Sex-denoting languages is ascribable to the same cause as in Hottentot.

2. THE NATURE OF THE CONCORD IN THE BÂ-NTU LANGUAGES.

405. In order to introduce the student at once to the structural peculiarities of the Bâ-ntu languages, I begin with sentences in ZULU, which are similar to the above-given English and German ones, and will exhibit the changes which the different parts of speech undergo when brought into reference to the different classes (or genders) of nouns. Without entering into any further explanation, I will merely mention that the part of the noun whereby the same is referred to a certain class (or gender) is marked here by being printed in Antique type, while those portions of the other parts of speech which indicate their concord with the noun are in Roman letters, to distinguish them from the *Italics*, in which native words and sentences are generally given here.

1. U-**mu**-*ntu* w-*etu* o-mu-*xle* u-*ya-bonakala,* si-m-*tanda*.
   Man (or woman) ours handsome appears, we him love.
   Our handsome man (or woman) appears, we love him (or her).

Thus also u-m-*fazi* woman, u-m-*fundisi* teacher, u-mu-*ne* elder brother, and almost all nouns of person formed with the derivative prefix mu-, or its abbreviations.

2. A-ba-*ntu* b-*etu* a-ba-*x̧le* ba-*ya-bonakala*, *si*-ba-*tanda*.
    People   ours handsome   appear,   we them love.
Our handsome people appear, we love them.

Thus *e.g.*, a-ba-*fazi* women, a-ba-*fundisi* teachers, a-ba-*ne* elder brothers, and all nouns formed with the prefix ba-, which are all plurals to personal nouns in mu-(1.)

3. U-mu-*ti* w-*etu* o-mu-*x̧le* u-*ya-bonakala*, *si*-wu-*tanda*.
    Tree   ours handsome   appears,   we it love.
Our handsome tree appears, we love it.

Thus *e.g.*, u-mu-*zi* kraal, u-mu-*nwe* finger, u-mu-*x̧la* day, u-m-*lilo* fire, and almost all impersonal nouns formed with the derivative prefix mu-.

4. I-mi-*ti* y-*etu* e-mi-*x̧le* i-*ya-bonakala*, *si*-yi-*tanda*.
    Trees   ours handsome   appear,   we them love.
Our handsome trees appear, we love them.

Thus *e.g.*, i-mi-*zi* kraals, i-mi-*nwe* fingers, i-mi-*x̧la* days, and all nouns formed with the derivative prefix mi-, which are all plurals of impersonal nouns in mu- (3.)

5. I-li-*zwe* l-*etu* e-li-*x̧le* li-*ya-bonakala*, *si*-li-*tanda*.
    Country ours   fine   appears,   we it love.
Our fine country appears, we love it.

Thus also i-li-*zwi* or i-*zwi* voice, i-li-*tye* or i-*tye* stone, i-*zulu* heaven, i-*gama* name, &c., &c.

6. A-ma-*zwe* etu a-ma-*x̧le* a-*ya-bonakala* si-wa-*tanda*.
    Countries ours   fine   appear,   we them love.
Our fine countries appear, we love them.

Thus also, a-ma-*zwi* words, a-ma-*tye* stones, a-ma-*zulu* heavens, a-ma-*gama* names, a-ma-*kosi* kings (sng. i-n-*kosi* 9. king), a-ma-*doda* men (sng. i-n-*doda* 9. man), and all other nouns formed with the derivative prefix ma-, be they plurals to nouns in the singular of the 5th (li-) class (as most of them are), or of the 9th (n-) class, or of other classes,—or be they without corresponding singular, as a-ma-*nzi* water, and similar nouns.

7. I-**si**-*zwe* s-*etu* e-si-x̌*le* si-*ya-bonakala*, *si*-si-*tanda*.
    Nation ours fine appears, we it love.
Our fine nation appears, we love it.

Thus also, i-**si**-*lo* wild animal, i-**si**-*tya* a vessel for eating or drinking, i-**si**-*ta* enemy, and all other nouns formed with the derivative prefix **si**-.

8. I-**zi**-*zwe* z-*etu* e-zi-x̌*le* zi-*ya-bonakala*, *si*-zi-*tanda*.
    Nations ours fine appear, we them love.
Our fine nations appear, we love them.

Thus also, i-**zi**-*lo* wild animals, i-**zi**-*tya* vessels for eating or drinking, i-**zi**-*ta* enemies, and all other plurals of nouns formed with **si**- in the singular.

9. I-**n**-*tombi* y-*etu* o-n-x̌*le* i-*ya-bonakala* si-yi-*tanda*.
    Girl ours handsome appears, we her love.
Our handsome girl appears, we love her.

Thus also, i-**n**-*to* thing, i-**m**-*vu* sheep, i-**n**-*kosi* king, i-**n**-*doda* man, &c., &c.

10. I-**zin**-*tombi* z-*etu* e-zin-x̌*le* zi-*ya-bonakala*, *si*-zi-*tanda*.
    Girls ours handsome appear, we them love.
Our handsome girls appear, we love them.

Thus also, i-**zin**-*to* things, i-**zim**-*vu* sheep, i-**zin**-*ti* sticks (sng. u-**lu**-*ti* 11. stick), and many other plurals to nouns of the 9th (**n**-) and 11th (**lu**-) classes.

11. U-**lu**-*ti* lw-*etu* o-lu-x̌*le* lu-*ya-bonakala*, *si*-lu-*tanda*.
    Stick ours handsome appears, we it love.
Our handsome stick appears, we love it.

Thus also, u-*bambo* rib, u-*nwele* hair, &c., &c.

The 12th and 13th classes of nouns are lost in the languages of the South-eastern Branch (of the South African Division of the Bâ-ntu languages), to which the Zulu belongs; but they are met with in the languages of the Middle Branch; and in Otyiherero, the most southern language of the South-western Genus, the 12th (**tu**-) class corresponds as plural to the 11th (**ru**-) class, and thus we have in Otyiherero:

11. *O*-**ru**-*vio* ru-*etu* o-r-ua* ru-*a*-*munika*, *ma*-*tu*-ru-ɜ'*uvere*.
    Knife   ours   fine   appears,   we   it   love.
Our fine knife appears, we love it.

Thus also, *o*-**ru**-*pati* rib, *o*-**ru**-*hingo* long kind of stick, *o*-**ru**-*huaku* thick ironwire, *o*-**ru**-*koro* breast (chest), and all other nouns formed with the derivative prefix **ru**-.

12. *O*-**tu**-*vio* tu-*etu* o-t-ua* tu-*a*-*munika*, *ma*-*tu*-tu-ɜ'*uvere*,
    Knives   ours   fine   appear,   we them love.
Our fine knives appear, we love them.

Thus also, *o*-**tu**-*pati* ribs, *o*-**tu**-*hingo* long sticks, *o*-**tu**-*huaka* bracelets of ironwire, *o*-**tu**-*koro* breasts (chests), and all other nouns formed with the derivative prefix **tu**-, which are almost all plurals of nouns formed in the singular with the prefix **ru**-.†

13. *O*-**ka**-*ti* k-*etu* o-ka-ua k-*a*-*munika*, *ma*-*tu*-ke-ɜ'*uvere*.
    Stick   ours   fine   appears,   we it love.
Our fine stick appears, we love it.

Thus also, *o*-**ka**-*puka* a little animal, *o*-**ka**-*rume*-*ndu* a little man, and all other nouns formed with the derivative prefix **ka**-, most of which are in Otyihereró diminutives.‡

14. *O*-**u**-*ti* u-*etu* o-u-ua u-*a*-*munika*, *ma*-*tu*-u-ɜ'*uvere*.
    Sticks   ours   fine   appear,   we them love.
Our fine sticks appear, we love them.

Thus, *o*-**u**-*puka* little animals, *o*-**u**-*rume*-*ndu* little men, and all other nouns formed with the derivative prefix **u**-, some of which are in Otyihereró plurals to nouns of the 13th (**ka**-) class, whilst others

---

* Contracted respectively from *o*-ru-*ua* and *o*-tu-*ua*.

† Mr. Rath enumerates the following Otyihereró nouns formed with the derivative prefix **tu**-, which have no singular corresponding to them, viz.: *O*-**tu**-*nda* elevation, *o*-**tu**-*ndu* mould, *o*-**tu**-*tumukua* death-rattle, *o*-**tu**-*pikua* field (as opposed to home), *o*-**tu**-*nde* a bone in the nape of the neck.

‡ Other nouns (not diminutives) formed with **ka**- in Otyihereró are according to Mr. Rath, the following: *O*-**ka**-*numaere* evening star, *o*-**ka**-*pute* hook, *o*-**ka**-*hikuinini* a kind of partridge, *o*-**ka**-*hue* cat, *o*-**ka**-*nduhanambaka* frog, toad, *o*-**ka**-*pendomuti* a bird, *o*-**ka**-*rumatavahona* a snake, *o*-**ka**-ɜ'*eni* kind of antelope, *o*-**ka**-*tyavui* spider.

are clearly of the singular number, *e.g. o-u-tuku* night (pl. *o-ma-u-tuku* 6. nights), *o-u-ta* bow (pl. *o-ma-u-tu* 6. bows), *o-u-kona* kingdom, *o-u-nene* greatness, and all similar abstract nouns in **u-**.

The 14th class is also found in ZULU, but the nouns included in it do not clearly imply the singular or the plural number; therefore this class does not correspond here to any other (as singular or plural), but includes mostly abstract nouns, as *u-***bu**-*kulu* greatness, *u-***bu**-*x̌le* beauty, u-**bu**-*bi* evil, u-**bu**-*kosi* chieftainship, &c.

14. U-**bu**-*suku* b-*etu* o-bu-*x̌le* bu-*ya-bonakala*, *si*-bu-*tanda*.
   Night   ours   fine   appears,   we it love.
Our fine night appears, we love it.

15. U-**ku**-*tanda* ku-*etu* o-ku-*kulu* ku-*ya-bonakala*, a-**ba**-*ntu*   Loving   ours   great   appears,   men
ba-ku-*bona*, *si*-ku-*bonakalisa*.
 it see,   we it appear make.
Our great love appears, men see it, we make it appear.

Thus, also, u-**ku**-*lunga* righteousness, u-**ku**-*x̌la* food, u-**ku**-*sa* dawn, morning, u-**ku**-*kanya* light, u-**ku**-*tyo* saying, and all other nouns formed with **ku-**, among which are found the infinitives of all verbs.

As the 16th **pa**- class (or gender) has disappeared in Zulu (§ 430) we give an example of this class in OTYIHEREBÓ, viz.:

16. O-**po**-*na* p-*etu* o-po-pa-*ua* pa-*munika* ma-*tu*-pe-*θ'uvere*.
   Place   ours   fine   appears,   we it love.
Our fine place appears, we love it.

406. A look at the above Zulu sentences will show us that in the examples which are given of the 11th (lu-) and 15th (**ku**-) classes (or genders), the concord between the noun and the other parts of speech consists in the full repetition of a part of the noun which we call its derivative prefix.[*] In the 2nd (**ba**-), 5th (li-), 7th (si-), 8th (zi-), and 14th (**bu**-) classes (or genders), the same rule holds

---

[*] We do not take here into consideration the initial vowels of the prefixes of the nouns, and of the adjectives, between which and the prefixes there is an evident agreement, as this will be further elucidated in the course of our researches. (§. 461—466.)

good, with the exception that the vowels of the syllables indicating the concord are elided before other vowels. Also in the other classes (or genders) the agreement between the forms of the nouns and of the other parts of speech is such as to favour the idea that there also, originally, a mere repetition of some part of the noun took place, and that it is only through wear and tear that the forms have assumed a somewhat reduced shape, which, though indicating a correspondence, no longer amounts to an actual repetition of some part of the noun. A comparison of all the various forms in the different dialects of this family of languages convinces us of the truth of this presumption; and as it is important to have this point at once cleared up, we will here give at least one proof by tracing some of those forms of the possessive adjective "our," which in Zulu seemed to deviate from this rule of actual bodily repetition.

407. Thus in the 3rd (**mu**-) class (or gender) instead of the Zulu u-**m**-*lenze* w-*etu* n-o-**mu**-*nwe* w-*ami*,
       leg ours and finger mine
the Isubu has **mo**-*indi* mo-*su* na **mu**-*ne* mo-*am*.

The corresponding plurals of the 4th (**mi**-) class are in Zulu i-**mi**.*lenze* y-*etu* n-e-**mi**-*nwe* y-*ami*,
      legs ours and fingers mine
but in Isubu **me**-*indi* mi-*asu* na **mi**-*ne* mi-*am*.

And though in the 3rd (**mu**-) class (or gender) the Kongo words **mu**-*tima etu* correspond exactly to the
         heart ours
Isubu words **mo**-*lema* mo-*su*, yet in the plural we find that the Kongo translates with **mi**-*tima* mi-*etu* what again the
           hearts ours
Isubu would express by **mi**-*lema* mi-*asu*. The Otyihereró has in this case preserved an intermediate stage in o-**mi**-*tima* vi-*etu* (our hearts).

408. Thus in the case of the 3rd (**mu**-) and 4th (**mi**-) classes (or genders), the Isubu forms (and in the latter class those of the old Kongo language also,) prove that

the Zulu forms w-*etu* 3. and y-*etu* 4. are here respectively derived from an original MU-ETU 3. and MI-ETU 4. This tends to make us believe that wherever in the 3rd class (or gender) we find now a *w* and in the 4th a *y*, as a sign of class, the *w* is derived from an original *mu*, and the *y* from an original *mi*.

409. Similarly in the 6th (**ma-**) class (or gender), the Zulu a-**ma**-*nzi* *etu* is translated literally in
         water   ours
Isubu **ma**-*diba* ma-*su*; and with this fuller form ma-*su* there agree also the corresponding forms of this possessive adjective in the 6th (**ma-**) class (or gender), in Kongo m-*etu* (our), and in Mpongwe ma-*ryo*.

410. As we have shown how the Zulu *etu* of the 6th (**ma-**) class (or gender) is derived from a former MAETU, —in the same manner all the other cases of concord between the nouns and other parts of speech (with a few particular exceptions which will afterwards be considered) can be proved to have arisen from an actual identity of the original forms of the derivative prefixes of the nouns with those portions of the other parts of speech which indicate the concord, or are, as we would call them, signs of the gender. The question is now, how this identity has arisen, and, consequently, what is the real cause of this peculiar division of the nouns into classes, or genders.

411. The most obvious explanation appears to be to assume that those portions which indicate the concord are pronouns, and that they were prefixed to the nouns in a similar manner as, for example, *he* and *she* are to *he-bear* and *she-goat*. Now, where these marks of concord, indicative of class (or gender), are found in other parts of speech, as referring these to nouns, it is true that they must be admitted and are to be considered as true pronouns,—*i.e.*, as mere representatives of the nouns to which they respectively refer. But if we assumed that the derivative prefixes of nouns were originally pronouns, this would not explain how there came to be such a

variety of different classes (or genders) of pronouns, or what was the principle on which they were respectively used for the formation, or for the classification, of the nouns. It has, indeed, been suggested by Sir GEORGE GREY that they were chosen mainly for euphony's sake,— *i.e.*, there being a variety of prefixes which could be used with nouns, those were selected which were most in harmony as to sound with the remaining part of the noun. This theory is probably true in a certain restricted sense,—*i.e.*, that where there were two or more forms of nouns with different prefixes which expressed very nearly the same meaning, that form would probably be generally retained which was the most euphonious, or at least the most easily pronounced.

412. But such an explanation does not, however, exclude the fact that every one of these different forms of the nouns conveyed originally a meaning of its own, and that each prefix possessed a distinct power. That this is really the case is clearly perceived even by a cursory glance at a variety of nouns in the Bâ-ntu languages belonging to different classes, though formed from the same stems. For example, in Zulu we have the noun u-mu-*ntu* (human being, person,) belonging to the 1st (mu-) class (or gender), and its plural a-ba-*ntu* (people) to the 2nd (ba-) class, and from the same stem i-si-*ntu* (human race, mankind,) of the 7th (si-) class, u-bu-*ntu* (human nature) of the 14th (bu-) class, besides which the Kafir language has u-lu-*ntu** of the 11th (lu-) class, which here means "human race, human kind," whilst i-si-*ntu* 7. in Kafir, according to Appleyard, indicates "human species."

413. In Se-*suto*, the name of the language itself belongs to the 7th (se-) class (or gender), whilst the people who speak it are called by a noun of the 2nd (ba-) class (or gender) Ba-*suto*, and one of them is a Mo-*suto*, which is

---

* In Zulu this word has the meaning of "outer covering of bowels," but a meaning similar to the Kafir one has also, though rarely, been observed. (Bishop of Natal's Grammar p. 16, Dictionary p. 354.)

a noun of the 1st (mo-) class. The name of their country is Le-*suto*, a noun of the 5th (le-) class. Similarly, a Mo-*tshuâna* (1st class) is one of the nation of the Be-*tshuâna* or Ba-*tshuâna* (2nd class), who speak Se-*tshuâna* (7th class)*; and an O-mu-*hereró* 1. is one of the O-va-*hereró*, 2. (Damaras), who speak O-tyi-*hereró* 7., *i.e.*, in Damara fashion.†

414. A chief is called in Kafir 1-n-*kosi* 9., and several a-ma-*kosi* 6., and chieftainship is u-bu-*kosi* 14. In Otyihereró, a chief is o-mu-*hona* 1., chiefs are o-va-*hona* 2., and chieftainship o-u-*hona* 14.

415. These specimens may suffice for the present to exemplify the fact that the derivative prefixes of the nouns in the Bâ-ntu languages have a similar power and meaning, as e.g., the English derivative suffixes -dom, -ship, -ness, -er, -hood, &c. Now, not even by the most strenuous upholders of the so-called Pronominal Theory‡ have these English derivative suffixes been deduced from pronouns; and there is no doubt that originally the nouns formed with these suffixes were compound nouns, and that these syllables (-dom,- ship, -ness, &c.) had almost all at an earlier period of the language the value and meaning of nouns, and were used separately as such.

416. It is, therefore, the most natural assumption, that the derivative prefixes of the nouns in the Bâ-ntu languages also, had originally a separate value and meaning, and that nouns formed with them were compounded, and

---

* *Vide* the note on pp. 109—112.

† That O-*tyi-hereró* does not mean merely the Damara Language, is clear from such sentences as o-n-*dyuo* y-a-*tungua* O-*tyi-hereró*, the house is built in Damara fashion.—(J. Rath).

‡ I here call by the name of Pronominal Theory a mania by which some of the most eminent philologists were once seized, of deriving all those grammatical elements of the language of which the explanation was not obvious, from so-called pronouns, really, however, from demonstrative particles.

that when the parts *to be determined** lost their meaning
as separate words, (*i.e.,* became obsolete,) these nouns,
originally compound, became derivatives.

417. Now, if the derivative particles of the nouns in
the Bâ-ntu languages were still merely parts of compound
nouns, and could still be used separately, there would be
nothing remarkable in their use as representatives of the
nouns which are compounded with them. This use is
found in all languages. In English, for example, in speaking of such compound nouns as *spyglass, lookingglass, wineglass,* &c., we may use the simple nouns *glass* for each of
them, though in a slightly different meaning from its
separate and independent use. Supposing, now, that this
word *glass* had lost its separate and independent meaning,
yet retained its power of representing those compound
nouns, of which it constitutes the principal nominal
element, it would have become a pronominal element, or
a particle to be used in order to refer other parts of
speech to the noun which it at the time represented.
Now, in the Bâ-ntu languages the derivative prefixes of
the nouns have done this; they have lost their separate
value as nouns, but retained the power of being used as
representatives of the nouns of which they form a part.

418. Or, to illustrate the case by another analogy.
Let us suppose that in English, for example, the syllable
dom could still be used by itself as representative of such
words as are compounded with it, and we could, therefore,
speak of *the fine dom* meaning *the fine kingdom* or *the fine
dukedom,* or any other *dom.* In olden times, of course,
when *dom* (related to *doom,*) was used as an independent noun, it could represent a noun of which it formed a

---

* In order not to be obscure, I should perhaps remind the general reader that in compound words one part is called the *determining, i.e.,* that which points out or determines more exactly the value of the other, which latter is called the part *to be determined.* For example, in the compound words "horse-shoe," "horse-flesh," "rail-way," "tram-way," &c., &c., *horse, rail,* and *tram,* are the determining elements, showing what kind of *shoe, flesh,* or *way,* is meant.

component part in the same manner, as, for example, the word *empire* can now stand for the fuller *king's empire*. But when it lost its independent position, it lost with it the representative power of standing instead of the nouns, of which it formed a component part. For, in the more advanced stages of morphological development, even in Pronominal Languages, it generally seems that the representative power of a noun is lost with its (the noun's) independent use. Thus we can no longer use the syllable *-ship* (German *-schaft*, which belongs originally to the same root as *shape*) for such nouns ending with it as, for example, *governorship, clerkship, stewardship,* &c.*; though we can, on the other hand, indicate a *governor's office* by the use of the latter noun *office*, because this has continued to be used as an independent noun, and has, when alone, a meaning of its own, which includes that of the more specified term; and for the same reason the independent noun *ship* (German *schiff*) can still be used in English as representative of nouns compounded with it,—as, *steamship, flagship,* &c.; for these nouns do not merely end with *ship*, but indicate ships. If, however, the noun *ship* had lost its independent meaning, the words compounded with it could no longer be referred to by this simple syllable, though they might continue to exist as derived nouns.

419. When the formation of the pronominal elements, (by which the concord of the noun with other parts of speech was effected,) first took place in the so-called Pronominal Languages,—syllables, after losing their independent value as nouns, were retained for the purpose of representing those nouns, of which they formed principal parts. Thus the Zulu sentence " u-bu-*kosi* b-*etu*

---

* It is true that by a satirical licence, such a word as *ology* is made to represent nouns ending with this termination. But this is an exception which rather tends to prove the rule that such formations (which appear, however, to differ entirely in their origin from that of the pronouns in the South African languages,) cannot be seriously employed at present in our languages.

o-bu-*kulu* bu-*ya-bonakala*, *si*-bu-*tanda*," would literally be in English "*the* king-dom, *our* dom, *which* dom *is the great* dom, *the* dom *appears, we love the* dom,"—a manner of speaking which sounds, of course, absurd in English; and so does also its most literal German translation "*das* könig-thum, *unser* thum, *welches* thum *ist ein grosses* thum, *das* thum *erscheint, wir lieben das* thum." But it becomes at least intelligible, if, instead of the derived noun *könig-thum* (kingdom), we use the compound noun *könig-reich* (king's empire), and say: "*das* könig-reich, *unser* reich, *welches* reich *ist ein grosses* reich, *das* reich *erscheint, wir lieben das* reich;" i.e. "*the king's* empire, *our* empire, *which* empire *is the great* empire, *the* empire *appears, we love the* empire." In like manner, though we cannot say "*the* steam-er, *our* er, *which* er *is a great* er, *the* er *appears, we love the* er," because the syllable *er* is here merely a derivative suffix which has no meaning of its own;—if we use instead of the derived word *steamer* the compound one *steamship*, the last syllable of this word may be employed to represent the whole, and thus we might say: "*the* steam-ship, *our* ship, *which* ship *is a great* ship, *the* ship *appears, we love the* ship." But in words where the syllable *ship* is a derivative suffix, it is incapacitated from being used by itself for the purpose of representing the whole compound noun. Thus it would be absurd to say, "*the friend*-ship, *our* ship, *which* ship *is a great* ship, *the* ship *appears, we love the* ship." The Zulu construction is, as far as regards the quality of the noun, (which is a derived one like *kingdom*, *königthum*, *steamer*, *friendship*, &c., not a compound one as *königreich*, *steamship*, &c.), similar to that of those sentences which are now impossible to us; but also like that of the other sentences (at least allowable,) in the power of representing the whole of a composite noun by means of its principal element.

420. There is an appearance of redundancy in this frequent repetition of the representative elements of the noun, when they are thus used with all parts of speech,

which have a reference to it. But this will not much astonish those who have studied the literature of primitive races, and know the construction of their compositions

> "With their frequent repetitions,
> And their wild reverberations."

The less people as yet express slight changes in their meaning by the mere position of words, by internal changes, or slight variations of pronunciation,—the more necessity there is for actual verbal expression, and repetition of that which is to be referred to. Besides, it must be remembered that these repetitions of parts of the noun take the place of pronominal elements, and a careful analysis of most of the highly civilized languages will show that in the grammatical forms indicating the concord, pronouns were originally used, which have now generally disappeared, though their influence continues to be felt. Still the Bâ-ntu languages far exceed in cumbersome repetition even the lowest known types of Sex-denoting languages.*

---

* Dr. LIVINGSTONE in his "ANALYSIS," page 9, says: "The chief use in the extraordinary repetition of the signs of nouns which occur in pure Setshuana, may be generally stated to be to give precision to the sentence. They impart energy and perspicuity to each member of a proposition, and prevent the possibility of a mistake as to the antecedent. They are the means by which with a single syllable or letter a recurrent allusion to the subject spoken of is made, which cannot be accomplished by our lawyers without the clumsy circumlocution of 'said defendant,' 'said subject matter,' &c., &c. They are, moreover, used as the articles are in Greek, but invariably follow, never precede the noun." [In Kafir and some other Bâ-ntu languages, they also precede the noun.—W. H. I. B.] "They are also demonstrative pronouns, &c., &c., as we shall hereafter show."

In a letter from Zanzibar, dated March, 2nd, 1866, he further remarks: "I cannot quite sympathize with you when you speak of that use as 'cumbersome repetition.' The absence of it, in the mouths of halfcastes, speaking an impure form of Setshuana, used to sound in my ears excessively harsh. And the fact of the sign being the easily recognizable initial sound of the noun, prevented any of that doubt which always clings to those abominations of the English language, 'former' and 'latter'. See how much difficulty you had to express yourself in Par. 403."

MO-TSHUANA, BE-TSHUANA, SE-TSHUANA.

[Note to § 413.]

With reference to the etymology of these words, the Rev. R. MOFFAT stated that the words Se-*tshuâna* 7., Be-*tshuâna* 2., and Mo-*tshuâna* 1., were not derived, as generally believed (*vide* "Livingstone's Travels," p. 200) from the verb *tshuâna* (be like each other, Kafir *funa*), but from the adjective-stem *tshuâna* (Kafir -mx̌*lotshana*) a little white, or inclining to white, light-coloured, (*i.e.*, not black, probably in opposition to the more dark-coloured tribes of the North,) a diminutive form from *tshueu* (Kafir -mx̌*lope*, Ki-kamba -*eu*, Mpongwe -*pupu*) white. (Sir G. Grey's Library, Vol. I. Part I. p. 184.)

This derivation was, however, rejected by the late Rev. J. FREDOUX, who said in a letter to the author : " Mo-*tshuâna* 1. is not the diminutive form from *tshueu* 9. (white), but from -*ntshu* (black), and means, therefore, not 'inclining to white,' but 'inclining to black,' as the colour of the Betshuâna. When an individual of that nation is rather whitish, he is sometimes said to be mo-*shuâna* (pronounced mo-*sheuana*) 1., and this is the diminutive form from *tshueu* 9. (mo-*shueu* 1.), meaning 'inclining to white.' "

Further, Dr. D. LIVINGSTONE, in a letter dated " Tette, 22nd February, 1859," made the following remarks on this subject : " Mr. Moffat's idea," he says, " is probably the right one, but as a philologist you may like to hear why some minds prefer the meaning of ' likeness or equality.'

" When sex is spoken of in connection with colour, the diminutive form is invariably applied (the diminutive being referred to the colour, not size). Thus *kxomu* e *tsheu* 9. a white ox, *i.e.*, altogether white ; *kxomu* e *tshuana* 9. a white cow, not a little, but entirely ; *kxomu* e e-*ntshu* 9. a black ox ; *kxomu* e *tshuâna* 9. black cow ; *kxomu* e *kxueba* 9. a speckled ox ; *kxomu* e *kxuebana* 9. a speckled cow. The idea of littleness seems to go to denote sex by the lesser size of the females, the males being denoted by *tôna* 9., in the same way.

" This point is not adverted to in the " ANALYSIS," but it is so distinctly adhered to in the language that an additional syllable is introduced to express a little of any colour. Thus Mo-*sheu* 1. a white man ; Mo-*sheunyana* 1. a little white man ; Mo-*ntshu* 1. a black one ; Mo-*ntshunyana* 1. a little black one. One of Sebituane's daughters is called *Montshunyana* from her colour, being as light as an Arab woman's, *i.e.*, only a little black.

" Were it not for the cow difficulty the term Ba-*tshuâna* 2. would be better translated ' a little black,' instead of ' a little white.' They were a little blacker than the Bushmen and Hottentots. They had intercourse with them, but they had none with the people beyond the Desert. To say they are a little whiter than these people is to reason from our own knowledge of what is only partially the case. The **Ba**-*tóka* 2., for instance, the **Ba**-*nyai* 2., and other tribes are as light as they are."

Then, Dr. Livingstone quotes one sentence, apparently in support of his first etymology. "A man was checked by Setshele for telling him some heathen story. He did not wish to hear it. 'You are under the Southern people,' said the man, in a pet. '*Re Batshuana*' [We are Betshuana, or alike ?], replied Setshele, 'I follow what I found in the book ; I am not inferior or under them.' If he had been applying a feminine term to himself, the assertion of equality would have been meaningless."

Lastly Mr. FREDOUX in a subsequent letter, dated Motito, February 16th, 1866, wrote as follows :

"As you have noticed in a note the various derivations given of the word **Be**-*tshuana*, I shall add here, on that account, the following remarks which may be of interest to you.

"I. *Objections which may be made to what is said in favour of the common derivation* (from χο *tshuana* 15. to be alike).

"1°. Dr. LIVINGSTONE says (in his book) that the Betshuana use that name as meaning *Equals*. I have never observed that, and I believe no Motshuana will say that such is the meaning of the word. In fact, Dr. L. himself admits nearly as much by saying a little farther, that the Betshuana cannot explain the derivation of their name, which would be the simplest thing in the world, *if they attached to it* the meaning expressed by a verb which they use continually. Thus they would say at once *Re Betshuana χone rea tshuana* (We are Betshuana, because we are like each other), or *Betshuana ki χo re ba ba tshuanah* (Betshuana that is to say those who are like each other).

"2°. Dr. Livingstone says in support of his derivation that the Betshuana call themselves by that name *exactly in the same sense* as Irishmen, &c., would say, 'We are Britons or Englishmen.' Now this would favour his derivation only if it could be shown that both the words *Britons* and *Englishmen* also mean *Equals*, since these are used exactly in the same sense as Betshuana is used. If Britons and Englishmen do not mean *Equals*, what he says here is rather against him.

"3°. But again χο *tshuana* 15. does not mean properly *to be equals*, but *to be alike*. Such being the case, the noun would mean *Those who are alike* or *those who are like each other*, rather than 'Equals.' Now it is difficult to understand how a nation could call itself by such a name, except its members distinguished themselves among other peoples by being so very much like each other in colour and forms, which is not the assumption.

"4°. I may add, without giving too much importance to this, that according to that derivation, Ba-*tshuana* 2. would be properly a phrase rather than a noun, and that the sing. would be O-*a-tshuana* 1. rather than **Mo**-*tshuana* 1.

" 5°. In the letter you quote, Setshele seems to be made to apply the name Batshuana not only to himself and his people, but even to the *Whites*. According to that, that word ought not to be considered any more as a proper name and as the particular name of the Betshuana. It would be a common word of the language. But there must be some mistake here, perhaps on my part. Setshele cannot have said, 'I and the Southern people are Betshuana,' except by 'Southern people' he meant Southern Betshuana, such as the BaXlapi.

" My opinion is that whatever may be the *root* of the name, it is now used *merely as a name*, without any other meaning being attached to it; and therefore, even if it was properly and originally a feminine, Setshele might with propriety apply it to himself.

" II. *What may be said in favour of the derivation which was proposed by me* (from *ntsho* black).

" 1°. The word *motshuana* 1. means : (1) A *blackish person*, without reference to sex or size ; (2) a *Motshuana*, a person of the Betshuana nation. Now it seems to be extremely natural to derive the second meaning from the first, without seeking for another etymology, when the word is taken in the second sense,—just as when we find the surname *Brown* in English, we think it is quite unnecessary to hunt for another root, when we have the adjective *brown*.

" 2°. We seem to be still more pressed to agree to the above explanation of the name Motshuana, when we consider that that word, when used in the first sense, denotes precisely the *typical* colour of the Betshuana. If you take a native who is rather dark-coloured for a Motshuana and ask what is his *colour*, the answer will be : *montsho* 1. (black) ; if you take one who is somewhat light-coloured, the answer will be: *moshueu* or *moshouana* (pronounced also *moshuaana*) ; if you take one who is of the usual colour, the answer will be : *motshuana*. This may be tried by any one ; the result is always the same.

" 3°. If it be asked why that explanation of the name of the Betshuana was not thought of from the first, and generally received, my answer will be : For the very simple and sufficient reason that the first meaning of the word *motshuana* had been noticed by few, if by any Europeans. You see from Livingstone's remarks that when he wrote his letter to you, he was not aware of that sense. Hence his 'cow difficulty.' That sense, however, is known to all the Betshuana, and there is no possibility of denying its existence, *when one has questioned the natives about it*. (See the late Rob. Moffat's work on Phonology, page 15.)

" You will perhaps be surprised, after all I have said above, to hear me add that, after all, I do not feel absolutely sure that my explanation of the name Betshuana was the right one, and that I am now somewhat inclined to confess my ignorance on that point, as the Betshuana themselves do.

" The word *motshuana* " a blackish person " is not pronounced exactly like *motshuana*, " a Mochuana." Had the two words had the same pronunciation, very likely the natives themselves might give to their name the above-mentioned derivation, which they do not do. According to the orthography followed in my "Sketch of Grammar," the first word is pronounced *mōchúana (mō-tshúana)*, whilst the other appears to be pronounced *Mōcúana (Mo-tsh'úana).* There may be besides some difference in the pronunciation of the first *a*. This, however, goes about as much against the derivation from χO-*tshuana* as against that from -*ntsho*. I confess this difference of pronunciation seems to me to be a great difficulty. To get over it, we would have to say that, in the course of time, the proper name was slightly altered, and this is not an impossibility.

"But has that name been in use for many generations? This may perhaps be doubted. It appears to be pretty certain that the word Betshuana originated in the South; that not very long ago, say 40 or 50 years ago, it was unknown among the Bahurutse, the Bahuaketsi, and the other northern tribes; and that these first heard it from the Baxlapis, who applied it to *them* (to the northern tribes), and *not* to themselves. This is what I am assured of by the natives, for instance by an old Mohurutse and an old Mohuaketsi, who live here. At the beginning of the present century, however, travellers found the word in existence at Lithakoń and Kuruman, and, it would seem, applied it to the Baxlapis as well as to the other tribes."

3. THE NATURE OF THE CONCORD IN THE HOTTENTOT LANGUAGE.

421. This appears at once, if we translate the first of the previous examples into the Hottentot language, and vary it according to the different classes (or genders).*

Masc. sing.   *Si-da   ē-sa   khoi-*p   *ta   khui,   /nam-bi-da-ra.*
     Our handsome man   does appear, love him we do.
Our handsome man (husband) appears, we love him.

* The Hottentot sentences given in this and the following paragraph are (with one exception, that illustrating the common sing. in § 421) taken from a manuscript in the Grey Library, kindly furnished by the late Rev. F. H. Vollmer. The orthography has been slightly altered. In their revision, use has been made of some valuable notes by the Superintendent of Missions in Great Namaqualand, the R. Rev. G. Krönlein. It must be borne in mind that the pronunciation of some words in the dialect of the *Gei-//khous*, or *Roode Volk*, among whom Mr. Vollmer resided, differs from that in which Krönlein's translation of the New Testament is written. The *Gei-//khous* for example, say *goma-*n (common sing.) "oxen" instead of *gama-*n (§ 226, note), /en-s (f. s.) "name" for ,/on-s, /geira-p (m. s.) "jackal" for /gūi-p, &c.

Masc. plur. *Si-da ē-sa khoi-***gu** *ra khui,* /*nam-gu-da-ra.*
  Our handsome men do appear, love them we do.
Our handsome men (husbands) appear, we love them.
Masc. dual. *Si-da /gam ē-sa khoi-***kha** *ra khui,* /*nam-kha-da-ra.*
  Our two handsome men do appear, love them we do.
Our two handsome men (husbands) appear, we love them.
Fem. sing. *Si-da ē-sa tara-***s** *ta khui,* /*nam-si-da-ra.*
  Our handsome woman does appear, love her we do.
Our handsome woman appears, we love her.
Fem. plur. *Si-da ē-sa tara-***ti** *ra khui,* /*nam-ti-da-ra.*
  Our handsome women do appear, love them we do.
Our handsome women appear, we love them.
Common sing. *Ēsa khoi-***ï** *ra khui,* /*nam-i-da-ra.*
  Handsome person any appears, we him love.
Any handsome person appears, we love him (or her.)
Common plur. *Si-da ē-sa khoi-***n** *ta khui,* /*nam-in-da-ra.*
  Our handsome people do appear, love them we do.
Our handsome people appear, we love them.
Common dual. *Si-da /gam ē-sa khoi-***ra** *ra khui,* /*nam-ra-da-ra.*
  Our two handsome persons do appear, love them we do.
Our two handsome persons appear, we love them.

422. In these sentences the concord is apparent in the objective pronouns only, not in the so-called possessive pronouns, or other adjectives, nor in the verb, as referring to its subject; the variation of *ta* for *ra* being entirely dependent upon the nature of the preceding letter.* The concord will, however, become more evident, if we take other sentences as examples, in which adjectival forms follow their nouns, &c.

MASCULINE SINGULAR.

//*Nä au-***p** *si-da !hau-s-di-*p, !*khu-hā-*p, /*nī lā-s-!na* //*an-hā-*p,
That man our tribe's he, rich being, another village-in dwelling,

---

* If emphasis is required, *gye-ra* is employed instead of *ra* or *ta.*

hō-bi-da-ra, gare-da-ra goma-n ă-b-a, tsī-p-ta |kai-da
find him we do, praise we do cattle of him, and he does present us
|gam tsău-n ||ēi-p-di-n-χa.
two calves his from.

The man who belongs to our tribe, who is rich, who dwells in that village, we find him, we praise his cattle, and he presents us with two of his calves.

||Nā !nau-p tara-s-di-p, ||nă-p gei-p, om-mi-!na ||goĕ-p, mū-bi-da-ra,
That beam woman's it, that large, house-in lying, see it we do,
||ēi-b-di |'ou-b-a da-ra mū-≠an, tsī-da ī-p ă-b-a ra |num,
its thickness we do see-know, and we appearance of it do like,
tsī-p-ta om-m-a ≠kă-!na.
and it does the house support.

The beam which belongs to the woman, which is large, which lies in the house, we perceive its thickness, and we like its appearance, and it supports the house.

This class or gender (masculine singular) includes all nouns terminating in -**p** (written -**b** by the Rhenish Missionaries), and a few ending in -**mi**, -**ni**, (and perhaps -**ri**,) as *om*-**mi** (Tindall and Krönlein's *omi*, Vollmer's *umi*) "house," &c. (*Vide* § 423.)

MASCULINE PLURAL.

||Nā au-**gu**, si-da !hau-s-di-gu, |ni !ā-s-!na ||an-hă-gu, ho-
Those men our tribe's they, another village-in dwelling, find
gu-da-ra, gare-da-ra goma-n ă-g-a, tsī-gu-gye-ra |kai-da |gam
them we do, praise we do cattle of them, and they do present us two
tsău-n ||ēi-gu-di-n-χa.
calves theirs from.

The men of our tribe who dwell in that village, we find them, we praise their cattle, and they present us with two of their calves.

||Nā !nau-**gu** tara-s-di- gu, ||nă-gu gei-gu, om-mi-!na ||goĕ-gu, mŭ-
Those beams woman's they, those large, house-in lying, see
gu-da-ra, ||ēi-gu-di ||ou-g-a da-ra mū≠an, tsī-da ī-p
them we do, their thicknesses we do perceive, and we appearance
ă-g-a ra |nam, tsī-gu-gye om-m-a ra ≠kă!na.
of them do like, and they house do support.

The beams which belong to the woman, which are large and lie in the house, we see them, we perceive their thickness, and like their appearance, they support the house.

To this class or gender (masculine plural) belong all nouns terminating in **-gu** (Knudsen's and Tindall's **-ku**, Schmelen's **-koe**), most of which are plurals to nouns of the preceding (**-p**) class or gender.

MASCULINE DUAL.

||Nā |gam au-**kha**, si-da !hau-s-di-kha, |nĭ̄ !ā-s-!na ||an-hā-kha,
Those two   men,   our tribe's they, another village-in dwelling,
hō-kha-da-ra, gare-da-ra goma-n ā-kha, tsĭ̄-kha-gye-ra /kai-da
find them we do, praise we do cattle of them, and they do present us
|gam tsaū-n ||ēi-kha-di-n-χa.
two calves   theirs from.

The two men of our tribe, who dwell in that village, we find them, we praise their cattle, and they present us with two of their calves.

||Nā |gam !nau-**kha**, ta-ra-s-di-kha, gei-hā-kha, om-mi-!na
Those two   beams,   woman's they,   large being, house-in
||goē-hā-kha, mū-kha-da-ra, ||ou-p ā-kha da-ra mū≠an, tsĭ̄-
   lying,   see them we do, thickness of them we do perceive, and
da   ĭ-p   ā-kha ra /nam, tsĭ̄-kha-gye om-m-a ra ≠hā-!na.
we appearance of them do love, and they the house do support.

The two beams which belong to the woman, which are large and lie in the house, seeing them we perceive their thickness, we like their appearance, they support the house.

This class or gender (masculine dual) includes all nouns terminating in **-kha**, which are all dual forms corresponding to nouns which in the singular end in **-p**, **-mi**, or **-ni**, &c.

FEMININE SINGULAR.

||Nā tara-**s** si-da !hau-s-di-s, !khu-hā-s, |nĭ̄ !a-s-!na ||an-hā-s,
That woman our tribe's she, rich being, another village-in dwelling,
ho-si-da-ra, gare-da-ra goma-n ā-s-a,   tsĭ̄-s-ta   /kai-da
find her we do, praise we do cattle of her, and she does present us
|gam tsaū-n ||ei-s-di-n-χa.
two calves   hers from.

The woman of our tribe, who is rich and lives in that village, we find her, we praise her cattle, and she presents us with two of her calves.

Hei-s tara-s-di-s, ǁēi-s gei-s, ǃhana-p-ǃna mã-s, mŭ-si-da-ra,
The tree woman's it, it large, garden-in standing, see it we do,
ǁēi-s-di ǁou-b-a da-ra mŭ≠an, tsi-da i-p ā-s-a ra ǀnam,
its thickness we do perceive, and we appearance of it do like,
tsī-s-gye ǃhana-b-a ra ē-ē.
and it the garden does make fine.

The tree which belongs to the woman, which is large, and stands in the garden, we see it, we perceive its thickness and like its appearance; it is an ornament to the garden.

To this class or gender (feminine singular) belong all nouns terminating in -s.

FEMININE PLURAL.

ǁNŭ tara-ti, sida ǃhau-s-di-ti, ǀni ǃā-s-ǃna ǁan-hā-ti, hō-ti-
Those women our tribe's they, another village-in dwelling, find them
da-ra, gare-da-ra goma-n ā-te, tsī-ti-gye-ra ǀkai-da ǀgam tsău-n
we do, praise we do cattle of them, and they do present us two calves
ǁēi-ti-di-n-χa.
theirsfrom.

The women of our tribe who live in that village, we find them, we praise their cattle, and they present us with two of their calves.

Hei-ti tara-s-di-ti, ǁēi-ti gei-ti, ǁēi-ti ǃhana-p-ǃna mā-ti, mŭ-
Trees woman's they, they large, they garden-in standing, see
ti-da-ra, ǁēi-ti-di ǁou-b-a da-ra mŭ≠an, tsi-da i-p
them we do, their thickness we do perceive, and we appearance
ā-te ra ǀnam, tsī-ti-gye ǃhana-b-a ra ē-ē.
of them do like, and they the garden do make fine.

The trees which belong to the woman, which are large, and stand in the garden, we see them, we perceive their thickness and like their appearance; they are an ornament to the garden.

This class or gender (feminine plural) comprehends all nouns with the termination -ti. They are plurals to nouns of the preceding (-s) class or gender.

COMMON SINGULAR.

Khoi-ĩ si-da !hau-s-di-i, !khu-hā-ĩ, ǀnĩ ǃā-s-ǃna ǁan-hā-ĩ, hō-
A person our tribe's he, rich being, another village-in dwelling, find
ĩ-da-ra, gare-da-ra goma-n ā-ĕ, tsĩ-i-gye-ra ǀkai-da ǀgam
him we do, praise we do cattle of him and he does present us two
tsāu-n ǁēi-i-di-n-χa.
calves his from.

A person of our tribe who is rich, and lives in that village, we find him (or her), we praise his (or her) cattle, and he (or she) presents us with two of his (or her) calves.

Hei-ĩ tara-s-di-ĩ, ǁēi-ĩ gei-ĩ, om-mi-ǃna ǁgoĕ-ĩ, mū-i-da-ra,
The stick woman's it, it large, house-in lying, see it we do,
ǁēi-ĩ-di ǁou-b-a da-ra mū≠an, tsĩ-da ĩ-p ā-ĕ ra ǀnam, tsi-
its thickness we do perceive, and we appearance of it do like, and
ĩ-gye om-m-a ra ĩ-ĕ.
it the house does make fine.

The stick which belongs to the woman, which is large and lies in the house, we see it, we perceive its thickness, and like its appearance; it is an ornament to the house.

To this class or gender (common singular) belong all nouns formed with the termination **-i**, exclusive, of course, of those in **-mi, -ni**, &c., of the masculine singular (**-p** class), and of those in **-ti** of the feminine plural. This termination **-i** imparts a kind of indefinite sense, in many cases corresponding in meaning to our indefinite article, or to the word "any," &c. Nouns formed with this termination are infrequent even in the Nama, and seem no longer to exist in the other Hottentot dialects. Also in the more Northern Sex-denoting languages, no trace of this class or gender has been, as yet, discovered.

COMMON PLURAL.

ǁNū khoi-n, si-da ǃhau-s-di-n, ǀnĩ ǃā-s-ǃna ǁan-hā-n, hō-
Those people our tribe's they, another village-in dwelling, find
ĩn-da-ra, gare-da-ra goma-n ā-n-a, tsĩ-ĩn-gye-ra ǀkai-da ǀgam
them we do, praise we do cattle of them, and they do present us two
tsāu-n ǁēi-n-din-χa.
calves theirs from.

The people of our tribe who dwell in that village, we find them, we praise their cattle, and they present us with two of their calves.

This class or gender (common plural) comprehends all nouns with the termination -n, most of which are plurals to nouns of the preceding (common singular) class.

COMMON DUAL.

||Nã |gam khoi-ra si-da /hau-s-di-ra, ¡ní /ā-s-!na ||an-hã-ra,
Those two persons our tribe's they, another village-in dwelling,
hō-ra-da-ra, gare-da-ra goma-n ã-ra, tsī-ra-gye-ra |kai-da
find them we do, praise we do cattle of them, and they do present us
|gam tsãu-n ||ēi-ra-di-n-χa.
two calves theirs from.

Those two (a man and a woman, or two women) of our tribe who dwell in that village, we find them, we praise their cattle, and they present us with two of their calves.

This class or gender (common dual) includes all nouns with the termination -ra. They are duals to nouns of the common and feminine singular classes (-i and -s).

423. Though the signs of the concord are not so frequently repeated here as in the Bâ-ntu languages, it is evident that its nature is the same; *viz.*, that it consists in the identity of the pronouns (or pronominal elements) with the derivative particles, (§ 406, 410,) which, however, in Hottentot are suffixed, not prefixed, as in the Bâ-ntu languages. This identity is even clearer in the Namaqua dialect, than in the Kafir and kindred languages; for, the forms of the pronouns in Namaqua, are either the same as those of the terminations of the nouns, or they are so manifestly derived from them as to render it hardly necessary to say a word in explanation of the slight variations which occur. The two chief exceptions to this rule are the forms of the objective pronominal suffixes of the verb in the masculine singular and feminine singular classes or genders. These forms (-*bi* and -*si*) have probably retained the ancient vowel which has

generally been lost in the forms of the pronouns, as well as in those of the derivative suffixes of the nouns. The original vowel of the termination of the masculine singular has again been preserved, as a derivative suffix, where the labial consonant of this termination is either assimilated to a consonant ending the stem (-m-, -n-, and perhaps -r-), or elided after it. For example, this is the case in om-mi house (objective om-m-a, pl. om-gu, dual om-kha), !hom-mi mountain (obj. !hom-m-a, pl. !hom-gu, dual !hom-kha), !nom-mi hillock (obj. !nom-m-a, pl. !nom-gu, dual !nom-kha), !om-mi hand (obj. !om-m-a, pl. !om-gu, dual !om-kha), χam-mi lion (obj. χam-m-a, pl. χam-gu), ǁgam-mi water (obj. ǁgam-m-a, dual ǁgam-kha), ausen-i perspiration (obj. ausen-a), &c.*

424. If the nature of the concord in the Hottentot language is thus similar to that in the Bâ-ntu Languages,—its peculiar sex-denoting character in the Hottentot might suggest that the identity of the pronouns and the derivative particles of the nouns (and, consequently, the cause of the division of the nouns into classes or genders,) may have a different origin in the two families of South African Languages; and that the derivative suffixes of the nouns in Hottentot were originally pronouns, as some grammarians (Knudsen, &c.) maintain.

* We do not find it noticed in any of the grammatical works on this language (by Messrs. Knudsen, Wallmann, and Tindall) that these nouns are of the masculine singular class or gender. On the contrary, the two first of these writers, at least, class them in the common singular gender. That this is an error, is evident from the fact that all pronouns referring to these nouns belong to the masculine singular class or gender. Another feature which distinguishes these nouns from those of the common singular class or gender, is that when they are used with the termination -a (indicating the objective, &c.), their end -i is suppressed before the -a, instead of (as in all nouns of the common singular class) being commuted by a process of vowel harmony, into -e, after which the suffix -a disappears. These nouns can be further recognized as belonging to the masculine singular class (or gender), from their exchanging their singular termination -mi or -i for -gu (masculine plural) and -kha (masculine dual).

(§ 411.) Such an explanation appears plausible, so long as we have only to do with nouns to which the distinction of sex is naturally applicable. Thus in *khoi*-p man (husband), *khoi*-gu men (husbands), *khoi*-kha two men (husbands), *khoi*-s woman, *khoi*-ti women, *khoi*-ï person, *khoi*-n people, *khoi*-ra two persons (man and woman, or two women), &c., the terminations might with some semblance of probability be concluded to be pronouns affixed for the purpose of distinguishing number and gender. But a similar explanation is inapplicable, when we observe the use of these terminations, with regard to nouns expressing objects, in which sex cannot be distinguished,—for example, *mũ*-p eye (as an object in space, *mũ*-p-*!na* in the eye, &c.), pl. *mũ*-gu, dual *mũ*-kha; *mũ*-s the organ of vision, pl. *mũ*-ti, dual *mũ*-ra; *hei*-p log of wood, beam, pl. *hei*-gu, dual *hei*-kha; *hei*-s tree (growing), pl. *hei*-ti, dual *hei*-ra; *hei*-ï' stick, pl. *hei*-n, dual *hei*-ra; *om*-mi house (οἶκός), pl. *om*-gu, dual *om*-kha; *om*-s habitation (οἰκία), pl. *om*-ti, dual *om*-ra; *om*-i any house, pl. *om*-n; *tsē*-p day (as a date, "jour"), pl. *tsē*-gu, dual *tsē*-kha; *tsē*-s day (as a period, "journée), pl. *tsē*-ti; *tsē*-i any day, pl. *tsē*-n, dual *tsē*-ra; &c. With many shades of meaning, the termination of the masculine singular class or gender most frequently indicates the idea of locality; that of the feminine singular implies causality, life, essence, &c. These meanings could only be derived with great violence from an original intention of transferring the sex-denoting distinctions to nouns, to which they are not strictly applicable.* On the

---

* As the translator of the New Testament into Namaqua is of a different opinion regarding the distinction of gender in Hottentot, the reader will thank me for subjoining his observations on the subject. Mr. Krönlein says: " In Bezug auf die Unterscheidung des Geschlechtes bemerke ich folgendes :

" Bei den lebendigen Wesen ergiebt sich das Geschlecht von selbst. Sie sind entweder Masculina oder Feminina. Kenne ich aber das Geschlecht des betreffenden Wesens noch nicht, so rede ich im Communis, z. B. *Mã !goa ë-s gye hõ?* (Was für ein Kind gebar sie?) Die Antwort

contrary, it is far more probable that the terminations

lautet entweder *ao-re-ro*-℔-*a* (ein Männlein) oder *ta-ra-re*-ʂ-*a* (ein Weiblein). *Ta-re-be hā-*ë̆ *kha ʀe-*ë̆? (Was für ein Pferd ist das?) ǂ*Kara-hā-*℔ *gymo.* (Es ist der Hengst.) ǂ*Nŭ hā-*ʂ *gymo.* (Es ist die schwarze Stute.) &c.

"In Bezug auf die leblosen Gegenstände gilt die Regel, welche ganz der subjectiven Ansicht des Redenden anheimgegeben ist:

"*a*. Dass alle Gegenstände, die man sich als *gross* und *hervorstechend* denkt, **männlich** aufgefasst werden, z. B. *hei*-℔ (m. s.) ist der Baum, der durch seinen schlanken, über die andern hinausgehenden Wuchs sich auszeichnet. *Om-*mĭ (m. s.) ist das Haus, welches durch seine Grösse und Ansehnlichkeit andere übertrifft, &c.

"β. Alle Gegenstände dagegen die *kleiner* oder *kürzer* sind, und mehr in die *Breite* gehen als in die Höhe, sind **Femininima**, z. B. *hei-*ʂ ist der Baum, der einen kurzen Stamm hat, aber seine Zweige gehörig ausbreitet (Bild der Hottentoten Frauen), oder auch wohl der gewöhnliche Busch oder Strauch. *Om-*ʂ (f. s.) ist das Haus, welches gegen andere in seiner Höhe und Dimension zurücksteht.

"In Bezug auf *mŭ-*ʂ (f. s.) und *mŭ-*℔ (m. s.) ist *mŭ-*ʂ am gebräuchlichsten. *Mŭ-*℔ wird nur in solchen Fäblen gebraucht, wo sich der Redende das Auge dessen, von dem er redet, als durch böse Einbildung oder Einflüsterung als *vergrössert* denkt, z. B. *sa mŭ-b-!na ta a* ǂ*kawa*, χ*awe-ta* //*na-ti-i tamu hā* (in deinem Auge bin ich böse, aber ich bins nicht). In den Abstractas kommt es nur darauf an wie sich der Gebrauch gebildet, oder wie sich der Redende den abstracten Begriff denkt: ǂ*gom-*ʂ (f. s., Glauben), ǂ*hanu-ei-si-*℔ (m. s., Gerechtichkeit), !*oŭ-ba-sgn-*ʂ (f. s., Hoffnung), /*nam-*mĭ (m. s., Liebe), &c.

"Der **Communis**: *om-*ĭ (ein Haus, pl. *om-*n), *hei-*ï̆ (ein Stock, pl. *hei-*n), *tsĕ-*ĭ (ein Tag, pl. *tsĕ-*n), ist selbst verständlich. Er lässt den Begriff unbestimmt.

"Ausser dem Gebrauch, der sich *fest*gebildet bei *einer grossen Anzahl von Wörtern*, hängt die Geschlechtsbestimmung also rein von der Anschauung und dem subjektiven Ermessen des Redenden ab, und er wird sogleich verstanden, warum er seinen Gegenstand so oder so auffasst."

To this I may add the remark that *mŭ-*p */na* ("moep na" "in the eye") is found in Schmelen's version of the Four Gospels, Matth. vii. 3 (twice), 4 (twice), and 5. In these places both Tindall and Krönlein have *mŭ-*ʂ-*/na*. The masculine form *mŭ-*p, &c., &c., is nowhere met with in Tindall's version of St. Matthew's Gospel, nor, I believe, in Krönlein's New Testament.

The gender may have to a certain extent the import which Mr. Krönlein ascribes to it; but this is clearly a derived faculty, and can by no means be said to apply to all, or even to the majority of nouns indicating inanimate things or ideas in Hottentot.

which indicate the class or gender of the nouns in the Namaqua language, were originally derivative particles, similar in their nature to the derivative prefixes in the Bâ-ntu languages; and that the origin of the division of the nouns in both languages into classes or genders is based upon the same principle. The apparent sex-denoting character which the classification of the nouns now has in the Hottentot language, was evidently imparted to it, after a division of the nouns into classes had taken place. It probably arose, in the first instance, from the possibly accidental circumstance that the nouns indicating (respectively) man and woman were formed with different derivative suffixes, and, consequently, belonged to different classes (or genders) of nouns, and that these suffixes thus began to indicate the distinctions of sex in nouns where it could be distinguished.

425. It may be assumed that the original meaning of the derivative suffixes of the nouns in Hottentot has been impaired and modified, and that they by no means impart as full a meaning as some of the prefixes in the Bâ-ntu languages, and are, therefore, still less equal in value to the derivative suffixes of modern languages. (§ 415.) Yet there can, however, be no doubt that their origin is similar, and that if our explanation of the nature and origin of the concord holds good for the Bâ-ntu languages, it is equally applicable to the Hottentot. But, in order to be more certain concerning this, we must proceed to examine how far we can ascertain the original meaning of the derivative prefixes and suffixes, on which the division of the nouns into classes or genders is respectively based in the Bâ-ntu and Hottentot languages.

II. ETYMOLOGY OF THE CONCORD-INDICATING DERIVATIVE PARTICLES OF THE NOUNS.

1. ETYMOLOGY OF THE BÂ-NTU DERIVATIVE PREFIXES.

426. As the derivative prefixes of the nouns in the Bâ-ntu languages are no longer used separately, it is now somewhat difficult to ascertain what was their exact meaning while so employed. There are two ways of ascertaining this, approximately. The power which these prefixes apparently possess for the formation of derivative nouns, and the general character of the nouns belonging to the same class or gender, tend to point towards the meaning which the prefix had, when still a separate word. But this alone is by no means a safe guide. It is possible that in many nouns, perhaps sometimes in the majority of those belonging to one class, the prefix has not its original value, but only that of a pronoun, from these words having been originally adjectival formations. For example, a great number of nouns of the 1st (**mu-**) class or gender may have been, originally, adjectives referred to u-**mu**-*ntu* "man;" and, in that case, the *mu-* in them would be only a pronoun used as representative of u-**mu**-*ntu*, whilst the *mu* in u-**mu**-*ntu* might originally have had quite a different meaning. (*Vide* § 412.) Yet, it is, of course, also possible that the original meaning of the **mu-** in u-**mu**-*ntu* is that of a single person, and that, on this account, the nouns of the 1st (**mu-**) class almost all represent personal beings in the singular number.

427. Similarly, a great number of names of rivers are formed in Zulu with the prefix **mu-** (3rd class)*. Yet

* *Umzimvubu*, (Sea-cow River), *Umzinto, Umzumbe, Umlazi, Umzimkulu, Umx'langa, Umx'loti, Umx'latuzane, Umx'lali, Umsunduze, Umtywati, Umkomazi, Umpanza, Umleku, Umkeze, Umvoti, Umgeni, Umnambiti, Umtwalume, Umbilo, Umzimayi, Umzimkulwana*, &c. (Colenso's Dictionary.)

it would be rash to infer from this that the original meaning of the prefix mu- (3rd class), when still an independent noun, was "river." It is indeed more probable that these nouns were either formed as adjectives referring to the Zulu noun *umfula* "river," (the Kafir *umlambo*, Setshuâna *molapo*, Tekeza *nambo*,)—or in mere analogy with this and similar nouns.

428. Still greater, perhaps, is the number of names of trees formed with this prefix mu- (3rd class). We find about a hundred such nouns in the Bishop of Natal's Zulu-English Dictionary, and about fifty in the considerably shorter Dictionary of the Otyihereró, or Damara language, by the Rev. C. H. Hahn. In many other South African languages equally numerous examples of names of trees formed with this prefix mu- occur; yet we are not, on this account, justified in asserting that the original meaning of this syllable mu-, when used separately, was that of a "tree" or "plant." It is, upon the whole, much more probable that these nouns were formed in analogy with the generally used noun u-mu-*ti* 3. "plant, herb, tree, wood, medicine," pl. i-mi-*ti* 4.* That the last syllable -*ti* has the meaning of vegetable matter here, is rendered probable by other nouns formed from this stem, such as Kafir u-lu-*ti* 11. "rod, stick," pl. i-zin-*ti* 10., Otyihereró o-ka-*ti* 13. "stick," pl. o-u-*ti* 14., Kafir and Zulu u-bu-*ti* 14. "poison, charm," Sena, Tette, and Cape Delgado ka-*mu-ti* 13. "shrub" (Kikámba ka-*mu-di* 13., pl. tu-*mi-di* 12.), &c.

429. How difficult it is in this manner to infer the original value of the prefixes of nouns from their present use, will be easily understood by any one who may have

* Kafir u-m-*ti* 3., pl. i-mi-*ti* 4., Southern Tekeza u-*tsi* 3., pl. i-mi-*tsi* 4., Lourenzo Marques and Quellimane *mure*, Inhambane *muri* (m), Tette, Sena, and Cape Delgado mú-*ti* 3., pl. mî-*ti* 4., Mosambique *mwiri*, Suahéli ma*ti* 3., pl. mi*ti* 4., Kiníka and Kipokómo mu*hi* 3., pl. mi*hi* 4., Kikámba mú-*di* 3., pl. mi-*di* 4., Otyihereró o-mu-*ti* 3., pl. o-mi-*ti* 4., Ovambo u-m-*ti* 3., Benguela o-u-*ti* 3., pl. o-vi-*ti* 4., Bunda mu-*shi* (muchi) 3., pl. mi-*shi* 4.

tried to ascertain the original meaning of such English suffixes as *-dom, -ness, -ship*, &c., from an analysis of the nouns formed with them. A comparison of such nouns as " kingdom, martyrdom, freedom," &c., may give us an idea of the present value of the suffix *-dom*, and of the meaning which it would give to such nouns as we can now form with it. But this is a very different thing from knowing what was the meaning of the syllable *-dom* when used independently; and we imagine that any guess at that meaning, without tracing it back historically, might be far from the truth.

430. This difficulty is the greater, as the different languages and dialects (though agreeing in the main regarding the value attached to each class of nouns and in the prefix denoting it,) exhibit much variety as to the exact force which each prefix has in them. To give an instance, whilst in the three other genera of the Middle Branch the prefix ka- of the 13th class is used for the purpose of forming diminutives, it appears not to have this force in the North Western (Kongo) genus. In the Kongo language the only nouns of the 13th (ka-) class (or gender,) enumerated in Brusciotto à Vetralla's Grammar, are ka-*ti-a-nzi* 13. " the middle " (*vide* § 436, note) and ka-*sasila* 13. " height." Curiously enough, diminutives are formed in this language with the prefix of the 7th class ki-, joined to a reduplication of the stem, as ki-*mu-ntu-mu-ntu* 7. "a little man" (§ 426), ki-*leke-leke* 7. "a little boy," pl. i-*lekeleke* 8. from mu-*leke* 1. "a boy," pl. a-*leke* 2; whilst this same 7th prefix in Tette (tshi- or shi-) and Sena (shi-) is employed for the purpose of indicating large objects, as Sena shi-*mu-ti* 7. "a large tree," pl. pi-*mi-ti* 8. (§ 428, note), Tette tshi-*u-ta* 7. " a large bow," tshi-*mā-zi* 7. " large water, river " (§ 452), tshi-*nyumba* 7. " large house." In Otyihereró again o-tyi-*ndu* 7. is " an old man or woman," whilst in Kafir the identical word i-si-*ntu* 7. means " human species," and in Zulu " human race, mankind." (§ 412.) It is clear that there is a very

great difference in the meanings which the 7th prefix has respectively in Kongo and Tette, in Otyihereró and Kafir.

431. Another circumstance which contributes much to complicate this mode of investigation, is that we cannot always be sure whether two or more classes or genders of nouns may not have been thrown together. This process would always be favoured by great similarity in the forms of the derivative prefixes and the pronouns derived from them, by similarity in the value of the prefixes, or by both causes combined. The history of the South African languages (as we shall see more especially hereafter,) shews many clear instances of these three ways, by which classes that were originally distinct, have been amalgamated.

432. Therefore we should probably be unable to ascertain anything of the original meanings of the derivative prefixes of the nouns in these South African languages, if this were the only method of discovering them. But although we do not now find the prefixes used in their separate state as independent nouns, some of them are still found as other parts of speech, particularly as prefixed directives or prepositions; or, as the case might also be represented, there are some other words, particularly prepositions, which seem to be closely related to, if not originally identical with, certain derivative prefixes of nouns.

433. Thus there cannot be the least doubt that the derivative prefix ku- of the 15th class or gender, is identical with the prefixed directive, or preposition *ku*- which means "to." In fact, the employment of this preposition for the formation of the infinitive of verbs, is analogous to that of the corresponding English preposition. Thus, in Zulu *ngi-ya-ku-tanda*, (I shall love,) which is literally " I go to love," (just as *ngi-ya ku-laba-bantu* means " I go to these people,") the *ku* is merely used as a directive like the " to " in "to love;" whilst in the sentence

u-**ku**-*tanda* ku-*mnandi*, "to love is sweet," the first *ku* is used as a derivative prefix, to which the second *ku* refers as a pronoun. But no one can doubt here that the prefixed directive (or preposition) and the derivative prefix are identical in origin.

434. Besides the clear infinitives of verbs used as nouns, there are, in almost all South African Bâ-ntu languages, a number of nouns belonging to this 15th class or gender, which were originally infinitives, but have now a more concrete meaning. Such are, for example, Kafir u-**ku**-x́*la* "food," (really "eat-ing,") u-**ku**-*sa* "morning," and u-**ku**-x́*lwa* "evening," which latter words both mean "dawn-ing," the one the early dawn, the other the growing dark at sunset. The Middle Branch languages also contain a number of nouns of this class or gender, which evidently were not infinitives of verbs originally, such as the Otyihereró nouns o-**ku**-*ngururu* "desert," o-**ku**-*ti* (Ovambo o-**ku**-*ti*) "field, country land," pl. o-**ma**-*ku-ti* 6., o-**ku**-*vare* "a great open place," o-**ku**-*yere* "flats, open place," o-**ku**-*ruo* "sacred place for the holy fire" &c., o-**ku**-*ara* "floor (of a hut)," o-**ku**-*pepera* "winter," o-**ku**-*roro* "rainy season (autumn)." In these nouns which indicate place and time, the common origin of that prefix **ku**- and the preposition *ku*- (to) is almost self-evident. This is not quite as clear in the following Otyihereró nouns, which also belong to the 15th class or gender, viz., o-**ku**-*iya* "thorn," pl. o-**ma**-*ku-iya* 6. (Ovambo o-**ku**-*edya* 15., pl. o-**ma**-*ku-edya* 6.), o-**ku**-*rama* (Ovambo o-**ku**-*lama*) "leg," o-**ku**-*oko* "arm," (Ovambo o-**ku**-*éko* 15., pl. o-**ma**-*éko* 6.), o-**ku**-*tui* "ear," pl. o-**ma**-*tui* 6.*

435. An almost equally strong case of original identity with a prefixed directive (or preposition) is presented by

---

* Ovambo o-**ko**-*tshui* 15. pl. o-**ma**-*ko-tshui* 6., Bashubea *kotoe*, Batoka *khotoe*, Maponda and Borotse *kutoe*, Banyenko *kutue*, Bayeiye *kuti*, Tette and Sena *kutu* pl. **ma**-*kutu* 6., Kikámba **ků**-*dŭ* 15. pl. **ma**-*ŭ-du* 6., Kongo **ku**-*tu* 15. pl. **ma**-*tu* 6., Mpongwe o-*roi*.

the derivative prefix (PA-) of the 16th class or gender. In the dialects of the South Eastern Branch of the South African Division of Bâ-ntu languages, (Kafir, Setshuâna, and Tekeza,) this prefix is obsolete, though clear traces of its former existence are still found, at all events, in the Kafir species and in Setshuâna. Some of the forms of the pronouns of the 15th (ku-) class or gender, in both species, evidently belonged originally to the 16th (pa-) class; and the 16th may be said in these languages to have been absorbed by the 15th (ku-) class. In Setshuâna this amalgamation was facilitated by the change of original *k* to χ or *h'*, and *p* to *h*. (§ 87 & 110.) Thus, it became difficult to distinguish apart those forms of the pronouns, in which the original vowels of these prefixes were elided. In many Middle Branch languages the 16th (pa-) class or gender has continued distinct, but generally contains a few nouns only, in some languages, perhaps, not more than one. Thus we find in the language of Nyungwe (Tette) pa-*zuru* pa-*muendo* "span of the foot," *i.e.*, " what is above the foot." (Dr. Peters' Mosambique Voc. No. 179.) In Kisuahéli the noun ma*háli* or pa*háli* belonging to this 16th (pa-) class* seems to indicate that the Setshuâna noun *hélo* " place " which is the only noun, not an infinitive, now belonging to the 15th class in this language, was originally a noun of the 16th class. In Kiníka we have the noun va*tu*,† in Kipokómo wa-*ntu*, in Kikámba wa-*ndu* (as wa-*ndu* w-*onde* " everywhere "), in Kihíau pa-*ndu* (as pa-*ndu* pa *motto* " fire place "), expressing the same meaning. The corresponding word in Otyihereró is o-po-*na* (as o-po-*na* pa-*ndye* o-po-*mba* " my place is here"), and in this language we have also a few other nouns of the 16th class

---

* Krapf's Outlines pp. 37, 43, 78, 81, 82, 84, 85, 90, 96, 97, as in ma*hali* or pa*hali* pa *raho* " place of rest." *Vide* Dr. Steere's " Table of Concords."

† Krapf's Outl. pp. 36, 38, 78, 81, 84, 85, 90, as in va-*tu* va *atu* " place of men."

or gender; whilst in the other Western languages of the Middle Branch, traces of this class have as yet been discovered in the old Kongo language only, and it cannot, even there, be proved to exist now as a distinct class of nouns. Among the dialects of the North Western Branch it is possible that the Isubu noun *oma* (as in *oma wa songgo* "place of graves," *wano oma* "this place") belongs to the 16th class or gender.

436. As to the origin of the prefix of the 16th class or gender, the nouns of which, few as they are, all indicate locality, there cannot be the least doubt that it is identical with the local preposition (or prefixed directive) *pa-*, found in so many South African Bâ-ntu languages. In Kafir and Zulu this *pa-* is no longer used as a regular directive, but occurs with the directive meaning in certain adverbial forms (used also as prepositions), which are derived from nouns, most of which are now obsolete. Appleyard (§ 319) derives *panxle* "outside" from *inxle* 9. "field," *pantsi* "beneath" from *izantsi* "lower part" (Zulu *inzansi*), *pezolo* "last night" from *izolo* "yesterday," *pezulu* "above" from *izulu* "heaven." But to these must be added the Kafir and Zulu preposition *pakati* (Setshuâna *haχare*) "within, between, among, inside, in the middle," which is a sort of locative form of an obsolete noun of the 14th (ka-) class*, (a gender which is now extinct in the South Eastern Branch;) also the Zulu and Kafir prepositions and adverbs *pambili* "in front of," *pambi* "before," *pesheya* (Zulu *petsheya* according to Colenso) "beyond, on the other side," &c. In Western Setshuâna this particle has the sound of *ha* and is still used as a preposition, as Mark xiv. 35, *a oéla ha hatsi* "he fell down *on* the ground." In some of the Middle Branch languages *pa* is more generally used either as a prefixed particle, or as a preposition, and has the same form *pa* in Inhambane, Sofala, Tette, Sena, Maravi, Kihiau, &c. In Otyihereró this preposition has, generally speaking,

---

* Compare also the Otyihereró prepositions *mokati* and *pokati*.

lost its vowel before the initial vowel of the noun (the article), but Hahn records its form as *pu-*, the labial quality of the vowel being probably in some manner due to the influence of the labial consonant which precedes it.

437. A third prefix, that of the 3rd class or gender, is also one in which the meaning of many of the nouns formed with it, renders it probable that it is allied to a directive bearing in most of these languages the same form. This prefix is **mu-** and **m-** in Zulu, **m-** in Kafir, **mo-** in Setshuâna, **mu-** in most Middle Branch languages (except in Mpongwe, which has shortened it to **o-**); in the North Western Branch, again, it is in Dualla and Isubu **mo-**, in Benga **mw-** and **u-**, in Fernando Po **bo-**, &c.

438. We claim for this prefix an original identity with the prefixed directive or preposition *mu-* of the Kongo language, as *mu-n-zo* 9. " in the house." This preposition occurs in the same or similar forms in many Middle Branch languages; it is for example *m-* or *mo-* in the South Western genus, as Otyihereró *m-o-n-dyuo* " in the house." In Setshuâna it has the form *mo* (*mo-X̌lu-ñ* "in the house"); but it is extinct in Kafir, which uses in its place a prefixed *se-* or *e-*, in conjunction with an affixed *-ini* or *-eni* (Setshuâna *-eñ*), as (*s*)*e-n-X̌lw-ini* " in the house."

439. The local meaning of many nouns formed with the derivative prefix of the 3rd (**mu-**) class (or gender) is still very clear, as in the following Kafir nouns: u-**m**-*pambili* "front" (*pambili* "before" § 436), u-**m**-*lima nX̌lela* "landmark" (*lima* "dig, plough, cultivate," i-**n**-*X̌lela* 9. " way, road "), u-**m**-*mango* " ridge," u-**m**-*nyango* " doorway," pl. i-**mi**-*nyango* 4., u-**m**-*X̌laba* " earth," u-**m**-*da* " boundary," pl. i-**mi**-*da* 4. (-*de* " long," vide § 362), u-**m**-*va* " back," u-**m**-*lomo* " mouth,"* u-**m**-*zi*. (Zulu u-**mu**-*zi*) " kraal,

---

* The Kafir and Zulu noun u-**m**-*lomo* "mouth" (Setshuâna **mo**-*lomo*, Tekeza *nomo* § 343, Sofala, Sena, and Tette **mau**-*romo*, Quellimane **mau**-*lomo*, Maravi **mo**-*lomo*, Dualla and Isubu **mo**-*lumbu*,) may be

place, residence," pl. i-**mi**-*zi* 4., u-**m**-*tombo* "fountain," pl. i-**mi**-*tombo* 4., and also such nouns as u-**m**-x̃*la* (Zulu u-**mu**-x̃*la*) "day," pl. i-**mi**-x̃*la*, u-*nyaka* 3. (Zulu u-**m**-*nyaka*) "year," pl. i-**mi**-*nyaka* 4., u-**m**-*zuzu* "some time, a-while," u-**m**-*so* (Zulu u-**mu**-*so*, Setshuâna **mo**-*sho*) "morrow, morning," from u-**ku**-*sa* 15. "to dawn." (§ 434.)

440. The number of nouns of the 3rd (**mu**-) class or gender, which have a clearly local meaning, is comparatively smaller in Otyihereró than in Kafir; but this may be because a large number of ancient nouns of this class have been lost in Otyihereró, and new ones have arisen, in which the prefix has not so much the original derivative meaning, as one of a reflected kind. (§ 426—428.) On the whole, however, it is not only possible, but probable, that two or more classes of nouns, originally distinct, have by similarity of their prefixes (and pronouns) coalesced (§ 431), and that one of these prefixes was identical with the directive (or preposition) *mu*- "in."

441. With regard to other derivative prefixes of nouns, all that can be said, is that more or less successful guesses may be made at the etymology of some of them. It may be that the prefix **li**- of the 5th class or gender was originally identical with the derivative suffix of respective verbs in -*el-a* (which, according to § 270 and 271, must originally have had the form -א- LE-A or -א- LI-A), and that, similarly, the prefix of the 11th class or gender

---

derived from Kafir and Zulu u-**ku**-*luma* 15. "to bite," (Setshuâna **xo**-*loma*, Tekeza e-**ko**-*luma*, Sena and Tette **ku**-*ruma*, Makua **u**-*luma*, Cape Delgado, Kihiau and Kiníka **ku**-*lúma*, Kikámba, Kisuaheli, and Kipokomo **ku**-*úma*, Otyihereró o-**ku**-*rumata*, Ovambo and Bunda o-**ku**-*lumata*, Mpongwe **go**-*noma*). This etymology will, however, appear doubtful to many, on account of the difference of the vowel of the stem in Kafir *um-lomo* and *uku-luma*; though the influences of vowel harmony will account for this change. In fact, in a noun of as ancient formation as *um-lomo* clearly is, the final passive suffix -*o* could hardly be expected not to have exerted an influence upon the preceding vowel of the stem. If this etymology is right, u-**m**-*lomo* originally indicated the place where there is biting, or rather, where there is being bitten, i.e., where one bites.

lu- is related to the suffix of inversive verbs in -*ul-a*
(originally -א- LU-A). There is, at all events, a probability that the prefix of the 7th class or gender (of
which the forms ki-, as found in Kikamba, Kinika,
Kisuaheli, Bunda, Kongo, and Kakongo, and si-, as
found in Kafir, se- in Setshuâna, z- in Mpongwe, are
most likely identical in their origin)*, is allied to the
suffixes of causative verbs in -*is-a* and -*ik-a*, of which the
primitive forms must be supposed to have been -א- SI-A
and -א- KI-A. The meaning of many nouns of the
7th class (as Kafir i-si-*vato* 7. "apparel," pl. i-zi-*vato* 8.
from u-ku-*vata* 15. " to dress," i-si-*fo* 7. " disease, sick-
ness," pl. i-zi-*fo* 8. from u-ku-*fa* 15. " to die," &c.,)
seems much to favour such a derivation. And with
regard to the derivative prefix ka- of the 13th class or
gender, which is now found only in the Middle Branch
languages, (*vide*, however, § 436,) and generally with a
diminutive meaning, we can hardly help comparing it
with the prefixed genitive particle *ka-* (" of "), employed
in Kafir with certain nouns (§ 463), and also (though
more restricted in its use) in Setshuâna, where it has the
form χ*a* (written *ga*) according to § 87 and 381.

442. All that can be said is that none of these derivations is impossible; but it must be observed that (as
stated in § 261—265) the formative or grammatical portions of most languages (and particularly of the South
African tongues) are reduced to a very small number of
sounds, and that the difficulties in pronunciation are
made to disappear much more rapidly here than in other
parts of speech. On this account, the cases of homophony of grammatical elements, quite distinct in their
origin, are of such frequent occurrence, that a coincidence
in form between two grammatical elements can by no
means be considered as a proof of their original identity,

---

* There are between them the intermediate forms, **tyi**- of the
Otyihereró and Benguela, **tshi**- and **shi**- of Lourenzo Marques, Tette
and Sena.

or even of their derivation from a common source. Etymology is, therefore, seldom more difficult than in the analysis of the formative or grammatical portions of a language, the suffixes and the prefixes, &c. It would, perhaps, hardly be necessary to lay any stress upon this evident rule, had it not been so frequently and flagrantly violated, particularly by advocates of the so-called Pronominal Theory. (*Vide* § 415, note.)

443. There can be little doubt that the original meaning of the prefixes has also been obscured by the custom of correspondence which established itself between prefixes of different numerical value, whereby the meaning of one prefix became affected by that of another, to which it corresponded, either as singular or plural. The prefixes of the plural number were naturally most affected in this way; and it may be on this account that their etymology is still less certain than that of those of the singular number. It is, indeed, possible that the derivative prefix ba- of the 2nd class (or gender), by which the plural of almost all nouns of the 1st (mu-) class (personal nouns) is formed, has something to do with the Setshuâna auxiliary verb *ba* "be again" (perfect *bile* or *be*, as *ki bile ki tsile* "I have come again") and also with the stem of the second numeral, of which the primitive form *-bali* (§ 361) is still used in the Benga language.

2. ETYMOLOGY OF THE HOTTENTOT DERIVATIVE SUFFIXES.

444. The number of the classes (or genders) of nouns in the Hottentot language, being, as we have seen, much smaller than in the Bâ-ntu languages, the cases in which (two or more) suffixes, originally distinct, and marking different classes, have coalesced, are probably more numerous. At the same time, the regularity in the numerical correspondence (as singular, plural, and dual) of

the different classes or genders to each other has been far more strictly carried through. These causes combine to render the etymology of the derivative suffixes which indicate the classes or genders in Hottentot, even more obscure than that of the prefixes in the Bâ-ntu languages. In fact, none of the derivations which suggest themselves with regard to these Hottentot terminations of nouns, is more than possible. Curiously enough, the terminations which can most easily be compared to other parts of speech, are those of the masculine plural and masculine dual classes. The form of the masculine plural -**gu** (Knudsen's and Tindall's -**ku**) is identical with the suffix, by which the reciprocal form of the verb is distinguished. Thus *mū-gu* is "see one another" (with reference to both plural and dual, and to all genders and persons), but *mū*-gu is "see them," or "they seeing," and *mū*-**gu** "eyes" (§ 424),—the termination *-gu* in the two latter cases belonging to the masculine plural class (or gender), in the one case as pronoun either objective or subjective, in the other as derivative suffix. It is quite possible that the plural and reciprocal meaning sprung from the same original idea; but it may be, also, that the identity is only apparent, just as in German the same form of pronoun (*sie*) does service now in the feminine singular (English "she") and common plural (English "they"), and the syllable *ihr* may either indicate the possessive adjectives of the feminine singular (English "her") and common plural (English "their"), or the dative case of the former (English "to her," &c.), or even be the so-called pronoun of the second person plural (English "you"). But such cases of homophony of forms which were originally distinct, are so numerous, that it ought to be superfluous to warn grammarians of the snares which they contain. With the same reservation, we may also compare the termination of the masculine dual -**kha** with the stem *kha-* in *khā-*p m. s. "war" (also "a bow"), *kha-koi-*p "an enemy." The Latin *bellum* (i.e.

duellum), German words like "Zwietracht, entzweien," and the English phrase "it takes two to make a quarrel," come forward as advocates for such a suggestion, but it cannot be considered as anything more. With regard to the other terminations of the classes or genders, we are even destitute of such hypothetical etymologies, excepting as far as the present general meaning of the suffix may be considered a safe guide. Thus the termination of the feminine singular, of which the original form appears to have been -si (§ 423), may have a causal meaning similar to that of the 7th prefix, of which the Kafir form is also si- (§ 447). In the Nama verb *dai-si* " to suckle," (compare *dai* "to suck,") the same suffix appears to have such a causal meaning; but, as yet, the above instance is the only one known in which this suffix is used for the formation of causative verbs. (*Sī* by itself, used as a verb, means "to go to, arrive at.") The identity of these terminations (the noun suffix -s and the verbal suffix -*si*) with that of the ǃKora causative, or rather permissive, verbs in -*kosi*,* (which seem to be unknown in the Nama dialect,) is still less clear. That the termination of nouns in the masculine singular -bi (§ 423) had originally a local signification, is rendered probable by the meaning of many nouns formed with it, and by those adverbial forms which were originally demonstrative and interrogative pronouns of this gender, as *ne*-b-*a* "here," ǁ*na*-b-*a* "there," *ma*-b-*a* "where;" whilst *ne*-s-*a* means "thus," *ma*-s-*a* "what, why," &c. These Hottentot adverbs are similar in their use and etymology to the Kafir adverbial expressions *a*-pa "here," *a*-p-*o* "there," and pi-*na* "where," which evidently were originally demonstrative and interrogative pronouns of the now obsolete 16th (pa-) class. (*Vide* § 435). But if it were allowable to identify derivative suffixes of the Hottentot nouns with the prefixes of the nouns in the Bâ-ntu languages,—then the suffix -b or -bi, in its junction of masculine and local meaning, would almost

* Appleyard, p. 25, XVIII.

suggest the hypothesis that the homophonous prefixes of the 1st and 3rd classes (mu-) had here been combined, so that the local meaning of the 3rd class had joined the personal one of the 1st, and that by an accidental exclusion of the feminine nouns (*vide* § 424), the latter class had been restricted to nouns indicating male beings. But we need not say that we do not ascribe the least weight to these comparisons, nor do we believe that we have proved even the probability of the identity of certain derivative suffixes of nouns in Hottentot, and similar prefixes in the Bâ-ntu languages. It is enough for us, here, to have ascertained that the principle, upon which the Concord in both these families of languages is based, is primarily the same. I do not, however, maintain that, before the question of any special identity of the suffixes of the one and the prefixes of the other family of languages can be mooted, it must first have become clear that one of these families of languages (either the Prefix-Pronominal or the Suffix-Pronominal) has inverted the original position of the derivative particles, and that thus, either the prefixes of the Bâ-ntu nouns, or the suffixes of the Hottentot, have to be regarded as articles originally descended from the derivative particles (which must now have wholly disappeared) rather than as derivative prefixes.* On the

---

* To make our meaning clearer, we may refer to the circumstance that nouns in the Bâ-ntu languages frequently lose their derivative prefixes, and merely indicate the concord by the pronominal elements referring to each noun. Let this practice be accompanied by the habit of placing demonstrative pronouns only at the end of the noun (as in Setshuána), and not prefixing them (as in Kafir),—then a simple pronominal element used as an article, at the end of the noun, may frequently become the chief mark, by which the class of each noun is distinguished. It must, of course, be supposed that the use of such a suffixed article had become so prevalent as to cause the original derivative prefix (no longer necessary as a mark of the concord) to disappear entirely,—before we can assume this to have been the origin of the concord-indicating suffixes of the nouns in Hottentot. Such a process is not impossible, but in the present state of our knowledge it would be wrong to look upon it as probable. If, however, it were to have taken place, then what we now call derivative

contrary, it is quite possible that in the primary stages of the Pronominal languages, the position of these derivative particles of the nouns was not fixed, and that they could either precede or follow the other parts of the noun. Their position, as prefixes or suffixes, may have afterwards fixed itself, and thus an original identity of some among such prefixes and suffixes is not impossible. But, of course, a few casual coincidences can by no means establish an actual identity.

445. Upon the whole, the etymology of almost all the derivative suffixes of the nouns in Hottentot, and of most of the derivative prefixes in the Bâ-ntu languages, may be said to be as uncertain as that of the most ancient derivative suffixes in our own languages. We do not doubt that these had originally an independent meaning, just as much as the more modern suffixes, of which we can still trace the derivation.

3. ANALOGIES.

446. Between some of the derivative prefixes of the Bâ-ntu languages, and certain derivative suffixes in our own, we notice a sort of correspondence. For example, in the formation of verbal nouns, the derivative prefix mu- of the 1st class or gender almost corresponds with the suffix -*er* in English and German. Thus, from Kafir u-ku-*fundisa* 15. "to teach" is derived u-m-*fundisi* 1. "teacher," from u-ku-*zinga* 15. "to tempt" u-m-*zingi*

suffixes of nouns in the Hottentot language, would have to be considered as pronouns, originally identical in form with derivative prefixes which have now disappeared. If this were the case, although it would alter our opinion regarding the status of the terminations indicating the gender of nouns in Hottentot, yet our explanation of the origin of the concord in that language would not be affected by it; for, if the present terminations are merely pronominal elements and not derivative particles, they must at all events be referred to derivative particles (either prefixed or suffixed), which were originally determinative of the class or gender, although they may now have disappeared.

" tempter," &c. A still more decided correspondence of meaning is found between the power of the prefix of the 14th class (**bu**- in Kafir, **bo**- in Setshuâna, **u**- in Otyihereró)* and our derivative suffixes -*ness*, -*ship*, -*hood*, -*dom*, and -*ing*, as u-**bu**-*nyakama* 14. "dampness" from u-**ku**-*nyakama* "to become damp," u-**bu**-*soka* 14. "bachelorship" from i-*soka* 5. "bachelor," u-**bu**-*ntwana* 14. "childhood" from u-**m**-*twana* 1. (Zulu u-**mu**-*ntwana* 1. pl. a-**ba**-*ntwana* 2.) "child," u-**bu**-*doda* 14. "manhood" from i-**n**-*doda* 9. "man" (pl. a-**ma**-*doda* 6. "men"), u-**bu**-*lumko* 14. "wisdom" from u-**ku**-*lumka* 15. "to heed, to care, to be wise," &c. Points of analogy may also be observed between other derivative prefixes in the Bâ-ntu languages, and the derivative suffixes of the nouns in ours; although none of these analogies are so extensive as to allow us to identify the meaning of any Bâ-ntu derivative particle, with that of one of our own.†

447. Correspondence does not exist to this extent between any of the sex-denoting suffixes in Hottentot, and the so-called derivative suffixes of nouns in our own languages. Evidently, the original power of those Hottentot derivative suffixes, (which indicate the concord,) has been

---

* In the Dakota Language, spoken by the Sioux in North America, the derivative prefix *wo*- is used for the purpose of forming abstract nouns from verbs and adjectives. (Dakota Grammar 4to, 1852, § 5, 5; § 62, 3.)

† The vowel terminating the nouns, in the Bâ-ntu languages, is in no way derived from, or connected with the derivative prefixes, and has no reference whatever to the concord. The nature of this vowel is, however, of importance to the meaning of the noun, particularly if derived from a verb. In this case the noun generally ends in one of the following vowels, -*a*, -*i* (or -*e*), and -*o*. The termination -*o* here clearly implies a passive meaning, the -*i* an active or causative, whilst the -*a* has a neutral force. It follows from the meaning which each of these vowels conveys, that certain prefixes are either constantly or generally accompanied by one of these terminations. For instance,—all, or almost all, the infinitives of verbs end in -*a*, and thus the great mass of the nouns of the 15*th* (**ku**-) class end also in -*a*. Similarly, most of the verbal nouns of the 1st (**mu**-) class (of personal beings) end in -*i*, and most of those of the 3rd (**mu**-) class have -*o* as their terminating vowel.

weakened, and their meaning obscured. They have, therefore, no longer that derivative force which they must have possessed formerly, and have become chiefly signs of gender (or class) and number. In fact, to some extent, the local and causal meanings which the two most important of these suffixes (those of the masculine and feminine singular) impart to many of the nouns formed with them, seem to place them almost in analogy with some case terminations in the Aryan languages. Yet these concord-indicating suffixes in Hottentot are sufficiently used for the purposes of derivation, and of delineating various shades of meaning, to render it evident that they (like the Bâ-ntu prefixes of nouns) were formerly employed as derivative particles, descended from words once independent.

III. THE GENDERS (OR CLASSES) AND NUMBERS OF NOUNS.

1. THE CLASSES AND NUMBERS OF NOUNS IN THE BÂ-NTU LANGUAGES.

a. NUMERICAL VALUE AND CORRESPONDENCE OF THE DERIVATIVE PREFIXES OF THE NOUNS.

448. With regard to the analogy, which we observed between the concord-indicating derivative prefixes in the Bâ-ntu languages, and the derivative suffixes of nouns in our own, this difference is, however, to be noted, that whilst our derivative suffixes do not by themselves indicate either the singular or plural (the number being marked by the declension of the noun), most of the Bâ-ntu derivative prefixes of nouns (like the terminations indicating the gender in the Hottentot and Semitic languages) imply a certain numerical value; and, as a general rule, one derivative prefix corresponds to another, either as singular or plural. Thus Zulu u-**m**-*fundisi* 1. (Nama

‖*khā*-‖*khā-au*-p m. s.) is "a teacher," and a-ba-*fundisi* 2. (Nama ‖*khā*-‖*khā-au*-ku m. pl.) "teachers," i-si-*fundiso* 7. (Nama ‖*khā*-‖*khā*-p m. s. or ‖*khā*-‖*khā*-s f. s.) "doctrine," and i-zi-*fundiso* 8. (Nama ‖*khā*-‖*khā-ei*-ti f. pl.) "doctrines," u-mu-*ti* 3. (Nama *hei*-s f. s.) "a tree," and i-mi-*ti* 4. (Nama *hei*-ti f. pl.) "trees," u-lu-ti 11. (Nama *hei*-i common s.) "a stick," and i-zin-*ti* 10. "sticks," i-li-*zwe* 5. "country," and a-ma-*zwe* 6. "countries," i-si-*zwe* 7. "nation," and i-zi-*zwe* 8. "nations," &c.

449. Although this is the general rule, it is by no means necessary that each prefix should convey a certain numerical value, or that a prefix indicating the plural number should only correspond to one of the singular. On the contrary, though the power of analogy, (particularly in the more advanced languages of the Bâ-ntu family,) has produced great regularity with regard to such correspondence, it still frequently occurs that one prefix of the plural number corresponds to two or more different prefixes of the singular number, and that two or three different plural prefixes are found in correspondence with one of the singular number.

450. Thus the (singular) prefix n- of the 9th class or gender is usually exchanged in the plural for zin- of the 10th class. Yet there are some nouns of the 9th class (as i-n-*doda* "man," i-n-*simu* "garden," i-n-*kosi* "chief,") the plurals of which are formed with the derivative prefix ma- of the 6th class, as a-ma-*doda* "men," a-ma-*simu* "gardens," a-ma-*kosi* "chiefs." (Colenso §§ 58—60.) Similarly, the prefix zin- of the 10th class generally corresponds as plural to lu- of the 11th class; but a few nouns in lu- have also their plurals formed with the prefix ma-, as u-*suku* (vocative lu-*suku*) 11. "day," pl. a-ma-*suku* 6.,* and in Kafir u-*bala* 11. "desert," pl. a-ma-*bala* 6.,

---

* In Zulu we find besides the form a-ma-*suku* 6. two other plurals corresponding to u-*suku* 11., viz, i-zim-*suku* or i-n-*suku* 10. and i-mi-*suku* 4. The latter is only used in the locative case, e-mi-*sukw-eni* or e-m-*sukw-eni* "every day." (Colenso's Dictionary p. 458.)

u-*lwalwa* 11. "rock," pl. a-ma-*lwalwa* 6. Examples of the latter kind of correspondence appear to be more frequent in Setshuâna than in the Kafir species, as lo-*uñuo* 11. "fruit," pl. ma-*uñuo* 6., lo-*loapa* 11. "court," pl. ma-*loapa* 6., lo-*humo* 11. "wealth," pl. ma-*humo* 6., lo-*rato* 11. "love," pl. ma-*rato* 6., &c.

451. The prefix ma- of the 6th class or gender corresponds most regularly as plural to the prefix of the singular number li- (of the 5th class), which li- is not exchanged for any other plural prefix. Besides this, the prefix ma- (as has just been stated § 450,) is used for forming plurals to certain nouns of the singular number with the prefixes n- of the 9th and lu- of the 11th classes (or genders). In Kafir, also, a few of the nouns formed with ma- (as a-ma-*pakati* 6. "councillors," A-ma-//*osa* "Frontier Kafirs," &c.,) are plurals to nouns of the 1st (mu-) class of personal beings, (u-m-*pakati* 1. "councillor," U-m-//*osa* 1. "a Frontier Kafir,") which generally has the 2nd (ba-) class as its corresponding plural. In Setshuâna, and in many of the more northern languages, this prefix ma- is also used for the formation of plurals to nouns having in the singular number the prefixes of the 14th (Setshuâna bo-, Otyihereró u-) and 15th (Setshuâna χo-, Otyihereró ku-) classes,—as Setshuâna bo-*sixo* 14. "night," pl. ma-*sixo* 6. (§ 453), Otyihereró o-ku-*tui* 15. "ear," pl. o-ma-*tui* 6.* (§ 434, note.)

452. We find also a number of nouns formed with the prefix ma- which do not correspond as plural to any singular nouns, but have a collective meaning. The nouns of this kind which are the most numerous and which are common to all languages of this family, are those

---

* With reference to the apparent probability that the ma- in these cases was originally prefixed to the prefixes of the 11th (lu-), 14th (bu-), and 15th (ku-) classes, rather than substituted for them, see below, § 454.

signifying liquids, as Kafir a-**ma**-*nzi** " water," a-**ma**-*si*†
" milk," a-**ma**-*futa* "oil, fat, butter"‡, a-**ma**-*te* "spittle,"
Setshuâna **ma**-*ri* "blood," &c.§ We also meet with a

* Sesuto *metsi*, Seχlapi *metse*, Tekeza and Inhambane **ma**-*ti*, Sofala and Kisuahéli **ma**-*dshi*, Tette, Sena, and Maravi **ma**-*dze* and **ma**-*dzi*, Quellimane **ma**-*ndshe* or **ma**-*inshe*, Makua **ma**-*zi*, Kihiau (Mudshau, Ajoua) *meze* (Peters) or *messi* (Koelle), Kikámba **ma**-*nsi*, Kiníka and Kipokomo **ma**-*zi*, Bashubea *menze*, Batonga **ma**-*nzi* (Chapman), Batoka *meye* (Livingstone), Borotse *mei*, Banyeǹko *meyo*, Bakhoba (Bayeiye) *ami*, Balojazi and Maponda *mema*, Otyihererro *omeva*, Ovambo *omea*, Nano (Benguela) *ovova*, Bunda (Angola) *menya*, Kongo *mdsa*, Dikele, Dualla, and Isubu **ma**-*diba*, Benga *miba*, Timneh, m'*antr*, Bullom *men*. The original form of this noun was probably similar to that still preserved in the North-western Branch (Dikele &c.), perhaps MA-NDIBA.

† Sesuto **ma**-*fi*, Seχlapi and Balojazi **ma**-*shi*, (Inhambane **ma**-*pisa*,) Suaheli and Kipokomo **ma**-*siwa*, Kinika *messia*, Ba-nyeǹko **ma**-*we*, Bashubea **ma**-*shue*, (Bayeiye **ma**-*shota*,) Otyihereró o-**ma**-*ihi*, Sindonga (Ovambo) o-**ma**-*x́ini*, (Batoka **ma**-*lile*, Nano or Benguela o-**va**-*vele*, Benga **ma**-*nyangã*, Dikele **ma**-*nyandiba*, Dualla **ma**-*nyongo-diba*,) &c.

‡ Sena, Tette, Cape Delgado, Batoka, and Bashubea **ma**-*futa*, Inhambane, Tekeza and Sesuto **ma**-*fura*, Seχlapi **ma**-*hura*, Makua **ma**-*kūra*, Suahéli **ma**-*fúda*, Kihiáu **ma**-*fúda* or **ma**-*búda*, Kinika and Kipokómo **ma**-*fuha*, Kikamba **ma**-*uda*; Banyeǹko, Barotse and Balojazi **ma**-*ǵé*, Bayeiye a-**ma**-*ze*, Baponda **ma**-*ze*, Otyihereró o-**ma**-*ǵ'e*, Bunda **ma**-*shi* (*magi*), &c.

§ This structural peculiarity, (viz. that a good number of nouns indicating liquids are formed with the derivative prefix **ma**-, and are, in consequence, represented by pronouns of which the original form was also **ma**-,) is so characteristic that it would be a most curious coincidence, if it originated in different languages independently of each other. It was on this account, that when nothing more was known to me of the BULLOM language than the short notice in Vater's "Mithridates" (Vol. IV. p. 438), the fact there mentioned of this language possessing a peculiar relative pronoun *ma* referring to liquids, seemed at once to suggest a relationship with the Bá-ntu languages. (De Nominum Generibus 1851, p. 39.) Soon afterwards, when Nyländer's publications became accessible to me, this hypothesis was converted into certainty. Subsequently, I found that the first Bishop of Sierra Leone (O. E. Vidal) had, about the same time, " discovered the Temneh (with its two cognates, the Sherbro and the Bullom) to be a branch" of what he calls "the South African family" of languages. (Crowther's Yoruba Vocabulary, 1852, Introd. Remarks, p. 7.) Later, I learnt, in perusing Hazelwood's Grammar of the FIJI language, that the genitive particle *mei* was especially

number of abstract nouns of the 6th (**ma-**) class without any corresponding singular or plural, particularly in the more northern of the South African Bâ-ntu languages.

453. Further, a derivative prefix may in some nouns have a plural value, and thus correspond to a prefix of the singular number, while in other nouns the same prefix may indicate the singular number, and have a plural prefix corresponding to it. Such is the case with the 14th prefix. This prefix (**bu-**) in Kafir and Zulu is of no definite number, and has no other prefix corresponding to it, either as singular or plural. Most of the nouns formed with it are abstract nouns. (§ 446.) In the kindred Setshuâna, however, the same prefix **bo-** is of the singular number, and the nouns formed with it exchange it in their plural for **ma-**, the derivative prefix of the 6th class. Similarly, many Middle Branch languages either displace the 14th prefix (in these languages generally abbreviated to **u-**) for the 6th prefix (**ma-**) in order to form the plural; or, for the same purpose, they prefix **ma-** to the form beginning with *u-*. Thus Otyihereró *o-u-tuku*[*] 14. (night) has as corresponding plural the

---

[*] used in this language to indicate "the possession of a thing to be drunk," as "*a me* (the drink) *i* (of) *Varani.*" ("Grammar" p. 19.) The natural inference suggested itself that this feature of the language was again to be considered as a trace of the common origin of the Fiji and the Bâ-ntu languages. This probability was then further confirmed by so many other evidences, particularly those met with in the Papuan languages, that no doubt could any longer remain as to the fact that the Papuan, Polynesian, and Malay languages are related to the Bâ-ntu languages, and that thus the Prefix-Pronominal Class forms almost one continuous belt of languages on both sides of the equator, from the mouth of the Senegal to the Sandwich Islands. The observations on the position of the Oceanic section of these languages were embodied in a treatise, which is in the possession of Sir George Grey.

[*] Kafir u-**bu**-*suku*, Sesuto **bo**-*sio*, Setshuâna **bo**-*siχo*, Tekeza (Lourenzo Marques) *besiko*, Inhambane **u**-*shiku* or **u**-*shigu*, Sofala **bu**-*shiku*, Tette **u**-*siku*, Maravi **u**-*siko*, Mosambique **u**-*htyu*, Kisuaheli, Kinika, and Kipokomo **u**-*siku*, Kikámba **ú**-*túku*, Banyenko **o**-*thiku*, Batoka and Borotse **bo**-*siko*, Bamponda **bo**-*tike*, Nano (Benguela) **u**-*tike*, Bunda (Angola) **u**-*súku*, Dualla and Isubu *bulu*.

form *o-**ma**-u-tuku** 6. (nights). But in Otyiherero (and also in several other Middle Branch languages,) the same prefix u- of the 14th class is not of the singular number only. It is also used for the purpose of forming nouns of the plural number, which correspond to singular nouns with the prefix **ka**- of the 13th class, as *o-**ka**-ti* 13. "stick," pl. *o-**u**-ti* 14. "sticks"; whilst the nouns of the 13th (**ka**-) class, in some of the Middle Branch languages, again have as corresponding plurals, nouns formed with the prefix of the 12th class **tu**-, which is used in Otyiherero and other languages as plural of the 11th (**ru**- or **lu**-) class. (§ 405.)

454. At an early period of the language, when the present derivative prefixes (or suffixes) were still used by themselves with an independent meaning, and when the nouns of which they formed part, were, therefore, not derivatives, but composites,—it seems that there was no general distinction of the number of nouns. The grammatical number of nouns is only a consequence of their distribution into classes; for, a regular indication of the number can only in this way have been effected. Few nouns in themselves necessarily implied either the singular or plural number, excepting those which stood in such relation to each other as some of our collectives stand to the single nouns corresponding to them,—"people" to "person," "army" to "soldier," "forest" to "tree," "fleet" to "ship," &c. In this way, when some of the present derivative prefixes (or suffixes) of nouns occupied this relative position, the habit may have gradually arisen of indicating that difference in the number of the nouns which was not yet a ruling principle in the structure of the language, by the contrast of these parts of the nouns which we may call their determinatives. But it does not, of course, follow that all those parts of the nouns which were

* Setshuána **ma**-*siχo*, Sena **ma**-*siko* or **ma**-*siku*, Bashubea (Livingstone) and Batonga (Chapman) **ma**-*siko*, Bakχoba (Bayeiye) **ma**-*suko*.

converted into derivative prefixes (or suffixes) indicating the concord, once stood in this relation to each other; though the progressive development of the language must have had the tendency to identify this grammatical classification of the nouns with general distinctions observed in nature. (§ 398—402.) But, to the regularity in the correspondence of the singular and plural prefixes, another exception is found in the numerous cases in which derivative prefixes of the plural number are prefixed to the corresponding singular prefixes, instead of replacing the latter. In such cases, the form with the prefix of the singular has to be considered as the stem from which (by the addition of its own prefix) the plural is formed. In the South-eastern genus of the Middle Branch languages, the prefix of the 6th class (ma-) is found prefixed in this manner to nouns formed with the prefixes of the 11th (lu-), 14th ((b)u-), and 15th (ku-) classes, as Bunda lu-*to* (Otyiherero o-ru-*tuo*) 11. "spoon" pl. ma-*lu-to* 6., u-*ta* (Otyiherero o-u-*ta*) 14. "bow" pl. ma-*u-ta* (Otyiherero o-ma-*u-ta*) 6., Sindonga (Ovambo) o-kó-*tshui*, 15. "ear" pl. o-ma-*kó-tshui* 6. (§ 434, note); &c. In the South-eastern Branch a similar case is only met with in Setshuâna, where the prefix bo- of the second class sometimes stands before forms of the 1st class with the prefix mo-, as bo-*mo-nnaue* 2. "younger brothers," sing. mo-*nnaue* (Kafir u-m-*nina-we*) "younger brother." It is not improbable that in these cases the forms with double prefixes are the originals, from which the forms with single plural prefixes, found in other dialects, are contracted. Yet the whole system of substituting a plural prefix for a singular one is certainly older than that of adding a particle indicating the plural to the form with a singular prefix. There are similar cases in some Middle Branch languages, where other concord-indicating prefixes precede the forms of full nouns, as in Kikamba ka-*mu-di* 13. "little tree," pl. tu-*mi-di* 12., Sena shi-*mu-ti* 7. "large tree," pl. **pl-**-*mi-ti* 8. (§ 428), &c. In all these instances, however, it must be remarked that the first prefix only is to be taken into consideration as regards the concord. In this respect, these cases differ entirely from that of the 10th (**TIN-**) class, if the latter was formed from the prefix of the 9th (**N-**) class, by an old plural prefix (**TI-**); for, the concord here takes account of the full form **TIN-**. But the correspondence of this 10th prefix as plural to the prefix of the 11th (**lu-**) class, of which examples are met with in many Bâ-ntu languages, is rather against the supposition that the tenth prefix (**TIN-**) is composed of an old plural prefix (**TI-**) and the singular prefix **N-** of the 9th class.

b. DISAPPEARANCE OF CLASSES OR GENDERS.

455. When the concord-indicating derivative prefixes first came into existence as such, (by ceasing to be used as independent words,) they were probably far more numerous than we now find them in those Bâ-ntu languages which have as yet come under our observation. Traces of some such extinct prefixes might possibly still be detected by careful analysis,—just as in Kafir we clearly find remains of demonstrative pronouns of the extinct 16th (**PA-**) class, which lie imbedded like petrefactions among the adverbs and conjunctions (§ 435 and 444), and as the remains of an obsolete noun, of the also extinct 13th (**KA-**) class, are met with among the prepositions. (§ 436.)

456. The disappearance of whole classes of nouns may have been produced in two ways,—either by the nouns belonging to them becoming obsolete, or by their derivative prefixes, and the pronouns referring to them, becoming assimilated to those of another class. For example, the latter is the case in Sesuto with the 11th class. This class is still perfectly distinct in Western Setshuâna, where its prefix is **lo-**; but by a phonetic

change of the *o* into *e* in Sesuto, (of which change other instances also occur,) this prefix has here become identical with that of the 5th (le-) class, and these two classes have thus coalesced. Of course, the mere homophony of the derivative prefixes does not in itself constitute the identity of two classes of nouns. Such a thorough amalgamation can only be said to exist, where all the different pronominal elements (or all the forms of concord referring respectively to nouns of the two originally different classes) have also assumed identical forms. Such appears to be the case with the 11th and 5th classes of nouns in Sesuto; it is, however, not so with regard to the 10th (zin-) and 8th (zi-) classes in Kafir (and Setshuâna), though the prefixes and the pronominal elements have in most instances assumed the same forms; but as this is not universal, the two classes are still to be viewed as distinct from each other.

457. Processes similar to these, which in comparatively recent times have reduced the number of classes (or genders) in many Bâ-ntu languages, may also safely be assumed to have been at work during the previous periods through which these languages passed. Thus the number of classes (or genders) of nouns, which was in all probability originally very large, has been reduced to less than a score; and these have assumed such relations to each other, that one class implying the singular number generally corresponds to another of the plural. This cannot have been the case at the beginning, nor is this rule, even now, strictly carried out in any Bâ-ntu language; but it indicates the direction in which the progress of the language tends. How this principle has been at work in the different Bâ-ntu languages which we are able to compare, will be seen from the tables, in which the different forms of the derivative prefixes of each language are so exhibited that the correspondence of the classes (or genders) of the singular and plural numbers can be perceived at once.

C. NOMENCLATURE.

458. For the purpose of identifying the several forms of the same class (or gender) in the different Bâ-ntu languages, it is necessary to indicate each class by a number. No other way of distinguishing the classes is equally capable of general application. Since they have *not* been connected with natural distinctions, as in the Sex-denoting languages, the only ways of clearly indicating them are either by numerals, or by employing for this purpose the most usual form of each derivative prefix. The latter nomenclature, however, would be useless for the purposes of comparison, or to say the least, very confusing; for, as the prefixes have different forms in the different languages, the same syllable is not infrequently used in one language as the prefix of one class, and in another as that of one wholly different. Thus li- in Kafir is the prefix of the 5th class (= Setshuâna le-), whilst li- in Setshuâna is the prefix of the 8th class of nouns,* of which the Kafir form is zi-. Such cases of apparent phonetic identity of different prefixes in different languages, as well as instances of different forms for the same prefix, are often met with in comparing these languages with one another. For example, whilst in the above instance the consonant *z* belongs in Kafir to the 8th (zi-) and 10th (zin-) classes,—in Mpongwe the same letter is characteristic of the 7th prefix (Kafir si-); and the 8th class in Mpongwe has *y*, and the 10th *s*, instead of this *z*.

459. Most Grammarians who describe these languages, have also distinguished by numbers what they call "principiations" (Brusciotto à Vetralla), "classes," "species," or "declensions" of the nouns; but they have generally combined the singular and plural forms corresponding to each other into one class, thereby greatly complicating their grammatical labours. For, as one (and the same)

---

* In his latest edition of the New Testament Mr. Moffat gives ŕi- as the form of this prefix, and also of the 10th; but in all former Setshuâna publications, and also in Mr. Frédoux's "Grammar," we find li-.

derivative prefix of the plural frequently corresponds to more than one prefix of the singular number, in such cases the grammatical forms referring to each plural prefix (as pronouns, adjectives, &c.,) must be twice or thrice repeated.

460. The order in which the classes (or genders) of nouns in the Bâ-ntu languages are placed here, is almost the same as that which is followed in my dissertation " De Nominum Generibus " &c. (Bonn, 1851); excepting that the 13th and 14th classes have changed their numbers. The present arrangement has been completely adhered to in my edition of Dr. Peters' Mosambique Vocabularies (London, 1856), in Hahn's Otyihereró Grammar and Dictionary (Berlin, 1857), and in Frédoux's " Sketch of the Sechuana Grammar " (Cape Town, 1864). It is, however, right to state that the Rev. C. H. Hahn objects to this order of the prefixes, and considers it arbitrary. ("Grammatik" p. 7, note.) It does not, however, appear to me that any better arrangement has been proposed; and ours has, at all events, the advantage that in Otyihereró (which language, as possessing the greatest number of classes of any known Bâ-ntu dialect, has been mostly considered in making this arrangement,) all the odd numbers from 1 to 13 indicate classes of the singular number, whilst the most usual plural class corresponding to each of these singular classes, is named by the even number following. The **mu-** class of personal nouns, with the corresponding **ba-** class, naturally head the series. Then follows, as third, the other **mu-** class with its corresponding plural as fourth; and with regard to the order in which the remaining classes have been arranged, certain reasons, either founded upon the present use of the prefixes, or upon their probable origin, have prevailed; but as they are chiefly of a practical nature, it is unnecessary to explain them here.

d. THE PREFIXES OF THE NOUNS IN THEIR DIFFERENT FORMS AND IN THEIR NUMERICAL CORRESPONDENCE.

A. IN THE SOUTH-EASTERN BRANCH.

THE KAFIR SPECIES.

461. The most usual forms in which the derivative prefixes of the nouns in the Kafir species occur, are those preceded by a vowel, which is always identical with the vowel ending the prefix itself, provided, of course, that this ends with a vowel. Such is everywhere the case in the Kafir language, excepting the prefixes of the 9th (n-) class, and those of the 1st and 3rd (m-) classes. In both the latter instances, however, the Zulu yet shews with monosyllabic stems the fuller and older form mu-. The initial vowel is chiefly absent in cases where the employment of an article would be inadmissible, — always in the vocative,* and in certain negative sentences.† We thus recognise in this vowel an article, which, according to its origin, is a pronoun that was in the first instance identical with the derivative prefix which it precedes.

462. That the article had originally the full form of the prefix is clear from an analysis of the so-called causal form (or case) of nouns in Kafir. (Appleyard § 114.) This case was originally formed by prefixing the preposition of identity and causality *ngi-* "it is, by" (Setshuâna *ki-*, Makua, Kihiau, Kinika, and Kisuahéli *ni-*, Otyihereró *i-*‡) to the form of the noun with the article. Thus with nouns of the 1st (m-), 2nd (ba-), 3rd (m-), and 6th (ma-) classes the vowel only of this *ngi-* has been suppressed, and, of the article, the vowel alone retained. We have thus *ng-u-*m*-fazi* 1. "it is a woman" (= Setshuâna

---

* Appleyard § 113, Colenso § 92, Grout § 123.

† Appleyard § 315 and 364, Colenso § 126.

‡ In the dialect of Sena, in Bunda, Kongo, Mpongwe, and Isubu this preposition appears to have merged into another preposition, common to most, if not all, Bâ-ntu languages, viz. *na-* "with, and."

ki mo-*sari*), *ng-a-ba-fazi* 2. "they are women" (= Setshuâna *ki* ba-*sari*), *ng-u-m-lomo* 3. "it is a mouth" (= Setshuâna *ki* mo-*lomo*), *ng-a-ma-fu* 6. "they are clouds" (= Setshuanâ *ki* ma-*ru*). But before nouns of the 5th (li-), 7th (si-), 8th (zi-), 10th (zin-), 11th (lu-), 14th (bu-), and 15th (ku-) classes, the preposition *ngi-* is now wholly elided, though its influence is felt in the retention of a fuller form of the article. This fuller form consists of the first two letters of that derivative prefix, from which each article has descended. Thus we find li-li-*fu* 5. "it is a cloud" (= Western Setshuâna *ki* le-*ru*), si-si-*fuba* 7. "it is the chest, breast" (= Setshuâna *ki* se-*huba*), zi-zi-*fuba* 8. "they are chests" (= Setshuâna *ki* li-*huba*), zi-zim-*vu* 10. "they are sheep" (= Setshuâna *ki* liñ-*ku*), lu-lu-*ti* 11. "it is a stick," lu-*nyawo** 11. "it is a foot" (= Setshuâna *ki* lo-*nao*), bu-bu-*suku* 14. "it is night" (= Setshuâna *ki* bo-*siχo*), ku-ku-*tanda* 15. "it is to love" (= Setshuâna *ki* χo-*rata*).†
We thus clearly see, that whilst in the former examples the preposition *ngi-* has amalgamated with the article (which, in this case, usually preserves only its vowel),—in the latter instances the preposition has disappeared before the consonant of the article, which consonant, by the influence of the preposition, has been retained. In the case of the 2nd (ba-) class both changes of form (dropping the preposition, and its amalgamation with the vowel of the article) are met with in different dialects of the Kafir language; the Amampondo dialect having the causal form ba-ba-, as in ba-ba-*ntu* (Boyce-Davis, § 25) = *ng-a-ba-ntu* of the Ama//osa (Frontier Kafirs). These two forms are equally derived from an ancient form *NGI-BA-BA-NTU* (Setshuâna *ki* ba-*thu*).

---

* Contracted from *NGI-*LU-LU-*NYAWO.* Vide § 465.

† In *y-i-*mai-*lambo* 4. "they are rivers" (= Setshuana *ki* mae-*lapo*), and *y-i-*ma-*vu* 9. "it is a sheep" (= Setshuâna *ki* ma-*ku*) the *y* is probably a weakened form of the *ng*. In Zulu we also find this *yi-* (= *ngi-*) used in several other classes. (Colenso § 138 — 140.)

463. Whilst the article is thus constantly retained in the causal case in Kafir, and appears either fully, or as a mere vowel,—it is as regularly omitted after some other prepositions (which form, as it were, cases of the nouns), particularly after *ka-* of the genitive, and *kwa-* of the locative, both of which prepositions are only used with personal nouns (Appleyard § 102, 104, and 112), being principally restricted to proper names*. If the article were employed in the examples given below, the vowel (*a*) of the preposition would have coalesced with the vowel *u* of the article of the 1st (m-) class, forming *o*, and with the *i* of the 9th (n-) class, forming *e*. (§ 328.) Such a contraction of the end *a* of the preposition with the vowel *i* of the article in the 4th (mi-), 5th (li-), 7th (si-), 8th (zi-), 9th (n-), and 10th (zin-) classes to *e*, and with the *u* of the 1st (m-), 3rd (m-), 11th (lu-), 14th (bu-), and 15th (ku-) classes to *o*, regularly occurs in the case of the usual genitive particle -*a*- "of," and in those of the prepositions *na*- "with, and," and *nga*- "by, through, with."† Again the omission of the article is sufficiently clear in the case of the local preposition (*s*)*e*-, the present use of which, as far as we know, is restricted to the Kafir species. (§ 438, Appleyard § 107.)

---

* For example, in the following instances taken from Appleyard (§ 104), u-m-*fazi ka-Pato* "the wife of Pato," a-ba-*fazi ba-ka-Pato* "the women of Pato," u-m-*ti ka-Kobi* "the tree of Kobi," i-mi-*ti ka-Kobi* "the trees of Kobi," i-*hashe li-ka-bawo* "the horse of my father," a-ma-*hashe ka-bawo* "the horses of my father," the article *u* of the 1st (m-) class does not precede the nouns u-*Pato*, u-*Kobi*, u-*bawo*, (my, or our father); and in i-m-*Xlu ka-m-kosi* "the house of the chief" and i-zim-*Xlu zi-ka-m-kosi* "the houses of the chief," the article *i* of i-m-*kosi* 9. "chief" is omitted. Similarly in *kwa-Pato* "at (to or from) Pato's place," *kwa-Mhala* "at (to or from) Umhala's place," the article *u* is again omitted.

† U-m-*fazi w-e-n-kosi* "the wife of the king," i-si-*tya s-o-m-fazi* "the dish of the woman," u-bu-*de b-e-li-zwe* "the length of the country," *n-o-m-fazi* "with the wife," *n-e-li-zwi* "and the word," *ng-o-m-ti* "through the tree," *ng-e-li-zwi* "by the word," &c.

464. Although it is clear that the initial vowel was originally a pronoun, (derived from and, at first, identical with the derivative prefix which it precedes, and) used with the force of an article, it can hardly be said now to have this power. Its employment appears mainly to depend upon usage, and scarcely upon any intention of thereby defining the noun. The position of this ancient article at the beginning of the noun accords with the general position of the demonstrative pronouns in Kafir, which in this language, as well as in Isubu, precede the noun, instead of being placed after it, as in Setshuâna and most of the other Bâ-ntu languages. Vestiges of this old article are also found in some other Bâ-ntu languages (as in Mpongwe); and this renders it probable that this form of article (originally identical with the prefix) was used at the period preceding the dispersion of the South African Bâ-ntu languages. We generally find, however, that, in these languages, either forms without an article are used, or that the demonstrative particle *o-* (which is *not* a pronominal element originally identical with a concord-indicating derivative prefix) precedes the prefixes with the force of an article, as is the case in the languages of the South-western genus (Otyiherer6, Bunda, &c.,).

465. A contraction of this ancient Kafir article with the derivative prefix which it precedes, (by which the latter appears to have been elided,) takes place frequently in those cases where the latter contains an *l*, viz. in the 5th (**li**-) and 11th (**lu**-) classes (or genders,) as

i-*zwe* 5. for i-**li**-*zwe* "land" (pl. a-**ma**-*zwe* 6.);
i-*gama* 5. "name" (pl. a-**ma**-*gama* 6.);
i-*soka* 5. "bachelor" (pl. a-**ma**-*soka* 6.);
i-*siko* 5. "custom, law" (pl. a-**ma**-*siko* 6);
i-*ziko* (Tekeza *tiko*) 5. "fire-place" (pl. a-**ma**-*ziko* 6.);

u-*ntu* for u-**lu**-*ntu* 11. "human race;"
u-*nwele* 11. "hair;"
u-*zwane* 11. "toe" (pl. a-**ma**-*zwane* 6.);
u-*kuko* 11. "mat;"
u-*bambo* 11. "rib;"
u-*pondo* 11. "horn;"
u-*sapo* 11. "child;"
u-*lwimi* 11. "tongue."

In the same manner the (bu-) of the 14th (bu-) and the
zi- of the 10th (zin-) classes of nouns may disappear in
combination with the article, and the forms of these
prefixes with the article may thus be reduced to u- and
i-n- (with its euphonic representatives according to
§ 214—216,)* as

u-*tyaloa* (Zulu u-bu-*tywola*, Se-   i-n-*kulo* 10. "mats;"
   tshuâna, bo-*yaloa*) 14. "Kafir   i-n-*nwele* 10. "hairs;"
   beer;"   i-n-*tsapo* 10. "children;"
u-*tyani* (Setshuâna bo-*yañ* 14.)   i-m-*bambo* 10. "ribs;"
   "grass;"   i-m-*pondo* 10. "horns;"
i-n-*komo* 10. for i-zin-*komo*   i-*lwimi* 10. "tongues"
   "cattle;"

All these cases of contraction are more frequent with
polysyllabic stems, and in some of the latter, such contractions are the rule, and the full form with the intermediate consonant the exception. But the form with the
consonant reappears in nouns of the 10th (zin-) and 11th
(lu-) classes, when they are used without the article
(§ 461), as zin-*komo* 10. "cows!" zim-*bambo* 10. "ribs!"
zi-*lwimi* 10. "tongues!" e-zi-*lwimi-ni* 10. "in the tongues," e-zin-*tsatsh-eni* 10. "among the children," lu-*sapo*
11. "child!" &c. Such a reappearance of the consonant
does not, however, take place in nouns of the 5th (li-)
class,† unless their stem is monosyllabic, as li-*zwe* 5.
"land!" Nor does it occur when the consonant which
has disappeared is the ending nasal of the prefix of the
9th (n-) or 10th (zin-) class; for, the nasal is suppressed
before the initial consonant of the stem when incompatible

---

* The nasal in the prefixes m- (9th) and zim- (10th class) is not
changed into ñ in Kafir, as was erroneously stated in Part I. of this
Grammar. For the correction of this mistake I am obliged to the kind
communication of the Rev. J. W. Appleyard, in a letter dated Mount
Coke, January 31, 1866.

† E-*haya* "at home" from i-*haya* 5. "home," Kafir *ndi-nye na-tyala
l-a-m-to* (I not being with guilt of thing, i-*tyala* 5. "guilt.") i-m-*to* 9.
"thing") "not having the guilt of the thing," Zulu u-*na-hashi* li-*nini-ná?*
(thou-with-horse-which? i-*hashi* 5. horse) "what horse hast thou?"

with the latter, as *hangu* 9. "pig!" *e-zi-gush-eni* "among the sheep" (i-*gusha* 10. "sheep"), &c. Here the forms without the article are equally devoid of the nasal with those which retain it. One case of this kind is also met with in the 3rd (m-) class, where the noun u-*nyaka* "a year" (pl. i-mi-*nyaka* 4.) has lost its prefixual m on account of the following nasal. (Appleyard § 75. 6. ii.)

466. Totally different, however, is the case with regard to those nouns of the 1st (m-) class, in which we find the article, but no derivative prefix. Here, as a rule, the prefix has not been elided, for the simple reason that these nouns have not been formed with the prefix of the 1st (m-) class. Some of them have not been formed with any of the concord-indicating derivative prefixes, but are remnants of an early formation of nouns, as u-*baba* "my father," u-*ma* (= Zulu u-*mame*) "my mother," &c. Others again are nouns from originally different classes (or even other parts of speech), which, used as proper names of persons, are on this account constructed like nouns of the 1st (m-) class (or gender), as U-*mboxla* 1. "Wildcat" (i-m-*boxla* 9.), U-*kala* 1. "Cry-out" (u-ku-*kala* 15.), u-*ewe* 1. "Yes," u-*hai* 1. "No," &c. (Appleyard § 75. 1.) These latter nouns were transferred to the 1st (m-) class by a logical tendency of the language, because they indicate (or are metaphorically conceived to indicate) persons in the singular. On this account they are preceded by the article of the 1st class, and used with the forms of concord of that class. Examples of a similar logical transference of nouns from one class or gender to another are frequently met with in different languages. In English this process has been fully developed by incorporating into the neuter class (or gender) those nouns, which, originally belonging to the masculine and feminine classes, contain no reference to the natural distinctions of sex. In the languages akin to the Kafir, instances of the transference of nouns by reason of their personal meaning from other classes to the first class occur

frequently; and in some of these instances the process of transition is still visible. For, whilst in Kafir these nouns are now constructed as belonging entirely to the 1st (**mu-**) class, in some other languages the forms of the pronouns and adjectives used with the nouns are partly those of the original class (or gender) to which their prefixes refer them. In Otyihereró those nouns of the 5th (**ri-**), 7th (**tyi-**), 9th (**n-**), and 13th (**ka-**) classes which indicate human beings, can either be constructed according to the class of their prefixes, or as if they were nouns of the 1st (**mu-**) class, with the pronouns, adjectives, &c., of that class; and the respective plural nouns of the 6th (**ma-**), 8th (**vi-**), 10th (**ʒ'on-**), and 14th (**u-**) classes can likewise be treated either as nouns of the 2nd (**va-**) class, or with reference to their own derivative prefixes. (Hahn § 34.)*
This is analogous to the occasional use in German of the pronoun *sie* in referring to such nouns as "Weib, Mädchen," instead of the more grammatically correct *es*. In the Swahéli language of Zanzibar not only names of persons, but also those of other *living beings*, originally belonging to other classes, can be in this

---

* In '**e**-*rumbí* r-*á-ndye* e-*kúru* r-*á-ya*' (my eldest brother has gone away) the pronominal elements are in concord with the derivative prefix of the 5th (**ri-**) class, with which the noun **e**-*rumbí* (i.e. *O-***RI**-*RUMBI*) is formed, but in '**e**-*rumbí* u-*ándye* o-mu-*kúru* u-*á-ya*' they belong to the 1st (**mu-**) class, to which the noun '**e**-*rumbí*' has been here logically transferred. In Otyihereró, a noun is not unfrequently used with both forms of concord at once; the possessive adjective, at all events, frequently following the class of the prefix of the noun, while the subjective pronoun of the verb agrees with the class to which the noun (on account of its meaning) has been transferred. Thus in Hahn's "Omahungi," &c. (1861) p. 47, in the sentence '*o*-**ma**-*rumbi o-a Yozev tyi* va-*ka-riʒ'ire*' (the sons of Joseph when they herded), the '*o-*' preceding the genitive particle '-*a-*' is a pronominal element of the 6th (**ma-**) class, whilst the '*va*' in '*va-ka-riʒ'ire*' (they herded) is a subjective pronoun of the 2nd (**va-**) class; and on p. 288, in the sentence '*Zaharias ihe y-e u-a-uriʒ'irue*' (Zacharias his father was filled), the '*y-e*' (his) is of the 9th (**n-**) class, to which '*ihe*' (father) appears to have belonged originally, and in '*u-a-uriʒ'irue*' (he was filled) the pronoun '*u*' is of the 1st (**mu-**) class.

manner transferred to the 1st (m-) and 2nd (wa-) classes, as n-*gombe* 9. "ox," pl. n-*gombe* 10. "oxen." (Dr. Steere's "Table of Concords" in his "Handbook of Swaheli.") Whilst the plurals of these nouns (in Otyiherero, Kisuahéli, &c.,) depend upon the usual rules of correspondence governing those prefixes with which the nouns were originally formed,—the Kafir nouns which have been transferred into the 1st (m-) class, form their plurals with the prefix bo-, which, when used with its article, is contracted to o-. The etymology of this form is not clear. It may be a mere modification of the 2nd prefix ba-, or a distinct prefix which originally marked a class of its own, but has now been absorbed by the 2nd class.

467. The mutual correspondence with regard to number, which takes place between the different concord-indicating derivative prefixes of nouns in the KAFIR language, is best shewn by the following tables. The cases in which the prefix has fallen off or been elided before the stem, are indicated by the mark (—).

DERIVATIVE PREFIXES OF THE NOUNS IN THE

	A. WITHOUT ARTICLE.		B. WITH ARTICLE.	
	SINGULAR.	PLURAL.	SINGULAR.	PLURAL.
PERSONAL.	1. m-, (—)	2. ba-, bo- b- be- 6. ma-	1. u-m-, u-	2. a-ba-, o- a-b- a-be- 6. a-ma-
	3. m- (—)	4. mi-	3. u-m- u-	4. i-mi-
	5. li-, (—)	6. ma- m-	5. i-li-, i- ··	6. a-ma- a-m-
	7. si- s-	8. zi- z-	7. i-si- i-s-	8. i-zi- i-z-
	9. n- m- (—)	10. zin- zim- zi- 6. ma-	9. i-n- i-m- i-	10. i-zin-, i-n- i-zim-, i-m- (i-zi-), i- 6. a-ma-
	11. lu-	10. zin- zim- zi- 6. ma-	11. u-lu-, u-	10. i-zin-, i-n- i-zim-, i-m- (i-zi-), i- 6. a-ma-
ABSTRACT.		14. bu- b-		14. u-bu-, u- u-b-
INFINITIVE AND LOCAL.		15. ku- kw-		15. u-ku- u-kw-

KAFIR LANGUAGE.

C. WITH ARTICLE AND PREPOSITION *NGI.*

SINGULAR.	PLURAL.
1. ng-u-m-, ng-u-	**2.** ng-a-ba-, ng-o-ng-a-b- ng-a-be- **6.** ng-a-ma-
3. ng-u-m- ng-u-	**4.** y-i-mi-
5. li-li-, li-	**6.** ng-a-ma- ng-a-m-
7. si-si- si-s-	**8.** zi-zi- zi-z-
9. y-i-n- y-i-m- y-i-	**10.** zi-zin-, zi-n- zi-zim-, zi-m- (zi-zi-), zi- **6.** ng-a-ma-
11. lu-lu-, lu-	**10.** zi-zin-, zi-n- zi-zim-, zi-m- (zi-zi-), zi- **6.** ng-a-ma-
ABSTRACT.	**14.** bu-bu-, bu- bu-b-
INFINITIVE AND LOCAL.	**15.** ku-ku- ku-kw-

KAFIR NOUNS.

u-m-*ntu* (Zulu u-mu-*ntu*) 1. "man, person," pl. a-ba-*ntu* (Z.) 2. "people;"

u-m-*fazi* (Z.) 1. "woman," pl. a-ba-*fazi* (Z.) 2.;

u-m-*enzi* 1. "maker," pl. a-b-*enzi* 2.;

u-m-*oni* (Z.) 1. "sinner," pl. a-b-*oni* (Z.) 2.;

u-m-*lungu* (Z.) 1. "European," pl. a-be-*lungu* (Z.) 2.;

u-*yise* (Z.) 1. " (his, &c.) father," pl. o-*yise* (Z.) 2.;

u-m-*pakati* (Z.) 1. "councillor," pl. a-ma-*pakati* (Z.) 6.;

U-m-*pondo* 1. "a Mpondo, a man of Faku's tribe," pl. A-ma-*mpondo* (Z.) 6.;

u-m-*bona* 1. "maize, Indian corn;"*

u-m-*ti* (Zulu u-mu-*ti*) 3. "tree, medicine," pl. i-mi-*ti* (Z.) 4.;

u-m-*zimba* (Z.) 3. "body," pl. i-mi-*zimba* (Z.) 4.;

---

* The corresponding word in Zulu u-m-*bila* belongs to the 3rd class; the natives say *si-ya*-wu-*tanda* (3.) "we like it," not *si-ya*-m-*tanda* (3.). That the word signifying "maize" is a personal being in Kafir has its parallel in the legend of *Mondamin*, told by the North American Indians (Longfellow's "Hiawatha" XIII.)

u-*nyaka* (Z.) 3. "year," pl. i-**mi**-*nyaka* (Z.) 4.;

*u-**m**-*melwane* 3. "neighbour," pl. i-**mi**-*melwane* 4. and a-**ba**-*melwane* 2.;

*u-**m**-x́*lobo* 3. "friend," pl i-**mi**-x́*lobo* 4. and a-**ba**-x́*lobo* 2.;

*u-**m**-*lwelwe* 3. "infirm person," pl. i-**mi**-*lwelwe* 4.;

i-**li**-*zwi* (Z.) 5. "word," pl. a-**ma**-*zwi* (Z.) 6.;

i-*siko* (Z.) 5. "custom," pl. a-**ma**-*siko* 6.;

i-*zulu* (Z.) 5. "heaven, sky," pl. a-**ma**-*zulu* (Z.) 6.;

a-**ma**-*si* (Z.) 6. "sour milk;"

a-**m**-*endu* 6. "speed;"

i-**si**-*fuba* (Z.) 7. "chest, breast," pl. i-**zi**-*fuba* (Z.) 8.;

i-**s**-*an*x́*la* (Z.) 7. "hand," pl. i-**z**-*an*x́*la* (Z.) 8.;

i-**s**-*onka* (Zulu i-*si-nkwa*) 7. "bread, loaf," pl. i-**z**-*onka* (Zulu i-**zi**-*nkwa*) 8.;

i-**n**-*to* (Z.) 9. "thing," pl. i-**zin**-*to* (Z.) 10.;

i-**m**-*vu* (Z.) 9. "sheep," pl. i-**zim**-*vu* (Z.) 10.;

i-*hangu* 9. (Hottentot *hagu*-p masc. sing.) "hog," pl. i-**zi**-*hangu* 10.;

i-**n**-*tombi* (Z.) 9. "girl," pl. i-**n**-*tombi* (Zulu i-**zin**-*tombi*) 10.;

i-**m**-*mini* (Z.) 9. "daytime, day," pl. i-**m**-*mini* 10.;

i-*mazi* (Zulu i-**n**-*kom-azi*, § 321, note) 9. "cow," pl. i-*mazi* 10.;

i-*gusha* 9. (Hottentot *gu*-**s**-*a* fem. sing. obj.) "sheep," pl. i-*gusha* 10.;

i-**n**-*doda* (Z.) 9. "man, husband," pl. a-**ma**-*doda* (Z) 6.;

u-**lu**-*ti* (Z.) 11. "stick," pl. i-**zin**-*ti* (Z.) 10.;

u-**lu**-*vo* 11. "feeling," pl. i-**zim**-*vo* 10.;

u-*suku* (Z.) "day," pl. i-**n**-*tsuku* 10. (Zulu i-**n**-*suku* 10. and a-**ma**-*suku* 6.);

u-*bambo* (Z.) 11. "rib," pl. i-**m**-*bambo* (Zulu i-**zim**-*bambo*) 10.;

u-*lwimi* (Zulu u-*limi*) 11. "tongue," pl. i-*lwimi* 10. (Zulu i-**zi**-*limi* 10. and a-**ma**-*limi* 6.);

u-*bala* (Z.) 11. "desert, wilderness," pl. a-**ma**-*bala* 6.;

u-*lwalwa* 11. "flat rock," pl. a-**ma**-*lwalwa* 6.;

u-**bu**-*so* (Z.) 14. "face;"

u-**bu**-*suku* (Z.) 14. "night;"

u-**bu**-*si* (Z.) 14. "honey;"

u-**bu**-*ze* (Z.) 14. "nakedness;"

u-**b**-*oni* 14. "evil;"

---

* These, the only nouns of persons which belong to the 3rd class, are occasionally construed according to their meaning, and not according to their grammatical class (or gender). Thus, with reference to u-**m**-*melwane* 3., u-**m**-x́*lobo* 3., or u-**ma**-*lwelwe* 3., I am informed (by the Rev. Tiyo Soga) that it is correct to say *ndi-m-tandile* (1.) "I have loved him," and not *ndi-wu-tandile* (3.). But on the other hand, with reference to u-**m**-*melwane* 3., the Kafirs do not say ye-*na* 1. "he," but w-*ona* 3., nor *a-ka-ko* 1. "he is not there," but *a-wu-ko* 3. In the latter case u-**m**-x́*lobo* 3. is said to be used with both forms, *a-wu-ko* 3. as well as *a-ka-ko* 1. (*Vide* § 466.)

Kafir and Zulu Derivative Prefixes of Nouns.

u-*tyani* (Z.*) 14. "grass;"
u-*tyalwa* (Zulu u-**bu**-*tywala* or u-*tywala**) 14. "Kafir beer;"
u-*boya* (Z.) 14. "hair of an animal;"
u-*bomi* (Z.) 14. "life, happiness;"
u-**ku**-*kanya* (Z.) 15. "light;"
u-**ku**-*teta* 15. "language" (Zulu "talk," &c.);
u-**kw**-*azi* (Z.) "knowledge;"
u-**kw**-*ona* (Zulu u-**kw**-*ona* or u-**k**-*ona*) 15. "to sin."

468. From the preceding list of nouns, in which those which are identical in form and meaning in ZULU are indicated by the letter "(Z.)," it will be seen that the correspondence of the classes of the singular and plural numbers does not differ much in Zulu from that in the language of the Frontier Kafirs (Ama//osa). In Zulu, however, we have to notice, that no nouns of the 9th (n-) class appear to exist in which the nasal has been entirely dropped. Those in Kafir, in which this is the case, are evidently late importations into the language.

* In the Bishop of Natal's Dictionary (p. 495 and 504) these nouns u-*tyani* and u-*tywala* are, by misprint, ascribed to the 11th (**lu**-) class.

ZULU PREFIXES.

WITH ARTICLE.

	SINGULAR.	PLURAL.
PERSONAL.	**1.** u-**mu**-, u- u-**m**-	**2.** a-**ba**-, o- a-**b**- a-**be**- **6.** a-**ma**-
	3. u-**mu**- u-**m**- u-	**4.** i-**mi**-
	5. i-**li**-, i-	**6.** a-**ma**- a-**m**-
	7. i-**si**- i-**s**-	**8.** i-**zi**- i-**z**-
	9. i-**n**- i-**m**-	**10.** i-**zin**-, i-**n**- i-**zim**-, i-**m**- **6.** a-**ma**-
	11. u-**lu**, ū-	**10.** i-**zin**-, i-**n**- i-**zim**-, i-**m**- i-**zi**- **6.** a-**ma**-
ABSTRACT.	**14.** u-**bu**-, u- u-**b**-	
INFINITIVE AND LOCAL.	**15.** u-**ku**- u-**kw**- u-**k**-	

THE SETSHUANA SPECIES.

469. In the Setshuâna and Tekeza dialects some of the prefixes coalesce more with the stem of the noun than they do in Kafir, and this either causes the suppression of the initial consonant of the stem, or the disappearance of the whole or a part of the prefix combined with a stronger explosive pronunciation of the initial of the stem. For example, the former is the case with the initial *b* in SETSHUANA when following the prefix **mo-** of the 1st or 3rd class. The **mo**-*b* is contracted here to **m-** (§ 113 and 343) as in **m**-*ŏpi* 1. "potter" (= Kafir u-**m**-*bumbi*), from χo *bopa* (Sesuto **h'o** *bopa*, Kafir u-**ku**-*bumba*) 15. "to make pottery," **m**-*ila* 3. "street" (Zulu u-**m**-*zila* "cattle track") pl. **me**-*bila* 4., **m**-*ele* (Sesuto) 3. "body" pl. **me**-*bele* 4. (compare Kafir i-**si**-*bili* 7. "substance of a body"), &c. Whilst the prefix has prevailed over the beginning of the stem in the instances given above,—we find again in the 9th (n-) and 10th (lin-) classes (according to the rules explained in § 218—220, and 335—337,) that the nasal of the prefix almost always disappears, excepting before monosyllabic stems. In these cases, however, the strengthened form of the initial consonant of the stem (when this is capable of being strengthened) which has in the first instance been called into existence by the nasal, remains, —becoming, as it were, characteristic of these classes, and, in the 9th (n-) class, almost representing the prefix. To indicate the presence of the consonant thus strengthened, the mark ·.· has been used.

The case is different in the SEχLAPI dialect, after the prefix of the 5th (le-) class. Here, as the nature of the vowel of the prefix is apparently favorable to a succeeding sibilant, we find that the initial of the stem, when a sibilant, is retained; while after the corresponding plural prefix **ma-** the same initial sibilant is converted into a liquid, as **le**-*sapo* 5. "bone," pl. **ma**-*rapo* 6. Also where there is a tendency towards palatalisation of a labial, it is

Seḱlapi Derivative Prefixes of Nouns.

carried through after the 5th (le-) prefix, whilst after the 6th (ma-) the original labial may be retained,—as *le-tsele* 5. "female breast," pl. ma-*bele* 6.

SEḰLAPI PREFIXES.

SINGULAR.	PLURAL.
PERSONAL.	
1. mo-, (—) mu- ṅu m- (**MO**-*B*-)	**2.** ba-, bō- be- b- ba-*b*- bo-*mo*-
3. mō- (o)m- m- (**MO**-*B*-) mu- (—)	**4.** me- me-*b*- **6.** ma-
5. le-, (—)	**6.** ma- m-
7. se-, (—)	**8.** li- (ŕi-), (—)
9. n-⋮ m-⋮ ṅ-⋮ (—)⋮	**10.** lin-⋮ lim-⋮ liṅ-⋮ li-⋮ (—)⋮ **6.** ma-
11. lo-, (—)	**10.** lin-⋮ lim-⋮ liṅ-⋮ li-⋮, (—)⋮ **6.** ma-
ABSTRACT	AND LOCAL.
14. bo-, (—)	**6.** ma-
INFINITIVE	AND LOCAL.
15. χo-(ɡo-), (—)	**6.** ma-

SEḰLAPI NOUNS.

mo-*thu* (Se-suto mo-*tu*, § 92) 1. "person," pl. ba-*thu* (Sesuto ba-*tu*, § 140) 2. "people;"

mạ-*saŕi* (Se-suto mo-*sali*, Kafir u-m-*fazi*), pl. ba-*saŕi* (Sesuto ba-*sali*) 2.;

mo-*loi* (Ses.) 1. "sorcerer," pl. ba-*loi* (Ses.) 2.;

m-*olai* (Ses., = Kafir u-m-*bulali*) 1. "a murderer," pl. ba-*bolai* (Ses., = Kafir a-ba-*bulali*) 2. from χo-*bolaea* (Sesuto h'o-*bolaïa*, Kafir u-ku-*bulala*) 15. "to kill," χo-m-*olaea* (Sesuto h'o-m-*olaïa*, Kafir u-ku-m-*bulala*) "to kill him;"

mo-*réna* (Ses.) 1. "lord, king," pl. ba-*réna* 2. (Sesuto ma-*réna* 6.);

m-*aba* 1. "enemy," pl. b-*aba* (i.e. **BA**-*BABA*) 2. (compare Kafir u-*tshaba* 11. "enemy");

mu-*ṅ* (Sesuto mo-*ṅ*, Kafir u-m-*nini*) 1. "master, owner," pl. be-*ṅ* (Sesuto be-*ṅ*, Kafir a-ba-*nini*) 2.;

mo-*ṅ* (*ka*) 1. "neighbour," pl. ba-*ṅ* (*ka*) 2.;

mo-*eṅ* 1. "stranger," pl. ba-*eṅ* 2.;

ntshé 1. (Zulu i-n-*tye* 9.) "ostrich," pl. bō-*ntshé* 2.;

tshụéne 1. (Kafir i-m-*fene* 9., pl. a-ma-m-*fene* 6.) "baboon," pl. bo-*tshụéne* 2.;

'ma Ses. (Kafir u-ma, Zulu u-mame)
1. "mother," pl. bo-ma Ses.
(Kafir o-ma, Zulu o-mame) 2;

mo-χolu (Kafir u-m-kulu-we)
1. "elder brother," pl. bo-mo-χolu (Kafir a-ba-kulu-we) 2.;

ńuana Ses. (Zulu u-mu-ntw-ana)
1. "child," pl. b-āna Ses. (Zulu a-ba-ntw-ana) 2.;

mo-tsi 3. "day," pl. me-tsi 4.;

mo-tse (Sesuto mo-tsi, Zulu u-mu-zi) 3. "village, kraal," pl. me-tse (Ses. me-tsi 4.);

mo-rimo (Sesuto mo-limo 3. "god," pl. me-rimo (Ses. me-limo) 4. (§ 395);

m-oea Ses. (Kafir u-m-moya) 3. "spirit," pl. me-oea (Sesuto me-ea, Kafir i-mi-moya) 4.;

m-ila 3. "street," pl. me-bila 4.;

mu-si or mo-si (Sesuto mō-si, Zulu u-mu-si) 3. "smoke";

mu-lelo (Sesuto mo-lelo, Kafir u-m-lilo, § 344) 3. "fire;"

(o)m-bu or mu-bu (Sesuto mo-bu) 3. "ground," pl. me-bu 4.;

ńuaχa (Sesuto ńuah'a, Kafir u-nyaka) 3. "year," pl. in Sesuto me-ńuah'a 4. (the Seχlapi plural li-ɲyaχa 10. "years" belongs to a singular of the 9th class);

mo-kăla 3. "camel-thorn," pl. ma-kala 6.;

le-ru Ses. (Kafir l-li-fu) 5. "cloud," pl. ma-ru 6.;

le-iχlo Ses. (Kafir i-li-so) 5. "eye," pl. ma-iχlo (Sesuto ma-χlo, Kafir a-m-eχlo, § 327) 6.;

le-ino Ses. (Kafir i-zinyo) 5. "tooth," pl. ma-ino (Sesuto m-eno, Kafir a-ma-zinyo or a-m-enyo, § 326) 6.;

le-intshue (Sesuto le-yoe, Kafir i-li-tye) 5. "stone," pl. ma-ye (Sesuto ma-yoe, Kafir a-ma-tye) 6.;

le-tséle (Kafir i-béle) 5. "female breast," pl. ma-béle (Sesuto ma-tsuele, Kafir a-ma-bele) 6.;*

le-tshoχo (Sesuto le-tshoh'o, Tekeza boho) 5. "arm," pl. ma-boχo (Sesuto ma-tshoh'o, Tekeza ma-boho) 6.;

le-sapo or sapo (Sesuto le-sapo, Kafir i-tambo) 5. "bone," pl. ma-rapo (Sesuto ma-sapo, Kafir a-ma-tambo) 6.;

le-huku or huku 5. "word," pl. ma-huku 6.;

le-hatsi or hatsi (Sesuto le-fatsi) 5. "land," pl. ma-hatsi 6. (compare Kafir pa-nsi "beneath," § 436);

ma-ri (Ses.) 6. "blood" (compare Kafir i-gazi "blood");

---

* Setshuána ma-béle (Zulu a-ma-bele) 6. means also "Kafir corn" (= Kafir a-ma-zimba 6.). In Zulu the singular of this noun, i-bele 5., has the meaning "ear of Kafir corn," and also that of "female breast, cow's udder." From the same stem there are in Zulu the following nouns, u-m-bele 3. "cow's teat," ("nipple of an animal" in Kafir, Ayliff,) i-si-bele 7. "man's nipple" (in Kafir "mercy," pl. i-zi-bele 8., Appleyard § 491, 2.), and u-bu-bele 14. "tenderness, compassion" (in Kafir "grace, pity, kindness, mercy, affection, compassion"). Colenso's Grammar p. viii, Dictionary p. 28.

Sex̱lapi Derivative Prefixes of Nouns.

se-*huba* (Sesuto se-*fuba*, Kafir i-si-*fuba*) 7. "breast, chest," pl. li-*huba* (Sesuto li-*fuba*) 8.;

se-ax̱la or ax̱la (Kafir i-s-anx̱la); 7. "hand," pl. li-ax̱la 8.;

se-x̱laku or x̱laku (Kafir i-si-x̱lañgu) 7. "shoe," pl. li-x̱laku 8.;

se-*ṅkhua* (Zulu i-si-*nkwa*, Kafir i-s-*onka*) 7. "bread, loaf," pl. li-*ṅkhua* (Zulu i-zi-*nkwa*, Kafir i-z-*onka*) 8.;

(e)n-*tsha* (Sesuto m-*ptsha*, Kafir i-n-*dsha*, § 277) 9. "dog," pl. lin-*tsha* (Ses. lim-*ptsha*) 10.;

(e)ṅ-*ku* Ses. (Kafir i-m-*vu*) 9. "sheep," pl. liṅ-*ku* 10.;

(e)ṅ-*ko* (Sesuto n-*kó*) 9. "nose," pl. liṅ-*ko* (Ses. lin-*ko*) 10.;

(e)m-*pa* (Ses.) 9. "belly," pl. lim-*pa* (Ses.) 10.;

phukuye (Sesuto *phōkōyoe*, Kafir i-m-*pungutye*) 9. "jackal," pl. li-*phukuye* (Sesuto li-*pōkōyoe*) 10.;

thuto (Ses.) 9. "doctrine," pl. li-*thuto* (Ses.) 10. (χo-*ruta* 15. "to teach");

tau Ses. (Lour. Marques i-n-*dao*) 9. "lion," pl. li-*tau* (Ses.) 10.;

ku-ana (Sesuto *konyana*, Kafir i-m-*vana*) 9. "lamb," pl. li-*kuana* (Sesuto li-*konyana*) 10.;

phiri (Sesuto *piri*, Zulu i-m-*piri*) 9. "hyena," pl. li-*phiri* (Sesuto li-*piri*) 10.;

kχomu (Sesuto *kh'omo*, § 226) 9. "cow, ox," pl. li-*kχomu* (Sesuto li-*kh'omo*) 10.;

(ei)n-*x̱lu* (Sesuto n-*x̱lu*, Kafir i-n-*x̱lu*) 9. "house," pl. ma-*x̱lu* (Ses.) 10.;

tsèphè (Zulu i-n-*sepe*) 9. "springbok," pl. ma-*sèphè* 6.;*

lo-*shu* 11. (Ses. le-*ju* 5.) "death," pl. lin-*tshu* 10. (χo-*shua* 15. "to die" = Kafir u-ku-*fa*);

lō-*ri* 11. "cord," pl. lin-*ti* 10.;

lō-*bu* 11. "saltpetre or brackish ground" (Livingstone), pl. lim-*pu* 10.;

lo-*leme* (Kafir u-*lwimi*, Zulu u-*limi*) 11. "tongue," pl. li-*teme* 10. (Sesuto le-*leme* 5., pl. ma-*leme* 6.);

lo-*naka* 1. (Sesuto le-*naka* 5.) "horn," pl. li-*naka* (Ses.) 10. (§ 472, note);

lo-*nao* (Kafir u-*nyawo*) 11. "foot," pl. li-*nao* 10.;

lo-χ*ata* 11. (Sesuto le-*h'ata* 5.) "skull," pl. li-*kχata* 10. (compare Zulu l-*kanda* 5. "head," i-si-*kanda* 7. "knob," u-*kanda* 11. "top of bullock's head, cut off with the horns");

---

* The prefix ma- of the 6th class (or gender) is sometimes used for the purpose of forming a sort of second plural to nouns of the 9th (m-) class besides their usual plural of the 10th (lim-) class. The ma- seems to denote "a collection or company" (I. Hughes, Manuscript Grammar), or "a large number" (Frédoux). Thus *pitse* 9. "a horse," li-*pitse* 10. "horses," ma-*bitse* 6. "troops of horses;" (e)ṅ-*ku* 9. "a sheep," liṅ-*ku* 10. "sheep," ma-*ṅ-ku* 6. "flocks of sheep." This explains, to some extent, how Archbell ("Grammar of the Bechuana Language" p. 10, § 6) fell into the mistake of considering the form with the prefix li- as the dual, and that beginning with ma- as the plural form.

166 *The Concord.*

lŏ-*lŏapa* 11. " yard," pl. **ma**-*lŏapa* 6.;

lo-*uñuo* 11. " fruit," pl. **ma**-*uñuo* 6 ;

lo-*humo* 11. "wealth," pl. **ma**-*humo* 6.;

lo-*rato* 11. (Sesuto **le**-*rato* 5., Kafir u-*tando* 11.) " love," pl. **ma**-*rato* 6.;

bō-*siχō* (Sesuto **bo**-*siho*, Kafir u-**bu**-*suku*) 14. " night," pl. **ma**-*siχō* (Sesuto **ma**-*siho*) 6.;

bo-*n'no* 14. " dwelling place," pl. **ma**-*nno* 6.;

bo-χ*osi* (Sesuto **bo**-*h'osi*, Kafir u-**bu**-*kosi*) 14. "chieftainship, kingdom," pl. **ma**-χ*osi* 6. (*k*χ*osi* 9. " chief" = Kafir i-**n**-*kosi*);

bo-*yañ* (Sesuto *dshoañ*, Kafir u-*tyani*) 14. " grass ;"

bo-*yaloa* (Sesuto *yoala*, Kafir u-*tyalwa*, Zulu u-*tywala*) 14. " Kafir beer ;"

hélo 15. " place," pl. **ma**-*hélo* 6. (§ 435) ;

χo-*rata* (Sesuto **h'o**-*rata*, Kafir u-**ku**-*tanda*) 15. " to love."

470. The SESUTO dialect thus varies little, either in the forms of the prefixes or in their mutual correspondence, from that of Western Setshuâna, the examples of which given here are taken from the Seχlapi dialect. How the 11th class or gender in Sesuto

SESUTO PREFIXES.

SINGULAR.	PLURAL.
PERSONAL.	
1. mŏ-, (—)	**2.** ba-, bo-, bo-*mo*-b-
'm- (**MO**-*B*-)	ba-*b*-
	6. ma-
3. mo- 'm- (**MO**-*B*-)	**4.** me- me-*b*-
5. (& 11.) le-, (—)	**6.** ma- m-
	10. li- ∵
7. se-	**8.** li-
9. n- ∵ m- ∵ (—) ∵	**10.** lin- ∵ lim- ∵ li- ∵
	6. ma-
ABSTRACT.	
14. bo-	**6.** ma-
INFINITIVE AND LOCAL.	
15. h'o- (go-)	

has become homophonically identical with the 5th (**le-**) class, has been previously explained, § 456. As all the grammatical forms of the 11th class now seem to coincide with those of the 5th, the 11th class or gender has virtually ceased to exist in Sesuto; many nouns originally belonging to the 11th class having even adopted the 6th (**ma-**) class as their corresponding plural, although the same nouns in Seẋlapi are always used with plurals of the 10th (**lin-**) class. But instances of the latter plural to nouns of the old 11th class are still occasionally to be found in Sesuto, and this causes it to appear as if the 5th (**le-**) class or gender were less exclusively restricted to plural forms of the 6th (**ma-**) class in Sesuto, than in any of the other South African Bâ-ntu languages. With regard to the 6th (**ma-**) class or gender, it is to be remarked that, in one case at least in this dialect, it is found corresponding to the 1st (**mo-**) class. Examples of local nouns of the 15th (**h'o-**) class with corresponding plurals have not, as yet, been found by me in Sesuto.

THE TEKEZA SPECIES.

471. The contraction of the form **mu-**l to **n-** in the first and third classes (§ 343) is the chief characteristic of the TEKEZA species. In other respects the forms of the prefixes are nearer to those in the Middle Branch languages than we find them to be in either of the remaining species of the South-eastern Branch (Kafir and Setshuâna). The following table shewing the correspondence of the derivative prefixes of nouns in the NORTHERN TEKEZA dialect spoken at LOURENZO MARQUES, Delagoa Bay, is, of course, incomplete. It is supposed that the form of the 8th prefix here is **psi-**, as in the dialect of Tette, but the vocabularies (as yet our only materials for the knowledge of these dialects) contain no positive evidence of this. An initial vowel (frequently a), which is evidently unconnected with the prefix, occasionally precedes the

noun in these vocabularies. The nature of this vowel is not clear. When an *a* it may be merely the genitive particle.

TEKEZA PREFIXES.

SINGULAR.	PLURAL.
PERSONAL.	
1. mu- n- (**MU**-*L*-) (—)	2. va-
3. mu- n- (**MU**-*L*-) m-	4. mi- mi-*l*-
5. ri- (—)	6. ma-
7. tshi- tshe-	8.
9. in-, en- im-, em- (—)	10. (ti-*in*-) thin-, tin- tim- thi-, the-
11. li-	10. tin- tim-
ABSTRACT. 14. bu- ? be-	
INFINITIVE. 15. ko- ku-	

TEKEZA NOUNS.

a-**mu**-*no* (Southern Tekeza **mû**-*nu*, Zulu u-**mu**-*ntu*) 1. "man, person," pl. **va**-*no* (S. T. **bâ**-*nu* or **va**-*nu*, Kafir a-**ba**-*ntu*) 2.;

n-*ánda* 1. "slave, poor follower," (from *e*-**ko**-*landa*, Kafir u-**ku**-*landa* 15. "to follow");

a-n-*oi* (Setshuâna **mo**-*loi*) 1. "sorcerer";

wana (Matonga *wuana*, Man/olosi *u*-*wana*, Zulu u-**mu**-*ntw-ana*) 1. "child;"

mu-*ti* (Zulu u-**mu**-*zi*) 3. "settlement, village," pl. **mi**-*ti* (Kafir i-**mi**-*zi*) 4.;

mu-*se* (Zulu u-**mu**-*si*) 3. "smoke;"

mu-*re* (Zulu u-**mu**-*ti*) 3. "tree;"

n-*ege* (Kafir u-**m**-*lenze*) 3. "leg" (?), pl. **mi**-*lenge* (Kafir i-**mi**-*lenze*) 4.;

n-*ambo* (Kafir u-**m**-*lambo*, Setshuâna **mo**-*lapo*) 3. "river";

n-*ambshana* (Kafir u-**m**-*landshana*) 3. "rivulet;"

n-*omo* (Kafir u-**m**-*lomo*) 3. "mouth";

(?) *a*-**m**-*iu* (Kafir u-**m**-*oya*, Setshuâna **m**-*oëa*) 3. "wind";

ri-*to* (Kafir i-**li**-*zwi*, Sesuto le-*ntshue*) 5. "voice";

ri-*bdsha* (Kafir i-**li**-*tye*, Sesuto **le**-*yoe*, Seχ̌lapi **le**-*intshuĕ*) 5. "stone";

tanda (Kafir i-*landa*) 5. "egg," pl. **ma**-*tanda* or *a*-**m**-*anda* (Kafir *a*-**ma**-*!anda*) 6.;

bito (Zulu i-*bizo*, Sesuto **le**-*bitso*) 5. "name," pl. *a*-**ma**-*bito* (Zulu *a*-**ma**-*bizo*, Sesuto **ma**-*bitso*) 6.;

tinyo (Kafir i-*zinyo*) 5. "tooth," pl. *a*-**ma**-*tinyo* (Kafir *a*-**ma**-*zinyo* or *a*-**m**-*enyo*) 6.;

tiχ̌lo (Kafir i-**li**-*so*, Setshuâna **le**-*iχ̌lo*) 5. "eye", pl. *a*-**ma**-*χ̌lo* (Kafir *a*-**m**-*eχ̌lo*, Sesuto **ma**-*χ̌lo*, Seχ̌lapi **ma**-*iχ̌lo*) 6.;

a-**ma**-*rre* (Kafir *a*-**ma**-*te*, Setshuâna **ma**-*the*) 6. "spittle";

tahi-*fuva* (Kafir i-**si**-*fuba*) 7. "breast, chest";

tshe-*vinde* (Kafir i-**si**-*bindi*) 7. "liver";

tahi-*londa* (Kafir i-**si**-*londa*) 7. "wound, sore";

in-*χ̌lo* (Kafir i-**n**-*χ̌lu*) 9. "house," pl. **ti**-*in*-*χ̌lo* (Kafir i-**zin**-*χ̌lu*) 10.

in-*χ̌loko* (Kafir i-**n**-*χ̌loko*) 9. "head";

in-*gue* (Kafir i-**n**-*gwe*) 9. "leopard";

im-*bilo* (Setshuâna *pelu*) 9. "heart";

en-*kollo* (Portuguese *colle*) 9. "neck";

em-*bute* (Kafir i-**m**-*buzi*) 9. "goat";

tin-*χ̌lamfe* (Zulu i-**zin**-*χ̌lanzi*, Setshuâna **li**-*χ̌lapi*) 10. "fishes";

omo (Kafir i-**n**-*komo*, Sesuto *kh'omo*, Seχ̌lapi *kχomu*) 9. "cow," pl. **te**-*omo* (Zulu i-**zin**-*komo*) 10. (§ 226);

uko (Kafir i-**n**-*kuku*, Seχ̌lapi *koku*) 9. "fowl," pl. **thi**-*uko* (Zulu i-**zin**-*kuku*) 10.

(*a*-)*kose* (Kafir i-**n**-*kosi*, Seχ̌lapi *kχosi*) 9. "king";

habo (Kafir i-**n**-*kawo*) 9. "monkey";

m-*isse* (Zulu i-**m**-*pisi*, Setshuâna *phiri*) 9. "hyena";

tin-*uala* (Kafir i-**n**-*twala*) 10. "lice";

li-*tiu* (Kafir u-*zipo*) 11. "finger, toe," pl. **tin**-*tio* (Kafir i-**n**-*zipo*) 10.;

li-*ondo* (Matonga **lu**-*pondo*, Kafir u-*pondo*) 11. "horn"; pl. **tim**-*ondo* (Zulu i-**zim**-*pondo*) 10.

li-*khuko* (Kafir u-*khuko*) 11. "mat";

bu-*χ̌lungo* 14. "powder" (Kafir u-**bu**-*χ̌lungu* 14. "poison, powder");

be-*siko* (Kafir u-**bu**-*suku*, Setshuâna **bo**-*siχo*) 14. "night";

i-**ku**-*fa* (Kafir u-**ku**-*fa*) 15. "to die";

e-**ko**-*tshava* (Zulu u-**ku**-*saba*) 15. "to be afraid" (Kafir u-**ku**-*saba* 15. "to flee").

B. IN THE MIDDLE BRANCH.

aa. *The Mosambique Genus.*

DIALECTS OF TETTE AND SENA.

472. The possession of the 12th (**tu-**), 13th (**ka-**), and 16th (**pa-**) classes distinguishes most of the languages of

the Middle Branch from those of the South-eastern. The dialects of the Middle Branch, which are the most nearly allied to the languages of the South-eastern Branch, are only known to us in vocabularies which do not enable us to construct any satisfactory tables of the prefixes. The languages of SENA and TETTE agree with the Kafir language in the forms of most of their prefixes, those of the 10th (**zin-**) class, for example, being remarkably similar. Where they differ from the Kafir prefixes they generally resemble those of the Tekeza, as in the 2nd (**va-**), 7th (**tshi-** or **shi-**), and 8th (**pi-** or **psi-**) classes. In the 14th (**BU-**) class the initial consonant has been almost invariably dropped in the Middle Branch languages; having been preserved in Sofala in a softened form (**vu-**). No certain evidence of the existence of the 11th (**LU-**) class has as yet been observed in the dialects of Tette and Sena. **Ri**-*rimi* "tongue" may belong to the 5th class (§ 351, note), although, if it be so, it is the only noun of this class as yet known to us in the dialect of Tette, in which the form of the prefix **ri-** has been preserved. In Sena, however, we find also **ri-***kombo* 5. "oyster," pl. **ma-***kombo* 6. In some nouns of the Tette dialect the prefix of the 5th class seems to have the form **zi-**, as **zi-***nyánga* (Sena *nyanga*) 5. "horn," pl. **ma-***nyanga* 6.*, **zi-***rûmi* 5. "wasp," pl. **ma-***rûmi* 6. In

* Seṣ̌lapi **le-***naka* 11. pl. **li-***naka* 10., Sesuto **le-***naka* 5. pl. **li-***naka* 10., Cape Delgado **lu-***nyanga* 11. pl. *nyanga* (10.), Quellimane **mau-***nyanga* 3. pl. **mi-***nyanga* 4. One might be inclined to derive the Kafir and Zulu noun i-**n-***yánga* 9. "moon" from this stem, thinking of the horns of the moon. Yet it is more probable that this noun has been fashioned from a Hottentot word for moon (*//khã*), as it has not been met with in this signification in any other Bâ-ntu languages. The very similar noun i-**n-***nyangá* 9. "doctor" is, on the contrary, common to most, if not all, of the South African Bâ-ntu languages. The Hottentot word for moon is written by Ludolf (1710) *t'Ga* and *k'chã*, by Kolb (1719) *Tchã* in the Cape dialect; *Kã* by Barrow (1806) in a more Eastern Hottentot dialect; in the !Kora dialect *t'gnam* by Borcherds (1801), *t'khaam* (m. s.) and *t"k'-haang-s* (f. s. "month") by Lichtenstein

some nouns (as *ziso* " eye "
§ 327, *zino* " tooth " § 326)
the initial *zi*, though disappearing in the plural (**ma**-*nu*
and **ma**-*so*), evidently belongs to the stem. In others
again it is difficult to say
whether *zi* is the prefix or
part of the stem of the noun.
The following tables of the
dialects of Tette and Sena
can but be more or less incomplete, and in need of correction. In the enumeration
of TETTE nouns, those which
have the same form in SENA,
are followed by the letter
" S."

TETTE NOUNS.

mú-*nttu* or **mu**-*ntto* S. (Zulu u-**mu**-*ntu*) 1. " man, person," pl. **vá**-*nttu*
(S.) 2.;
mu-*kázi* S. (Zulu u-**m**-*fazi*) 1.
" woman," pl. **va**-*kázi* or **a**-*kazi*
(S.) 2.;
mu-*ána* S. (Zulu u-**mu**-*ntwana*)
1. " child," pl. **w**-*ana* (S.) 2.;
Mu-*mbo* 1. (an inhabitant of **Ku**-*mbo* 15.), pl. **Va**-*mbo* 2.;
bába S. (Zulu u-*baba*) 1. " father";
mu-*éne* or **mo**-*ene* S. (Zulu u-**m**-*nini*) 1. " master;"
máma S. (Zulu u-*mame*) 1. " mother";
mu-*shinda* (S.) 1. " prince," (Sena pl. **ma**-*shinda* 6.);

TETTE PREFIXES.

SINGULAR.	PLURAL.
PERSONAL.	
1. mŭ-, (—) mo-	2. va- wa- a-
3. mū-	4. mi-
5. (—) zi-	6. ma-
7. tshi- shi-	8. psi-
9. n- m- (—)	10. zin- zim- zi- (—)
	6. ma-
DIMINUTIVE.	
13. ka-	12. tu-
ABSTRACT.	
14. u-	
INFINITIVE AND LOCAL.	
15. ku-	
LOCAL.	
16. pa-	

(1812), '*kaam* by Burchell (1824), *qchaam* (m. s.) by Wurm (1850);
whilst in the Namaqua dialect the noun has still the derivative suffix
of the masculine singular in the form ||*khã*-**p**.

nyarûgwe (S.) 1. "tiger";

mû-ti S. (Zulu u-**mu**-*ti*) 3. "tree," pl. **mî**-*ti* (S.) 4.

mú-nwe (Zulu u-**mú**-*nwe*) 3. "finger," pl. **mí**-*nwe* 4.;

mu-sĕve (Sofala **mu**-*sheve*) 3. "arrow," pl. **mi**-*sĕve* 4.;

mû-zi (Sena **mu**-*tshitsi*) 3. "root," pl. **mî**-*zi* 4.;

mu-aka (Zulu u-**m**-*nyaka*) 3. "year," pl. **mi**-*aka* 4.;

zíno S. (Zulu i-*zinyo*) 5. "tooth," pl. **ma**-*nu* S. (Zulu a-**ma**-*zinyo*) 6. (§ 326);

ziso (Sena *diso*, Zulu i-**li**-*so*, Setshuâna **le**-*iX̌lo*, Lourenzo Marques *tiX̌lo*) 5. "eye," pl. *ma-so* (Zulu a-**m**-*eX̌lo*, Setshuâna **ma**-*iX̌lo*, Lour. Marq. **ma**-*X̌lo*) 6. (§ 327);

zansha 5. "hand," pl. **ma**-*nsha* 6.;

zina S. (Setshuâna **le**-*ina*, Bunda o-**ri**-*shina*) 5. "name";

zirûmi 5. "wasp," pl. **ma**-*rûmi* 6.;

zirua (Sena *rua*) 5. "flower," pl. **ma**-*rua* (S.) 6.;

zûku 5. "female breast," pl. **ma**-*zûku* 6.;

ziko 5. "kingdom";

zuro S. (Zulu i-*zolo*) 5. "yesterday";

zaï 5. "egg," pl. **ma**-*zaï* 6.;

sĕzi 5. "toad," pl. **ma**-*sĕzi* 6.;

zindwe 5. "pig-nut," pl. **ma**-*ndwe* 6.;

tsosi 5. "tear," pl. **mă**-*tsosi* 6.;

tûpi 5. "body";

shira (S.) 5. "native cloth," pl. **ma**-*shira* (S.) 6.;

tsâmba (S) 5. "leaf," pl. **ma**-*tsamba* (S.) 6.;

tonshe (S.) 5. "cotton";

tenga 5. "feather," pl. **ma**-*tenga* 6.;

tondo 5. (fruit of **mu**-*tondo* 3.), pl. **ma**-*tondo* 6.;

fara (S.) 5. "voice";

guni (S.) 5. "cloth";

fûpa (S.) 5. "bone," pl. **ma**-*fûpa* (S.) 6.;

pūtu (S.) 5. "cheek," pl. **ma**-*pūtu* (S.) 6.;

bondo (S.) 5. "knee," pl. **ma**-*bondo* (S.) 6.;

papídwe (S.) 5. "wing," pl. **ma**-*papidwe* (S.) 6. (Zulu u-**ku**-*papa*, Setshuâna χ*o-hoha*, Tekeza *iko-haha* 15. "to fly as a bird," § 360);

piri (S.) 5. "hill," pl. **ma**-*piri* 6.;

bĕte 5. "cockroach," pl. **ma**-*bĕte* 6. (Sena *pémpe* 5., pl. **ma**-*pempe* 6.);

ma-*pira* (S.) 6. "millet";

mâ-ta S. (Kafir a-**ma**-*te*) 6. "saliva";

shi-*kópe* 7. "eyelash," pl. **psi**-*kópe* 8. (Kafir u-*kope* 11. "eyelash," pl. i-**zin**-*kope* 10.);

shi-*poropóro* (Sena **dshi**-*poroporo*) 7. "ball," pl. **psi**-*poropóro* 8.;

Sena **shi**-*mu-ti* 7. "large tree," pl. **pi**-*mi-ti* (S.) 8. (§ 430 and 454);

(t)**shi**-*ū-ta* 7. "great bow";

(t)**shi**-*mā-zi* 7. "large water, river";

(t)**shi**-*nyumba* 7. "large house";

n-*yumba* (S.) 9. "house," pl. **zi**-*nyumba* 10. and **ma**-*nyumba* 6.;

(i)**n**-*yoka* S. (Zulu i-**n**-*nyoka*) 9. "snake," pl. **zin**-*yoka* (S.) 10.;

dzòu S. (Zulu i-**n**-*X̌lovu*) 9. "elephant," (Sena pl. *dzòu* 10.);

Tette and Sena Derivative Prefixes of Nouns. 173

kúmba (S.) 9. "tame pig," pl.
zin-kúmba (S.) 10. ;

m-páka (Zulu i-m-paka) 9.
"cat," pl. zim-páka 10. ;

m-búdu (Sena im-bu) 9. "mosquito," pl. zim-búdu 10. ;

m-pete (S.) 9. "ring," pl. zim-pete 10. ;

zomba (Sena nsómba or somba, Zulu i-n-x̂lanzi, Setshuâna x̂lapi) 9. "fish," pl. zi-zomba 10. ;

(n)gûo S. (Kafir i-n-gubo) 9. "cloth," Sena pl. gúo 10. ;

ka-piri 13. "hillock ;"

ka-dzámba 13. "small leaf," pl. tu-ma-dzámba 12. (+ 6.) ;

ka-mūti (S.) 13. (+ 3.) "a shrub ;"

ka-mā-dzi 13. (+ 6.) "a rivulet ;"

ka-nyumba 13. (+ 9.) "a hut ;"

u-shi (Sena u-dshi, Kafir u-bu-si) 14. "honey ;"

ú-zua (Sena u-dzu, pl. ma-u-dzu) 14. "straw" (Sofala vu-shua 14., Kafir u-tyani 14. "grass") ;

u-tāre S. (Sofala vu-tare) 14. "iron ;"

u-siku or u-siko (Kafir u-bu-suku) 14. "night," (Sena pl. ma-siko or ma-siku 6.) ;

u-ta S. (Setshuâna bo-ra) 14 "bow ;"

u-nga (S.) 14. "powder ;"

ku-dia S. (Kafir u-ku-tya) 15. "food ;"

ku-pūma S. (Zulu u-ku-pefumula "to breathe") 15. "breath ;"

ku-roára S. (Zulu u-ku-lobola "to settle for a wife with the girl's father") 15. "marriage ;"

ku-nungha S. (Zulu u-ku-nuka) 15. "bad smell ;"

pa-nsi 16. "land, country, kingdom" (Kafir preposition pansi "below, beneath," § 436) ;

pa-kati p-a u-siku (Sena pa-kati p-a tsiku) 16. "midnight ;"

pa-dzuru p-a muendo 15. "span of the foot" (zuru = Kafir i-zulu 5. "heaven"), § 435.

473. The difference between the dialects of Sena and Tette is very small, the derivative prefixes in both languages being almost identical. **Psi-**, the form of the 8th prefix in Tette, is intermediate between the Sena form **pi-** and the Kafir **zi-** (Setshuâna **li-** or **ŕi-**). It may be well to observe here that the language spoken at Tette and Sena extends also to MARAVI, to SOFALA, and to Andersson's[*] CHJILIMANSE. The dialect of the latter agrees most nearly with that of Tette, and next to it with Sofala. A few Chjilimanse words, however, shew a close resemblance to the dialect of Inhambane.

[*] "Journey to Lake 'Ngami."—(Reprinted from the *S. A. Commercial Advertiser* and *C. T. Mail.*) 1854. p. 20.

SENA PREFIXES.

SINGULAR.	PLURAL.
PERSONAL.	
1. mu-, (—)	2. a-va-wa-
	6. ma-
3. mu-	4. mi-
5. ri-(d)zi-(—)	6. ma-
7. tshi-tsh-dsh-	8. psi-
9. n-, in-m-(—)	10. n-, zin-m-(—)
13. ka-	12. tu-
ABSTRACT. 14. u-	
INFINITIVE AND LOCAL. 15. ku-	
LOCAL. 16. pa-	

MAKUA LANGUAGE.

474. We notice in the language of the Makua a remarkable form of the 5th prefix, in which the liquid consonant (l) has been changed into a nasal (n). We

MAKUA PREFIXES.

SINGULAR.	PLURAL.
PERSONAL.	
1. mu-m-	2. a-
3. mu-m-	4. mi-
5. ni-n-in-	6. ma-m-
7. iki-ik-i-	
9. n-, in-(—)	
13. ka-	
14. u-	6. ma-
INFINITIVE. 15. u-w-	

also find here that the 15th prefix has lost its consonant, and has thus become identical in form with the 14th. On the other hand, the 7th (**ki-**) prefix appears to have retained a more primitive form than either in Sena or Tette. Of the 8th, 10th, and 12th classes the forms are uncertain, and we are thus ignorant as to the corresponding plurals of the 7th (**ki-**), 9th (**n**), and 13th (**ka-**) classes. That the 11th class may have merged into the 5th is not an unnatural hypothesis. Traces of the old initial articles are apparently met with in some of the forms of the prefixes.

MAKUA NOUNS.

mû-*ttu* (Zulu u-**mu**-*ntu*) 1. "person," pl. **a**-*ttu* (Zulu **a**-**ba**-*ntu*) 2.;

m-*bewe* 1. "king," pl. **a**-*bewe* 2.;

mu-*ríma* (Sena and Tette **mu**-*tima*) 3. "heart," pl. **mi**-*ríma* 4.;

m-*ŏno* (Cape Delgado **mu**-*hóno*) 3. "arm," pl. **mi**-*no* 4.;

mu-*tęthe* 3. "feather," pl. **mi**-*tęthe* 4.;

mu-*íshi* (Zulu u-**mu**-si) 3. "smoke;"

mu-*íri* (Zulu u-**mu**-*ti*) 3. "tree;"

m-*óro* (Tette, Sena, Kihiau, and Suáheli **m**-*otto*) 3. "fire;"

ni-*kuva* (Tette and Sena *fúpa*) 5. "bone," pl. **ma**-*kuva* (T. and S. **ma**-*fúpa*) 6.;

n-*íto* (Kafir i-**li**-*so*) 5. "eye," pl. **me**-*to* (Kafir a-**me**-*x̌lo*) 6.;

n-*rama* 5. "cheek," pl. **ma**-*rama* 6.;

i-**n**-*lako* 5. "lip," pl. **ma**-*lako* 6.;

i-**n**-*zu* (Zulu i-**li**-*zwi*, Delagoa Bay **a**-**ri**-*to*, Sena **ri**-*bze*) 5. "voice," pl. **ma**-*zu* 6.;

ni-*parári* 5. "rib," pl. **ma**-*parári* 6.;

ni-*odshe* 5. "egg," pl. **m**-*odshe* 6.;

i-**k**-*arari* 7. "hair" (dz-*a reru* "of the chin," i.e. beard);

i-**ki**-*námbo* (Tette and Sena **dshi**-*nambo*, Cape Delgado **ki**-*námbo*) 7. "lime;"

i-*reru̇* (Kafir i-**si**-*levu*, Sena and Tette [t]**shi**-*děvu*, Cape Delgado **ki**-*rebvu*) 7. "chin;"

i-**n**-*yŏpe* 9. "ox" (§ 226);

i-*núpa* (in all other Eastern dialects of the Middle Branch *nyumba*) 9. "house;"

i-*gúo* (Kafir i-**n**-*gubo*, Sena and Tette [**n**]*guo*) 9. "cloth;"

gulúë (Kafir i-**n**-*gu-lube*) 9. "pig;"

i-*puri* (Kafir i-**m**-*buzi*) 9. "goat;"

i-*púla* (Kafir i-**m**-*vula*) 9. "rain;"

n-*darama* (Inhambane, Tette, and Sena *daráma*) 9. "gold;"

ka-*puti* 13. "gun". (Sofala, Sena, and Tette *futi*);

u-*hiyu* (Kafir u-**bu**-*suku*) 14. "night;"

u-*ga* or **u**-*ka* (Sofala **vu**-*nga*, Inhambane, Sena, and Tette *ú-nga*) 14. "gunpowder;"

u-*liala* (Kafir u-**ku**-*libála*, Se-tshuâna χo-*lebala*, Tekeza e-**ko**-*dzirala*, Inhambane **ku**-*dívala*, Tette and Sena **ku**-*divâra*, Cape Delgado **ku**-*riwála*) 15. "to forget;"

w-*ama* (Sena and Tette **ku**-*káma*) 15. "to milk" (Zulu u-**ku**-*kama* 15. "to squeeze, drain out as a milkpail," &c.)

KIHIAU.

475. The fuller table which we have of the prefixes of the nouns in the **Ki**-*hiáu* language, contains but one class which has not been preserved in Kafir. This is the 16th (**pa-**) class. The 12th (**TU-**) and 13th (**KA-**) classes (which are also lost in Kafir) have either disappeared in Kihiau, or are so rarely used as not to occur in Krapf's extensive vocabulary. We notice in this language a number of abstract nouns formed with the derivative prefix of the 6th class (**ma-**) which, in these cases, does not correspond as plural to any singular prefix. **Ki**-*hiáu* 7. is spoken by the **Wa**-*hiáu* or **Vé**-*iáo* 2. who live in **Kú**-*yáo* 15. and are called *Inkiaua* by the Maravi, and **A**-*dshóua* or **A**-*dshâwa* 2. (sing. **Mu**-*dshau* 1.) by other foreigners.

KIHIAU PREFIXES.

SINGULAR.	PLURAL.
PERSONAL.	
1. mu-, (—) m-	2. va- (wa-)
3. mu- m-	4. mi-
5. li- ri- (—)	6. ma- m-
7. dshi- ki-	8. hi- vi- (wi-)
9. n- m- (—)	10. n- m- (—)
11. lu-	10. (—)
ABSTRACT.	
14. u- (—)	6. ma-
INFINITIVE. 15. ku-	
LOCAL. 16. pa-	

KIHIAU NOUNS.

mu-*ndu* (Zulu u-**mu**-*ntu*) 1. "person," pl. **vá**-*ndu* 2;

mu-*ihi* (§ 325) 1. "thief";

m-*ana-dshe* (Otyihereró o-**m**-*a-tye*) 1. "child," pl. **v**-*ana-dshe* (Otyihereró o-**v**-*ana-tye*) 2.;

Kihiáu Derivative Prefixes of Nouns.

m-*limi* 1. "farmer," (from ku-*lima* = Kafir u-ku-*lima* 15. "to cultivate");

dúde 1. "father," pl. va-*dúde* 2.;

mu-*aka* (Zulu u-mu-*nyaka*) 3. "year," pl. mi-*aka* (Zulu i-mi-*nyaka*) 4.;

mu-*hi* (Zulu u-mu-*ti*, § 428 note) 3. "tree;"

mu-*dshi* (Zulu u-mu-*zi*) 3. "village;"

m-*lómo* (Kafir u-m-*lomo*, § 439 note) 3. "lip;"

m-*otto* 3. "fire" (the same in Maravi, Tette, Sena, and Kisuaheli);

li-*verre* (Kafir i-*bele*) 5. "teat," pl. ma-*verre* 6. (p. 164, note);

samba 5. "branch," pl. ma-*samba* 6.;

rémbo 5. "grave," pl. ma-*rémbo* 6.;

lúa (Tette zi-*rûa*) 5. "flower," pl. ma-*lua* 6.;

li-*yére* 5. "egg," pl. ma-*yere* 6.;

r-*íno* (Zulu i-*zinyo*, § 326) 5. "tooth," pl. m-*eno* 6.;

r-*isso* (Zulu i-li-*so*, § 327) 5. "eye," pl. m-*esso* 6.;

li-*óka* or ri-*dshóka* (Koelle's li-*dshoya*) 5. (Ovambo e-*oka* 5. pl. o-ma-*oka*, 6.) "serpent, viper;"

ma-*tumbako* 6. "wrath," (ku-*tumbaka* 15. "to be angry");

ma-*sáko* 6. "love, will" (ku-*saka* 15. "to love, to will");

dshi-*ndu* or ki-*ndu* (Ki-kamba ki-*ndu*) 7. "thing," pl. vi-*ndu* 8.;

dshi-*gombo* 7. "utensil," pl. hi-*gombo* (Suaheli vi-*ombo*) 8.;

ki-*nólo* (the same in Kinika, ki-*nóo* in Kisuaheli and Kipokomo) 7. "whetstone;"

ki-*sídshi* (the same in Kipokomo, ki-*siki* in Kisuaheli and Kinika) 7. "stem;"

dshi-*híru* 7. "body;"

dshi-*dshondsho* 7. "potsherd;"

dshi-*viga* 7. "pan;"

ṅ-*gombe* 9. "cow, ox" (§ 226);

*m-*buzi* (Kafir i-m-*buzi*) 9. "goat;"

*m-*bua* 9. "dog" (§ 235 and 277);

n-*ióta* 9. "star;"

m-*bebo* or m-*bevo* (Setshuána *pheho*) 9. "wind;"

n-*gŏnya* (Kafir i-n-*gwenya*) 9. "alligator;"

niáma (Kafir i-n-*nyama*) 9. "flesh, meat;"

niúmba or *nyumba* (the same at Sofala, Sena, Tette, Maravi, and in all Zangian dialects) 9.- "house;"

somba (Tette *zomba*, Sena *sómba* or *nsomba*) 9. "fish;"

lu-*húmbo* 11. "hair," pl. *humbo* 10.;

l-*úiko* (Sena and Tette r-*úko*) 11. "spoon," pl. *uiko* 10. (Setshuána lu-*sho* 11., pl. lin-*tsho* 10.);†

---

* These nouns indicating animals are also found construed as nouns of the 1st (mau-) class. (§ 466.)

† Inhambane and Sofala ma-*ukó* 3., Suaheli, Kinika, and Kipokomo m-*iko* 3, pl. mi-*iko* 4., Kikamba ma-*ui* 3. ; Cape Delgado ki-*ko* 7.

lu-*wembe* 11. "fly," pl. *wembe* 10. (Cape Delgado *membe*);
lu-*góno* 11. "sleep;"*
lu-*póta* 11. "yarn;"
u-*tumbo* 14. "gut," pl. ma-*tumbo* (Kafir a-ma-*tumbu*, with sng. i-*tumbu* 5.) 6. "bowels;"
u-*mi* (Kafir u-*bomi*) 14. "life;"
u-*gono* 14. "bed;"*

u-*imbo* 14. "song" (Kihiau, Kinika, Suaheli, Sena, Tette, Sofala, Tekeza, and Otyihereró *imba*, Makua *ipa*, Mpongwe *jemba* "sing");
u-*kulúngwa* 14. "greatness;"
oga 14. "fear" (Kafir u-*ku-oyika* 15. "to fear," Kihiau *ogopa* "be afraid");
pa-*ndu* (§ 435) 16. "place."†

bb. *The Zangian Genus.*

476. Our limited knowledge of the Eastern members of the Middle Branch does not enable us to define clearly the characteristics by which the different genera of this Branch may be distinguished from each other. Upon the whole, our division of the genera into a South-eastern or Mosambique Genus, and a North-eastern or Zangian Genus is mainly geographical. Yet *Kikámba, Kiníka, Kisuáheli, Kipokómo,* and *Kisambála* are certainly more closely related to each other than they are to the dialects of Sena and Tette, to Kihiau, or to the Makua language.

* From ku-*góna* 15. "to sleep" in Kihiau, Maravi, Tette, Sena, and Quellimane.

† The preceding specimens of the Kihiáu language are taken from Dr. Krapf's vocabularies, in which the pronunciation of some of the consonants is not quite clear. Dr. Steere (in a letter dated Dec. 22nd, 1866,) has furnished the following examples of this language, which he calls **Tshi**-*yao* (*Chiyao*) 7. These examples give a few different forms of the prefixes. It also appears from them that the 6th (ma-) prefix may in this language correspond as plural to the 11th (lu-) prefix.

SINGULAR.
1. mu-*ndu* "man,"
3. m-*tera* "tree,"
5. { li-*simba* } "lion," { li-*wago* } "axe,"
7. tshi-*ndu* (*chindu*) "thing,"
9. m-*yumba* "house,"
11. lu godshi (*lugoji*) "rope,"
15. ku-*tu-nónyera* "to love us;"
16. pa-*ndu* "place and places."

PLURAL.
2. wa-*ndu* "people;"
4. mi-*tera* "trees;"
6. { ma-*simba* } "lions;" { ma-*wago* } "axes;"
8. i-*ndu* "things;"
10. m-*yumba* "houses;"
6. ma-*godshi* "ropes;"

477. In the Zangian Genus, we see that the prefix of the 10th class has invariably lost the initial part preceding its ending nasal, having been reduced to the latter, with or without a following vowel (n-, or ni-). In some cases, the nasal of the 10th prefix has a strong effect upon the initial of the stem which follows. Thus in KIKAMBA and KINIKA an initial *ts* may disappear after this n- (§ 349 and 350), and after the same prefix in KISUAHELI the initial *l* is changed into *d*, and the initial *w* into *b*. (§ 351.) The rule that nouns of the 9th (n-) and 10th (n-) classes indicating persons or animals are construed as nouns of the 1st (mu-) and 2nd (va-) classes is of extensive application in the Zangian Genus. (§ 466.)

478. It is a most singular trait in the languages of this genus that nouns of whatsoever class, when standing in the locative case (which is indicated by the suffix *-ni*) are construed as if they belonged to one of two local classes, viz. the 15th (ku-), or 18th (MU-) class. According to Dr. Steere's "Table of Concords," this locative case in Swaheli is in concord with forms in *ku* "when implying *motion to, or distance from*" a thing, and with forms "in *mu*, if it merely expresses *being within*."

In the Kikámba sentence *y-u-naikie tu-ala* ma-*ddu-ni* ku-*a-ke* (Mark vii. 33) "he put the fingers into his ears," the ku-*a-ke* "his" belongs to the 15th (ku-) class, although the noun ma-*ddu* "ears" is of the 6th (ma-) class, and, as such, usually requires the form m-*ake* 6. "his," as (Mark. vii. 35.) ma-*ddu* m-*a-ke* ma-*na-winguiwe* "his ears were opened." (Compare Kinika ma-*sikiro-ni* mu-*enu* 18. "in your ears," Luke ix. 44, with ma-*sikiro* g-*enu** 6. "your ears," Luke iv. 21.) Further in Kikamba the noun ma-*u* "feet" is of the 6th (ma-) class, and, as such, rules forms like m-*a-gu* "thy," m-*a-ke* "his, her," m-*eniu* "your,"—notwithstanding which, we read *iwiaiyei* (shake ye off) *mu* (the dust) ma-*u-ni* ku-*eniu* (from your feet), Mark. vi. 11, and yu-*na walukile* ma-*u-ni* mu-*a-ke* (Mark. v. 22, "he fell

* This *g* in Kinika is a pronominal representative of the *m* of the 6th (ma-) prefix, pointing to an original form of this prefix (perhaps *NGA*), in which probably the nasal and the guttural explosive (*g*) were both represented, as will be more clearly explained in a succeeding chapter.

to his feet ")—the ku-*eniu* "your" belonging to the 15th (**ku**-), and the mu-*a-ke* "his" to the 18th (**mu**-) class. (Compare Kiníka **ma**-*gulu-ni* mu-*a-kwe* 18. "to his feet" with **ma**-*gulu*-g-*e* 6. "his feet," Luke vii. 38.) Similarly, although *niumba* "house" in the singular is of the 9th, and in the plural of the 10th class, we find that "go into thine house" (Mark v. 19) is translated into Kikámba thus, *di niumba-ni* ku-*a-gu* 15., and "into their houses" (Mark viii. 3) *niumba-ni* mu-*a-o* 18. (Kiníka *niumba-ni* mu-*a-kwe* 18. "in his house," Luke v. 29, *niumba-ni* mu-*a-ko* 18. "in thy house," Luke vii. 44.) It must, however, be remarked that in Krapf's translations this rule is by no means strictly carried out; for sometimes the genitives following nouns in the locative case are in concord with the class of the nouns, instead of having the genitive form of one of the two locative classes (15th or 18th) mentioned above. Thus we find (Mark. xi. 15 &c.) *niumba-ni* y-*a Mulungu* 9. "into or in the house of God," and (Mark xi. 1) **ki**-*ima-ni* dsh-*a ma-pela* 7. "at the mount of Olives," &c. It will also be perceived, in the examples taken from Dr. Krapf's translations, that the distinction which Dr. Steere has observed with regard to the use of *mu* and *ku*, has not been followed throughout.

479. As far as we know, the locative suffix -*ni* is only met with in the languages of the Zangian Genus of the Middle Branch and in those of the South-eastern Branch,—where its form in the Kafir species is -*ini* or -*eni*, in the Tekeza -*ine* or -*ene*, and in the Setshuâna -*eñ*, &c. (§ 309 and 273.) In the languages of the South-eastern Branch the nouns with this suffix are always to be construed according to the class of their prefixes, without reference to their local meaning. There is, however, an analogous case in Kafir in the concord required by the majority of prepositions. These are mostly local or other forms of nouns which are either still used as such or have lately become obsolete. Such a noun would naturally require the genitive following it to agree with its own prefix; and, accordingly, in the Middle Branch languages these prepositions are still generally followed by a genitive form in accordance with the class of that noun from which the preposition has been formed. But in Kafir, Zulu, and Setshuâna, almost all those prepositions which were originally nouns, require a genitive form of

the local 15th (Kafir ku-, Setshuâna χo-) class to follow them. (Appleyard § 491, Colenso § 270.) A case which completely resembles that of the Zangian locatives is met with in the Zulu sentence e-/al-eni kw-O-m-geni " on one side of the Umgeni " (Colenso's Grammar p. 82), from i-/ala, a noun of the 5th (li-) class, which according to its prefix would require after it the form l-O-m-geni. In such cases, I formerly believed that the ku- was not to be considered as a pronominal element, but as a directive. In fact, I assumed (as Grout does) that the form kwa- which occurs here, was identical with the prefixed directive kwa- (Appleyard § 112; § 165, 3; § 172, 3; Colenso § 130)* ; but the fact that before proper names of persons, where otherwise kwa has its most usual place, it is replaced by ku-ka- (pa-m-bi ku-ka-Faku "before Faku," Grout § 326), renders it more probable that the " ku " in these cases is to be regarded as a pronominal element. Still more convincing proofs are furnished by a comparison of Setshuâna; for, similar prepositions in this language are followed by χ-a-, which is clearly the genitive form referring to the 15th (χo-) class (Kafir kw-a-),—whilst the Kafir preposition kwa- has been retained in Setshuâna in the form kúa.

480. In trying to explain this curious feature of the language, we must bear in mind that in Kafir and Zulu the suffix -ini or -eni is only found when the noun is preceded by the prefixed directive (s)e-, which latter has, as yet, been met with only in these two languages.† In

---

* Forms in -eni-kw-eni, as e-mn-v-eni-kw-eni "after" (= e-mn-v-eni from u-mn-va 3. "back part of an object"), //-eni-kw-eni "at the time when" (i-//a 5. "time"), e-mn-χ̇l-eni-kw-eni "in the day when" (u-mn-χla 3. "day"), //esh-eni-kw-eni "at the time when" (i-//esha 5. "time"), seem only to add to the perplexity which surrounds the construction of forms in -ini or -eni. (Appleyard § 322; 336, 1.)

† In the Tekeza dialect of Lourenzo Marques, however, if our vocabularies can be trusted, the suffix -ine or -ene is used with a prefixed a-, which may be identical with the Kafir prefixed directive (s)e-. Tekeza

Setshuâna, on the contrary, we find that the prefixed directives *mo* "in" (§ 438), *ha* "at" (Kafir *pa*, § 436), and *kuá* "in the direction of, to, till, in, at" (Kafir *kwa*), are always followed by the form with the suffix *-eṅ*, which, also, frequently occurs with nouns which are not preceded by any preposition. In the latter case, however, Livingstone (Analysis p. 17) and Frédoux (§ 7) consider this termination to imply the presence of such a prefixed directive (or preposition). In the Zangian languages, nouns with the suffix *-ni* are not now preceded by any of these prefixed directives; but the forms of concord used with nouns in this locative case appear to indicate that it was formerly preceded by one of two (or more) prefixed directives, which were, in this instance, promoted to the rank of concord-indicating prefixes of nouns. These prefixed particles (which were originally case-indicating directives preceding the regular derivative prefix of the noun) have now fallen off, but the concord still indicates their former presence. Let us take for an example the Kikamba phrase *y·u-na-walukile ma-u-ni mu-a-ke* 18. "he fell at his feet" (Mark. v. 22), and compare it with the Setshuâna translation *a oéla mo nao-n ts-a χaχue* 10. The prefixed directive MU- (which probably originally preceded the **ma-u-ni**) has been lost in Kikamba, but is still indicated by the pronominal element "mu,"—(the prefixed directive having become here the concord-indicating element). In Setshuâna, in which (as we have seen in these cases) the forms of concord always agree with the derivative prefix of the noun, the latter has been dropped, *nao* being an abbreviation of li-*nao* (Kafir i-zin-*nyawo* or i-n-*nyawo*) 10., the plural of lo-*nao* (Kafir u-*nyawo*) 11. The concord also here is visible in the pronominal element "ts"

*a-*maĭ*-ti-ne* = Kafir *e-*maĭ*-zi-ni* (Setshuâna *mo-*me*-tse-ṅ*) "in the settlements, kraals," Tekeza *a-*maṡa*-*χ̌*lo-ene* = Kafir *e-*ma*-e*χ̌*lw-eni* (Setshuâna *mo-*maṡa*-i*χ̌*lo-ṅ*) "in the eyes," Tekeza *a-*m*-dolo-ene* = Kafir *e-*ma*-lilw-eni* (Setshuâna *mo-*matu*-lelo-ṅ*) "on the fire."

(Kafir " z "), which is a representative of the derivative prefix li- or ri- (Kafir zi-). The translations of this phrase into both languages (Kikámba and Setshuâna) thus agree in making the concord only visible in the forms following the noun, whilst the prefixed particle, which may be considered as the source of the concord, has been dropped. In fact we conclude that Kikamba *ma-u-ni* mu-*a-ke* stands for MU-*ma-u-ni* mu-*a-ke*, just as Setshuâna *mo na-o-ṅ* ts-*a χaχue* is an abbreviation of *mo li-nao-ṅ* ts-*a χaχue*. But the two languages differ in this— that in Setshuâna the concord-indicating particle was a derivative prefix, and in Kikamba a directive, prefixed to the form of the noun with its own derivative prefix.* In the latter instance, the local directive has assumed the position of a concord-indicating prefix, and thus the forms of concord refer to it, and not to the regular derivative prefix of the noun.†

480. The prefixed directives mentioned above as having assumed the character of concord-indicating derivative prefixes of nouns, were probably originally not quite identical with the prefixes **mu-** of the 3rd, and **ku-** of the 15th class. At all events, the forms of concord required by the Zangian locative case in MU- are different from those of the 3rd (**mu-**) class, and we have, therefore, provisionally identified these MU- forms with the 18th (**mo-**) class in Otyihereró. Similarly, it is not improbable that the Zangian forms in " ku-" which are in concord with the locative case, may have originally belonged to the 17th (Otyihereró **ko-**) class; but as their forms are, as far as we know, the same as those employed in the 15th (**ku-**) class, we have placed them under the head of this latter class.

* Just as we find plural or diminutive prefixes prefixed to nouns formed with other prefixes. (*Vide* p. 145.)

† That local derivative particles of nouns may impart to the nouns formed with them a meaning analogous to our case terminations, has been already remarked with regard to some Hottentot derivative suffixes. (§ 447.)

KIKAMBA PREFIXES.

SINGULAR.	PLURAL.
PERSONAL.	
1. mu-, (—) m-	2. a- 6. ? (—)
3. mu- m-	4. mi-
5. i-, (—) y-	6. ma- m-
7. ki- dsh-	8. i-
9. n- m- (—)	10. n- m- (—) 12. tu-
11. u-, u-*ts*-	10. n- m- (—)
13. (+ 3.) ka-, ka-*mu*-k-	12. (+ 4.) tu-, tu-*mi*-
ABSTRACT.	
14. u-	6. (+ 14.) ma-*u*-
INFINITIVE AND LOCAL.	
15. ku-	6. ma-
LOCAL. 16. wa-	
LOCATIVE: 15. (? 17.) (—) .... -*ni*	
18. (—) .... -*ni*	

KIKAMBA.

481. Ki-*kámba* 7. (spoken by the A-*kámba* 2.) has more fully preserved the original distribution of the nouns into classes or genders than either Kiníka or Kisuáheli. In the two latter languages we have not, as yet, met with any traces of the 12th (tu-) class. Kikamba agrees with the languages of the Mosambique Genus in making the 12th (tu-) class correspond as plural to the 13th (ka-). As we shall see hereafter, the Angola language is distinguished by the same peculiarity, although in this respect it appears to stand alone among the members of the South-western or Bunda Genus, in which the 14th (u-) class generally corresponds as plural to the 13th (ka-).

KIKAMBA NOUNS.

mú-*ndu* (Zulu u-mu-*ntu*, Kisambala mu-*ntu*, Kiníka mu-*tu*, Suáheli m-*tu*) 1. "man, person," pl. a-*ndu* (Kafir a-ba-*ntu*, Kisambala wa-*ntu*, Kiníka a-*tu*, Suáheli wa-*tu*) 2.;

Kikámba Derivative Prefixes of Nouns. 185

mu-*ka* 1. (Zulu u-m-*ka*- 1., pl. o-*m*-*ka*- 2. Colenso's Dict. p. 119; Kiníka mu-*dshe*, Suaheli m-*ke* 1.) "wife," pl. a-*ka* (Kiníka a-*dshe*, Suáheli a-*ke*) 2.;

mu-*ina* (Kafir u-m-*nina*-*we* "younger br.") 1. "brother," pl. a-*ina* 2.;

m-*úme* (Kiníka mu-*lúme*, Suaheli m-*úme*) 1. "husband," pl. a-*ume* 2.;

ide (w-*a*-*o*) 1. "(their) father," pl. *ide* (m-*a*-*o*) 6.;

mu-*dshi* (Zulu u-mú-*zi* Kiníka mu-*tsi*, Suaheli m-*dshi*) 3. "town," pl. mi-*dshi* Suah. (Kiníka mi-*tri*) 4.;

mu-*tue* (Kihiau m-*tue*, Batoka and Banyenko mo-*thos*, Borotse mo-*thu*, Balojazi mo-*thue*, Maponda and Bashubea mo-*tue*) 3. "head," pl. mi-*tue* 4.;

mu-*di* (Zulu u-mu-*ti*, Kisambala mu-*ti*, Kinika mú-*hi*, Suáheli m-*ti*) 3. "tree," pl. mi-*di* (Kisambala mi-*ti*, Kiníka mi-*hi*, Suáheli mi-*ti*) 4. (§ 428);

mu-*denia* 3. "day," pl. mi-*denia* 4.;

m-*oko* (Sofala mu-*voko*) 3. "arm," pl. mi-*oko* 4. (Setshuâna le-*tshoχo* 5. "arm," pl. ma-*boχo* 6.);

mu-*iwa* (Kinika m-*ia*, Kisuaheli m-*iba*) 3. "thistle," pl. m-*iwa* (Kinika m-*ia*, Kisuaheli m-*iba*) 4.;

mú-*io* (Kinika, Kisuáheli, Kipokomo, and Kihiau m-*sigo*) 3. "load," pl. mi-*io* 4.;

i-*temma* 5. "liver," pl. ma-*temma* 6.;

i-*dŭmo* (Inhambane li-*fumo*, Kinika, Suaheli, Kipokomo, Kihiau *fumo*) 5. "lance, spear," pl. ma-*dŭmo* 6.;

i-*modoi* 5. "tear," pl. ma-*modoi* 6.;

i-*woi* (Setshuâna le-*phui*) 5. "pigeon," pl. ma-*woi* 6.;

i-*wói* 5. "lung," pl. ma-*wói* 6.;

i-*londu* 5. "sheep," pl. ma-*londu* 6.;

i-*kúyu* 5. "fish," pl. ma-*kúyu* 6.;

i-*dangu* 5. "leaf," pl. ma-*dangu* 6.;

i-*wia** 5. "stone," pl. ma-*wia* 6.;

i-*do* 5. "eye," pl. me-*do* 6. (§ 327);

i-*o* 5. "tooth," pl. ma-*yo* 6. (§ 326);

yi-*u* 5. "knee," pl. mú-*u* 6.;

i 5. "door," pl. ma-*i* 6.;

jua (Tette zi-*rúa*, Sena and Kinika *rua*, Kihiau *lúa*, Suaheli *úa*) 5. "flower," pl. ma-*úa* (Sofala ma-*ruva*, Tette, Sena, and Kinika ma-*rúa*, Cape Delgado and Kihiau ma-*lúa*, Suaheli ma-*úa*) 6.;

---

* Probably from LI-*BUA*, Batóka le-*bue*, Borotse li-*ue* (pl. ma-*biwe* or maa-*oúa*), Banyeńko li-*ue* (pl. mu-*ue*), Balojazi li-*ove* (pl. maa-*ue*), Otyihercró e-*oe* (pl. o-maa-*oe*), Batoka *tshue* (pl. maa-*ue*), Kinika *dziwe* (pl. maa-*we*), Kisuaheli *dshiwe* (pl. maa-*we*), Cape Delgado rí-*we* (pl. maá-*we*), Quellimane li-*bue*, Sofala *búe*, Tekeza (Lourenzo Marques) ri-*bdsha*, Seχlapi le-*ntshue* (pl. maa-*ye*), Sesuto le-*yoe* (pl. maa-*yoe*), Kafir i-li-*tye* (pl. a-maa-*tye*). *Vide* § 176.

lema (Kinika *rema*) 5. "net," pl. **ma**-*lema* (Kinika **ma**-*rema*) 6.;

ki-*tuo* (Kinika **ki**-*túrro*) 7. "shoulder," pl. **i**-*tuo*, 8.

n-*sia* (Kafir i-**n**-*xlela*, Kinika [e-] **n**-*dshira*, Kipokómo **n**-*dshia*, Suáheli **n**-*sia*), 9. "way, path," pl. **n**-*sia* (Kinika [e-]**n**-*dshira*) 10.;

m-*béwo* (Kafir i-**m**-*pepo*, "cold wind," Setshuána *pheho* "wind") 9. "wind," pl. **m**-*béwo* 10. (Zulu i-**si**-*pepo* 7. "gust, gale, storm");

(?)**n**-*dumba* 9. "slave," pl. **tu**-*dumba* 12.;

u-*kú* (Kafir u-*kuni*) 11. "wood," pl. **n**-*gú* (Kafir i-**n**-*kuni*) 10. (§ 348);

u-*tsea* 11. "wing," pl. **n**-*tsea* 10.;

u-*báu* (Kafir u-*bambo*) 11. "rib," pl. **m**-*báu* (Kafir i-**m**-*bambo*) 10.;

u-*tsigi* 11. "mule," pl. **n**-*igi* 10.;

u-*tsiégi* (u-*smu*) 11. "(dry) straw," pl. **n**-*iegi* (ni-*smu*) 10.;

ka-*míloa* 13. "thorn," pl. **tu**-*míloa* 12.;

ka-*ka* (k-*a mu-aki*) 13. "spark (of fire)," pl. **tu**-*ka* (tu-*a mu-aki*) 12.;

k-*ana* 13. "child, son, &c.," pl. **tu**-*ána* 12.;

k-*ala* 13. "claw," pl. **tu**-*ala* 12.;

ka-*mu-di* 13. "shrub," pl. **tu**-*mi-di* 12. (§ 454);

u-*ndu* 14. "state, thing," pl. **ma**-*u-ndu* 6.;

u-*ta* (Setshuána **bo**-*ra*, Otyihereró o-**u**-*ta*) 14. "bow";

u-*dio* (Kinika, Kisuaheli, &c. **u**-*sso*, Kihiau **u**-*ssio*, Kafir u-**bu**-*so*) 14. "face;"

u-*tsumbe* (Kinika) 14. "kingdom;"

kŭ-*du* 15. "ear," pl. **mä**-*ddŭ* 6. (§ 434, note);

ku-*u* 15. "foot, leg," pl. **ma**-*ú* 6.;

wa-*ndu* 16. "place" (§ 435).

KINIKA AND KISUAHELI.

482. In KINIKA and KISUAHELI the decay of the original grammatical structure is far greater than in Kikámba. We find in Kiníka that a noun which originally belonged to the 3rd (**mu-**) class, is now, on account of the loss of its initial nasal, in concord with forms of the 14th (**u-**) class, although retaining a plural form of the 4th (**mi-**) class, which latter thus appears in Kiníka to correspond to the 14th (**u-**) class. It is also remarkable in Kiníka and Kisuáheli that the 10th prefix may precede instead of replacing the 11th, which in this case always loses its initial liquid (*l*), which is otherwise retained in Kiníka. When the 10th prefix either precedes the **u-** of the 11th, or replaces the latter, it (the 10th prefix) assumes in

KINIKA PREFIXES.

SINGULAR.	PLURAL.
PERSONAL.	
1. mu-, (—) m-	2. a- (—)
3. mu- m-	4. mi-
5. (—), (—)-tsi	6. ma- m-
7. ki- dshi-, dsh-	8. vi- (wi-)
9. (e)n-, un- (e)m- (—)	10. (e)n-, un- (e)m- (—)
11. lu- lu-u-	10. ni-u- ni- mi- (—)
DIMINUTIVE.	
13. ka-	
ABSTRACT.	
14. u-, (—)	4. mi-
INFINITIVE.	
15. ku-	
LOCAL.	
16. va-	
LOCATIVE. 15. (? 17.) (—) .... -ni	
18. (—) .... -ni	

Kiníka (and sometimes in Kisuáheli) the form **ni-**, and in Kinika, before labials, **mi-**.

KINIKA NOUNS.

mu-*hoho* (Suaheli **m**-*toto*) 1. "child," pl. **a**-*hoho* (Suaheli **wa**-*toto*) 2.;

mu-*ínyi* (Suah.) 1. "possessor," pl. *enyi* (Suaheli **w**-*enyi*) 2.;

m-*ana* Suah. (Zulu u-**mu**-*ntwana*) 1. "son, daughter, child," pl. *ana* (Zulu a-**ba**-*ntwana*, Suaheli **w**-*ana*) 2.;

mú-*ho* (Suaheli **m**-*to*, Cape Delgado **mu**-*to*, Anjuane **mu**-*rró*) 3. "river," pl. **mí**-*ho* (Suaheli **mi**-*to*) 4.;

m-*oyo* Suah. (Kipokomo **m**-*otsho*, Cape Delgado and Sofala **m**-*oïo*) 3. "heart," pl. **mi**-*oyo* (Suah.) 4.;

tsína (Setshuâna **le**-*ina*, Suaheli *dshina*) 5. "name," pl. **ma**-*tsína* (Setshuâna **ma**-*ina*, Suaheli **ma**-*dshina*) 6.;

néno (Suah.) 5. "word," pl. **ma**-*néno* (Suah.) 6.;

tsósi (Suaheli *tosi*, Kipokomo and Tette *tsosi*, Kihiau **li**-*ndshósi*,) Makua **ni**-*tori*) 5. "tear," pl. **ma**-*tsosi* (Suaheli **ma**-*tori* Tette **mă**-*tsosi*, Kihiau **ma**-*ndshósi*, Makua **me**-*tori*) 6.;

triwe (Suaheli *dshiwe*, note to § 481) 5. "stone," pl. **ma**-*we* (Suah.) 6.;

tsino (Suaheli *dshino*) 5. "tooth," pl. **m**-*eno* (Suah.) 6. (§ 326);

hotsa 5. "leaf," pl. **ma**-*hotsa* 6.;

kí-*tu* Suah. (Kikamba **ki**-*ndu*, Kihiau **dshí**-*ndu*) 7. "thing," pl. **vi**-*tu* (Suah.) 8.;

ki-*tsoa* (Suaheli ki-*toa*, Cape Delgado ki-*súa*) 7. "head," pl. vi-*tsoa* (Suaheli vi-*toa*) 8.;

dsh-*ala* (Suaheli dsh-*ánda*, Sena and Tette tsh-*ara*, Maravi ki-*ála*) "finger," pl. vi-*ala* (Suaheli vi-*ánda*, Sena pi-*ara*, Maravi dz-*ala*) 8.;

dshi-*a* (Kipokómo ki-*dsha*) 7. "vessel, instrument, utensil," pl. vi-*a* (Kipokómo vi-*dsha*) 8.;

ki-*hi* (Suaheli ki-*ti*, Kipokomo dshi-*hi*) 7. "throne," pl. vi-*hi* (wi-*hi*) 8.;

(e)n-*dugu* (Suah. and Kipokómo) 9. "brother," pl. (e)n-*dugu* 10.;

(e)m-*bíra* (Kikamba m-*bia*, Kipokomo m-*béra*) 9. "grave, tomb," pl. (e)m-*bíra* 10.;

tsiku (Suaheli, Kipokomo, and Kihiau *siku*, Sena n-*tsiku*) 9. "day," pl. *tsiku* 10. (Kafir u-*suku* 11. "day [including night]"), pl. i-m-*tsuku* 10. (Compare § 453 notes, and § 450 note);

baba (Suah.) 9. "father," pl. *baba* 10.;

(u)n-*gúo* Suah. &c. (Kafir i-n-*gubo*, Setshuána *kobo*, Sofala *guvo*, Tette, Sena, Cape Delgado n-*gúo* or *gúo*, Kikamba [u]n-*gwa*) 9. "cloth, cloak," pl. (u)n-*gúo* (Suah.) 10.;

tsi (Suaheli n-*ti*, Kikámba n-*di*, Kipokomo n-*si*) 9. "land, country," pl. *tsi* (Suaheli n-*ti*) 10.;

lu-*rimi* (Suaheli u-*limi*) 11. "tongue," pl. ni-u-*rími* (Suah. n-*dimi*) 10. (§ 351);

lu-*tsoa* 11. "worm," pl. ni-u-*tsoa* 10. (Suaheli m-*toa* 3. "white coloured worm," pl. mi-*toa* 4.);

lu-*ffu** 11. "dead," pl. ni-u-*ffu* 10. (Suaheli m-*fu* 1. pl. wá-*fu* 2.; but in Setshuána lo-*shu* 11. is "death," pl. lin-*tshu* 10.);

lu-*áyo* (Suaheli w-*ayo*, Kipokomo tsu-*atsho*) 11. "trace," pl. ni-*áyo* Suah. (Kipokomo ni-*átsho*) 10.;

lu-*tsérre* (Suaheli u-*nuelle*) 11. "hair," pl. ni-*erre* (Suaheli *nuelle*) 10.;

lu-*nióga* (Kipokomo u-*niodsha*) 11. "feather, wing," pl. *nióga* 10.;

lu-*fúsi* 11. "wool," pl. mi-*fusi* 10. (Suaheli *fusi* 5.);

ka-*hoho* (Kipokomo ka-*dudu*) 13. "a young one;"

u-*miro* 14. "voice," pl. mi-*miro* 4.;

ku-*londa* 15. "desire;"

ku-*loha* (Suaheli ku-*óta*) 15. "dream;"

va-*tu* 16. "place" (§ 435).

---

* From ku-*ffua* (Suaheli and Kipokomo ku-*ffa*, Kisambala ku-*fa*, Kikamba ku-*gwa*, Kihiau kú-*húa*, Makua ú-*kwa* or u-*ókwa*, Sena, Tette, Sofala, Inhambane, and Delagoa Bay kú-*fa*, Kafir u-ku-*fu*, Sesuto h'o-*fua*, Seχlapi χo-*shua*, Batoka ko-*fua*, Otyihereró o-ku-*ta*, Sindonga [Ovambo] o-ku-э'*a* or o-ku-*fa*, Nano o-gu-*fa*, Bunda [Angola] ku-*fud*, Kongo ku-*fua*) 15. "to die" (Mpongwe *dshuwa*, Dikele *gwa*, Dualla and Isubu *wa* "die").

483. By the loss of its initial lingual (*l*), the 11th prefix in KISUAHELI has become identical with the 14th (u); and the 11th and 14th classes have thus coalesced. (§ 456 and 457.) This transference has gone so far, that nouns which formerly clearly belonged to the 14th class, as u-*sso* (Kafir u-bu-*so* 14.) "face," have adopted a plural of the 10th (n-) class. It is probable that this peculiar correspondence of the classes is not an ancient feature in the structure of the Bâ-ntu languages, but due to the influence of modern false analogies. On account of this plural correspondence, I considered it practically more convenient to call this amalgamated (u-) class the 11th, although it includes a great number of abstract nouns which originally belonged to the 14th class. To the Kisuáheli nouns previously given in the Kikámba and Kiníka lists, it is only necessary to add the few which follow. They are all taken from Krapf's publications; but, in the construction of the Table of the Kisuáheli prefixes, Dr. Steere's "Table of Concords" has been of much assistance. The latter work

KISUAHELI PREFIXES.

SINGULAR.	PLURAL.
PERSONAL.	
1. m-, (—) mu-	2. wa-, (—) w-
3. mu- m-	4. mi-
5. (—), (—) -*dshi*-	6. ma- m-
7. ki- dsh-	8. vi- (wi-)
9. n-, (u)n- m- (—)	10. n-, (u)n- m- (—)
11. (& 14.) u-, w-	10. n-, ni- m-, ni-u- (—) 6. ma-
INFINITIVE. 15. ku-, kw-	
LOCAL. 16. ma-, pa-	
LOCATIVE.	18. (? 17.) (—) ...... -*ni*
	18. (—) ...... -*ni*

illustrates the Swaheli language as spoken at Zanzibar, whilst Dr. Krapf's publications represent the same language as spoken at Mombas (Ki-*suáheli* dsh-*a Om-wita*). A vocabulary of the Swaheli dialect of Cape Delgado is in Dr. Peter's Collection; and manuscripts containing pieces of native literature exist in the purest and most ancient of the Swaheli dialects,—that which is spoken on the Islands of Patta and Lamu.

KISUAHELI NOUNS.

u-*báfu* (Kinĭka lu-*báfu*, Kikamba u-*báu*, Kipokomo yu-*afu*, Kafir u-*bambo*) 11. "rib," pl. ma-*bafu* (Kikámba m-*báu*, Kafir i-m-*bambo*) 10.;

u-*wíngu* (Kipokómo yu-*wingo*) 11. "heaven," pl. m-*bingu* 10.;

u-*nióya* 11. "wool," pl. ma-*nióya* 6.;

u-*kúni* (Kafir u-*kúni*) 11. (Kinika u-*kúni* 14.) "wood," pl. *kuni* (Kafir i-n-*kuni*) 10. (§ 348);

u-*tu* (Kafir u-lu-*to*) 11. (Kinika u-*tu* 14.) "thing," pl. ni-u-*tu* 10.;

u-*sso* 11. (Kinika u-*sso*, Kafir u-bu-*so* 14.) "face," pl. ni-u-*sso* 10.

w-*aráka* 11. (14. in Kinika) "letter," pl. ni-*araka* 10.;

ku-*ffa* 15. "death" (§ 482 note);

kw-*ansa* 15. "beginning;"

ma-*hali* or pa-*hali* 16. "place" (§ 435).

KISAMBALA.

484. Ki-*sambala* 7. is spoken in U-*sambala* 14. by a people called by Dr. Krapf Wa-*sambára*. The following nouns, given in a letter from Dr. Steere (dated Dec. 22nd, 1866), are my only materials for forming an outline table of the derivative prefixes of the nouns in the Kisambala language. It appears as if false analogies had also extended their influence to this language. At least, we attribute to this cause the fact that the 8th (vi-) prefix corresponds here as plural not only to the 7th (ki-), but also to the 13th (ka-). The identity of the consonant of the two singular prefixes ki- and ka- appears to have been the misleading element. The use of the 10th (ny-) prefix as plural to the 14th (u-) is also ascribable to the identity of the vowel of this latter prefix with that of the 11th (lu-); the 11th prefix being properly entitled to the 10th (n-) as its corresponding plural. It has

Kisambala Derivative Prefixes of Nouns. 191

already been remarked that the prefix of the 11th (lu-) class has in the Zangian dialects a strong tendency to lose its initial letter, thus becoming identical in form with the 14th (u-) prefix. The Kisambala language appears, phonetically speaking, to stand nearest to Ki-*pokomo* 7. (spoken by the Wa-*pokomo* 2.); in fact many words in the two languages are identical.

KISAMBALA PREFIXES.

SINGULAR.	PLURAL.
PERSONAL.	
1. mu-, (—)	2. wa-, (—)
3. mu-	4. mi-
5. (—)	6. ma-
7. ki-	8. vi-
9. n-	10. n-
11. lu-	10. (—)
13. ka-	8. vi-
14. u-	10. ny-
INFINITIVE. 15. ku-	
LOCAL. 16. ha-	

KISAMBALA NOUNS.

mu-*ntu* (note after § 494) 1. "man," pl. wa-*ntu* 2. "people;" ṅgombe 1. "ox," pl. ṅgombe 2. (§ 226 and 466);
mu-*ti* (Zulu u-mu-*ti*) 3. "tree," pl. mi-*ti* 4. (§ 428);
zina* 5. "name," pl. ma-*zina* 6.;
ki-*ntu* (Kipokomo) 7. "thing," pl. vi-*ntu* 8.;
n-*yumba* (Kipokomo, &c.) 9. "house," pl. n-*yumba* 10.;
lu-*zixi* 11. "rope," pl. *zixi* 10. (Kipokomo *msidshi*);
ka-*xoshi* 13. "youth," pl. vi-*xoshi* 8.;
u-*ila* (Kipokomo w-*ia*) 14. "song," pl. ny-*ila* 10.;
ku-*fa* (Kipokómo ku-*ffa*, § 482 note) 15. "dying;"
ha-*ntu* (Kipokómo va-*ntu*, § 435) 16. "place and places."

* Maravi, Quellimane, Sena, and Tette (d)*zina*, Makua m-*zina*, Cape Delgado *sina*, Suáheli *dshina* (pl. ma-*dshina* 6.), Kiníka *tsina* (pl. ma-*tsina* 6.), Kíhiáu r-*ina*, Inhambane l-*ind*, Setshuána le-*ina* (pl. ma-*ina* 6.), Otyihereró e-*na* (pl. o-ma-*na* 6.), Sindonga e-*'ina* (e-*sina*), Angola o-ri-*shina* (pl. o-ma-*shina* 6.), Mpongwe i-*na* (pl. a-*na* 6.), Dikele, Benga, Dualla, and Isubu d-*ina* (pl. ma-*ina* 6.).

cc. *Languages of the Interior.*

485. Comparative philology can only follow at a distance the march of geographical discovery. The extensive vocabularies collected by DR. LIVINGSTONE in the course of his travels, and preserved in manuscript in the Grey Library, are most valuable in affording a knowledge of the languages of the region between those tracts of country in which the better known languages of the Mosambique and Bunda genera are spoken. But we must know more with regard to the plural forms of the nouns, and also have the forms of concord illustrated by some phrases, before it be possible to construct reliable tables illustrating the correspondence of the derivative prefixes in these intermediate languages*. Among the latter, the dialects of the Ba-*lojazi* 2. (? Lobale) and Ma-*ponda* 6. (Ba-*maponda* or Ba-*ponda* 2.) are evidently varieties of one language, which can be recognised as belonging to the South-western or Bunda Genus. To define the exact position which the dialects of the Ba-*nyeṅko*, Ba-*toka*, Ba-*rotse*, Ba-*shubea*, and Ba-*yeiye* or Ba-*k͟χoba* would occupy in a classification of the languages of the Middle Branch, must be the work of further research.

We find that **mo-** is the prefix of the 3rd class in all these dialects, and corresponds to **mi-** of the 4th class in the dialects of the Balojazi, Batoka, and Bashubea. In the dialects of the Maponda and Banyeṅko the 4th prefix bears the form of **me-**. The 5th prefix is **li-** in the dialects of the Balojazi, Banyeṅko, and Borotse, **li-** or **le-** in those of the Maponda and Bayeiye, and **li-** or **i-** in that of the Bashubea. Its plural is (as always) formed by the 6th prefix, which is **ma-** in all these dialects, with a variation to **me-**, which at least occurs in the dialects of the Batoka, Bashubea, and Bayeiye. The 11th prefix has the form **lo-** in the dialects of the Maponda, Banyeṅko, and Bashubea, **do-** in that of the Borotse, and **ro-** in that of the Bayeiye.

* When Livingstone's more extensive vocabulary of the language of the BAROTSE (which is accompanied by a Setshuâna translation only) has been fully deciphered, we shall doubtless be able to construct a fairly satisfactory table of the derivative prefixes of the nouns in this language.

486. Of the derivative prefixes of nouns in the language of the Ba-*yeiye* 2. (a people called Ba-*kχoba* 2. or Ma-*kχoba* 6. by the Betshuana) I have drawn up the following table, which I give here as a mere attempt. The table is incomplete, as the plurals corresponding to the 7th (se-) and 11th (ro-) classes have not yet been ascertained. The correspondence of the 10th (zin-) class as plural to the 13th (ka-) is still doubtful; having been established in one instance only, and it is possible that the plural zín-*kone* 10. corresponds here (as in most kindred languages, § 348) to a singular of the 11th (ro- or lo-) class, and that the word with the prefix ka- (ka-*kone* 13.) given in Dr. Livingstone's vocabulary is merely a diminutive. But, on the other hand, we have to take into consideration the fact that also in the Nano language of Benguela at least one case occurs in which the 10th (9'o-) class forms the plural to a noun of the 13th (ka-) class. (§ 495.)

BAYEIYE PREFIXES.

SINGULAR.	PLURAL.
1. mo-	2. ba-
3. mo-, om- mu- m-(*b*)-	4. me-
5. le- li-	6. ma-, ama-
7. se-	
9. n-, *o*-n-, en- m-, *u*-m-	10. zin-
11. ro- (lo-)	
13. ka-	10. zin-
14. o-	
15. ko-	

BAYEIYE NOUNS.

mo-*rume* (Otyihereró o-mu-*rume* "male," Benguela u-*lome*, Angola mu-*lumi*, Kinika and Kihiau mu-*lúme*, Kipokómo mu-*yúme*, Kikamba and Kisuá-heli m-*une*, Mpongwe o-*nomí*, Dikele n-*9'omi*, Benga, Dualla, and Isubu m-*omi*, Fernando Po bo-*obe*) 1. "man, husband;"

mo-*kazi* 1. " woman," (*vide* note at end of § 494);

mo-*via* (Borotse mo-*bika*, Sindonga u-m-*pika*, Angola mu-*bika*, Kongo o-mu-*bhiga*) 1. "servant, slave;"

mo-*rumb-one* (Sofala and Sena mu-*rumbu-āna*) 1. "a lad;"

mo-*ka-na* (Bashubea mo-*kasana*, Otyihereró o-mu-*kaϑ'-ona*, Sindonga u-m-*kaϑ'-ona*) 1. "girl;"

mo-*yene* (Setshuána mo-*eñ*, Dualla mo-*en* or mw-*en*) 1. "stranger;"

mo-*nziri* (Bashubea mo-*nϑure*) 1. "teacher;"

ba-*zimo* Baponda (Bashubea ba-*ϑimo*, § 395) 2. "ancestral spirits;"

mo-*nwe* (Otyihereró o-mu-*nue*, § 494) 3. "finger," pl. me-*n'* (*añga*) 4. "(my) fingers;"

mo-*shoro* (Sofala mu-*shoro*, Tette and Sena mu-*sóro*) 3. "head;"

mo-*shana* (Batoka and Bashubea mo-*sana*, Setshuána mo-*klana*) 3. "back;"

mo-*sinza* (Borotse and Baponda mo-*sindshe*) 3. "whey;"

mu-*si* (Zulu u-mu-*si*, Otyihereró o-mu-*ise*, § 494) 3. "smoke;"

mo-*zi* or mo-*si* (Zulu u-mu-*zi*, Setshuána, Bashubea, Balojazi mo-*tse*, Banyeńko and Borotse mo-*nde*) 3. "town;"

me-*aka* (the same in the dialects of the Banyeńko, Batoka, Borotse, Bashubea, Balojazi, Baponda, u-m-*nyaka* in Zulu, ñuaχa in Setahuána, mu-*aka* in Manika, Tette, Kihiau, Kisuaheli, Kinika, Kikamba, and Kipokomo) 3. "year;"

mo-*tshu* (Setshuána mo-*tshui*, Sofala mu-*sheve*, Tette mu-*zēve*, Quellimane mu-*ve*) 3. "arrow;"

mo-*ndiro* (Banyeńko and Bashubea me-*lilo*, Setshuána and Barotse mo-*lelo*, § 344) 3. "fire;"

mo-*roñka* (Borotse and Batoka mo-*roñga*, Banyeńko mo-*loñka*) 3. "river bed;"

m-*biri* (Setshuána m-*ele*, § 469, Banyeńko mo-*iri*, Batoka and Bashubea mo-*biri*, Balojazi mo-*bila*, Bamaponda mo-*bela*) 3. "body;"

o-m-*oio* (Sofala and Batoka m-*oio*, Kinika and Kisuaheli m-*oyo*, Kipokomo m-*otsho*) 3. "heart;"

o-m-*oa* (Kafir u-*moya*, Setshuána mo-*ea*, Batoka mo-*ia*, Borotse mo-*iya*, &c.) 3. "soul, breath;"

li-*dzi* 5. "knee," pl. ma-*dz'*[a] (Bashubea ma-*dzue*) 6.;

le-*ueri* or *tshue* 5. "stone," pl. ma-*we* 6. (p. 185, note);

le-*iro* (Otyihereró e-*uru*, § 494) 5. "nose;"

le-*oko* (Balojazi li-*boko*, Setshuána le-*tshoχo*) 5. "arm;"

li-*ua* or le-*oa* (Otyihereró e-*yuva*, § 494) 5. "sun;"

li-*ru* (Otyihereró e-*yuru*, § 494) 5. "sky;"

ma-*dzunza* 6. "clouds;"

ma-*shota* or ma-*shuta* 6. "sweet-milk;"

ma-*ropa* 6. "blood;"

a-ma-*dze* 6. "butter, fat" (p. 142, end of third note);

a-m-*i* 6. "water," (p. 142, first note);

Bayeiye Derivative Prefixes of Nouns. 195

se-*kabi* (Bashubea ki-*kabi*) 7. "skin or hide;"

se-*rapo* (Banyeṅko se-*labo*, Borotse si-*rabo*, Bamaponda she-*lapo*, Bashubea ki-*raho*) 7. "paddle;"

n-*kombe* Baponda (Banyeṅko, Bashubea, Balojazi n-*gombe*) 9. "ox," pl. zin-*gombe* 10. (§ 226);

n-*ko* (Kafir i-n-*gubo*, Setshuâna *kobo*, Batoka n-*kobo*, Bashubea and Balojazi n-*gobo*) 9 "a kaross, cloak;"

n-*koku* (Kafir i-n-*kuku*, Setshuâna *koku*, Barotse n-*oku*, Bashubea n-*kobu*) 9. "fowl;"

n-*dshera* 9. "path" (§ 493, note);

m-*bua* (Banyeṅko, Batoka, Bashubea, and Bayeiye) 9. "dog" (§ 235 and 277);

o-n-*dshovo* (Kafir i-n-x́*lovu*, Setshuâna x́*lou*, Lourenzo Marques i-n-x́*lófo*, Sofala i-n-*dshóu*, Tette, Sena, and Makanga *dzou*, Quellimane *dóu*, Kisuâheli n-*dófu*, Kinika and Kipokomo n-*tsófu*, Kikámba n-*sóu*, Batoka n-*dshovo*, Borotse *dshovo* or n-*dobo*, Bashubea 9*ovo*, Otyihereró o-n-*dyou*, Kongo n-*zau*, Mpongwe n-*dshǎgu*, Dikele n-*dsháki* l., Isubu n-*dshoku*) 9. "elephant;"

o-n-*tavo* (Setshuâna *tau*, Lourenzo Marques i-n-*dão*, Batoka n-*daku*, Bashubea n-*tavo*) 9. "lion;"

o-n-*yati* (Setshuâna *nari*, Banyeṅko, Borotse, Bashubea, and Isubu n-*yati*, Balojazi h-*gati*, § 226, note) 9. "buffalo;"

i-n-*yene* (Zulu i-n-*nyoni*, Inhambane n-*yoni*, Kihiau *dshiúni*, Kikamba, Kinika, Kipokomo, and Kisuaheli n-*iúni*, Banyeṅko *eyunye*, Kongo *nuni*, Mpongwe n-*yǎni*, pl. in-*yǎni*) 9. "bird" (Dikele vi-*nǎni*, pl. la-*nǎni*, Benga i-*nǎni*, pl. lo-*nǎni*, Dualla i-*nun*, pl. bi-*nun*, Isubu i-*noni*, pl. lo-*noni*, Fernando Po si-*nodi*, pl. to-*nodi*);

m-*peo* (Setshuâna *pex́lo*, Bashubea and Batoka m-*bezo*, Zulu i-m-*bazo*, Tette *bāzo*, Sena *badzo*, Makua i-*bazo*, "an axe") 9. "an adze;"

e-n-*fera* (Banyeṅko m-*vula*, Bashubea n-*fula*, § 118) 9. "rain;"

i-n-*shoe* (Batōka and Bashubea i-n-*shue*) 9. "fish," pl. zin-*shue* 10.;

o-m-*vuvu* (Otyihereró o-n-*tvu*, § 494) 9. "hippopotamus;"

n-*tshu* or n-*dshu* (Kafir i-n-x́*lu*, Setshuâna n-x́*lu*, Tekeza i-n-x́*lo*, Banyeṅko n-*duo*, Borotse n-*do*, Bashubea n-θ*obo*, Balojazi and Bamaponda n-*dshobo*, Otyihereró o-n-*dyuo*, Sindonga o-n-*dshuo*, Angola and Kongo n-*zo*) 9. "house;"

ro-*reme* (Banyeṅko lo-*lime*, Borotse do-*leme*, Bashubea lo-*leme*, Maponda lo-*limi*, § 351) 11. "the tongue;"

lo-*aṅga* (Andersson's ro-*aṅga*) 11. "spear" (Balojazi and Baponda li-*oṅga* 5., Banyeṅko plur. ma-*oṅga* 6.);

ka-*kone* 13. "stick," pl. zin-*kone* 10. (Bashubea and Batoka lo-*kone*, Borotse lo-*konye* 11., § 348);

ka-*émbe* 13. "an axe" (Kafir i-*zembe* 5.);

o-ra (Otyihereró o-u-ra "entrails, intestines") 14. " belly ;"
ko-koa Borotse (Kafir u-ku-wa, Setshuána xo-oa, Lourenzo Marques i-k-ua, Tette and Sena kú-gua, Cape Delgado kú-bwa, Otyihereró o-ku-ua)

15. "to fall on the ground" (Kihiáu gŭa, Kipokomo gŏa, Kinika bŭa and gua, Kongo bua, Mpongwe, Dikele, and Isubu kwa, Dualla ko "fall"); ko-esha 15 "to roast."

dd. *The Bunda Genus.*

487. The languages of the South-western or Bunda Genus are distinguished by the use of the demonstrative particle *o-* as prefixed article. This article itself, in the Bunda Genus, is only slightly affected by the prefix which follows it; but the vowel of the derivative prefix of the noun has been, in more than one instance, assimilated to the vowel of the article; and the prefix may even adopt the latter vowel when used without the article. This is chiefly the case with the 10th prefix, of which the vowel *i* (supposed, as we shall see hereafter, to have descended from an original *a*) has been converted into *o* in most Bunda languages. In the case of this prefix (Otyihereró **9'on-**), and in those of the Otyihereró 16th (**po**), 17th (**ko-**), and 18th (**mo-**) prefixes, we are not sure whether it is a merely euphonic influence which has commuted the vowels of these prefixes, or whether we have to do here with demonstrative pronouns preceding nouns which have lost their original derivative prefixes, or, at least the main portion of them. Thus Otyihereró 9'on- might be really 9'-o-n-, the n- being in this case to be considered as the only remnant of the original derivative prefix, whilst the 9'- would be a pronominal element of the 10th class forming with the demonstrative particle *-o* a demonstrative pronoun. However, it must be remembered that this explanation is merely hypothetical, and I should prefer to ascribe the *-o* which is now found in these prefixes, to the force of euphonic assimilation which had moulded vowels, originally different, into likeness with the article which so frequently preceded them.

488. It may also be that the article *o-*, like the English article *the*, is only the remainder of an old demonstrative pronoun,* which originally had different forms agreeing with the various classes of nouns to which it referred. Admitting that the pronominal element may be reduced to a mere vowel (as we have seen it to be in Kafir),—such a vowel would be exceedingly liable to amalgamate with the demonstrative particle *o*. It may be that further investigations will afford historical proof of this combination; but until such proof has been found, it will be safer merely to consider this *o-* as a demonstrative particle used as an article.

489. In the Bunda Genus the article *o-* precedes nouns in similar circumstances to those in which the Kafir article is employed. The latter was, as we have seen, originally a pronominal element identical with the derivative prefix. (§ 461—464.) Usage must, upon the whole, determine in which instances this article is to be employed, and in which to be omitted, in the Bunda languages. As a general rule it may be stated that this *o-* in the Bunda Genus possesses more clearly the power of an article than the initial vowel which precedes the derivative prefixes in Kafir; and that it has far less become a part of the derivative prefix than is the case with the initial vowel in Kafir.

OTYIHERERO.

490. The *O-tyi-hereró* or Damara language (spoken by the *O-va-hereró* 2. and *O-va-mbandierú* 2.) is richer in classes of nouns than any other known Bâ-ntu language. Besides the sixteen classes which originally belonged to the Middle Branch languages, Otyihereró has two others which are apparently the individual property of

---

* Formed by the combination of a demonstrative particle with the pronominal element.

the language. It may be that the 17th (**ko-**) and 18th (**mo-**) classes are only later modifications of the 15th (**ku-**) and 3rd (**mu-**) classes respectively; for, the forms in *o* may have been originally demonstrative pronouns rather than true derivative prefixes. But at the present time, at all events, the 17th (**ko-**) and 18th (**mo-**) prefixes have—by certain distinct forms of concord in which they respectively differ from the 15th (**ku-**) and 3rd (**mu-**) classes,—gained the right to be considered as distinct classes; nor can it be denied that the **ko-** and **mo-** may originally have been distinct prefixes. It may, however, also be, that the vowel *o* of these prefixes is due to that process of assimilation of the vowel of the prefix to that of the article, which has been noticed in § 487, and which, as regards Otyihereró, appears to have permanently affected the forms of the prefixes of the 10th (**ɤ'on-**) and 16th (**po-**) classes.

491. It is remarkable that the 5th prefix (which originally must have had the form **RI-**) is always contracted in Otyihereró to **e-**, before which form the article *o-* disappears. The same contraction occurs in Sindonga (Ovambo) and Nano (Benguela), also in Angola and Kongo, although the two last-named old languages have retained in many cases the original form **ri-** (with the article, *o-***ri-** in Angola and *e-***ri** in Kongo).* In no other Otyihereró class is the prefix omitted, or as strongly contracted as in the 5th (**ri-**) class. In the 10th (**ɤ'on-**) class the two first letters of the prefix (**ɤ'o-**) are always retained in Otyihereró nouns, and the ending nasal only is modified. (§ 321.) The few plurals to singular nouns of the 14th (**u-**) class are all formed by placing the 6th (**ma-**) prefix before the full form with the 14th prefix **u-**, whilst the plurals of singular nouns of the 15th (**ku-**)

---

* It may, however, also be that the **e-** is a contraction of *o-***ri**, and not merely an abbreviation of **ri-**, and that the contracted form with the article (**e-**) superseded the form **ri-** without the article in Otyihereró and other languages.

class either substitute **ma-** for **ku-**, or add **ma-** to the form with **ku-**. (§ 454.)

492. With regard to nouns which indicate personal beings, they may be transferred from any class to the first, and may be used, either wholly or partly, with forms of concord of the 1st (**mu-**) class and in the plural of the 2nd (**va-**) class. The nouns indicating "father" and "mother" appear to have been originally treated as if of the 9th (**n-**) and 10th (**ȣ'on-**) classes, although the prefixual *n* does not appear in them, and they may not even have been originally formed with one of these prefixes. When transferred in the plural to the 2nd (**va-**) class they usually have **o-** as their prefix, which appears to be identical with the Kafir and Setshuâna prefix **bo-** used with the same nouns. (§ 466.) This derivation, at all events, appears more probable than that this Otyiherero plural prefix **o-** is derived from an original ȣ'o- of the 10th class, as Hahn seems to suggest.

493. The Missionaries who first learned and described this language are more positive with regard to the meaning which they ascribe to the derivative prefixes of the nouns, than any other observers of the peculiarities of the Bâ-ntu languages. Although some of their distinctions are fanciful, and others at least subject to numerous exceptions, it cannot be denied that in more than one instance they have given, if not the original meaning of the prefix, at least that which it now chiefly possesses in the language. What the Rev. C. H. Hahn thinks about the prefixes is to be found in his "Grammatik;" it may, however, be interesting to the student to hear what the Revd. J. RATH says upon the same subject in his Manuscript Vocabulary preserved in the Grey Library, and in order to state this in his own words, I shall give the German untranslated.

1. mu- (pl. **2. va-**). " Dieses Präfix hat nur der Mensch. Vor ein Verbum gesetzt, bezeichnet das dadurch gebildete Substantiv den oder die, welche die Handlung verrichten oder in dem Zustande sich befinden, welche im Verbum liegen." (MSS. p. 446.)

3. mu- (pl. **4. mi-**). "Die meisten Pflanzen haben dieses Präfix." (§ 428.) "Die damit vorhandenen abstracten Worte geben den Eindruck, dass der Begriff einer gewissen Vollständigkeit damit verbunden ist." (MSS. p. 446).

5. e- (pl. **6. ma-**). "Das Präfix **e-** findet sich häufig an solchen Gegenständen, welche nur in der Einzahl oder paarweise vorhanden sind: **e-**yuru Himmel; Nase" (vide § 494, list of Otyihereró nouns); "**e-**hi Erde; **e-**tambo Rücken; **e-**akoti Nacken, Genick; **e-**yo, o-**ma-**yo Zahn, Zähne, die beiden Reihen; **e-**ke, o-**ma-**ke Hand, Hände; **e-**punga, o-**ma-**punga Lunge, Lungen. Möglich, dass ersteres die Ursache ist, dass es auch abstract und anders für Gegenstände gebraucht wird, welche einzig in ihrer Art sind, sowohl im guten als bösen Sinn; und dass durch letzteres der Plural gewissermassen zum Dual wird. Steigbügel nennen die Damara o-**ma-**poha, und da sie diese erst nach der Ankunft der Europäer, oder doch nicht vor ihrer genauern Bekanntschaft mit den Namaqua kennen gelernt, so sollte man vermuthen, dass sie noch das Gefühl haben, **ma-**sei dass passende Präfix für paarweise existirende Sachen." (MSS. pp. 94 and 95.) *Vide* p. 165, note.

6. ma-. "Zu dem bei **e-** bemerkten, dass es nämlich häufig bei paarweise vorhandenen Gegenständen angewandt wird, lässt sich noch hinzufügen.

"*a.* Dass es oft mit Verbas verbunden wird um einen Ort anzuzeigen, wo eine derartige Handlung statt findet, z. B. o-**ma-**pambero" (Nath, pamba flechten; dicht zusammenkommen, vereinigen), "o-**ma-**ke-turiko" (Aufhängestelle, *turika* aufhängen), "o-**ma-**kondero" (Übergangstelle, Furth, *konda* übersetzen, übergehen), "&c. In diesem Falle ist das Präfix wahrscheinlich von o-**mo-**na 18. abgeleitet." (The last suggestion is very doubtful.)

"*b.* Bei Worten wie o-**ma-**indyombo, o-**ma-**yambe" (Verläumdung, *yamba* verläumden), "und derlei hängt das Präfix wahrscheinlich mit o-**ma-**mbo" (Worte) "zusammen, so dass solche Worte eigentlich bedeuten: Lügenworte, Verläumdungsworte." (§ 426.)

"*c.* Die meisten Sammelnamen haben dieses Präfix." (MSS. p. 421.)

7. tyi- (pl. **8. vi-**). "Für dieses Präfix passt am besten die Bezeichnung: 'sächlich.' Es findet seine Anwendung bei Werkzeugen, als *Dingen*, womit die in der Wurzel liegende Handlung bewirkt wird, oder die dazu verwandt werden, z. B. o-**tyi-**havero Sitzding" (Stuhl, Bank); "o-**tyi-**kamo Deckel; o-**tyi-**hupuro Spaten; von *havera*" (sitzen), "*kama*" (drücken, auswinden), "*hupura*" (graben). "In diesem Falle hängt das Präfix wohl mit o-**tyi-**na, Ding, zusammen." (§ 441.) "Auch auf andere Gegenstände, wie Menschen, &c., angewandt, werden diese zur blossen Sache erniedrigt, wie *o-tyi-mu-ndu* alter, unbrauchbarer Mensch" (§ 430), "*o-tyi-ñ-gombe* alter Ochs" (§ 226), "*o-tyi-ϑ'u* altes Schaf" (*o-n-tu* or *o-n-dϑ'u* 9. "sheep" = Kafir i-m-vu, Setshuâna ñ-ku). "Ausser dem zweifelhaften *o-tyi-angapara*" (Glück) "ist bis jetzt kein abstractes Wort mit diesem Präfix gefunden, das einen guten Begriff hat. Dasselbe gilt auch von dem Plural **vi-**, mit dem sich mehrere Worte finden, welche keinen Singular haben. In einigen wenigen Fällen kommt **tyi-** auch bei Platzeigennamen vor, wo es mit *o-tyi-roñgo*, Platz, zusammenhängt, und eigentlich Adjektiv ist." (MSS. pp. 554 and 555.)

9. ñ- (pl. **10. ϑ'on-**). "Die meisten Thiernamen haben dieses Präfix; die damit versehenen abstracten Worte haben vorwaltend einen guten Begriff." (MSS. p. 391.)

11. ru- (pl. **tu-**). "Die bis jetzt mit diesem Präfix aufgefundenen concreten Wörter geben den Eindruck, dass damit der Begriff der Länge, Höhe, Ausgestrecktheit und Ausgedehntheit, Dünne verbunden ist. Aehnliches zeigt sich auch bei den abstracten Wörtern, bei denen häufig der Begriff der Übertragung auf andere scheint statt zu finden. Vergleiche **e-***pondo*" (5. Bedächtigkeit, Langsamkeit, Gelassenheit, Geduld) "mit *o-ru-a-ponda*" (11., *u-n-o-ru-a-ponda*, wenn jemand sehr lange krank ist, ohne sich zu bessern; auch wenn ein Kind lange nicht ans Gehen kommt); "*e-ho-ϑ'e*" (5. Thräne) "mit *o-ru-hoϑ'e*" (11. Traurigkeit, Betrübniss; das Weinen); "*o-ndy-ira*" (9. Weg, Pfad) "mit *o-ru-ira*" (11. Fusspfad*); "*o-mu-tyira*" (3. Schwanz, &c.) "mit *o-ru-tyira*" (11. langer, dünn gestreckter Schwanz)", "*o-u-vara*" (14. Ansehen, Macht, Herrschaft über Dinge) "mit *o-ru-vara*"

---

* It appears to me, however, probable that the nouns *o-n-dyira* 9. "way, path" and *o-ru-ira* 11. "footpath" are formed from different stems. I identify the stem of the latter noun (*o-ru ira* 11.) with that of Zulu u-m-*zila* 3. "cattle track" = Setshuâna m-*ila* (i.e. **MO-BILA**) 3. "street," pl. me-*bila* 4. The former noun (*o-m-dyira* 9.) occurs in the same meaning as in Otyihereró and in forms varying only slightly, in almost all the South African Bâ-ntu languages: Kafir and Tekeza i-m-x́léla (Zulu pl. i-zim-x́léla 10.), Setshuâna *tsela* (pl. li-*tsela* 10.), Inhambane *dshílla*, Tette *dshíra*, Sena *shira*, Quellimane m-*díla*, Cape Delgado m-*shira*, Kisuáheli (Mombas) m-*día*, Swáheli (Zanzibar) and Kipokómo m-*dshía*, Kinika (e)u-*dshíra* (pl. [e]m-*dshíra* 10.), Kikámba m-*sia* (pl. u-*sia* 10.), Banyeñko m-ϑera (or m-*dshela*), Batoka m-*zela*, Bashubea m-*zera* (m-*zela*, or *tsera*), Bayeiye m-*dshera*, Borotse m-*dera* or m-*dela*, Balojazi and Baponda m-χela (Livingstone's ñgela), Otyihereró o-m-*dyira* (pl. o-ϑ'om-*dyira* 10.), Sindonga (Ovambo) *o-m-dyíla*, Nano (Benguela) *o-m-dyilla* (pl. o-ϑ'om-*dyilla* 10.), Angola *o-m-shila* (Cannecattim's *ngílla*, pl. *jingílla* 10.), Kongo m-*shílla* (Cann.), Dikele m-*zyeϑ'a* (pl. mim-n-*zyeϑ'a* 6.), Benga m-*dshea* (pl. m-*dshea* 10.), Dualla m-*gia* (pl. mim-n-*gia* 6.), Isubu m-*dshea* (pl. mim-n-*dshea* 6.).

(11. "Macht, Ansehen über andere Menschen, dabei kann mann aber arm an Gütern sein"). "Auch ist zu bemerken, dass Adverbia der Zeit, wie *a-ru-he* 'immer' mit diesem Präfix zusammenhangen; siehe *o-ru-ve*9'*e*" (11. Raum, Gegend, Stelle, Zeit). "Ebenso werden die Wiederholungszahlen damit gebildet; ru-*mue* einmal, tu-*vari* zweimal." (MSS. p. 525.)

13. ka- (pl. **14. u-**). *a.* "Verkleinerungs-Präfix, *o-***mu**-*ndu* (1.) Mensch, *o-***ka**-*ndu* Menschlein; *o-***n**-*tu* (9.) Schaf, *o-***ka**-9*'u* Schäflein; *o-***n**-*dyuo* (9.) Haus, *o-***ka**-*n-dyuo* Häuslein."

"*b.* Mit **ka**- werden abstracte Worte gebildet, welche in ihrer Art auch eine Verkleinerung ausdrücken; *o-***ka**-*nye* scheint kleiner Hass zu sein, von *nyeṅgua*" (passive Form mit activer und passiver Bedeutung, hassen, verachten); "*o-***ka**-9*'uva-tui* feines, scharfes, gutes Gehör" (9*'uva* hören, verstehen, *o-***ku**-*tui* 15. Ohr); "*o-***ka**-*tarera* wenn einer meint alles sehen zu müssen" (das Zusehen, von *tarera* aufpassen, sich vorsehen, die respective Form von *tara* sehen).

"*c.* Mit *ka*- beginnen im Otyihereró fast alle Eigennamen." (The proper names of persons formed with *ka*- do not however belong to the 14th [**ka**-], but to the 1st [**mu**-] class of nouns.) "Ob es das Anrede-Präfix ist? In einer Erzählung wird ein Fluss angeredet *ka-ndundu!*" (*o-***n**-*dundu* 9. mountain, hill.) "Hat es etwa Ähnlichkeit mit der deutschen Nachsilbe -*chen*, Fritz, Fritzchen? Bei einer Frage, warum ein Häuptling *Hukanun*, und nicht wie fast alle andern mit einem Namen genannt ist, der mit *ka*- beginnt, wurde geantwortet, er sei ja ein sehr angesehener Mann. Ganz richtig war die Antwort nicht, denn es gab mächtigere Häuptlinge, als dieser war, deren Namen mit *ka*- begannen. Vielleicht aber hat sich vom Sprachgefühl etwas in der Antwort ausgesprochen." (MSS. p. 405.)

14. u-. "Bei diesem Präfix lässt sich ein dreifacher Gebrauch unterscheiden.

"1. Ist es Plural-Präfix von **ka-**: *o-***ka**-*kambe*" (Pferd) "pl. *o-***u**-*kambe*; *o-***ka**-*ti*" (Stock) "pl. *o-***u**-*ti*;

"2. Bei einigen wenigen Worten ist es Singular-Präfix, und nimmt dann das Präfix **ma**- als Plural-Präfix an.

*o-***u**-*ta* (Bogen) "plur. *o-***ma**-*u-ta* (6.);

*o-***u**-*tuku* (Nacht) " 14. *o-***ma**-*u-tuku* (6.);

"3. Finden sich mit diesem Präfix verhältnissmässig die meisten abstracten Worte; und es ist nicht unmöglich, dass es sich dem grössten Theil der Wurzeln vorsetzen lässt, um ein Abstractum davon zu bilden." (MSS. p. 587.)

15. ku- (plur. **6. ma-**). "Präfix des Infinitiv. Bei manchen Worten bleibt die Silbe *ku*- auch im Plural, z. B. *o-***ku**-*ti*" (Feld, Land, Gegend) "pl. *o-***ma**-*kuti;* bei andern fällt sie aus, *o-***ku**-*rama*" (Bein, Englisch "leg") "pl. *o-***ma**-*rama*." (MSS. p. 415.)

OTYIHERERO PREFIXES.

SINGULAR.	PLURAL.
PERSONAL.	
1. o-mu-, o-o-m-, u- (—)	2. o-va-, o-o-o-v-, o-
3. o-mu-	4. o-mi-
5. e-	6. o-ma- o-me-
7. o-tyi- o-ty-	8. o-vi-
9. o-n- o-ṅ- o-m- o-	10. o-ɜ'on- o-ɜ'oṅ- o-ɜ'om- o-ɜ'o-
11. o-ru-	12. o-tu- 10. o-ɜ'on- o-ɜ'oṅ- o-ɜ'om- o-ɜ'o-
DIMINUTIVE.	
13. o-ka-	14. o-u-
ABSTRACT.	
14. o-u-	6. (+14.) o-ma-u-
INFINITIVE.	
15. o-ku- o-k-	6. o-ma- o-ma-ku-
LOCAL.	16. o-po-
	17. o-ko-
	18. o-mo-

494. As the Otyihereró forms of the derivative prefixes are not contracted when combined with the article *o-*, excepting in the 5th (**ri-**) class,—it appears superfluous to give more than the table of the prefixes with the article; for, the forms without articles can in all cases (excepting, of course, the 5th class) be arrived at, by merely eliding the *o-*. As regards the vocative, it is worthy of remark that not only the article, but even the derivative prefix is occasionally omitted in this case. The nasal of the prefixes of the 9th (**n-**) and 10th (**ɜ'on-**) classes falls off before stems beginning with *h* and *ɜ'* (*s*), as stated § 230; while in some other cases the nature of the initial consonant of the stem is in its turn affected by the nasal, as described in § 352.

OTYIHERERO NOUNS.

*o-***mu**-*kaɜ'e-ndu** 1. "wife," pl.
*o-***va**-*kaɜ'e-ndu* 2.;
*o-***mu**-*rume-ndu* 1. "man," pl.
*o-***va**-*rume-ndu* 2.;

* Vide note at the end of this paragraph.

o-m-a-tye (for *o-mu-na-tye*, Kihiau **m**-*ana-dshe*) 1. "child," pl. *o-v-ana-tye* (Kihiau **v**-*ana-dshe*) 2.;

o-m-irityimuke 1. "a presumptuous, audacious one," pl. *o-v-erityimuke* 2.;

o-mu-ini (Kafir u-**m**-*nini*) 1. "owner, possessor," pl. *o-v-eni* (Kafir a-**ba**-*nini*) 2.;

o-m-angu 1. "younger brother or sister," pl. *o-v-angu* 2.;

o-tate (Bunda *tata*) 9. and 1. "(my, our) father," pl. *o-o-tate* 2.;

o-mama (Zulu u-*mame*) 9. and 1. "(my, our) mother," pl. *o-o-mama* (Zulu o-*mame*) 2.;

u-nyoko (Kafir u-*nyoko*) 9. and 1. "(your) mother;"

ina (Kafir u-*nina*) 9. and 1. "(his, her, their) mother," pl. *o-o-ina* (Kafir o-*nina*) 2;

iƛo (Kafir u-*yiƛ̃lo*) 9. and 1. "(your) father;"

ihe (Kafir u-*yise*) 9. and 1. "(his, her, their) father," pl. *o-o-ihe* (Kafir o-*yise*) 2.;

o-mu-ti 3. "tree, plant, medicine," pl. *o-mi-ti* (§ 428);

o-mu-tima (Sena and Tette **mu**-*tima*, Makua **mu**-*rima*, Kihiau **m**-*tima*, Banyenko **mo**-*tima*, Sindonga *u-m-tima* "breath," Nano **u**-*tima*, Angola **mu**-*shima*, Kongo **mu**-*tima*, Mpongwe *o-rema*, Dikele *lema*, Dualla and Isubu **mo**-*lema*) 3. "heart," pl. *o-mi-tima* (Makua **mi**-*rima*, Nano *o-vi-tima*, Angola **mi**-*shima*, Kongo **mi**-*tima*, Dikele, Dualla, and Isubu **mi**-*lema*) 4.;

o-mu-eʒ'e* 3. "moon, month," pl. *o-mi-eʒ'e* 4.;

o-mu-ise (Zulu u-**mu**-*si*, Kafir u-**m**-*si*, Setshuâna **mō**-*si* or **mu**-*si*, Tekeza **mo**-*se*, Makua **mw**-*ishi*, Kiníka and Kipokómo **mo**-*ssi*, Kisuáheli **mó**-*shi*, Banyenko and Bayeiye **mu**-*si*, Batoka **m**-*busi*, Balojazi **mo**-*ezi*) 3. "smoke;"

o-mu-nue (Zulu u-**mu**-*nwe*, Kafir u-**m**-*nwe*, Tette **mu**-*nwe*, Barotse and Bayeiye **mo**-

---

* Sofala **mu**-*edzĕ*, Manika, Sena, Tette, Maravi, Anjoane, and Cape Delgado **mu**-*ézi* or **mu**-*eze*, Makua **mu**-*éri* or **mu**-*ere*, Kíkamba **mu**-*ti*, Kisuáheli, Kiníka, Kipokómo, and Kihiáu **m**-*ezi*, Batoka and Borotse **mo**-*ezi*, Bashubea **mo**-*edzi*, Sindonga *u*-**mu**-*ezi*, Mpongwe **o**-*gwĕli*, Dikele **mi**-*ĕli* ("moonlight"), Dualla **mo**-*ădi* (pl. **mi**-*ădi* 4.), Isubu **mw**-*eri* ('moonbeam, moonlight"). Compare also Seƛlapí *ƛxueri* 9. (pl. **li**-*ƛxueri* or *ƛxueri* 10.) or *ńgueri*, Sesuto *ƛƛ'ueli* 9. (pl. **li** *ƛƛ'ueli* 10.), Tekeza *uéte* 9., Angola *o-m-beshi* 9. "moon, month;" Kafir i-**m**-*kwe-n-kwezi* 9 and 10. "star and stars;" Kafir and Zulu i-*kwezi* 5. "morning-star;" Zulu a-**ma**-*kwezi-kwezi* 6. "bright stripes." The original Kafir noun for "moon" (which may be presumed to have been I-N-*KWEZI* 9.) seems to have disappeared early, perhaps in consequence of the custom of "u **lu**-*ƛlonipa*" 15. (Ayliff's Vocabulary p. vi), and the corresponding Hottentot word for this venerated object may have been introduced into Kafir by the captured Hottentot women. (*Vide* § 472 note, and *Cape Monthly Magazine*, vol. I. April 1857, p. 203.)

nwe, Sindonga u-m-nwe, Mpongwe om-enlo, Dualla and Isubu mu-ne) 3. "finger, toe," pl. o-mi-nwe Sindonga (Kafir i-mi-nwe, Tette mi-nwe, Banyeńko me-nwe, Batoka mi-noe, Bashubea mi-nwe, Balojazi mi-nye, Maponda me-nye, Dikele mi-na, Dualla and Isubu mi-ne) 4.;

o-mu-na 3. "lip," pl. o-mi-na 4. (o-mu-na 1. = Zulu u-mu-ntw-ana 1. "child," vide note at the end of this paragraph);

o-mu-ko 3. "bowstring," pl. o-mi-ko 4.;

o-mu-ruṅgu 3. "face," pl. o-mi-ruṅgu 4.;

e-mu-tyira (Kafir u-m-sila) 3. "tail," pl. o-mi-tyira 4.;

e-yuva (Sofala and Tette zuva, Sena dzuwa, Maravi dzúa, Makua in-zún, Kikámba, Kisuáheli, and Anjoane dıhwa, Kiníka tsua, Batoka le-zuva, Banyeńko li-oua, Borotse le-shoba, Bayeiye li-va, Sindonga e-úya, Dikele di-oba) 5. "sun, day," pl. o-ma-yuva 6.;

e-ɜ'uko or e-ruko (Kafir i-ziko) 5. "fireplace," pl. o-ma-ɜ'uko 6.;

e-teteoe (Zulu i-titikoya) 5. "peewit," pl. o-ma-teteoe 6.;

e-vere (Zulu i-bele) 5. "female breast," pl. o-ma-vere 6. (p. 164, note);

e-uru (Banyeńko and Borotse li-olo, Balojazi li-yolo, Maponda le-olo, Bashubea i-tholo, Sindonga e-yulu, Angola ri-zúlo) 5. "nose," pl. o-ma-uru 6.;

e-yuru (Kafir i-zulu, Banyeńko li-olo, Batoka le-dıkuru, Borotse li-uilo, Bashubea li-ulo, Balojazi lilo, Bayeiye liru or lıru, Sindonga e-úlu, Angola 6-ulu or o-ri-éulu) 5. "heaven, sky," pl. o-ma-yuru (Angola o-má-ulu) 6.;

e-tupa (Tette and Sena fúpa, Makua ni-kuva) 5 "bone," pl. o-ma-tupa (Tette and Sena ma-fúpa, Makua ma-kuva) 6.;

e-tha (Kafir i-li-fa) 5. "inheritance, property left by one deceased," pl. o-ma-tha 6. (from o-ku-tha 15. "to die," § 482, note);

e-ṅga (Sindonga e-onga) 5. "assagay," pl. o-ma-ṅga 6;

e-rumbi 5. and 1. "brother," pl. o-ma-rumbi 6. and 2. (§ 466, note);

e-ke (or e-rie) 5. "hand," pl. o-ma-ke 6.;

e-pia 5. "gum, resin," pl. o-ma-pia 6.;

e-raka (Sindonga e-laka) 5. "tongue, language," pl. o-ma-raka 6.;

e-kaɜ'e-ndu 5. and 1. "very tall woman," pl. o-ma-kaɜ'e-ndu 6. (vide note at the end of this paragraph);

o-me-va (MA-NDIBA, p. 142, first note) 6. "water;"

o-ma-hakiɜ'e 6. "sour milk, shaken in the calabash;"

o-ma-henda 6. "thick milk;"

o-ma-iki or o-ma-iɜ'i 6. "sweet milk;"

o-ma-kande 6. "thick milk;"

o-ma-torero 6. "last bad milk, before a cow dries up;"

o-**ma**-*tuka* 6. "buttermilk;"

o-**ma**-*yere* or *o*-**ma**-*ire* (Sindonga *o*-**má**-*le*) 6. "sour milk;"

o-**ma**-*eve* 6. "a sort of boochoo;"

o-**ma**-*hoϑ'e* (Kiníka **ma**-*tsori*, p. 187) 6. "tears;"

o-**ma**-*kaya* (Sindonga *o*-**ma**-*káya*) 6. "tobacco;"

o-**ma**-*ṅgeka* 6. "wild hemp;"

o-**ma**-*ni* 6. "honey which sticks to one's body;"

o-**ma**-*nina* 6. "mucus from the nose;"

o-**ma**-*nyenya* 6. "Scotch mist, misty rain;"

o-**ma**-*nyune* 6. "soup;"

o-**ma**-*pupe* 6. "running water;"

o-**ma**-*te* 6. "saliva;"

o-**ma**-*ϑ'e* 6. "melted fat;"

o-**ma**-*ϑ'a* (Kafir a-**ma**-*nx̱la*, Setshuâna **ma**-*x̱la* "power") 6. "marrow, strength, power;"

o-**tyi**-*na* 7. "thing," pl. *o*-**vi**-*na* 8.;

o-**tyi**-*nyo* 7. "mouth," pl. *o*-**vi**-*nyo* 8.;

o-**tyi**-*pa* (Zulu i-**si**-pa) 7. "branch," pl. *o*-**vi**-*pa* (Zulu i-**zi**-pa) 8. (Otyihereró *o*-**ru**-*pa* 11. "branch," Zulu u-**mu**-*pa* 3. "stalk of maize with cob");

o-**tyi**-*vere* (Zulu i-**si**-*bele* "man's nipple") 7. "large female breast," pl. *o*-**vi**-*vere* 8. (p. 164, note);

o-**tyi**-*ϑ'ire* (Kafir i-**si**-*tunzi*) 7. "shadow of man, &c.," pl. *o*-**vi**-*ϑ'ire* 8. (Otyihereró *o*-**mu**-*ϑ'ire* = Kafir u-**m**-*tunzi*, Setshuâna **mo**-*ruti* or **mo**-*roti*, 3. "shadow of a tree, &c.;" Kafir i-*tunzi* 5. "shadow of a cloud, &c.");

o-**ty**-*oϑ'e* 7. "the Pleiades;"

o-**ty**-*unda* 7. "fence," pl. *o*-**vi**-*o-ty*-*unda* 8.;

o-**tyi**-*rongo* (Sindonga *o*-**shi**-*lóngo*) 7. "place," pl. *o*-**vi**-*roṅgo* (Sindonga *o*-**i**-*longo*) 8.;

o-**tyi**-*vava* 7. "wing," pl. *o*-**vi**-*vava* 8. (§ 360);

o-**tyi**-*n*-*dyuo* 7. "old house" (*o*-**n**-*dyuo*, Kafir i-**n**-*x̱lu* 9. "house");

o-**tyi**-*ṅ*-*gaϑ'e* 7. "old woman;"

o-**ṅ**-*gaϑ'e* 9. "a female," pl. *o*-**ϑ'oṅ**-*gaϑ'e* 10. (*vide* note at the end of this paragraph);

o-**n**-*tuu* (Kafir i-**m**-*vubu*, Setshuâna *kx̱ubu* or *kubu*, Lourenzo Marques in-*fúvo*, Inhambane im-*vúo*, Sofala **m**-*vúo*, Sena **m**-*vu*, Tette *vû*, Kipokómo un-*guu*, Banyeṅko **n**-*ru*, Barotse **m**-*bo*, Bashubea **n**-*vuvu*, Bayeiye *o*-**n**-*vuvu*, Balojazi *govo*, Batoka **n**-*tshoko*, Mpongwe **n**-*guŭ*, Dikele **n**-*gubi*, Dualla and Isubu **n**-*gubu*) 9. "hippopotamus," pl. *o*-**ϑ'on**-*tuu* 10.;

o-**n**-*ya* 9. "horn," pl. *o*-**ϑ'on**-*ya* 10. (§ 472);

o-**ṅ**-*gaṅga* (Kafir i-**n**-*nyangá*, Setshuâna *ṅaka*, Inhambane in-*yaṅga*, Sena, Banyeṅko, Batoka, Borotse, and Bayeiye **ṅ**-*gaṅga*, Nano *o*-**ṅ**-*gaṅga*) 9. "doctor," pl. *o*-**ϑ'oṅ**-*gaṅga* 10. (Kisuáheli, Kiníka, Kihiau **m**-*gaṅga*, Mpongwe **o**-*gaṅga*, Dikele *nga* 1.; Isubu **mo**-*tu* a *ṅgaṅga* 1., pl. **ba**-*tu* ba *ṅgaṅga* 2.);

o-n-dyuo (Bayelye **n**-*tshu* or **n**-*dshu*, § 486) 9. "house," pl. *o*-**ʒ'on**-*dyuo* (Kafir i-**zin**-*ślu*, Angola *o*-**shin**-*zo*) 10.;

o-m-bua 9. "dog," pl. *o*-**ʒ'om**-*bua* 10. (§§ 235 and 277);

o-honi (Kafir i-**n**-*śloni*) 9. "shame" (*o*-**ku**-*honipara* = Kafir u-**ku**-*ślonipa* 15. "to be ashamed");

o-**ʒ'on**-*dyeru* (Kafir i-**zin**-*devu*) 10. "whiskers;"

o-**ru**-*kune* (Kafir u-*kuni*, Sindonga *o*-**ru**-*kuni*) 11. "large piece of firewood," pl. *o*-**ʒ'on**-*gune* (Kafir i-**n**-*kuni*) 10. (§ 348);

o-**ru**-*roto* 11. "dream," pl. *o*-**tu**-*roto* 12.;

o-**ru**-*tuo* (Angola **lu**-*to*, § 497) 11. "spoon," pl. *o*-**tu**-*tuo* 12. (pp. 145 and 177);

o-**ru**-*u* 11. "reed," pl *o*-**tu**-*u* 12.;

o-**ru**-*tenda* 11. "long thin iron chain," pl. *o*-**tu**-*tenda* 12. (*o*-**tyi**-*tenda* 7. "iron, metal");

o-**ru**-*vio* 11. "knife, lot," pl. *o*-**tu**-*vio* 12.;

o-**ka**-*ti* 13. "stick," pl. *o*-**u**-*ti* 14. (§ 428);

o-**ka**-*na*-*tye* 13. "little child," pl. *o*-**u**-*na*-*tye* 14. (*o*-**m**-*a*-*tye* 1. child," pl. *o*-**v**-*ana*-*tye* 2.);

o-**ka**-**ʒ'***era* 13. "little bird," pl. *o*-**u**-**ʒ'***era* 14. (*o*-**n**-*dʒ'era* or *o*-**n**-*tera* 9. "bird");

o-**ka**-*puka* 13. "little animal," pl. *o*-**u**-*puka* 14. (*o*-**tyi**-*puka* 7. "game");

o-**u**-*tuku* 14. "night," pl. *o*-**ma**-*u*-*tuku* 6 (§ 453, notes);

o-**u**-*ta* (Sindonga) 14. "bow," pl. *o*-**ma**-*u*-*ta* 6. (§ 496);

o-**u**-*vi* (Kafir u-**bu**-*bi*) 14. "evil;"

o-**u**-*re* (Kafir u-**bu**-*de*) 14. "length, depth, height" (§ 362);

o-**u**-*tyi* (Kafir u-**bu**-*si*) 14. "honey;"

o-**u**-*ye* 14. "world, land;"

o-**u**-*pe* (Kafir u-**bu**-*tsha*) 14. "youth, state of freshness, newness" (§ 177);

o-**ku**-*ti* (Sindonga *o*-**kú**-*ti*) 15. "field," pl. *o*-**ma**-*kuti* 6.;

o-**ku**-*tui* 15. (Sindonga *o*-**ko**-*tshui*) "ear," pl. *o*-**ma**-*tui* (Sindonga *o*-**ma**-*ko*-*tshui*) 6. (§ 434, note);

o-**ku**-*rama* (Sindonga *o*-**ku**-*lama*) 15. "leg," pl. *o*-**ma**-*rama* 6.;

o-**ku**-*oko* (Sindonga *o*-**ku**-*éko*) 15. "arm," pl. *o*-**ma**-*uko* (Sindonga *o*-**ma**-*eko*) 6.;

o-**ku**-*iya* (Sindonga *o*-**ku**-*édsha*) 15. "thorn," pl. *o*-**ma**-*ku*-*iya* (Sindonga *o*-**ma**-*ku*-*edsha*) 6.;

o-**ku**-*ara* 15. "floor;"

o-**ku**-*roro* 15. "autumn, rainy season;"

o-**ku**-*ni* 15. "spring;"

o-**ku**-*pepera* 15. "winter;"

o-**ku**-*ruo* 15. "altar;"

o-**ku**-*ha* 15. "opinion;"

o-**ku**-*lua* (Kafir u-**ku**-*lwa*) 15. "quarrel;"

o-**po**-*na* 16. "place;"

o-**ko**-*na* 17. "a distant place;"

o-**mo**-*nu* 18. "place where one is."

OMUKAϑ'ENDU, OVAKAϑ'ENDU, &c.

[Note to p. 203.]

The Otyihereró noun o-**mu**-*kaϑ'e*-*ndu* 1. is composed of the stem -*kaϑ'e** and the noun o-**mu**-*ndu* 1. "man, person, human being." The latter noun is met with in almost all South African Bâ-ntu languages; and, in fact, the name of this family of languages is the plural form of the identical Kafir noun **mu**-*ntu*. The terms u-**mu**-*ntu* and a-**ba**-*ntu*, and the corresponding words in the kindred languages, are frequently used in the restricted sense of indicating the black inhabitants only,—in contradistinction to the Europeans, Arabs, Hottentots, and Bushmen, to whom the word a-**ba**-*ntu* only applies in a wider sense. We may consider the most original forms of this noun to be those used in Zulu and Kafir (u-**mu**-*ntu* or u-**m**-*ntu* 1., pl. a-**ba**-*ntu* 2.), Sofala (pl. **va**-*ntu* 2.), Sena and Tette (**mû**-*nttu* or **mu**-*ntto* 1., pl. **va**-*nttu* or **va**-*ntto* 2.), Quellimane (**mu**-*ntu* 1., pl. **a**-*ntu* 2.), Maravi (**mu**-*ntu* 1., pl. **wa**-*nthu* 2.), Kisambala and Kipokómo (**mu**-*ntu* 1., pl. **wa**-*ntu* 2.), Batoka (**mo**-*ntu* 1.), Bashubea (**mo**-*nto* 1.), Sindonga or Ovambo (u-**m**-*tu* 1., pl. o-**a**-*ntu* 2.), and Kongo (o-**mu**-*ntu* 1., pl. o-**a**-*ntu* 2.). The *nt* of the stem has become *nd* in Kikámba (**mu**-*ndu* 1., pl. **a**-*ndu* 2.), Kihiáu (**mu**-*ndu* 1., pl. **wá**-*ndu* 2.), Anjoane (**mu**-*ndu* 1.), and Otyihereró (o-**mu**-*ndu* 1., pl. o-**va**-*ndu* 2.). The nasal of the *nt* has been lost (with or without subsequent aspiration of the *t*) in Setshuâna (**mo**-*thu* 1., pl. **ba**-*thu* 2.), Inhambane (**mu**-*tu* 1.), Quellimane (**mú**-*ttu* 1., pl. **á**-*ttu* 2.), Kinika (**mu**-*tu* 1., pl. **a**-*tu* 2.), Suábeli (**m**-*tu* 1., pl. **wa**-*tu* 2.), Angola (o-**mu**-*tu* 1., pl. o-**a**-*tu* 2.), Benga (**mo**-*to* 1., pl. **ba**-*to* 2.), Dualla and Isubu (**mo**-*tu* 1., pl. **ba**-*tu* 2.). A palatalisation of the *t* has produced such forms as we find used in Dikele (**mu**-*tyī* 1., pl. **bo**-*tyī* 2.) and in Fernando Po (**bo**-*tshu* 1., pl. **bu**-*tshu* 2.). Finally the nasal of the stem (*n*) has prevailed over the *t* in Tekeza (**mu**-*no* or **mû**-*nu* 1., pl. **vâ**-*nu* or **ba**-*nu* 2.), Barotse and Balojazi (**mo**-*nu* 1.), Banyeñko and Baponda (**mo**-*no* 1.), and in the Nano language of Benguela (o-**mu**-*no* 1., pl. o-**ma**-*no* 2.). *Vide* §§ 140, 141, 412, 426. The diminutive which is formed from the stem **mu**-*ntu* (&c.) is subject to various and very strong contractions. Even in Zulu, the unabbreviated form u-**mu**-*ntw-ana* 1. "child, prince" (pl. a-**ba**-*ntw-ana* 2.) is chiefly used when speaking of royal children, and has thus become almost synonymous with the Spanish *infante* and *infanta*. When applied to common children, u-**mu**-*ntw-ana* is abbreviated to u-**m**-*twana* or u-**m**-*tana*, and even to u-**m**-*ta*. In the Mosambique

---

* Compare o-**n**-*gaϑ'e* 9. "female," and ϑ-*kaϑ'e* 5. "tendency of a woman to produce none but female offspring,"—ϑ-*rume* 5. indicating the tendency of bringing forth boys only.

Genus the same diminutive noun passes through various stages of abbreviation, such as *muana*, *mua*, &c., and in Lourenzo Marques *wana* (Matonga *wuana*, Man/olosi u-*nuana*) 1. "child" appears to be contracted to *wa*. The Setshuâna form of this noun is ñ*uana* 1. (pl. **b**-*ana* 2.), and in the Middle Branch languages it is generally **mu**-*ana* 1., as in Inhambane, Tette, Sena (pl. **w**-*âna* 2.), Makua, Cape Delgado, Batoka, and Kongo (pl. *ana* 2.),—or **m**-*ána* 1., as in Kipokómo, Kinika (pl. *ana* 2.), and Kisuaheli (pl. **w**-*ana* 2.). Other variations of this noun in the Middle Branch are Sindonga u-**m**-*nona* 1., Angola **mo**-*na* 1. (pl. **a**-*na* 2.), and Mpongwe **o**-*nwana* 1. (pl. **a**-*nwana* 2.). The North-western Branch has **mw**-*ana* 1. in Benga and Isubu, **mi**-*ana* or **m**-*ana* 1. in Dikele, and **mu**-*na* in Dualla,—with the plural form **b**-*ana* 2. in all these dialects. From the same stem, with an affix, is derived the Kihiáu **m**-*ana-dshe* 1. "child" (pl **v**-*ana-dshe* 2.), and also the identical Otyihereró noun o-**m**-*a-tye* 1. (pl. o-**v**-*ana-tye* 2.), whence the diminutive o-**ka**-*na-tye* 13. "little child," with which we may compare the Kikamba diminutive (without the affix) **k**-*ana* 13. "child" (pl. **tu**-*ana* 12.).

The stem -*kaṣ'e*, which occupies in the Otyihereró word o-**mu**-*kaṣ'e-ndu*, as well as in others, a position in the middle of the word, is in other languages frequently used as a suffix for the purpose of indicating the female sex. As such, it has in Kafir the form -*kazi*, in Sesuto -*k'ali* (-*gali*), in Sexlapi -χ*ari* (-*gari*), &c. Nouns of the 1st and 2nd classes are formed from this stem by the mere addition of the derivative prefixes of these classes, as Tette and Sena **mu**-*kâzi* 1. (pl. **va**-*kâzi* and **a**-*kâzi* 2.), Bayeiye **mo**-*kazi* 1., Borotse **mo**-*kati* 1., Banyenko **mo**-*kathi* 1., Cape Delgado **mú**-*ka* 1., Kikámba **mu**-*ka* 1. (pl. **a**-*ka* 2.), Kipokómo **mu**-*ke* 1., Kisuáheli **m**-*ke* 1. (pl. **a**-*ke* 2.), Kiníka **mu**-*dshe* 1. (pl. **a**-*dshe* 2.), Setshuâna **mo**-χ*ats'*- 1., Kafir u-**m**-*ka* 1. (pl. o-**m**-*ka* 2.). This last may be a contracted form of u-**MU**-*KAZI ka*-, or u-**m**-*fazi ka*- (wife of-); for, the original *k* in this noun has been softened to *f* in the Kafir and Zulu pronunciation, and we thus have in these languages u-**m**-*fazi* 1. "woman" (pl. a-**ba**-*fazi* 2.; Zulu i-**si**-*faz-ana* 7. "collection of females, womankind"). The original *k* is still preserved in the Kafir diminutive i-**n**-*kaz-ana* 9. "young woman" (pl. a-**ma**-*n-kaz-ana* 6.; i-**si**-*n-kaz-ana* 7. "genitalia muliebria"). Still greater is the change in the Setshuâna form **mo**-*sari* (Sesuto **mo**-*sali*) 1. "woman," pl. **ba**-*sari* (Sesuto **ba**-*sali*) 2. (**se**-*sari* 7. "womankind," kχosi e-a **se**-*sari* 9. "a female king," i.e. a queen; *tsari* 9. "female of animals"). The Tekeza forms *fati** and -*sate*†

---

* The Ma-n/olosi use the noun *fati* for the Kafir u-**m**-*fazi*.

† The suffix -*sate* seems to correspond in the dialects of the Matonga and Maχloenga to the Kafir suffix -*kazi* = Man/olosi -*kati*.

appear to connect the above Setshuâna nouns with the others, notwithstanding the great change of *k* to *s* which this identification presupposes. However, I cannot yet consider it as fully proved that the above Setshuâna forms are derived from the same root.

The compound noun for "woman" (which has in Otyihereró the form *o-***mu**-*kaϑ'e-ndu*) occurs in most of the Western members of the South African Division of Bántu languages. In some of these languages the compound form only is met with, whilst in others we also find the more simple form, which is identical with Tette and Sena **mu**-*kázi* 1. "wife, woman" (pl. **va**-*kazi* 2.). In almost all these languages the compound form is more or less strongly contracted, sometimes so greatly as to cause the middle portion of the noun (which corresponds to Otyihereró -*kaϑ'e*, = Kafir -*kazi*) to disappear; and in consequence of this contraction, the Dualla form for *o-***mu**-*kaϑ'e-ndu* (which is **mu**-*tu* 1., pl. **b**-*i-tu* 2.) differs little in appearance from the Dualla noun **mo**-*tu* 1. (pl. **ba**-*tu* 2.), which is identical with Zulu u-**mu**-*ntu* 1. (pl. a-**ba**-*ntu* 2.). The following table exhibits the forms which correspond in the different Western languages to Otyihereró *o-***mu**-*kaϑ'e-ndu* 1. (woman), *o-***va**-*kaϑ'e-ndu* 2. (women), *o-***mu**-*ndu* 1. (man, person), and *o-***va**-*ndu* 2. (people), and to Tette **mu**-*kázi* 1. (wife), and **va**-*kázi* 2. (wives).

Languages.	WIFE (WOMAN) 1.	WIVES (WOMEN) 2.	WOMAN (WIFE) 1.	WOMEN (WIVES) 2.	MAN (PERSON) 1.	PEOPLE 2.	Authorities.
TETE.........	mu-kázi...	va-kázi......	....	....	mú-ntu...	vá-ntu...	Peters.
OTYIHERERÓ..	....	....	o-mu-kaɜ'e-ndu	o-va-kaɜ'e-ndu	o-mu-ndu	o-va-ndu	Rath.
SINDONGA...	....	....	u-m-ke-ntu...	....	u-m-tu...	o-a-ntu...	Hahn.
BALOJAZI	....	....	mo-ke-no ...	....	mo-nu ...	....	Livingstone.
ANGOLA....... {	mu-káshi...	....	mu-hái-tu...	a-hái-tu......	o-mu-tu...	o-a-tu......	Dias.
	....	....	mu-χa-tu	a-χa-tu	....	....	Canncoattim.
	....	....	mu-χe-tu	a-χe-tu	....	....	Hahn.
MONGO.........	....	....	mu-ke-ntu	a-ke-ntu	o-mu-ntu..	o-a-ntu...	Vetralla.
MPONGWE.....	....	....	om-a-nto	a-nto	....	....	Wilson.
DIKELE.........	ml-ali (3.).	(ml-ali 4.)	mu-a-ddsho...	....	mu-tyî...	bo-tyî...	Preston & Best.
BENGA.........	mw-adi	....	mu-tu...	b-i-tu	mo-lo......	ba-lo	Mackey.
DUALLA.......	(m-odi 3.)..	(ml-odi 4.)..	mu-ai-tu...	b-ai-tu	mo-tu	ba-tu	Saker.
ISUBU	(mw-ariɜ.)	b-ari (ml-ari 4.)	mu-ai-tu	b-ai-tu	mo-tu	ba-tu	Merrick.
FERNANDO PO.	bw-adi.....	b-adi	bw-ai-su	b-ai-su	bo-tshu...	bu-tshu...	Clarke.

SINDONGA PREFIXES.

SINGULAR.	PLURAL.
PERSONAL.	
1. u-mu-, mu- u-m- u-, (—)	**2.** o-a-, a-
3. u-mu-, o-mu- u-m-	**4.** o-mi-
5. e-	**6.** o-ma-
7. o-shi- o-sh-	**8.** o-vi- o-i-, i- **6.** o-ma-
9. o-n- o-ń- o-m- o-	**10.** o-n- o-ń- o-m- o-ɜ'o-
11. o-ru- o-lu-	**12.** o-tu- **10.** o-n-
DIMINUTIVE. **13.** o-ka-	
ABSTRACT. **14.** o-u-	
INFINITIVE. **15.** o-ku- o-ko-	**6.** (+ 15.) o-ma-ku- o-ma-ko- o-ma-

SINDONGA.

495. Sindonga, or the language of the O-va-*mbo* (2.),* differs but little from Otyihereró in the forms of the prefixes. In Sindonga the 10th prefix generally appears in a contracted form, in which it is identical with the 9th. Nouns of the 9th (n-) class, therefore, have for their plurals (of the 10th class) the same form as the singular. Plurals corresponding to singular nouns of the 13th (ka-) and 14th (u-) classes are not met with in the specimens of the Sindonga language in our possession. These are contained in a manuscript vocabulary, presented to the Grey Library by the Rev. C. H. HAHN. The following list of nouns taken from

* Mr. Palgrave informs me that there are between the Cunene river and the 18th degree of South Latitude about fourteen tribes, distinct from each other, although preserving to an unusual extent similar characteristics. Of these, five speak Sindonga, viz. the O-va-*mbo* of O-m-*donga*, the O-va-*kua-mbi* (Chief *Nayuma*), O-va-*kua-n-dshera* (late Chief *Tshipaka*), O-va-*nguaruiɜ'e* or O-karuɜ'e (Chief *Tshikongo*), and *Okorongaɜ'e* (no Chief).

this vocabulary has been revised by Wm. Coates Palgrave Esq., whose emendations are distinguished by the letter "P." As we find that most of the nouns are given *with* the article, we have placed the few forms of the prefixes which occur without it in the same table.

SINDONGA NOUNS.

ú-**m**-*tu* 1. "man, person," pl. *o*-**á**-*ntu* 2. (p. 208);

u-**m**-*ké-ntu* 1. "woman" (p. 211);

u-**mu**-*hungú* 1. "married man," pl. **a**-*hungu* 2.;

u-**m**-*píka* (Bayeiye **mo**-*via*, § 486) 1. "servant," pl. **a**-*pika* (Angola **a**-*bika*) 2.;

u-**mu**-*máti* or *u*-*máti* 1. "young unmarried man, youth, boy," pl. **a**-*máti* 2.;

u-**m**-*samáni* 1. "old man;"

u-**m**-*nóna* (Zulu u-**mu**-*ntwana*, p. 209) 1. "child;"

u-**m**-*kaϑ'ona* (Otyihereró *o*-**mu**-*kaϑ'ona*) 1. "girl;"

u-**m**-*fúko* (Otyihereró *o*-**mu**-*ϑ'uko*) 1. "young woman;"

u-**m**-*kulú-ndu* 1. "eldest brother" (compare Kafir u-**m**-*kulu-we*, Setshuâna **mo**-*xolu* 1. "elder brother");

o-**mu**-*ϑ'ióna* (Otyihereró) "poor man;"

u-**m**-*lumbu* (Kafir u-**m**-*lungu?*) 1. "white man;"

u-*mburusháta* 1. "a Portuguese," pl. **a**-*mburushata* 2.;

u-**m**-*rúϑ'i* 1. "black man;"

mu-*ini* (Otyihereró *o*-**mu**-*ini*) 1. "owner;"

ú-*mua* 1. "king;"

u-**m**-*kaníloa* 1. "king;"

u-**m**-*ϑ'ίϑ'i* 1. "God;"

kalúnga 1. "God;"

o-**mu**-*ϑ'íma* 3. "fountain," pl. *o*-**mi**-*ϑ'íma* 4.;

ú-**m**-*ti* 3. "tree" (§ 428);

u-**m**-*shila* (Kafir u-**m**-*sila*, Tette **mu**-*shira*, Quellimane **mw**-*ira*, Kihiáu **m**-*dshiru*, Kipokómo **mu**-*dshía*, Kinika **m**-*kíra*, Suáheli **m**-*kía*, Otyihereró *o*-**mu**-*tyira*, Angola **mu**-*kíla*) 3. "tail;"

u-**m**-*lilo* (Otyihereró *o*-**mu**-*riro*, § 344) 3. "fire;"

u-**m**-*lúnga* (Otyihereró *o*-**mu**-*ruṅga*) 3. "palm-tree;"

u-**m**-*lúngu* (Otyihereró *o*-**mu**-*ruṅgu*) 3. "face;"

u-**mu**-*éle* or *o*-**mu**-*eϑ'e* (*u*-**m**-*ěrě* P.) 3. "dagger, knife;"

c-**mu**-*χo*, *o*-**mu**-*ho*, or *o*-**mu**-*sho* (Otyihereró *o*-**mu**-*ho*) 3. "calf of leg;"

o-**mu**-*énge* 3. "sugar-cane;"

u-**m**-*ténya* 3. "day;"

ú-**m**-*tsē̃* (Benguela **u**-*tue*, Kikamba **mú**-*tue*, p. 185) 3. "head;"

o-**mu**-*ϑ'ímba* (Kafir u-**m**-*zimba* "body") 3. "dead body;"

u-**m**-*ϑ'iré* (Kafir u-**m**-*tunzi*, Otyihereró *o*-**mu**-*ϑ'ire*, p. 206) 3. "shadow;"

u-**m**-*tara* 3. "bellows;"

o-**mu**-*fϑ'i* 3. "grass;"

u-**m**-*tóko* 3. and *ú*-**m**-*te* 3. "ashes;"

ú-**m**-*ϑ'ia* 3. "giraffe acacia;"

e-*shendyo* 5. "tooth," pl. o-**ma**-*shendyo* 6. (Kafir i-*zinyo* 5., pl. a-**m**-*enyo* 6., § 326);

e-*témo* 5. "a pick," pl. o-**ma**-*temo* 6.;

ó-*yi* (e-*we* P., Otyihereró e-*i*) 5. "egg," pl. o-**ma**-*yi* 6.;

e-*kakara* 5. "large eatable lizard," pl. o-**ma**-*kakara* 6.;

e-*káχa* (Nano e-*ka*, Otyihereró e-*ke*) 5. "hand" (also o-**shi**-*kaχa* 7.), pl. o-**ma**-*kaχa* (Nano o-**va**-*ka*) 6.;

e-*hínga* or e-*shínga* 5. "leopard," pl. o-**ma**-*hínga* or o-**ma**-*shínga* 6.;

e-*óka* (Kihiáu **li**-*oka* or **ri**-*dshóka*) 5. "snake," pl. o-**ma**-*yoka* 6. (Otyihereró o-**n**-*yoka* 9.);

e-ϑ'*ína* (= e-*zína*, not e-ϑ'*ina* = e-*sina*, as stated wrongly § 484, note) 5. "name;"

e-*pepé* 5. "shoulder;"

e-*tángo* 5. "sun;"

ó-*u* 5. "seed of sugar-cane;"

e-*ténga* 5. "a bamboos (vessel for milking);"

é-*pia* (Nano) 5. "garden, field;"

e-*kúya* (Otyihereró e-*kuva*) 5. "hatchet;"

ó-*sho* (e-*ho* P.) 5. "eye" (§ 327);

e-*úmbo* 5. "kraal" (Otyihereró o-**ru**-*mbo* 11.);

ó-*la* 5. "belly;"

ó-*wi* (e-*hi* or e-*shi*) 5. "earth;"

ó-ϑ'*ia* 5. "pool, fountain;"

e-*totúno* 5. "wild cat;"

e-*húmbu* 5. "a commando;"

e-*nyanda* 5. "cattle;"

e-*póra* 5. "way;"

e-χoϑ'*énye* 5. "love;"

e-*pénda* (Otyihereró) 5. "hero, brave one;"

e-ϑ'*íro* 5. "dirt;"

o-**ma**-ϑ'*úϑ'u* 6. "hair;"

o-**ma**-*kúnde* (Otyihereró) 6. "beans;"

o-**ma**-*púngu* 6. "maize;"

o-**má**-*oe* or o-**ma**-*we* 6. "stones" (§ 481, note);

o-**ma**-*hángu* 6. "millet;"

o-**má**-*mbo* (Otyihereró) 6. "words;"

o-**ma**-*χíni* 6. "milk;"

o-**ma**-*nyeñge* 6. "rushes;"

o-**ma**-*rovu* 6. "beer;"

o-**shi**-*koö* 7. "cloud," pl. **i**-*koö* 8.;

o-**shi**-*témba* 7. "a trough," pl. o-**ma**-*témba* 6. (Otyihereró e-*temba* 5.);

o-**shi**-*kómbo* 7. "goat" (Otyihereró o-**ri**-*gombo* 9.);

o-**sh**-*éla* 7. "iron," pl. **i**-*yera* 8.;

o-**shi**-*pakoroa* s-o-ϑ'*énya* 7. "snuff-horn;"

o-**shi**-*ti* s-o-ϑ'*éna* 7. "snuff-spoon;"

o-**shi**-*fufuta* 7. "gun;"

o-**shi**-*móna* 7. "pearl;"

o-**sh**-*ana* (Otyihereró o-**ty**-*ana*) 7. "a plain, flats;"

o-**shi**-*nima* 7. "thing," pl. o-**í**-*na* 8.;

o-**vi**-*lya* (o-**vi**-*dia* P.) 8. "Kafir corn;"

o-**vi**-*yéra* 8. "rings" (= o-**vi**-*garinge* 8. P.);

i-**i**-*ta* (Otyihereró o-**vi**-*ta*) 8. "war" (Zulu u-**bu**-*ta* 14. "enmity," i-**si**-*ta* 7. "enemy;" vide Nano **u**-*ta* 14. "bow," § 496);

ó-χ*i* or ó-*shi* (Nano o-*ssi*) 9. "fish," pl. o-**lo**-*shi* 10.;

Sindonga (Ovambo) Derivative Prefixes of Nouns. 215

o-n-ϑ'ímbo 9. "stick," pl. o-n-ϑ'ímbo 10.;
o-n-gómbe 9. "ox, cow," pl. o-n-gombe 10. (§ 226);
o-ϑ'ena 9. "snuff;"
o-m-baϑ'e (Otyihereró) 9. "foot;"
o-ϑ'ona 9. "wether;"
o-fukua 9. "potatoe;"
o-n-dzhála or o-n-dyála (Otyihereró o-n-dyara) 9. "hunger;"
o-n-yota (Otyihereró) 9. "thirst;"
o-n-dyámba (o-n-djamba P.) Benguela 9. "elephant;"
o-n-dϑ'ira (Otyihereró o-n-tera) 9. "bird;"
o-n-dumetána 9. "large ox;"
o-m-vúla (Otyihereró o-m-bura, § 118) 9. "rain;"
o-n-guru-ϑ'ímbo 9. "knobstick;"
ó-n-ϑ'i (Otyihereró o-n-tui) 9. "seed;"
o-n-ϑ'i (o-n-si, Otyihereró o-n-tu or o-n-tϑ'u, Setshuána n-ku, Kafir i-m-vu) 9. "sheep," pl. o-n-ϑ'i (Otyihereró o-ϑ'on-tu or o-ϑ'on-tϑ'u, Setshuána lin-ku, Kafir i-zim-vu) 10.;
o-m-bila 9. "grave;"
o-n-sha (o-en-na P.) 9. "food" (= 1-ku-lyia 8.);
o-m-binda (Otyihereró) 9. "pig;"
o-n-dyúshua (Otyihereró o-n-dyuhua) 9. "fool;"
o-n-dundu (Otyihereró) 9. "mountain;"
(o-n-dendu 9. "river" P.);
o-n-yúshi (Nano o-n-yihi, § 496) 9. "bee;"
o-n-yóϑ'i (Otyihereró o-n-yoϑ'e) 9. "star," pl. o-n-yóϑ'i 10.;
o-m-bépo (Otyihereró) 9. "wind;"
o-niχó 9. "needle;"

o-n-tána (Otyihereró o-n-tana) 9. "calf;"
o-shélo 9. "door;"
o-n-déte 9. "breast;"
o-n-túlo 9. "breast;"
o-n-yáti (Otyihereró and Bayeiye, p. 195) 9. "buffalo," pl. o-n-yáti 10. (§ 226, note);
o-m-báshe (Otyihcrero o-m-báhe P.) 9. "giraffe;"
o-shoróngo (Otyihcreró o-horongo) 9. "koodoo;"
o-n-garagombe (Otyihereró o-n-garangombe) 9. "eland;"
o-m-pánda 9. "rhinoceros;"
ó-n-goro (Otyihereró o-n-goro) 9. "zebra;"
o-m-pukúlu 9. "guu;"
o-ϑ'ínó 9. "gemsbok;"
ó-m-po (Otyihereró o-m-bo) 9. "ostrich;"
o-n-dyambamea (o-n-djamba-meva "water-elephant" P.; Kihiau, Kikamba, Kiníka, and Kisuáheli mamba) 9. "hippopotamus;"
ó-n-gwe (Kafir i-n-gwe, Otyihereró o-n-gue) 9. "leopard;"
o-nimé 9. "lion;"
i-m-búngu (Otyihereró o-m-bungu) 9. "hyena;"
o-m-pampáni 9. "old man;"
o-m-biχa (o-m-bika P., Nano o-m-bia, § 496) 9. "pot;"
o-m-biχa y-o-ku-teréka 9. "cooking-pot;"
o-m-biχa y-o-ma-kaya 9. "tobacco pipe;"
o-m-búnda 9. "back;"
o-nyekéshua 9. "pod;"
ó-n-guo (Kafir i-n-gubo, Bayeiye n-ko, § 486) 9. "apron;"
o-n-géndyo or o-n-génsho or o-n-genzo 9. "bell;"

o-*shángi* 9. " peace ;"
o-**n**-*dúko* 9. " speed ;"
o-**n**-*dytla* (Otyihereró o-**n**-*dshira* p. 201, note) 9. " way ;"
o-*nyánya* 9. " malice, hatred ;"
o-**n**-*gula* 9. " morning, morrow ;"
o-χ*éla* 9. " yesterday ;"
o-*néna* 9. " to-day ;"
o-**lu**-*káku* (Otyihereró o-**ru**-*haku*) 11. or o-**n**-*gaku* 9. " sandal," pl. o-**n**-*gaku* (Otyihereró o-Ƨ'*oñ-gaku*) 10. ;
o-**ru**-*tutu* (Otyihereró o-**ru**-*tu*) 11. " body," pl. o-**tu**-*tu* 12. ;
o-**ru**-*lúra* 11. " meal, flour ;"
o-**ru**-*shindo* 11. " spoon ;"
o-**ru**-*áƧ'i* 11. " lightning ;"
o-**ru**-*panda* 11. " cheek ;"
o-**ru**-*kúla* 11. " ochre ;"
o-**ka**-*talilo* 13. " looking-glass ;"

o-**ka**-χ*anóna* 13. " baby ;"
o-**ka**-*nóno* 13. " little child ;"
o-**ka**-χ*úmba* or o-**ka**-*h'umba* (Otyihereró o-**ka**-*kambe*) 13. " hartebeest ;"
o-**ká**-*na* 13. " moon ;"
o-**u**-*énda* (Otyihereró) 14. " journey ;"
o-**u**-Ƨ'*áno* 14. " play, dance ;"
o-**u**-*tarará* 14. " cold, wet ;"
u-Ƨ'*íla* 14. " flour ;"
o-**u**-*yóni* 14. " world ;"
o-**kó**-*tshui* 15. " ear," pl. o-**ma**-*kó-tshui* 6. (§ 434) ;
o-**kú**-*ti* (Otyihereró o-**ku**-*ti*) 15. " field ;"
i-**kú**-*ti* 15. " arrow ;"
o-**ku**-Ƨ'*a* or o-**ku**-*fa* 15. " to die, death " (§ 482, note).

THE NANO LANGUAGE.

496. The language of BENGUELA, of which NANO is one variety, is distinct from that of Angola as well as from the more Southern members of the Bunda Genus (Otyihereró and Sindonga). With regard to the forms of the prefixes, it is to be remarked that the **m** of the 4th prefix has not unfrequently become **v**; and also, that the same change has throughout affected the 6th prefix,—which has thus become identical in form with the 2nd (**va-**). Again, in one noun, at least, the **v** of the 2nd prefix has been converted (by the influence of a following nasal) into the labial nasal **m**. Thus the 2nd (**va-**) prefix has adopted in this one noun o-**ma**-*no* (Otyihereró o-**va**-*ndu* § 140) the form which the 6th prefix has relinquished in this language. With regard to the correspondence of the prefixes, we have to notice that the 6th (**va-**) and 10th (Ƨ'**o-**) prefixes correspond here as plurals to the 13th prefix (**ga-**)[*],

---

[*] Regarding an apparent case of correspondence of the 10th prefix as plural to the 13th, in the Bayeiye language, *vide* § 486.

and the 8th (**vi-**) to the 14th (**u-**). But the **vi-** in this instance may be merely the softened form of the 4th prefix (**mi-**), which in Kiníka (§ 482), and also in some languages of the North-western Branch (§ 504), corresponds as plural to the 14th (**u-**). The reason for this correspondence may be, that the form of the 14th prefix has been mistaken for the homophonous abbreviated form of the 3rd prefix **mu-** (to which the 4th forms the usual plural); but it may also be that this is an ancient manner of correspondence which has been retained here. The absence of the 12th prefix (**TU-**) from our list of Nano nouns is remarkable; —the 10th (**S'o-**) has apparently taken its place. But the incompleteness of our material allows of no certainty with regard to the non-existence of any class in the Nano language; nor am I even sure that I have assigned each noun to the right class. The specimens of the language given below were obtained by me from one of the **Va-**kua-nano or **Va-**nano (2.); but they agree in all essentials with the Nano words given by Mr. Rath in a manuscript of the Grey Library, also with the **Ba-**rondu (2.) and *O-*tyi-vanda (7.) vocabularies in Hahn's "Grammatik des Hereró," and with the *Pangela* words in Koelle's "Polyglotta Africana."

NANO PREFIXES.

SINGULAR.	PLURAL.
PERSONAL.	
1. o-mu-, (—) u-	2. o-va- o-ma-
3. o-mu- u-	4. o-mi- o-vi-
5. e- i-	6. o-va- o-v-
7. o-tyi-	8. o-vi-
9. o-n- o-ñ- o-m- o-	10. o-S'on- o-S'oñ- o-S'om- o-S'o-
11. o-lu-, o-	(?) 10. o-S'o-
DIMINUTIVE.	
13. o-ga- o-ka-	6. o-va-
	10. o-S'o-
14. u-	8. o-vi-
INFINITIVE.	
15. o-gu-	

NANO NOUNS.

o-**mu**-*no* (Otyihereró o-**mu**-*ndu*) 1. "person," pl. o-**ma**-*no* (Otyihereró o-**va**-*ndu*) 2. (note at the end of § 494);

u-*lome* (Bayeiye **mo**-*rume*, § 486) 1. "man," pl. o-**va**-*lome* 2.;

tate 9. and 1. "my father;"

mandyange 1. "sister," pl. o-**va**-*mandyange* 2.;

kotaliange 1. "brother," pl. o-**va**-*kotaliange* 2.;

o-**mu**-*tu* 3. "pumpkin," pl. o-**mi**-*tu* 4.;

u-*ti* 3. "tree," pl. o-**vi**-*ti* 4. (§ 428, note);

u-*tanga* 3. "day," pl. o-**vi**-*tanga* 4.;

u-*tue* (Kikámba **mú**-*tue*, § 481) 3. "head," pl. o-**vi**-*tue* 4.;

u-*tima* (Otyihereró o-**mu**-*tima*, § 494) 3. "heart," pl. o-**vi**-*tima* 4.;

e-*kála* Sindonga (Otyihereró e-*kara*) 5. "coal," pl. o-**va**-*kala* 6.;

e-*laχa* (Sindonga e-*laka*, Otyihereró e-*raka*) 5. "tongue," pl. o-**va**-*laχa* 6.;

e-*tama* (Sesuto **le**-*rama*, Seχlapi **le**-*sama*, Makua **n**-*rama*, Dualla and Isubu **i**-*lama* or **i**-*tama*) 5. "cheek," pl. o-**va**-*tama* (Setshuána and Makua **ma**-*rama*, Isubu **ma**-*tama* or **ma**-*lama*) 6.;

e-*tui* (Angola **rí**-*tui*, Balojazi **li**-*twi*-*twi*, Dualla **i**-*toi*, Isubu **di**-*to*, **i**-*to*, or **i**-*toi*) 5. "car," pl. o-**va**-*tui* (Angola **ma**-*tui*, Dualla **ma**-*toi*, Isubu **ma**-*toi* or **ma**-*to*) 6. (§ 434, note);

e-*timba* 5. "carcase," pl. o-**va**-*timba* 6. (Kafir u-**m**-*zimba* 3. "body");

e-*yo* 5. "tooth," pl. o-**va**-*yo* 6. (§ 326);

i-*lu* (Otyihereró e-*yuru*, § 494) 5. "sky, heaven;"

i-*iso* 5. "eye," pl. o-**va**-*iso* 6. (§ 327);

e-*kumbi* (Angola *kumbi* "hour") 5. "sun;"

e-*pungo* 5. "maize;"

o-**va**-*vele* 6. "milk;"

o-**v**-*ova* 6. "water" (§ 452, first note);

o-**va**-*kaya* (Otyihereró o-**ma**-*kaya*) 6. "tobacco;"

o-**tyi**-*ngere* 7. "earring," pl. o-**vi**-*ngere* 8.;

o-**tyi**-*ntere* 7. "European," pl. o-**vi**-*ntere* 8.;

o-**tyi**-*buki* 7. "bean;"

o-**tyi**-*bomba* 7. "native beer;"

o-**n**-*guru* (Kafir i-**n**-*gulube*, Setshuána *kolobe*, Lourenzo Marques i-**n**-*goluve*, Makua *gulúě*, Kihiáu and Kinika un-*gulúe*, Kipokomo un-*guyúe*, Kikámba and Kisuáheli un-*gúe*, Otyihereró o-**n**-*guruve*, Angola and Kongo **n**-*gulu*, Mpongwe **n**-*gowa* or **n**-*goa*, Dikele **n**-*goya*, Dualla and Isubu **ń**-*goa*) 9. "pig," pl. o-ϑ'**on**-*guru* 10.;

o-**ŋ**-*gundi* 9. "door," pl. o-ϑ'**oń**-*gundi* 10.;

o-**ń**-*gandu* (Otyihereró) 9. "alligator," pl. o-ϑ'**oń**-*gandu* (Otyihereró) 10.;

o-**ń**-*ganga* (Otyihereró, § 494) 9. "poison-doctor;"

Nano (Benguela) Derivative Prefixes of Nouns. 219

o-ṅ-guli 9. " lion ;"
o-n-dyilla (Sindonga o-n-dyíla) 9. "way," pl. o-Ȝ'on-dyilla 10. (p. 201, note) ;
o-n-yoka Otyihereró and Angola (Kafir, Tekeza, Sena, and Tette i-n-yoka, Setshuâna noχa, Inhambane, Sofala, Kinika, Kipokomo, and Kisuáheli n-yoka or n-ioka, Kikámba n-soka, Makua n-óa or i-n-oa, Dikele nyō) 9. "snake, serpent," pl. o-Ȝ'on-yoka (Otyihereró) 10. ;
o-n-yihi (Kafir i-n-yosi, Sena n-yūdshi, Makua núī, Kihiau, Kipokomo, and Kinika n-iúdshi, Kikamba n-suki, Kisuáheli n-ioki, Otyihereró o-n-yuityi, Sindonga o-n-yushi, Angola n-yúki, Kongo n-yossi, Mpongwe n-yowe) 9. "bee," pl. o-Ȝ'on-yihi (Setshuâna li-notse, Lourenzo Marques tin-yoshe, Dikele n-yui) 10. ;
o-ṅ-gombe 9. "cow," pl. o-Ȝ'oṅ-gombe 10. (§ 226) ;
o-n-dalu or o-n-dalo 9. "fire ;"
o-m-bongulu 9. "star," pl. o-Ȝ'om-bongulu 10. ;
o-m-bia (Kafir i-m-biza, Setshuâna pitsa, Kinika m-biga, Sindonga o-m-bidya, Angola im-bia) 9. "pot," pl. o-Ȝ'om-bia 10. ;
o-m-bela (Bayeiye e-n-fera, § 486) 9. "rain " (§ 118) ;
o-m-bambi (Otyihereró) 9, "kind of antelope (much resembling the roe)," pl. o-Ȝ'om-bambi 10.;
o-moko (Tekeza mukwa, Banyeṅko and Balojazi moko, Angola poku) 9. "knife," pl. o-Ȝ'o-moko 10. ;

o-m-bevo 9. "tortoise," pl. o-Ȝ'om-bevo 10. ;
o-mota 9. "bead," pl. o-Ȝ'o-mota 10. ;
o-mai 9. "toe," pl. o-Ȝ'o-mai 10. ;
o-mela 9. "mouth," pl. o-Ȝ'o-mela 10.;
o-messi 9. "tobacco pipe," pl. o-Ȝ'o-messi 10. ;
o-memi 9. "sheep," pl. o-Ȝ'o-memi 10. (Kongo e-meme, Kakongo li-meme 5.) ;
o-mela 9. "leaf," pl. o-Ȝ'o-mela 10.;
o-munda 9. "mountain," pl. o-Ȝ'o-munda 10. ;
o-nanga (Balojazi nanga, Baponda ntanga) 9. "dress, apron," pl. o-Ȝ'o-nanga 10. ;
o-ssi (Sindonga ó-xi or ó-shi) 9. "fish," pl. o-Ȝ'o-ssi 10. ;
o-ssive 9. "hair," pl. o-Ȝ'o-ssive 10. ;
o-sapi 9. "dish," pl. o-Ȝ'o-sapi 10. ;
o-ssima (Tette and Sena in-shima, Otyihereró o-n-dyimá, Angola h'ima, Mpongwe n-kěma, Dikele kiema) 9. "monkey," pl. o-Ȝ'o-ssima (Otyihereró o-Ȝ'on-dyima) 10. (Otyihereró o-ka-ima 13. "little baboon ") ;
o-ssai 9. "moon ; "
o-zanye 9. "fowl," pl. o-Ȝ'o-zanye 10. ;
o-fela 9. "wind ;"
o-hita 9. "porridge," pl. o-Ȝ'o-hita 10. ;
(?) o-rui 9. "river," pl. o-Ȝ'o-rui 10. (Otyihereró o-ru-i 11. "spring, fountain," pl. o-tu-i 12.) ;
sekulu 9. "chief," pl. o-Ȝ'o-sekulu 10. ;
o-lu-kongoro 11. "rainbow ;"

o-kuru 11. "leg," pl. *o-ȝ'o-kuru* 10. (Kinika *gúlu*, Kisuáheli *gu* pl. **ma**-*gu* 6., Kikámba *hú-u* 15. pl. **ma**-*u* 6.);

o-**ka**-*n-dyu* (Otyihereró *o*-**ka**-*n-dyuo*) 13. "small house," pl. *o*-**va**-*n-dyu* 6.;

o-**ka**-*ntimba* 13. "hare," pl. *o*-**va**-*ntimba* 6.;

o-**ga**-*kwendye* 13. "young man," pl. *o*-**va**-*kwendye* (6. or 2.);

o-**ga**-*veko* 13. "girl," pl. *o*-**va**-*veko* (6. or 2.);

o-**ka**-*r̄ui* (Otyihereró) 13. "rivulet," pl. *o*-**va**-*r̄ui* or *o*-**ve**-*r̄ui* 6.;

o-**ka**-*n-dyila* 13. "bird," pl. *o*-ȝ'**on**-*dyila* 10.;

o-**ka**-*n-dyilla* 13. "little way;"

o-**ka**-*n-yonki* 13. "flower," pl. *o*-ȝ'**on**-*yonki* 10.;

o-**ga**-*mora* 13. "little child," pl. *o*-ȝ'**o**-*mora* 10.;

u-*lela* 14. "fat;"

u-*ta* (Setshuána **bo**-*ra*, Sofala **vu**-*ta*, Sena and Tette **û**-*ta*, Anjoane **u**-*tá*, Makua **ū**-*ra*, Otyihereró, Sindonga, and Angola *o*-**u**-*ta*) 14. "bow (gun?)," pl. *o*-**vi**-*ta* 8. (Otyihereró *o*-**vi**-*ta* = Sindonga i-**i**-*ta* 8. "enmity, commando, war;" Zulu i-**ai**-*tu* 7. "enemy" pl. i-**zi**-*ta* 8., u-**bu**-*ta* 14. "enmity");

u-*teke* (§ 453, note) 14. "night," pl. *o*-**vi**-*teke* 8.;

o-**gu**-*lila* (Kafir u-**ku**-*lila*, Otyihereró *o*-**ku**-*rira*) 15. "weeping;"

o-**gu**-*lima* (Kafir u-**ku**-*lima*) 15. "to plough, dig."

THE ANGOLA LANGUAGE.

497. The old Angola language* has, upon the whole, retained older forms of the prefixes than the other Bunda tongues, although only fifteen of the classes of nouns have been found here. The double forms of the prefixes of the 10th (**shin-**) class are remarkable. In these we find forms with the vowel *i*, and also with the vowel *o*. In the 5th (**ri-**) class we find the form *o*-**ri-** instead of the contracted **e-** of the other Bunda languages. (*Vide* § 491, and first note on p. 222.) The fact of the correspondence of the 12th (**tu-**) prefix to the 13th (**ka-**), and not, as in the other Bunda tongues, to the 11th (**lu-**), has already been remarked. (§ 453.) The 14th prefix (which in Otyihereró corresponds as plural to the 13th) is in Angola of the singular number only. The 15th (**ku-**) class in Angola appears only to include infinitives, and has, therefore, no plural corresponding to it.

*The **ku**-*amba* ku-*a Ngola* 15. is represented by the Jesuit Catechism (1643, 1661, 1784, 1855), and by Dias' Grammar ("Arte," 1697).

ANGOLA DERIVATIVE PREFIXES OF NOUNS.

WITHOUT ARTICLE.		WITH ARTICLE.	
SINGULAR.	PLURAL.	SINGULAR.	PLURAL.
PERSONAL.		**PERSONAL.**	
1. mŭ-, (—) mo-	2. a-	1. o-mŭ-, o-o-mo-	2. o-a-
	10. shi-, sho-		10. o-shi-, o-sho-
3. mŭ-	4. mi-	3. o-mŭ-	4. o-mi-
5. ri-, (—)	6. ma- m-	5. o-ri-	6. o-ma- o-m-
7. ki- (qui-)	8. i- hi- y-	7. o-ki-	8. o-i- o-hi- o-y-
9. n- (i)m- (—)	10. shin- (gin-), shon- shim-, shom- shi-, sho-, (—)	9. o-n- o-m- o-	10. o-shin-, o-shon- o-shim-, o-shom- o-shi-, o-sho-
11. lu-	6. (+ 11.) ma-*lu*-	11. o-lu-	6. (+ 11.) o-ma-*lu*-
DIMINUTIVE.		**DIMINUTIVE.**	
13. ka-	12. tu-	13. o-ka-	12. o-tu-
ABSTRACT.		**ABSTRACT.**	
14. u- w-	6. (+ 14.) ma-*u*- ma-*w*-	14. o-u-	6. (+ 14.) o-ma-*u*-
INFINITIVE.		**INFINITIVE.**	
15. ku-		15. o-ku-	

ANGOLA NOUNS.

mu-*tu* 1. "man, person," pl. **a**-*tu* 2. (note at the end of § 494);

mu-*bika* (Bayeiye **mo**-*via*, § 486) 1. "slave," pl. **a**-*bika* 2.;

mu-*haï-tu* 1. "woman," pl. **a**-*haï-tu* 2. (note at end of § 494);

mu-*kashi* 1. "wife" (note at end of § 494);

mu-*lumi* (Bayeiye **mo**-*rume*, § 486) 1. "man," pl. **a**-*lumi* 2.;

mu-*biri* 1. "herdsman," pl. **a**-*biri* 2.;

mu-*lambi* 1. "cook," pl. **a**-*lambi* 2.;

mu-*kwǎ* 1. "inhabitant;"

mo-*na* 1. "son, child," pl. **a**-*na* 2. (p. 209);

Fula 1. "Francis," pl. **Shi**-*fula* 10.;

ngana 1. "master," pl. **shi**-*ngana* 10.;

mu-*shi* 3. "piece of wood, stick," pl. **mi**-*shi* 4. (§ 428);

mu-*shima* (Otyihereró o-**mu**-*tima* "heart," § 494) 3. "will, wish;"

mu-*longa* 3. "word," pl. **mi**-*longa* 4.;

mǎ-*kwa* 3. "a certain kind of fruit;"

o-**ri**-*éulu* or *éulu** (Otyihereró e-*yuru*, § 494) 5. "heaven," pl. o-**má**-*ulu* 6.;

o-**ri**-*shina* or *shina*† (Kisambala *zina*, § 484) 5. "name," pl. o-**ma**-*shina* 6.;

ri-*embe* or *embe* 5. "pigeon," pl. **ma**-*embe* 6.;

nbata† 5. "house," pl. **ma**-*bata* 6.;

nbuba† 5. "whirlpool," pl. **ma**-*buba* 6.;

nbombelo 5. "flattery," pl. **ma**-*nbombelo* 6. (**ku**-*nbomba* 15. "to flatter," **ku**-*nbombela* 15. "to pet, to be kind");

yala 5. "man, male," pl. **ma**-*yala* 6.;

soshi (Otyihereró **e**-*hoϑ'e*, Kinika *tsosi*, § 482) 5. "tear (lagrima)," pl. **ma**-*soshi* (Otyihereró o-**ma**-*hoϑ'e*) 6.;

sote 5. "frog," pl. **ma**-*sote* 6.;

fuma 5. "notice," pl. **ma**-*fuma* 6.;

ri-*nongwenna* 5. "chameleon;"

ri-*zúlo* (Otyihereró **e**-*uru*, § 494) 5. "nose;"

ki-*kalakalo* 7. "work," pl. **i**-*kalakalo* 8. (o-**ku**-*kala-kala* 15. "to work," from o-**ku**-*kǎla* 15. "to be," § 208);

---

* I had first believed the *e* in this form *éulu* to be a contraction of the 5th prefix, with or without the article,—like the **e**- which occurs in Otyihereró, Sindonga, and Nano. (§ 491.) But it is now clear to me that the *e* of *éulu* belongs to the stem of the noun, and corresponds to the Otyihereró *y*-. And, as far as our examples go, the existence of **e**- as a form of the 5th prefix in Angola is not proved.

† The forms *nshina*, *nbata*, and *nbuba* have as yet been found only in Dias' "Arte." They may either be misprints for **ri**-*shina*, **ri**-*bata*, and **ri**-*buba*, or the *n* in them may be the first consonant of the stem, before which the derivative prefix has fallen away. It is, at all events, unlikely that the 5th prefix in Angola should (as in Makua) have adopted a nasal form.

ki-*tushi* 7. "debt," pl. **i**-*tushi* 8.;
ki-*ûma* (Kongo) 7. "thing," pl. **y**-*uma* (Kongo) 8.;
ki-*lwishi* 7. "river;"
ki-*yàla* 7. "a great, strong man" (vide *yala* 5.);
n-*dandu* 9. "relative," pl. **shin**-*dandu* 10.;
N-*zambi* 9. "God," pl. **shin**-*zambi* 10.;
i**m**-*bia* (Nano o-**m**-*bidya*, § 496) 9. "pot," pl. **shim**-*bia* 10.;
fuba (§§ 116 and 353) 9. "flour, meal," pl. **shi**-*fuba* 10.;
hanga 9. "partridge," pl. **shi**-*hanga* 10.;

tulo 9. "breast," pl. **shi**-*tulo* 10.;
shitu (Nano o-*ssitu*) 9. "flesh," pl. **shi**-*shitu* 10.;
lu-*to* (Otyihereró o-**ru**-*tuo*) 11. "spoon," pl. **ma**-*luto* 6. (pp. 145 and 177);
lu-*bango* 11. "stick," pl. **ma**-*lubango* 6.;
ka-*musete* 13. "little box," pl. **tu**-*musete* 12.;
u-*ta* (Nano, § 496) 14. "bow," pl. **ma**-**u**-*ta* 6.;
w-*anga* 14. "fetish," pl. **ma**-*wanga* 6.;
ku-*zola* 15. "to love."

ee. *The Kongo Genus.*

498. The Kongo Genus is represented by two languages, which exhibit remarkable differences from each other by reason of the widely removed stages of development in which they appear. The old Kongo language, as spoken in that empire two hundred years ago, shews the prefixes in forms almost equally full with those generally possessed by the other Middle Branch languages; while Mpongwe, modernised probably not only by time, but situation and other circumstances, has abbreviated most of the forms of the prefixes, usually retaining only their vowels. Hence, in Mpongwe, several originally distinct prefixes and forms of concord having become homophonous, some of the classes of nouns have coalesced, and one, at least, seems to have disappeared. It is certain that the old Kongo language possesses fifteen of the sixteen classes of nouns generally inherited by the Middle Branch; but Mpongwe appears to have reduced this number to ten, chiefly by processes of amalgamation. As article in Kongo, we only meet with the demonstrative particle *o-* with its euphonic modifications; whilst in Mpongwe we find initial vowels, which (like the Kafir articles, § 464) appear to have been

pronouns, originally identical in form with the derivative prefixes themselves. In one case, (that of a noun of the 6th class) it appears as if the article derived from the pronoun were also met with in Kongo; but as this noun (a-ma-*ko*) occurs only once, it is doubtful whether it may not be a misprint for *o*-ma-*ko*.

THE KONGO LANGUAGE.

499. The Kongo language shares with the members of the Bunda Genus the use of the prefixed *o*- as a sort of article; but in Kongo this *o*- is always changed into an *e*- before prefixes which contain the vowel *i*, such as the 4th (mi-), 5th (ri-), 7th (ki-), 8th (i-), and 10th (zin-), —also when preceding a prefix in which *i* was the vowel, although now suppressed, such as the 9th (n-). But before prefixes containing the vowels *u*, *o*, or *a*, the article *o*- remains unaltered. With regard to the prefixes, it is to be

KONGO PREFIXES.

SINGULAR.	PLURAL.
PERSONAL.	
1. mu-, *o*-mu-m-u- (—)	2. a-, *o*-a- (—)
	6. ma-, a-ma-
3. mu-, *o*-mu-m-	4. mi-, *e*-mi-
5. e-, *e*-ri- e-ye-	6. ma-, *o*-ma-m- 2. a-
7. ki-, *e*-ki-ke-	8. i-, *e*-i-y-, *e*-y-
9. n-'.', *e*-n-'.' *o*-n-'.'	10. n-'.', *e*-zin-'.' 2. a-n-'.', *o*-a-n-'.'
11. lu- lu-*l*- l- u-	12. tu-, *o*-tu- tu-*n*- 10. n-'.'
13. ka-	
ABSTRACT. 14. u-, *o*-u- o-, *o*-o-	6. ma-, *o*-ma-
INFINITIVE. 15. ku-, *o*-ku-	6. ma-, *o*-ma-

remarked that, excepting the disappearance of the labial explosive consonant in the 2nd (**BA-**), 8th (**PI-**), and 14th (**BU-**) prefixes, their forms are as original as those to be met with in any of the other Middle Branch languages. That the 6th (**ma-**) prefix corresponds here, in some cases, as plural to the first (**mu-**), appears to be an ancient feature of the language; for, it also occurs in Kafir (§ 451), Sesuto, Sena, and perhaps in Kikamba. Those of the nouns of the 5th (**ri-**) and 9th (**n-**) classes which indicate persons are frequently treated as if of the 1st (**mu-**) class, and in this case they adopt the 2nd (**a-**) prefix as their plural. (§ 466.) The forms with the article are, as far as they can be ascertained, placed by the side of those without it.

KONGO NOUNS.

o-**mu**-*ntu* 1. "man, person," pl. o-**a**-*ntu* 2. "people" (p. 208);

mu-*tinu* or **m**-*tinu* 1. "king;"

o-**mu**-*bhiga* (Bayeiye **mo**-*via*, § 486) 1. "servant;"

mu-*ana* 1. "son, child, descendant, nephew," pl. *ana* 2. (p. 209);

o-**mu**-*leke* 1. "boy," pl. o-**a**-*leke* 2.;

mu-*ke-ntu* 1. "woman," pl. **a**-*ke-ntu* 2. (p. 211);

mu-*tangi* 1. "teacher," pl. **a**-*tangi* 2.;

mú-*iwi* 1. "thief," pl. *ewi* 2. (§§ 325 & 326);

mu-*bhangi* 1. "doer, actor," pl. **a**-*bhangi* 2.;

mu-*bhobheri* or **m**-*bhobheri* 1. "advocate;"

mu-*te-kúlú* 1. "grandchild," pl. **a**-*te-kúlú* 2.;

Npetelo 1. "Peter;"

u-*ko* 1. "father-in-law, mother-in-law, son-in-law, daughter-in-law," pl. a-**ma**-*ko* or **ma**-*ko* 6.;

o-**mu**-*kunga* 3. "song," pl. e-**mi**-*kunga* 4.;

o-**mu**-*funu* (**m**-*funu*) 3. "work," pl. e-**mi**-*funu* (**m**-*funu*) 4.;

mu-*saka* 3. "ear of corn," pl. **mi**-*saka* 4.;

mu-*ngua* 3. "salt," pl. **mi**-*ngua* 4.;

mu-*wu* 3. "year," pl. **mi**-*wu* 4.;

mu-*sangu* 3. "tribute;"

mu-*zála* 3. "hunger;"

mu-*anu* 3. "manner, mode," pl. **mi**-*anu* 4.;

mu-*tima* (**m**-*tima*, Otyihereró o-**mu**-*tima*, § 494) 3. "heart, consciousness," pl. **mi**-*tima* 4.;

e-**ri**-*tondo* or e-(n)*tondo* 5. "praise," pl. o-**ma**-*tondo* 6.;

e-**ri**-*bhitu* and e-*bhitu* 5. "door;"

e-*sarikwa* 5. "beginning," pl. **ma**-*sarikwa* 6.;

e-*kesa* 5. "soldier," pl. **ma**-*kesa* 6.;

e-*bhanda* 5. "branch," pl. **ma**-*bhanda* 6.;

m-*esso* (Kafir a-**m**-*exlo*) 6. "eyes" (§ 327);

e-*sse* 5. & 1. "father," pl. **ma**-*sse* 6. & 2. (Kafir u-*yise* 1. "his or their father," pl. o-*yise* 2.);

e-*yekala* 5. "human being," pl. **a**-*kala* 2.;

e-*meme* (Kakongo **li**-*meme*) 5. "sheep" (Nano o-*meme* 9.);

e-**ki**-*lumbu* 7. "day," pl. e-**i**-*lumbu* 8.;

e-**ki**-*kuma* 7. "debt," pl. e-**i**-*kuma* 8.;

e-**ki**-(w)uma (Angola **ki**-úma) 7. "thing," pl. **e**-**y**-*uma* (Angola **y**-*uma*) 8.;

ki-*fu* 7. "custom," pl. **i**-*fu* 8.;

ki-*nkete* 7. "a mechanic," pl. **i**-*nkete* 8.;

ki-*sunga* 7. "memory," pl. **i**-*sunga* 8.;

ke-*ndika* 7. "obstacle," pl. **i**-*ndika* 8.;

ki-*bhenzo* 7. "brightness," pl. **i**-*bhenzo* 8.;

ki-*nbungu* 7. "hyena" (Otyihereró o-**m**-*buṅgu* 9.);

ki-*tanga* 7. "teacher;"

ki-*tangilu* 7. "manner of teaching, counting, reading;"

ki-*rilu* 7. "lamentation;"

ki-*ririlú* 7. "manner of mourning;"

ki-*bhangua* 7. "a thing done;"

ki-*bhanga* 7. "doer," pl. **i**-*bhanga* 8.;

ki-*zitirua* 7. "a beloved object;"

ki-*zitisa* 7. "a lover," pl. **i**-*zitisa* 8.;*

ki-*ta* 7. "one who goes home," pl. **i**-*ta* 8.;*

ki-*mu-ntu-mu-ntu* 7. "a little man" (§ 430);

ki-*leke-leke* 7. "a little boy" (§ 430);

ki-*mu-ana-mu-ana* 7. "a little child" (**ki**-*mu-ana-mu-ana* **ki**-e-*meme* "a little child of a sheep," i.e. "a little lamb"), pl. **y**-*ana-ana* 8. (§ 430);

ki-*tumbu* 7. "correction;"

ki-*kula* 7. "friendship;"

ki-*sonekelo* 7. "manner of writing;"

ki-*tarilú* 7. "manner of laughing;"

e-**n**-*bongo* 9. "seed, fruit," pl. e-**zin**-*bongo* 10.;

n-*bhele* 9. "knife," pl. e-**zin**-*bhele* 10.;

n-*wula* (§ 118) 9. "rain," pl. e-**zin**-*wula* 10.;

e-**n**-*tazi* 9. "hour, sun;"

n-*zo* (Bayeiye **n**-*tshu*, § 486) 9. "house," pl. **n**-*zo* (Angola **shin**-*zo*) 10.;

n-*za* 9. "world;"

n-*pobho* 9. "language," pl. **n**-*pobho* 10. (**ku**-*bhobha* 15. "to speak," § 355);

n-*dogi* 9. "teacher," pl. **n**-*dongi* 10. (§ 354);

n-*dínga* 9. "voice," pl. **n**-*dínga* 10.;

n-*butete* 9. "star," pl. **n**-*butete* 10.;

---

* Vetralha (p. 75) gives as additional plurals of these nouns (**ki**-*zitisa* 7. and **ki**-*ta* 7.) the forms **sa**-*mi-nzitisa* or **sa**-*inzitisa*, and **sa**-*minta* or **sa**-*inta*, which evidently belong to the 2nd (**sa**-) class.

n-*kubu* or n-*kunbu* 9. "time (German *mal*)," pl n-*kubu* or n-*kunbu* 10.;

n-*gonde* (Balojazi n-*gonde*, Bamaponda *gonde* "moon") 9. "month," pl. n-*gonde* 10.;

n-*kosi* (perhaps = Kafir i-n-*kosi*, Setshuâna *kχosi*, Tckeza *hose* "chief") 9. "lion;"

n-*banza* (Angola n-*bata* "house") 9. "town;"

n-*susu* (Bayeiye n-*koku*, § 486) 9. "fowl," pl. n-*susu* 10.;

n-*pangi* 9. "brother," pl. n-*pangi* 10. (§ 185);

n-*zari* 9. "relation," pl. n-*zari* 10. or a-n-*zari* 2.;

o-n-*fumu* 9. "lord, master," pl. n-*fumu* 10. and o-a-n-*fumu* 2.;

lu-*tumu* 11. "proscription," pl. tu-*tumu* or o-tu-*tumu* 12.;

lu-*azimu* 11. "splendour," pl. tu-*azimu* 12.;

lu-*langanime* 11. "obstinacy," pl. tu-*nanganime* 12.;

lu-*ilu* 11. "fervour," pl. tu-*ilu* 12.;

lu-*ina* 11. "perspiration," pl. tu-*ina* 12.;

u-*ssolo* 11. "choice," pl. tu-*ssolo* 12.;

lu-*zolo* 11. "desire, wish," pl. tu-*zolo* 12.;

lu-*tangu* 11. "computation;"

lu-*fumu* 11. "chapter;"

lu-*zaisa* 11. "news;"

l-*oko* 11. "act of drying;"

l-*ondeko* 11. "act of wetting;"

lu-*sangu* 11. "tribute;"

lu-*tumbu* 11. "correction;"

lu-*akirilu* 11. "support;"

lu-*kanu* 11. "determination;"

lu-*fuku* 11. "ten thousand," pl. n-*fuku* 10.;

lu-*bhebhe* 11. "hundred thousand," pl. n-*pebhe* 10.;

tu-*bhia* or tu-*bia* 12. "fire and fires;"

tu-*lu* 12. "sleep;"

ka-*ti-a-nzi* 13. "middle, centre;"

ka-*sasila* 13. "height;"

o-u-*lungu* 14. "ship," pl. o-ma-*lungu* 6.;

u-*zitu* or o-*zitu* 14. "honour;"

o-*nga* or o-o-*nga* 14. "fear;"

u-*ntu* (Kafir u-bu-*ntu* § 412, Otyihereró o-u-*ndu*) 14. "humanity;"

u-*ingi* (Zulu u-bu-*ningi*) 14. "multitude;"

u-*ndima* 14. "badness;"

u-*ita* 14. "war" (*vide* Nano u-*ta* 14. "bow," p. 220);

ku-*tu* 15. "ear," pl. ma-*tu* 6. (§ 434, note);

o-ku-*ria* (Kafir u-ku-*tya*) 15. "food;"

ku-*lenda* 15. "power;"

ku-*soneka* or ku-*zoneka* 15. "writing;"

ku-*tanga* 15. "reading, lesson;"

ku-*angalala* 15. "joyfulness;"

ku-*nunkua* (Kafir u-ku-*nukwa*) "prophecy, the being smelt out;"

ku-*bkinga* 15. "service."

THE MPONGWE LANGUAGE.

500. In their present form, the derivative prefixes of the nouns in the Mpongwe language consist of a vowel, which is rarely preceded, although sometimes followed, by a

consonant. These vowels seem to have been articles, rather than original derivative prefixes. The derivative prefixes themselves appear to have been so contracted with their articles that they have either wholly disappeared, or retained their consonant only. It can hardly be supposed that the initial vowels of the Mpongwe prefixes can have descended from the article *o-* which we find in the Kongo language; for, in that case this *o-* must have entirely assimilated itself to the vowel of each prefix in Mpongwe,—changing into an *a* before prefixes containing this vowel (such as the 6th), &c. It is far more probable that we meet here with remnants of the old Bântu article derived from pronominal elements originally identical with the prefixes,—that article which we find also in Kafir, &c. (§ 464.) As a third explanation, we would suggest that forms of the prefixes such as **am-** (6.) and **ow-** (14.) may have been mere transpositions of **MA-** and **WO-**; but, however this may be, the present forms have now no trace of the meaning of an article in themselves, and have practically to be looked upon entirely in the light of derivative prefixes; and have, therefore, been noted as such.

501. By this mutilation of the forms of the prefixes, those of the 11th, 14th, and 15th classes have become identical with that of the 3rd (O-) class; and as the other forms of concord of these classes appear also to have assimilated, we can now only discern by the different plural prefixes that a noun belonged originally to the 11th, 14th, or 15th class,—instead of to the 3rd (O-) class. Thus in Mpongwe the 11th, 14th, and 15th classes appear to have been incorporated into the 3rd (O-) class, and to have practically ceased to exist. It is, therefore only for purposes of comparison that we have assigned to them separate places here. It is remarkable that whilst the **k** of the 7th class has become **z** (and not **s**, as in the corresponding Kafir prefix), the 10th prefix has a form **sin-** corresponding to the Kafir **zin-**; so that *s* and *z* seem

to have reversed their respective positions in these two languages. (§ 385.) The strengthened form of the initial consonant of the stem (indicated by the mark ʻ.ʻ) occurs in Mpongwe after the prefixes of the 9th (n-) and 10th (sin-) classes, and also after that of the 6th (am-) class, when the latter is placed in its full form before a labial fricative. (§§ 360 & 361.) The formation of abstract nouns of the 10th (sin-) class in this language also deserves notice.

MPONGWE PREFIXES.

SINGULAR.	PLURAL.
PERSONAL.	
1. o- om-	2. a- (—)
3. o- om-	4. i- in-
5. i-	6. a- am- ʻ.ʻ
7. ez- e-	8. y- (—) i-
9. n- ʻ.ʻ m- ʻ.ʻ (—) ʻ.ʻ	10. in- ʻ.ʻ, sin- ʻ.ʻ im- ʻ.ʻ i- ʻ.ʻ, si- ʻ.ʻ
3. (11.) o-	10. i- ʻ.ʻ, shi- ʻ.ʻ
3. (14. or 15.) o- ow-	6. a- am-

MPONGWE NOUNS.

o-*nomi* (Bayeiye **mo**-*rune*, § 486) 1. "man," pl. **a**-*nomi* 2.;

o-*nw-ana* 1. "child," pl. **a**-*nw-ana* 2. (p. 209);

om-*a-nto* 1. "woman," pl. **a**-*nto* 2. (note at end of § 494);

o-*nw-a-nto* 1. "girl;"

o-*ma* 1. "person," pl. **a**-*nlaga* 2.;

o-*noki* 1. "liar;"

o-*lǎvi* 3. "river," pl. *i*-*lǎvi* 4.;

o-*londa* 3. "bud, nut," pl. *i*-*londa* 4.;

o-*tondo* 3. "basket," pl. *i*-*tondo* 4.;

o-*rĕma* (Otyiherero o-**mu**-*tima*, § 494) 3. "heart," pl. *i*-*rĕma* 4.;

o-*ronginu* 3. "grave," pl. *i*-*ronginu* 4.;

o-*gweli* (Otyiherero o-**mu**-*eɔ'e*, § 494) 3. "moon;"

o-*lumbu* (Kafir u-**m**-*lomo*, § 439 note) 3. "lip," pl. **in**-*lumbu* 4.;

o-*gwěra* 3. "night," pl. *i*-*gwěra* 4.;

om-*enlo* (Otyiherero o-**mu**-*nue*, § 494) 3. "finger;"

o-*ramba* 3. "root," pl. *i*-*ramba* 4.;

i-*dǎmbe* 5. "sheep," pl. **a**-*dǎmbe* 6.;

i-*zǎge* 5. "duck," pl. **a**-*zǎge* 6.;

i-*vanga* 5. "law," pl. am-*panga* 6.;

i-*vava* 5. "wing," pl. am-*pava* 6. (§ 360);

i-*vare* 5. "branch," pl. am-*pare* 6.;

i-*wugu* 5. "cheek," pl. am-*bugu* 6.;

i-*ntyå* 5. "eye," pl. a-*ntyå* 6. (§ 327);

i-*do* (§ 481, note) 5. "stone," pl. a-*do* 6.;

i-*nå* 5. "tooth," pl. a-*nå* 6. (§ 326);

i-*gåvi* 5. "war," pl. a-*gåvi* 6.;

i-*gamba* 5. "word," pl. a-*gamba* 6. (§ 366);

a-*ningo* 6. "water;"

a-*lugu* 6. "rum;"

a-*gali* 6. "oil;"

ez-*ango* 7. "book," pl. y-*ango* 8.;

ez-*a* 7. "thing," pl. y-*a* 8.;

ez-*åma* 7. "thing," pl. y-*åma* 8.;

ez-*åmbålålå* 7. "broom," pl. y-*åmbålålå* 8.;

e-*gara* 7. "chest, box," pl. *gara* 8.;

e-*rere* 7. "tree," pl. *rere* 8. (Dikele dsh-*eli* 13., pl. bi-*eli* 8., § 507);

e-*rem* 7. "axe;"

e-*wondsho* 7. "head," pl. *wondsho* 8.;

e-*kĕikĕi* 7. "babe, infant," pl. *kĕikĕi* 8.;

e-*gåmba* 7. "allegory, parable," pl. *gåmba* 8.;

e-*gombe* 7. "time," pl. *gombe* 8.;

e-*keva* 7. "wave," pl. i-*keva* 8.;

e-*pa* 7. "bone," pl. *pa* 8.;

e-*vindi* 7. "cloud," pl. *vindi* 8.;

n-*yare* or n-*yari* 9. "cow, bullock, ox," pl. in-*yare* or sin-*yare* 10. (§ 226, note);

swaka 9. "knife," pl. i-*swaka* or si-*swaka* 10.;

tondo 9. "basket," pl. i-*tondo* or si-*tondo* 10.;

m-*boni* (Kafir i-m-*buzi*, Sesuto *pulii*, Sex̌lapi *puri*,* Tekeza em-*bute*, Inhambane *buti*, Sofala *budshi*, Tette, Quellimane, Kihiau, Kinika, and Kisuábeli m-*buzi*, Makua i-*púri* or i-*burri*, Kikamba m-*bui*, Dikele am-*boli*, Benga and Dualla m-*bodi*, Isubu m-*bori*) 9. "goat," pl. im-*boni* 10. (Tumale yimbǔte "goats");

m-*boa* (§§ 235 & 277) 9. "dog," pl. im-*boa* 10.;

---

* Hence the word for "goat," used by the !Korana, Namaqua, and Bushmen: viz. !Kora *birii*-b (m. s.) of Lichtenstein, or *bri* (*bree*) of Burchell,—Nama *bri*-i (c. s.) and *bri*-s (f. s.) of Le Vaillant, *plii*-ti (f. p.) and *pli-ro*-i (c. s. of diminutive) of Schmelen, *biri-ro*-e (c. s. obj. of diminutive) of Knudsen, *piri*-p (m. s.) and *piri-ro*-i (c. s. of dimin.) of Tindall, *beri*-b (m. s.) and *beri-ro*-i (c. s. of dim.) of Krönlein,— Bushman *piri* (Lichtenstein), *bri* or *bli* (own observation). It is probable that these nations (the Hottentots and Bushmen) became first acquainted with goats by means of the Western Betshuána, from whom they seem to have borrowed the name, and whom they call the "goat people," *Bri*-qu-*a* or *Brii*-ku-*ah* (m. pl. obj., Lichtenstein) and *Piri*-ku (m. pl. Tindall). This term has now, however, a meaning so extended as to indicate not only the Betshuána but also the kindred Kafir tribes.

m-pânlâ 9. "path, road," pl. im-pânlâ 10.;
m-bora 9. "place," pl. im-bora 10.;
n-ago 9. "house," pl. in-ago 10.;
n-kala 9. "town, village," pl. in-kala 10.;
n-tyâni (Kafir i-n-xloni, Otyihereró o-honi, p. 207) 9. "shame;"
n-yâni (Bayeiye i-n-yene, p. 195) 9. "bird," pl. in-yâni 10.;
n-tyina 9. "blood;"
n-gowa 9. "hog," pl. in-goa 10.;
n-tyozyo 9. "foot," pl. in-tyozyo 10.;
n-dego 9. "friend," pl. in-dego 10.;
n-omba 9. "mountain, hill," pl. in-omba 10.;
shape 9. "key," pl. i-shape 10.;

i-numba 10. "hatred;"
i-tŏnda 10. "love" (rŏnda "love thou," §§ 365—368);
i-benda 10. "wrath;"
o-wowa 3. (11.) "feather," pl. i-bowa 10.;
o-rue 11. "hair," pl. i-tue or i-tui (or shi-tue) 10.;
o-gâ 3. (14.) "arm," pl. a-gâ 6.;
ow-atanga 3. (14.) "ship," pl. am-atanga 6.;
ow-aro 3. (Dikele bi-ali 14., § 507) "canoe," pl. am-aro 6.;
o-roi 3. (15.) "ear," pl. a-roi 6. (§ 434, note);
o-zyo 3. (Kikamba u-dio 14., § 481) "face," pl. a-zyo 6.;
o-golu 3. (Kikamba ku-u 15.) "leg," pl. a-golu (Kikamba ma-u) 6.

C. IN THE NORTH-WESTERN BRANCH.

502. The derivative prefixes of the nouns in the languages of the North-western Branch exhibit a strong preference for the letter *b*. This is shown, not only as in Kafir and Setshuâna, by the retention of the letter in those prefixes which originally possessed it,* but also by a tendency to convert other labials into this media. In the languages of the North-western Branch generally, the consonant of the 8th prefix (PI-) has been thus transformed. But in one of these languages (that of Fernando Po), the labial nasal of the prefixes of the 1st (MU-), 3rd (MU-), 4th (MI-), and 6th (MA-) classes has also been changed into the labial media *b*. On the other hand, the letter *k* is no longer met with in the prefixes of the nouns which are used in these languages. It has either been entirely dropped, or it appears in the form of some other letter,—for instance, as *dsh* in the 13th Dikele prefix,

* *Viz.* the 2nd (ba-) and 14th (bu-).

s in the 7th Fernandian prefix, and *v* in the same 7th prefix in Benga and Dikele.

503. The recognition of the 7th and 13th prefixes in these languages was difficult, especially as here the 7th prefix has generally the 12th, and the 13th the 8th, as corresponding plural; whilst in all other known South African Bântu languages the 8th prefix always forms the plural of the 7th, and the 12th (in those languages which possess it) is plural to the 11th or 13th. Nor are the forms in which these prefixes more usually occur, such as to render their identification an easy task. The singular prefix e- or y-, to which, in most of these languages, the 8th (be-) prefix corresponds as plural, would naturally suggest an identification with the 7th prefix (as usually found in correspondence with the 8th), especially as we have seen in Mpongwe that the form of the 7th prefix has dwindled to e-. However, the very same nouns which in the other languages of the North-western Branch possess this e- prefix, begin, in Dikele, with a-, which can but be identified with the 13th (KA-) prefix of the Middle Branch languages. Therefore the e- of the other languages of the North-western Branch is evidently to be ascribed to a darkening of the vowel of the 13th prefix. On the other hand, I was long doubtful as to which class to assign a prefix which generally corresponds as singular to the 12th (lo-). The form of this prefix is i- in Isubu and Dualla, i- and vi- in Benga, and vi- in Dikele. However, the Fernandian form of this prefix (which is si- or s-) renders it probable that the 7th prefix is to be discovered here. This 7th prefix (in Fernandian certainly, and probably also in some other languages of the North-western Branch) possesses the power of forming diminutives,—a feature which we also occasionally meet with among the other South African Bântu languages. (§ 430.)

504. The various correspondences of the singular and plural prefixes in the languages of the North-western

Branch (which languages, in this respect, differ from each other, as well as from those of the Middle and South-eastern Branches) seem to shew that the original range of correspondence of many of the plural prefixes was a far wider one than would have been concluded from a comparison of the more Southern Bântu languages only. Yet, even in the latter, we meet with occasional traces of some unusual methods of correspondence which are only found to occur with regularity in the North-western Branch. Thus, in Kisambala (§ 484) we find the 8th (vi-) prefix corresponding as plural to the 13th (ka-), just as it does in the languages of the North-western Branch,—and it appears hardly probable now, that this can be referred (as I formerly suggested) to a confusion of the 13th (ka-) prefix with the 7th (ki-). Similarly, in the languages of the North-western Branch,* the frequent occurrence of the 4th (mi-) prefix as plural to the 14th (bo-) renders it highly probable that the similar case in Kiníka is to be explained as a remnant of an old mode of correspondence which has become obsolete in the other known members of the Middle Branch.

505. As to the forms of the prefixes, besides the preference for the *b*, and the avoidance of the *k* sound, the prefixes of the North-western Branch generally retain the labial nasal *m*, excepting in the case of the Fernandian language. In the 5th prefix, instead of *l* or *r*, we usually find the dental media *d*. On the other hand, the dental tenuis of the 12th prefix (TU-) has been converted into the liquid *l* in all the North-western Branch languages, excepting the Fernandian; and the same liquid has also been retained as the consonant of the 11th prefix.

506. We have admitted that some of the correspondences between singular and plural prefixes which are peculiar to the North-western Branch, or only shared by

---

* In Benga, Dualla, and Isubu.

one or two other Bântu languages, are probably not innovations,—but retentions from a former period, when, as yet, many of the plural prefixes had not regularly attached themselves to certain singular forms. We also, on one or more occasions, meet with a prefixual form which appears to be more original than those found in the other two Branches of the Bântu languages. But all the peculiarities which are distinctive of the North-western Branch do not admit of this explanation. The forms of some of the prefixes have been so strongly contracted as almost to defy identification. Thus prefixes may have been confounded with each other, and correspondences differing from the original ones may have arisen through the force of analogy. At the same time, the concord appears to be frequently employed in the North-western languages rather as an alliterative process, than in its original grammatical sense, or as a division of the nouns into classes. The incompleteness of our materials for a knowledge of these languages renders it probable that the rules based upon them will have to be altered or modified in some of their details.

DIKELE.

507. Di-*kĕle* 5. is spoken by the Ba-*kĕle* 2., sing. N-*kĕlĕ* (Mpongwe O-*kĕlĕ*) 1. In this language, as in Kafir, the forms of the 1st and 3rd prefixes are usually contracted to a mere consonant. Dikele, however, proceeds a step farther than Kafir, and adapts this m- to the nature of the initial consonant of the stem. Thus the m- frequently becomes an n-, or in some cases falls off entirely. The most usual forms of the 1st and 3rd prefixes are, therefore, identical with those of the 9th, and these three classes are frequently only to be distinguished by means of the forms of concord which refer to them. Many nouns which indicate animals, parts of the body, &c., have evidently been transferred from the 9th (or some other) class to the 1st, and now have plurals of the 2nd (ba-) class. In cases where the vowel of the 1st and 3rd classes is retained,

the *u* sound is usually converted into *i*, which renders these prefixes homophonous with the 4th (**mi-**). In one instance (*gwana* 3. " mouth ") it almost seems as if the 3rd prefix had in Dikele the unusual form **gw-**, but a comparison of Mpongwe shews that the *gw* here is part of the stem, although it falls off before the plural prefix **mi-**. It is remarkable that the vowel *u* of the 11th and 12th prefixes has been changed into *a* in Dikele. This renders it a little doubtful whether the prefix **a-** or **dsh-** is really identical with the **ka-** of the Middle Branch, and to be assigned to the 13th class. It is possible that the letter *a*, as given by the missionaries, may be more of an indistinct short sound, derived from any other original vowel. Very curious, if true, is the case of a noun which beginning with **m-** in the singular, is said to belong to the 6th class, and forms its plural with the 4th prefix **mi-**. The *i* of the 5th (**di-**) prefix is retained in Dikele before *a*, *ă*, *o*, and *e*,— but is suppressed before *i* and *u*; whilst the *a* of the 6th prefix (**ma-**) always disappears when the stem before which it is placed begins with a vowel.

DIKELE PREFIXES.

SINGULAR.	PLURAL.
1. (—), **mu-** **n-** **m-** **mi-**	2. **ba-**, **bo-** **b-**
3. (—), *gw-* **mi-** **m-** **n-**	4. **mi-** 6. **ma-**
5. **di-** **d-**	6. **ma-** **m-**
6. **m-**	4. **mi-**
7. **vi-** **v-**	12. **la-** **l-** 4. **mi-**
9. **n-** **m-** (—)	6. (+ 9.) **ma-***n*- **ma-***m*- **ma-**
11. **la-** **ɟ'a-**	6. **ma-** 10. (—)
13. **dsh-**, **a-**	8. **bi-** 6. **ma-**
14. **bi-** **b-** **bo-**	6. **ma-**, **ma-***bi*- **m-** **ma-***bo*-

DIKELE NOUNS.

mu-*tyī* 1. "man, person," pl. bo-*tyi* 2. (p. 208);

mi-*ana* or m-*ana* 1. "child," pl. b-*ana* 2. (p. 209);

m-*ǎnǎ* (Mpongwe m-*ǎnlǎ*) 1. "mullet," pl. b-*ǎnǎ* 2.;

n-*kǎɜ'ǎ* 1. "a bachelor," pl. ba-*kǎɜ'ǎ* 2.;

n-*lŏṅ* (Mpongwe o-*nlogi*) 1. "builder," pl. ba-*lŏṅ* 2.;

n-*dʃhoɜ'i* (Mpongwe o-*yonisi*) 1. "killer," pl. ba-*dʃhoɜ'i* 2.;

koshě 1. "parrot," pl. ba-*koshě* 2. (Mpongwe n-*gozyo*, Benga *koho* 9.);

gwǎlě 1. "ear," pl. ba-*gwǎlě* 2.;

lema (Otyiheréro o-mu-*tima*, § 494) 3. "heart," pl. mi-*lema* 4.;

mbeka 3. "hill," pl. mi-*mbeka* 4.;

nkoma 3. "ring," pl. mi-*nkoma* 4.;

ɜ'*ali* or n-ɜ'*ali* 3. "law," pl. mi-ɜ'*ali* 4.;

gwana (Mpongwe o-*gwana*) 3. "mouth," pl. mi-*ana* 4.;

m-*ǎi* 3. "belly, womb," pl. mi-*ǎi* 4.;

m-*ulǐě* 3. "head," pl. mi-*ulǐě* 4.;

m-*ūṅ* 3. "a corpse," pl. mi-*ūṅ* 4.;

mi-*aka* 3. "a castrated animal," pl. mi-*aka* 4.;

mi-*aya* 3. "white ant," pl. mi-*aya* 4.;

mi-*ǎṅyǎ* 3. "fur, hair of the body," pl. mi-*ǎṅyǎ* 4.;

mi-*ěṅye* 3. "lunatic," pl. mi-*ěṅye* 4.;

mi-*endshi* 3. "messenger," pl. mi-*endshi* 4.;

mi-*ěbě* 3. "a swelling," pl. mi-*ěbě* 4.;

m-*iěli* 3. "moonlight," pl. mi-*ěli* 4. (p. 204, note);

mi-*ěliǎ* 3. "measure (of length)," pl. mi-*ěliǎ* 4.;

mi-*ěɜ'e* 4. "entrails;"

mi-*nyungwa* 3. "fragment," pl. mi-*nyungwa* 4.;

m-*bŏ* 3. "arm," pl. ma-*bŏ* 6.;

n-*koɜ'i* (Mpongwe o-*golu*) 3. "leg," pl. ma-*koɜ'i* 6.;

di-*kǎki* 5. "stone," pl. ma-*kǎki* 6.;

di-*ashika* 5. "a door, doorway," pl. m-*ashika* 6.;

di-*ǎli* 5. "nape," pl. m-*ǎli* 6.;

di-*eki* or di-*ekě* 5. "law," pl. m-*eki* 6.;

di-*oi* (Zulu i-*li-zwi*, Mpongwe i*nyoi*) 5. "voice," pl. m-*oi* 6. (Isubu *do*, Dualla *doi* pl. ma-*doi* 6.);

d-*ishī* (Benga d-*ihǎ*, Dualla and Isubu d-*iso*) 5. "eye," pl. m-*ishī* (Benga m-*ihǎ*, Dualla and Isubu m-*iso*) 6. (Kafir i-*li-so* 5., &c., § 327);

d-*u* 5. "fire," pl. m-*u* 6.;

d-*umba* (Mpongwe i-*gumba*) 5. "cargo," pl. m-*umba* 6.;

d-*ushī* 5. "a brush," pl. m-*ushī* 6.;

ma-*kiemba* 6. "salt;"

m-*anga* (Mpongwe) 6. "manatus, seal, and seals;"

m-*oka* 6. "sole fish," pl. mi-*oka* 4.;

vi-*nǎni* (Benga i-*nǎni*, Dualla i-*nun*, Isubu i-*noni*, Fernando Po si-*nodi*) 7. "bird," pl. la-*nǎni* (Benga lo-*nǎni*, Isubu lo-*noni*, Fernando Po to-*nodi*) 12. (Bayciye i-n-*yene* 9., § 486, p. 195);

vi-*lambě* 7. "a trap, snare," pl. la-*lambe* 12.;

vi-*ondshi* 7. "hatchet," pl. 1-*ondshi* 12. (Isubu e-*ondo* 13. "axe," pl. be-*ondo* 8.);
v-*eia* 7. "firewood," pl. 1-*eia* 12. (Dualla and Isubu *wea*);
vi-*na* 7. "finger," pl. mi-*na* (Otyihereró o-mi-*nwe*, § 494) 4.;
n-*dshali* (Mpongwe) 9. "gun," pl. ma-n-*dshali* 6.;
m-*bute* (Mpongwe) 9. "bottle," pl. ma-m-*bute* 6.;
pĕndshe 9. "world, earth, land, woods," pl. ma-*pĕndshe* 6.;
sheba 9. "ivory," pl. ma-*sheba* 6.;
la-*ngăkă* 11. "head," pl. ma-*ngăkă* 6.;
s'a-*pas'a* 11. "hoof," pl. ma-*pas'a* 6. (? Mpongwe m-*pănda* 9., Isubu *fala*);
la-*nyui* 11. "honey-bee," pl. *nyui* 10. (Mpongwe *nyowe*);
la-*nyas'a* 11. "a flea;"
la-*ndănga* 11. "the end," pl. *ndănga* 10. and ma-*ndănga* 6.;
dsh-*eli* (Benga e-*le*) 13. "tree," pl. bi-*eli* (Benga be-*le*) 8. (Mpongwe e-*rere* 7. pl. *rere* 8., Setshuâna se-χla-re 7. pl. li-χla-re 8., Zulu u-mu-*ti* 3. pl.

i-mi-*ti* 4. § 428 note, Dualla bo-*eli* 14. pl. mi-*eli* 4., Isubu bw-*eli* 14. pl. ma-*li* 6.);
a-*vata* (Benga e-*gala*) 13. "chest," pl. bi-*vata* (Benga be-*gala*) 8. (Mpongwe e-*gara* 7.);
a-*bobi* 13. "hat," pl. bi-*bobi* 8.;
a-*shu* 13. "day (of 24 hours)," pl. bi-*shu* 8. and ma-*shu* 6.;
bi-*ali* (Mpongwe o-*waro*, Isubu b-*olo*) 14. "a canoe," pl. m-*ali* (Mpongwe am-*aro*, Isubu m-*olo*) 6. (Benga bw-*alu* 14. pl. mi-*alu* 4., Dualla b-*olo* 14. pl. mi-*olo* 4.);
bo-shĕ (Mpongwe o-*zye*, Isubu bo-*so*) 14. "face," pl. ma-bo-shĕ (Isubu ma-*so*) 6. (Benga bo-*ho* 14. pl. mi-o-*ho* 4., Dualla bo-*so* 14. pl. mi-o-*so* 4., Kafir u-bu-*so* 14., Makua w-itó 14., Kihiau u-*ssio* 14., Kikámba u-*dio* 14., Kinika u-*sso* 14., Kisuáheli u-*sso* 11. pl. ni-u-*sso* 10. § 483);*
bi-*wobi* 14. "a piece of cloth," pl. ma-*wobi* 6.;
bi-ău (Dualla and Isubu bo-*ngo*) 14. "brain," pl. m-ău 6.;
bi-shikwĕ 14. "back-yard," pl. ma-bi-shikwĕ 6.;
b-*uli* 14. "cavern," pl. m-*uli* 6.

THE BENGA LANGUAGE.

508. The Benga language, spoken on the islands of Corisco Bay, belongs to a different species from Dikele. In our limited specimens of Benga, no trace of the 11th

* This noun evidently belongs to the same stem as d-*ishi* (= Kafir i-li-*so*) 5. "eye." (*Vide* p. 236 and § 327.) The plural forms mai-o-*ho* and mai-o-*so* 4. in Benga and Dualla are very suggestive, when compared with the Kisuáheli plural mi-u-*sso* 10.

class of nouns has, as yet, been discovered. The 10th (n-) class appears to be in regular correspondence with the 9th (n-). The Benga language agrees with Dualla in using the prefix of the 4th class (mi-) as plural to the 14th (bo-). One noun of the 14th class is, however, irregular, and appears to possess a plural of the 10th (n-) class. It is remarkable that the prefix (mw-) of the 3rd class frequently loses its consonant, and that the vowel u- then represents in Benga the same 3rd prefix which we often find in Dikele converted into an n-. The 5th (di-) and 7th (vi-) prefixes frequently lose their consonants, and become, in this shorter form, apparently homophonous. This may sometimes have occasioned the transference of nouns from one of these two classes to the other.

BENGA PREFIXES.

SINGULAR.	PLURAL.
1. PERSONAL. 2. mo-, (—) mw- m-	ba- b-
3. mw- m- n-	4. mi- me-
5. di- dy- d- i-	6. ma- m-
7. i- vi- v-	12. lo- l-
9. n- m- (—)	10. n- m- (—)
13. e- y-	8. be- bi-
14. bw- b- bo- bu-	4. mi- me- mi-o- 10. (—)

BENGA NOUNS.

mo-*to* 1. "man, person," pl. ba-*to* 2. "people" (p. 208);

mw-*ana* 1. "child," pl. b-*ána* 2. (p. 209);

mo-*m-o* (? = Otyihereró o-mu-*rumendu*) 1. "man," pl. ba-*m-o* 2.;

mw-*a-dsho* 1. "woman," pl b-*a-dyo* 2. (p. 211);

Anyambi (Dikele *Anyambie*) 1. "God" (§ 396);

mw-*adi* (Dikele mi-*adi*) 3. "female" (p. 211);

u-*dumbu* (Dualla and Isubu mo-*lumbu*, § 439 note) 3. "mouth," pl. me-*dumbu* 4.;

u-*báki* 3. "axe," pl. me-*báki* 4.;

u-*vándá* (Dikele n-*wándá*) 3. "cassada," pl. me-*vándá* 4.;

Benga Derivative Prefixes of Nouns.

u-*diki* (Dikele n-*dushiki*) 3. "pestle," pl. me-*diki* 4.;

u-*kwala* (Dikele n-*kwata*, Mpongwe o-*kwara*) 3. "cutlass," pl. me-*kwala* 4.;

u-*vătă* 3. "body hair," pl. me-*vătă* 4.;

u-*namba* (Dikele n-*damba*, Mpongwe o-*lamba*) 3. "cloth," pl. me-*namba* 4.;

u-*ngoko* (Dikele n-*kokwĕ*) 3. "sugar-cane," pl. me-*ngoko* 4. (Mpongwe i-*koko*);

mw-*anga* 3. "garden," pl. mi-*anga* 4.;

m-*olo* 3. "head," pl. mi-*olo* 4.;

i-*kadu* (Dikele di-*handshi* = ? Sena and Tette z-*ansha*) 5. "hand," pl. ma-*kadu* (? Sena m-*ansha*) 6.;

i-*tătă* Mpongwe (Dikele di-*tătă*) 5. "banana," pl. ma-*tătă* 6.;

i-*paki* (Mpongwe) 5. "cap," pl. ma-*paki* 6. (Dikele a-*paki* 13.);

i-*bătă* 5. "dress," pl. ma-*b tă* 6. (*bătă-kă*, Dualla bo̱to, "to dress");

i-*dyăge* 5. "duck," pl. ma-*dyăge* 6.;

i-*kĕngă* 5. "razor," pl. ma-*kengă* 6. (Dikele vi-*kiĕn* 7.);

i-*tăi* (Isubu i-*toi*) 5. "drop," pl. ma-*tăi* (Isubu ma-*toi*) 6.;

i-*ngongo* (Mpongwe) 5. "tin," pl. ma-*ngongo* 6. (Dikele a-*ngwengwe* 13.);

i-*bongo* 5. "boat," pl. ma-*bongo* 6.;

i-*lali* Isubu (Dualla i-*dali*) 5. "stone," pl. ma-*lali* Isubu (Dualla ma-*dali*) 6.;

i-*bĕkĕ* 5. "shoulder," pl. ma-*bĕkĕ* 6. (Dikele a-*bekĕ* 13.);

di-*tă* (Dualla i-*toi*, Nano e-*twi*, p. 218) 5. "ear," pl. ma-*tă* (Dualla ma-*toi*) 6. (§ 434, note);

di-*ke* (Dikele di-*aki*, Mpongwe i-*ki*, Sindonga ĕ-*yi*, p. 214) 5. "egg," pl. ma-*ke* 6.;

d-*ina* (Dikele, Dualla, and Isubu) 5. "name," pl. m-*ina* (Dikele, Dualla, and Isubu) 6. (§ 484, note);

dy-*oba* (Dikele di-*oba*, Otyihererö e-*yuva*, p. 205) 5. "sun," pl. m-*oba* 6.;

dy-*ămbi* (Dualla dsh-*ombe*, Isubu dy-*ombe*) 5. "door," pl. m-*umbi* (Isubu m-*ombe*) 6.;

d-*iă* (Dualla and Isubu d-*io*, Otyiherero e-*ɔ'uko* p. 205) 5. "fire-place," pl. m-*iă* (Isubu m-*io*) 6.;

m-*iba* (Dikele, Dualla, and Isubu ma-*diba*, p. 142, first note) 6. "water;"

ma-*vule* (Isubu ma-*ula*, Kafir a-ma-*futa*, p. 142, third note) 6. "oil;"

ma-*kăndă* (Dikele ma-*kăndshika*, Mpongwe a-*ka*) 6. "sap;"

ma-*ku* (Dikele ma-*ɔ'ak'*, Mpongwe a-*lugu*) 6 "rum;"

ma-*kia* Isubu (Dualla ma-*iya*) 6 "blood;"

m-*ănyangă* 6. "milk;"

i-*boko* 7. "place," pl. lo-*boko* 12.;

i-*kadada* 7. "pepper," pl. lo-*kadada* 12.;

i-*bobĕli* 7. "spider," pl. lo-*bobĕli* 12. (Mpongwe i-*boboti* 5.);

vi-*aha* 7. "a lime," pl. 1-*aha* 12. (Dikele di-*loshi* 5., Mpongwe o-*loshi* 3.);

vi-*anga* (Mpongwe ez-*anga*) 7. "salt," pl. 1-*anga* 12.;

v-*itua* 7. "candle," pl. 1-*itua* 12.;

n-*dabo* (= Bashubea n-*dobo*, Bayeiye n-*tshu* or n-*dshu*, &c., p. 195) 9. "house," pl. n-*dabo* 10. (Dualla and Isubu n-*dabo* 9., pl. ma-n-*dabo* 6.);

n-*dshea* 9. "path," pl. n-*dshea* 10. (p. 201, note);

m-*boka* Isubu (Dualla m-*boa*) 9. "town," pl. m-*boka* 10. (Dikele m-*bokĕ* 3.);

m-*bwia* (Dikele m-*buɜ'a*, Dualla and Isubu m-*bua*, Bayeiye e-n-*fera* p. 195) 9. "rain" (§ 118);

m-*bandsha* 9. "bamboo," pl. m-*bandsha* 10. (Dikele a-*bandshika* 13.);

pavo 9. "knife," pl. *pavo* 10.;

e-*lombo* (Dikele a-*lombi*) 13. "thing," pl. be-*lombo* 8.;

e-*lendi* (Dikele a-*lendshi*) 13. "boat," pl. be-*lendi* 8. (Mpongwe e-*lende*);

e-*linga* (Dikele a-*linga*) 13. "dress," pl. be-*linga* 8. (Mpongwe e-*linga* 7.);

e-*huka* (Dikele a-*shuka*) 13. "jug," pl. be-*huka* 8. (Mpongwe n-*tyuga* 9.);

e-*bonga* 13. "chair," pl. be-*bonga* 8.;

e-*kăi* (Dikele a-*kăndă*) 13. "plantain," pl. be-*kăi* 8. (Mpongwe i-*kăla* 5.);

e-*pokolo* 13. "hat," pl. be-*pokolo* 8. (Mpongwe e-*pokolu* 7.);

e-*dyaka* 13. "fish," pl. be-*dyaka* 8.;

e-*nă* 13. "arm," pl. be-*nă* 8.;

y-*apa* (Dikele dsh-*apa*) 13. "a flat basket," pl. bi-*apa* 8.;

y-*ăkă* 13. "a large family fetish," pl. bi-*ăkă* 8.;

y-*alu* 13. "a boat of peculiar form," pl. bi-*alu* 8.;

bw-*alu* (Dikele bi-*ali*, § 507) 14. "canoe," pl. mi-*alu* (Dualla mi-*olo*) 4.;

bo-*ho* (Dikele bo-*shĕ*, § 507) 14. "face," pl. mi-*o-ho* (Dualla mi-*o-so*) 4.;

b-*okă* 14. "rainy season," pl. mi-*okă* 4.;

bw-*anga* Dualla (Dikele bi-*áŭ*) 14. "medicine," pl. mi-*anga* 4.;

bo-*lohi* 14. "orange," pl. me-*lohi* 4. (Mpongwe o-*lasha* 3., Dikele di-*liasa* 5.);

bu-*wha* 14. "day," pl. *whi* 10. (Isubu and Dualla bu-*nya* 14., pl. mi-*nya* 4.).

DUALLA AND ISUBU.

509. In Dualla and Isubu we perceive an irregular correspondence of the 2nd (ba-) prefix, which we occasionally find here as plural to the 3rd (mo-); and in each language, in one case at least, the 4th prefix (mi-) corresponds as plural to the 1st (mo-). It is probable that these irregularities are in some way connected with the existence in these dialects of personal nouns of the 3rd and 4th classes. It is clearly shown by

the few Kafir nouns of persons which belong to the 3rd (m-) and to the 4th (mi-) class that it is natural for such nouns to be either partly or wholly treated as if they belonged to one of the two personal classes. (*Vide* p. 160, note.) The contest between grammatical and logical gender, between ancient usage and modern analogy, continually produces similar apparent irregularities.

510. It is a second peculiarity of these dialects that in them the 12th (lo-) prefix corresponds, in a few cases, as plural to the 5th (di-). The 5th prefix in the Bântu languages almost universally has the 6th as its corresponding plural; the only exception besides the present being that of one personal noun in Kongo, which belongs to the 5th (ri-) class, but forms its plural with the 2nd prefix (a-). As the 5th prefix in Dualla and Isubu is, when abbreviated, homophonous with the usual form of the 7th i- (to which here the 12th prefix generally corresponds), it may be that this circumstance has led, by error or analogy, to the above-mentioned exceptional correspondence. The 9th (n-) class in these dialects has not only the 10th (n-), but also the 6th (ma-), and 2nd (ba-), as corresponding plurals. The respective prefix of each of the two latter classes is placed before the form with the 9th (n-) prefix. We notice in Dualla, as in Benga, that the 4th (mi-) prefix corresponds as plural to the 14th; whilst in Isubu (as well as Dikele and Fernandian) the 14th class more usually forms its plural with the 6th prefix. A few Isubu nouns of the 14th (bo-) class have, however, plurals of the 4th.

511. The DUALLA (or Cameroons) language differs but slightly from Isubu. In a few Dualla words we find the palatalised form (dsh-) of the 5th (di-) prefix. The 11th (l-) class appears to be distinct from the 5th. The 7th prefix (i-), in a few nouns at least, has the 8th (bi-) as its corresponding plural, although the 12th (lo-) is the usual plural in Dualla. Of this

partial agreement with the general rule of correspondence of the 7th and 8th classes in the Bântu languages, Dualla and Fernandian afford, as far as we know, the only instances among the languages of the North-western Branch.

DUALLA PREFIXES.

SINGULAR.	PLURAL.
PERSONAL.	
1. mo- mu- m-	**2.** ba- b- **4.** mi-
3. mo- m-	**4.** mi- **2.** b-
5. di-, dsh- d- i-	**6.** ma- m- **12.** lo-
7. i-	**12.** lo- **8.** bi-
9. n-, m-, (—)	**10.** n-, (—) **6.** (+ 9.) ma-n-, ma-m- **2.** ba-
11. l-	**6.** m-
13. e-	**8.** be-
14. bo- b-	**4.** mi- mi-o-

DUALLA NOUNS.

mo-*tu* (Isubu) 1. "man," pl. ba-*tu* (Isubu) 2. (p. 208);

mu-*tu* (Isubu mw-*ai-tu*) 1. "woman," pl. b-*i-tu* (Isubu b-*ai-tu*) 2. (pp. 210 and 211);

mo-*kum* (Isubu mo-*komi*) 1. "slave," pl. ba-*kum* (Isubu ba-*komi*) 2.;

mo-*longeri* 1. "singer," pl. ba-*longeri* 2.;

mo-*abedi* 1. "divider," pl. ba-*abedi* 2.;

mo-*abuedi* 1. "climber," pl. ba-*abuedi* 2.;

mo-*aledi* 1. "holder, peacemaker," pl. ba-*aledi* 2.;

mo-*anedi* 1. "ruler, governor," pl. ba-*anedi* 2.;

mo-*dimo* (Isubu) 1. "demon, apparition, ghost, spirit," pl. ba-*dimo* (Bayeiye ba-*zimo* p. 194) 2. (§ 395);

mo-*dieri* 1. "leader, guide," pl. ba-*dieri* 2.;

mo-*dun* 1. "aged," pl. ba-*dun* 2. (Isubu mo-*luni*, pl. mi-*luni* 4.);

mo-*ibedi* (Isubu mo-*iba*) 1. "thief," pl. ba-*ibedi* (Isubu ba-*iba*) 2. (§ 325);

mo-*biedi* 1. "learned person, doctor," pl. ba-*biedi* 2.;

mo-*boedi* 1. "sick person," pl. ba-*boedi* 2.;

mo-*boledi* 1. "worker, labourer," pl. ba-*boledi* 2.;

Dualla Derivative Prefixes of Nouns. 243

mo-*langedi* 1. "calculator," pl. ba-*langedi* 2.;
mo-*leedi* 1. "teacher," pl. ba-*leedi* 2.;
mo-*loedi* 1. "curser, swearer," pl. ba-*loedi* 2.;
mu-*na* (Isubu mw-*ana*) 1. "child, son, offspring," pl. ba-*na* (Isubu b-*ana*) 2. (p. 209);
mo-*okeli* (Isubu mo-*okoa*) 1. "learner," pl. ba-*okeli* (Isubu ba-*okoa*) 2.;
mo-*en*(i) or mw-*en* (Bayeiye mo-*yene*, Setshuâna mo-*en* pl. ba-*en* 2.) 1. "stranger," pl. mi-*en* 4.;
mo-*lopo* (Isubu) 3. "head," pl. mi-*lopo* 4.;
mo-*lema* Isubu (Otyihereró o-mu-*tima*, § 494) 3. "heart," pl. mi-*lema* (Isubu) 4.;
mo-*nia* 3. "parable," pl. mi-*nia* 4.;
m-*benga* (Isubu) 3. "dove," pl. mi-*benga* 4.;
m-*bia* (Isubu) 3. "palm-nut," pl. mi-*bia* 4.;
m-*pimba* (Isubu m-*bemba*) 3. "nose," pl. mi-*pimba* 4.;
m-*odi* 3. "female," pl. mi-*odi* 4. (p. 211);
mo-*anu* or mw-*anu* 3. "thought," pl. mi-*anu* 4.;
mo-*lumbu* (Isubu) 3. "mouth," pl. mi-*lumbu* (Isubu) 4. (§ 439, note);
m-*omi* (Benga) 3. "male," pl. b-*omi* (Isubu) 2. (Isubu m-*omi* 1., Bayeiye mo-*rume*, § 486);
di-*kom* 5. "friend," pl. ma-*kom* 6.;
di-*bondi* (Isubu) 5. "cup, mug," pl. ma-*bondi* (Isubu) 6.;
di-*bongo* (Isubu di-*bongo-bongo*) 5. "knee," pl. ma-*bongo* (Isubu ma-*bongo-bongo*) 6.;
di-*a* (Isubu di-*ka*, Sindonga e-*káxa*, Nano e-*ka*, Otyihereró e-*ke*) 5. "hand," pl. ma-*a* (Isubu ma-*ka*, Sindonga o-ma-*kaxa*, Nano o-va-*ka*, Otyihereró o-ma-*ke*) 6.;
dah-*ongise* 5. "salvation," pl. ma-*ongise* 6.;
d-*iso* (Isubu) 5. "eye," pl. m-*iso* (Isubu) 6. (§ 327);
d-*umbu* (Isubu) 5. "a bird's nest," pl. m-*umbu* (Isubu) 6.;
i-*du* (Isubu) 5. "cork," pl. ma-*du* (Isubu ma-*du* or ma-*lu*) 6.;
i-*tanga* 5. "foot," pl. ma-*tanga* 6.;
i-*nama* 5. "arm," pl. ma-*nama* 6.;
di-*kongo* 5. "shot," pl. lo-*kongo* 12.;
i-*bon* (Isubu i-*boni*) 7. "a ball," pl. lo-*bon* (Isubu lo-*boni*) 12.;
i-*sangu* 7. "idol," pl. lo-*sangu* 12.;
i-*sun* 7. "a drop," pl. lo-*sun* 12.;
i-*nun* (Isubu i-*noni*, Dikele vi-*náni*, p. 236) 7. "bird," pl. bi-*nun* 8. (vide Bayeiye i-n-*yene* 9., p. 195);
i-*lipa* 7. "fleecy cloud," pl. bi-*lipa* 8.;
i-*tambi* 7. or e-*tambi* 13. "shoe," pl. be-*tambi* 8.;
n-*dabo* (Isubu and Benga, § 508) 9. "house," pl. ma-n-*dabo* 6.;
m-*boa* (Isubu and Benga m-*boka*, § 508) 9. "abode," pl. ma-*m-boa* (Isubu ma-*m-boka*) 6.;

m-*basi* (Isubu) 9. "corn," pl. ma-m-*basi* (Isubu) 6.;

m-*bimba* 9. "corpse," pl. ma-m-*bimba* 6.,—Isubu m-*bimba*, (Kafir u-m-*zimba*, Southern Tekeza u-*timba* "body") 3., pl. m-*bimba* 4.;

n-*yaka* (Isubu) 9. "ox," pl. n-*yaka* (Isubu) 10.;

n-*denge* 9. "suffering, distress;"

kalati (Isubu) 9. "book," pl. *kalati* (Isubu) 10.;

kunga (Isubu *konga* or *kunga*) 9. "boat;"

l-*oko* (Isubu) 11. "game, play, sport," pl. m-*oko* (Isubu) 6.;

l-*ongo* (Isubu l-*ongo*) 11. "a part, portion, share," pl. m-*ongo* (Isubu m-*ongo*) 6.;

l-*ambu* (Isubu) 11. "thing," pl. m-*ambu* 6.;

e-*puma* Isubu (Dikele a-*buma*) 13. "fruit," pl. be-*puma* (Isubu) 8.;

e-*kotu* (Isubu e-*koto*) 13. "cap," pl. be-*kotu* (Isubu be-*koto*) 8.;

e-*bolu* (Dikele a-*shali*) 13. "work," pl. be-*bolu* 8.;

e-*idi* or e-*ili* (Isubu e-*eli* "bush, thick shrub," Dikele dsh-*eli* "tree," § 507) 13. "forest, wilderness," pl. be-*idi* (Isubu be-*eli*) 8.;

e-*yala* 13. "word," pl. be-*yala* 8.;

bu-*nya* (Isubu) 14. "day," pl. mi-*nya* (Isubu) 4.;

bo-*eli* (Isubu bw-*eli*) 14. "tree," pl. mi-*eli* 4. (Zulu u-mu-*ti* 3., pl. i-mi-*ti* 4., § 428 note; Dikele dsh-*eli* 13. pl. bi-*eli* 8., § 507);

bo-*ambu* (Isubu) 13. "language," pl. mi-*ambu* 4.;

bo-*anga* 14. "breast," pl. mi-*anga* 4.;

bo-*so* Isubu (Benga bo-*ho*, Dikele bo-*shĕ*, § 507) 14 "face," pl. mi-*o-so* (Benga mi-*o-ho*) 4.;

b-*olo* (Isubu b-*olo*, Benga bw-*alu*, Dikele bi-*ali*, § 507) 14. "canoe," pl. mi-*olo* (Benga mi-*alu*) 4.

512. The characteristics which distinguish ISUBU from its variety, Dualla, are few. Among the North-western Branch languages, Isubu alone has retained the ancient feature of a local class (o-), which is probably to be identified with the 16th (PA-) class. (§ 435.) The 11th (l-) class, on the contrary, can hardly (if at all) be distinguished in its concord from the 5th (dl-). Although the prefix of this latter class occasionally dwindles to y-, it has never been palatalised in Isubu, as it has in Dualla. On the contrary, the prefix dsh- in Isubu belongs to the 7th (l-) class, being derived from an ancient k. (*Vide* § 502.) To the Isubu nouns given in the Dualla list, we add the following.

ISUBU PREFIXES.

SINGULAR.	PLURAL.
1. PERSONAL. mo- mw- m-	**2.** ba- b- **4.** mi-
3. mo- mu- m- mw-	**4.** mi- me- m- **2.** ba-
5. di- d- i- y-	**6.** ma- m- **12.** lo-
7. i- y- dsh-	**12.** lo- l-
9. n-, m-, ñ-, (—)	**10.** n-, m-, ñ-, (—) **6.** ma-n-, ma-m-, m- **2.** ba-n-, ba-m-, ba-
11. l-	**6.** ma-l- m-
13. e- y-	**8.** be- bi-
ABSTRACT. **14.** bo-, bw- b- bu-	**6.** ma- m- **4.** mi-
LOCAL. **16.** (**15.**) o-	

Bleek, S. Afr. Comp. Grammar.

ISUBU NOUNS.

mo-*kutu* (Dualla **mo**-*utu*) 1. "child," pl. **ba**-*kutu* (Dualla **ba**-*utu*) 2.;

mo-*kanea* (Dualla **mo**-*anedi*) 1. "ruler," pl. **ba**-*kanea* (Dualla **ba**-*anedi*) 2.;

mw-*ai-tu* 1. "woman," pl. **b**-*ai-tu* 2. (p. 211);

m-*omi* 1. "male," pl. **b**-*omi* (Dualla) 2. (Dualla and Benga **m**-*omi* 3., Bayeiye **mo**-*rume*, § 486);

m-*om-ana* (Dualla **m**-*om-a*) 1. "husband," pl. **b**-*om-ana* 2.;

mo-*ongise* (Dualla **mo**-*ongiseri*) 1. "saviour," pl. **ba**-*ongise* 2.;

mo-*nya* 1. "brother-in-law, sister-in-law," pl. **ba**-*nye* 2. or **mi**-*nye* 4.;

mo-*ñgombi* 3. "garment," pl. **mi**-*ñgombi* 4.;

m-*ulu* or **m**-*uru* (Dualla **mo**-*udi*) 3. "breath," pl. **mi**-*uru* 4.;

m-*bu* (Dualla) 3. "year," pl. **m**-*bu* (Dualla **mi**-*bu*) 4.;

mu-*ni* (Dualla **mu**-*ne*, Otyihereró *o*-**mu**-*nue*, § 494) 3. "finger," pl. **mi**-*ni* (Dualla **mi**-*ne*) 4.;

mw-*iri* 3. "side," pl. **mi**-*iri* 4.;

1 K

me-aṅgo (Dualla) 4. "news;"
m-ea (Dualla mi-ea) 4. "bowels;"
m-bimba (Dualla) 3. "carcase," pl. mi-bimba 4.;
mw-andsha 3. "sea," pl. mi-andsha 4.;
mo-kaki 3. "giant," pl. mi-kaki 4.;
mw-ari 3. "female," pl. b-ari 2. or mi-ari 4. (p. 211);
mo-kuta 3. "bag," pl. mi-kuta 4.;
mo-kita 3. "body or trunk of a tree," pl. mi-kita 4.;
mo-ese (Dualla) or mw-ese 3. "daylight," pl. mi-ese 4.;
mo-ke 3. "egg," pl. me-ke 4.;
mo-seba 3. "horn," pl. mi-seba 4.;
mo-indi (Dualla mo-endi) 3. "leg," pl. me-indi (Dualla mi-endi) 4.;
di-kaki (Dualla) 5. "promise," pl. ma-kaki (Dualla) 6.;
di-kondi 5. "a post," pl. ma-kondi 6.;
di-kosi 5. "bow," pl. ma-kosi 6.;
di-koṅgo 5. "dart," pl. ma-koṅgo 6.;
di-indu 5. "cloud," pl. ma-indu 6.;
di-bondu 5. "hut," pl. ma-bondu 6.;
d-iebo 5. "grindstone," pl. m-iebo 6.;
d-uwendi (Dualla di-windi) 5. "knife," pl. ma-wendi (Dualla ma-windi, ma-wendi or ma-endi) 6.;
i-angane 5. "supplication," pl. ma-angane 6.;
i-tama or i-lama (Dualla i-lama, Nano e-tama p. 218) 5. "cheek," pl. ma-lama (Dualla) 6.;

i-ombe or di-ombe (= dy-ombe, Dualla dsh-ombe) 5. "door," pl. m-ombe 6.;
i-obi or y-obi 5. or 1-obi 11. "hook," pl. ma-obi 6.;
i-noṅgo 5. "bed," pl. ma-noṅgo 6.;
i-tutu (Dualla) 5. "a bamboo palm," pl. ma-tutu (Dualla) 6.;
i-teke 5. "dirt, mud," pl. ma-teke 6.;
i-tua l-a bw-eli 5. "gum," pl. lo-tua lo bw-eli 12.;
i-boṅgo 7. "a box," pl. lo-boṅgo 12.;
i-obi, y-obi, or dsh-obi 7. "fish-hook," pl. l-obi 12.;
i-duwa 7. "basket used by fishermen," pl. lo-duwa 12.;
i-toti 7. "hissing," pl. lo-toti 12.;
i-ya 7. "the little ant-eater," pl. lo-ya 12.;
i-oṅgo or y-oṅgo 7. "pot," pl. lo-oṅgo 12.;
i-tololo 7. "frog," pl. lo-tololo 12.;
i-miti 7. "a small stinging fly," pl. lo-miti 12.;
n-doki 9. "folly," pl. n-doki 10.;
n-dshoku (Bayeiye o-n-dshovo, p. 195) 9. "elephant," pl. n-dshoku 10.;
ñ-bwa or m-bwa (Dualla m-bọ, Fernandian m-pwa) 9. "dog," pl. ñ-bwa or m-bwa 10. (§§ 235 and 277, Dikele m-bia 1., pl. ba-m-bia 2.);
m-bori (Mpongwe m-boni, § 501) 9. "goat," pl. m-bori 10.;
faki (Fernandian n-kapi) 9. "paddle," pl. faki (Fernandian i-kapi) 10.;

Isubu Derivative Prefixes of Nouns.

tambu (Dualla) 9. "hat," pl. *tamba* 10.;
soe 9. "hair," pl. *soe* 10.;
waṅga 9. "bush," pl. *waṅga* 10.;
konda (Dualla) 9. "chair," pl. *konda* 10.;
n-*dabo* (Dualla) 9. "house," pl. ma-n-*dabo* (Dualla) 6. or n-*dabo* 10.;
m-*boka* (Dualla m-*boa*) 9. "abode," pl. ma-m-*boka* (Dualla ma-m-*boa*) 6.;
akwasa 9. "boil," pl. m-*akwasa* 6.;
n-*yaṅgo* 9. "mother," pl. ba-n-*yaṅgo* 2. (Dualla *nyango* 1., pl. ba-*nyango* 2.);
m-*bamba* 9. "grandfather, grandchild," pl. ba-m-*bamba* 2.;
saṅgo 9. "father," pl. ba-*saṅgo* 2. (Dualla *sango* 1., pl. ba-*sango* 2.);
l-*oṅgo* 11. "trade," pl. ma-l-*oṅgo* 6.;
l-*oṅgo* (Dualla) 11. "part, share," pl. m-*oṅgo* (Dualla) 6.;
l-*obo* 11. "charm," pl. m-*obo* 6.;
e-*kwali* (Dualla) 13. "word," pl. be-*kwali* (Dualla) 8.;
e-*bambu* (Dualla) 13. "board," pl. be-*bambu* (Dualla) 8.;
e-*boliri* 13. "custom, manner," pl. be-*boliri* 8.;
e-*wesi* (Dualla e-*isi* or e-*wisi*, Dikele a-*vesha*) 13. "bone," pl. be-*wesi* (Dualla be-*isi*) 8.;
e-*koni* (Dualla e-*kon*, Dikele a-ϑ'*oni*) 13. "enmity," pl. be-*koni* 8.;
e-*sai* (Dualla e-*sau*, Dikele a-*shaϑ'a*) 13. "a feather," pl. be-*sui* (Dualla bi-*sau*) 8.;

y-*oma* 13. "thing," pl. be-*ma* (Dualla bi-*ma*) 8. (Angola and Kongo e-ki-[w]*uma* 7. pl. e-y-*uma* 8., Mpongwe ez-*ǎma* 7. pl. y-*ǎma* 8.);
e-*lela* (Dualla e-*lele*) 13. "duck," pl. be-*lela* 8.;
e-*embi* (Dualla) 13. "cattle," pl. bi-*embi* (Dualla be-*embi*) 8.;
e-*wake* (Dualla) 13. "baboon," pl. be-*wake* (Dualla) 8.;
e-*wolu* (Dualla) 13. "bread," pl. be-*wolu* (Dualla) 8.;
e-*ondo* 13. "axe," pl. be-*ondo* 8.;
e-*dimo* 13. "ghost, spirit of a dead person," pl. be-*dimo* 8. (§ 395);
e-*dshieli* or e-*gieli* 13. "abiding place," pl. bi-*dshieli* or bi-*gieli* 8.;
e-*ondi* 13. "island," pl. be-*ondi* 8.;
bo-*ndene* Dualla (Otyihereró o-u-*nene*, Kikámba u-*nene*) 14. "greatness," pl. ma-*ndene* (Dualla) 6.;
bo-*loṅgi* 14. "building," pl. ma-*loṅgi* 6.;
bo-*tumba* 14. "colour, sort," pl. ma-*tumba* 6.;
bo-*endi* 14. "cotton," pl. m-*endi* 6.;
bo-*ambu* or bw-*ambu* (Dualla) 14. "language, dialect, tongue, dialogue," pl. m-*ambi* 6.;
b-*uma* (Dualla) 14. "the cotton tree, ceiba," pl. m-*uma* 6.;
bu-*luwe* 14. "loin," pl. ma-*luwe* 6.;
bu-*ten*(i) 14. "night," pl. mi-*ten*(i) 4.;
o-*ma* 16. (or 15.) "place."

FERNANDIAN.

513. The striking peculiarity of the Fernandian derivative prefixes of nouns is the change of the labial nasal (*m*) into the labial media (*b*). By this, the 1st and 3rd prefixes have become homophonous with the 14th (**bo-**), the 6th prefix with the 2nd (**ba-**), and the 4th with the 8th (**bi-**). The number of the prefixes has thus been practically reduced to eleven; but it has been deemed better, for the purpose of comparison, to separate in the table of the prefixes those classes which have now virtually coalesced, *viz.* the 2nd and 6th (**ba-**), the 3rd and 14th (**bo-**), and the 4th and 8th (**bi-**). This change of *m* into *b* does not, however, appear to take place in all the dialects spoken on the island of Fernando Po. At least, the usual forms of the numerals in the Southern part of the island abound in the letter *m*, where those employed in other parts of the island have a *b*. (J. Clarke's Introduction to the Fernandian Tongue, 1848, pp. 22 and 23.) The nouns given in the appended list probably belong to dialects spoken near Clarence, in the North of the island. An analogy to the general change of the *m* into *b* in Fernandian, is met with in the Nano language, in which the *m* of the 6th prefix is always changed into *v*, whilst the *m* of the other prefixes is in some cases retained, but in others also converted into *v*, or, before *u*, falls off entirely. Thus in Nano, the 6th prefix cannot be distinguished from the 2nd (**va-**), and the 4th has, besides its own ancient form (**mi-**), a softened one (**vi-**) which is homophonous with that of the 8th prefix. The 1st and 3rd classes in Nano also possess, in addition to the regular form of their prefix (**mu-**), a second form (**u-**), which is identical with the 14th prefix in Nano. (§ 496.) In Fernandian, also, the 1st and 3rd prefixes (**bo-**) occasionally lose their consonant entirely.

514. Another characteristic of the Fernandian language is the form of the 7th prefix (**si-**), in which, curiously enough, Fernandian agrees with Kafir, although the

diminutive meaning which the 7th prefix possesses in Fernandian is not to be met with in this prefix in Kafir. In Kongo, however, the same 7th prefix (ki-) appears to possess some sort of diminutive force. (§ 430.) Fernandian is also distinguished from the other languages of the North-western Branch by the retention of the original consonant (*t*) of the 12th prefix, which consonant, in this Branch, has been generally converted into *l*. The *l* of the 11th prefix has also been retained in Fernandian; the *r* in r-*oto* "bag" belonging probably to the 5th (di-) class, as the 6th (ba-) class (to which b-*oto* "bags" belongs) has not yet been met with in any other Fernandian noun in plural correspondence with the 11th (lo-) class. A case in which the 8th (bi-) prefix occurs as plural to the 5th (di-) is unique in its kind and exceedingly doubtful. In fact, we dare not draw any stringent conclusion from the insufficient materials which have as yet been published in the Fernandian tongue. Full as they are of misprints and inconsistencies, they are still valuable in furnishing us with a certain kind of knowledge of a language which, in some ways, has been very peculiarly shaped.

FERNANDIAN PREFIXES.

SINGULAR.	PLURAL.
PERSONAL.	
1. bo-, (—) bw- bu- mo- o-	**2.** ba- b- be- (bu-) (?) bi-
3. bo-, (—) bu- b- o-	**4.** bi- (bii-) be-
5. di-, i- d- r-	**6.** ba- b- **8.** bi-
DIMINUTIVE.	
7. si- s-	**12.** to- tw- t-
9. n- m-	**10.** i-
11. lo- lu- l-	**10.** n-, i- m-
13. e-	**8.** bi- i-
14. bo- bu-	**6.** ba-

FERNANDIAN NOUNS.

bo-*tukwe* 1. "king," pl. ba-*tukwe* 2.;

bo-*riba* 1. "stranger," pl. ba-*riba* 2.;

bo-*ie* 1. "man," pl. ba-*ie* 2.;

bo-*obe* or b-*obe* (Benga, Dualla, and Isubu m-*omi*, Bayeiye mo-*rume*, § 486) 1. "male, man," pl. ba-*obe* (Dualla and Isubu b-*omi*) 2.;

bw-*adi* (Benga mw-*adi*) 1. "female," pl. b-*adi* (Isubu b-*ari*) 2. (p. 211);

bw-*ai-so* (Isubu mw-*ai-tu*) 1. "woman," pl. b-*ai-so* (Isubu b-*ai-tu*) 2. (p. 211);

bo-*tshu* (Dualla and Isubu mo-*tu*) 1. "man, person," pl. bu-*tshu* or be-*tshu* (Dualla and Isubu ba-*tu*) 2. (p. 208);

bu-*eta* or bw-*eta* 1. "sister," pl. be-*eta* 2.;

bw-*itshi* (? tw-*itshi*) 1. "brother," pl. bi-*itshi* 2.;

mo-*ube* (Isubu mo-*iba*, vide Dualla mo-*ibedi* p. 242) 1. "thief," pl. be-*ube* (Isubu ba-*iba*) 2. (§ 325);

o-*bola* 1. "a poor mau," pl. a-*bola* 2.;

o-*bedi* or o-*beri* (Shambala m-*vele*) 1. "woman, mother," pl. a-*bedi* (Shambala wa-*vele*) 2.;

o-*bitsha* 1. "rat," pl. a-*bitsha* 2.;

omi 1. "mother," pl. b-*omi* 2.;

bo-*tshika* 3. "spear," pl. bi-*tshika* 4.;

bo-*mpo* 3. "nose," pl. bi-*mpo* 4.;

bo-*so* 3. "fire," pl. be-*so* 4.;

bu-*ee* 3. "mouth," pl. bi-*ee* 4.;

b-*oba* 3. "ground," pl. bi-*oba* 4.;

o-*pelo* 3. "bolt," pl. be-*pelo* 4.;

oko 3. "owl," pl. bi-*oko* 4.;

di-*ala* (Dualla di-*a*, § 511) 5. "hand," pl. ba-*ala* (Dualla ma-*a*) 6.;

di-*koto* (Isubu di-*koso* ?) 5. "foot," pl. ba-*koto* (ba-*kota* ?) 6.;

d-*aatshi* 5. "bed," pl. b-*aatshi* 6.;

r-*oto* 5. (?) "bag," pl. b-*oto* 6.;

i-*te* (Kafir i-li-*tye*, § 176, and § 481 note) 5. "stone," pl. ba-*te* 6. or bi-*te* 8.;

si-*nodi* (Dikele vi-*nâni*, Benga i-*nâni*, Dualla i-*nun*, Isubu i-*noni*) 7. "a small bird," pl. to-*nodi* (Dikele la-*nâni*, Benga lo-*nâni*, Isubu lo-*noni*) 12. (Bayeiye i-n-*yene* 9., p. 195);

si-*pa* 7. "a small ring or armlet," (e-*pa* 13. "an armlet");

si-*so* 7. "a small fire" (bo-*so* 14. "fire");

si-*neneheh* 7. "a babe;"

s-*inki* 7. "a small fly," pl. to-*inki* 12.;

s-*oto* 7. "a small bag," pl. t-*oto* 12.;

s-*ahah* 7. "staff," pl. tw-*ahah* 12.;

s-*etshi* 7. "gazelle," pl. tw-*etshi* 12.;

si-*lu* 7. "yam" (e-*lu* 13., pl. bi-*lu* 8.);

n-*tshobo* 9. "house," pl. i-*tshobo* 10.;

n-*tshodu* 9. "sheep," pl. i-*tshodu* 10.;

n-*kapi* (Isubu *faki*, Mpongwe n-*kabi*) 9. "paddle," pl. i-*kapi* 10. (Dikele la-*kapi* 11., pl. *kapi* 10.);

n-*ko* (Isubu ñ-*goso*, Mpongwe n-*gozyo*) 9. "parrot," pl. i-*ko* 10. (Dikele *koshĕ* 1. pl. ba-*koshĕ* 2.);

n-*kopo* or *kopo* 9. "ox;"

m-*podi* (Mpongwe m-*boni*, p. 230) 9. "goat," pl. i-*podi* 10.;

m-*pela* 9. "snake, eel," pl. i-*pela* 10.;

lo-*oba* 11. "gourd," pl. n-*kobe* 10.;

lo-*bebo* 11. "tongue," pl. i-*bebo* or m-*bebo* 10.;

lu-*kate* 11. "bat," pl. n-*kate* 10.;

l-*oba* 11. "knife," pl. n-*koba* 10.;

l-*ua* 11. "clothes," pl. n-*kue* 10.;

e-*aou* 13. "hatchet," pl. bi-*aou* 8.;

e-*lu* 13. "yam," pl. bi-*lu* 8.;

e-*tata* 13. "gun," pl. i-*tata* 8.;

e-*tshi* (or i-*tshi*) 13. "country," pl. bi-*tshi* 8.;

e-*buta* 13. "hat," pl. i-*buta* 8.;

bo-*ti* or bu-*ti* (Isubu bw-*eli*, Dualla bo-*eli*, p. 244) 14. "tree," pl. ba-*ti* (Isubu ma-*li*) 6.

e. REVIEW OF THE DERIVATIVE PREFIXES OF THE NOUNS.

515. Having thus gone through the known South African Bântu languages, and shown the different systems of correspondence between the concord-indicating derivative prefixes of the nouns, which obtain in each,—we can now pass these prefixes in review. Of each prefix it will be stated in what languages it occurs, in what forms it appears, and what is (as far as these can be ascertained) its etymology, force, and meaning; also to what other class or classes the class indicated by it corresponds either as singular or plural. We shall thus furnish a kind of descriptive catalogue of the different South African Bântu Prefixes of the nouns, giving, as it were, a *resumé* of their Natural History. We shall see the general constancy in the form of each prefix, with many minor phonetic variations, and also how far the different languages agree or vary in their modes of replacing each singular prefix by a corresponding plural one.

1. FIRST PREFIX: MŬ-.

516. The first prefix (MŬ-) is common to all South African Bântu languages.

FORMS OF THE FIRST (MŬ-) PREFIX.

Branch	Language	Forms		
SOUTH-EASTERN BRANCH.	KAFIR.		m-	
	ZULU.	mu-		
	SEĆLAPI.		mo-, m-	
	SESUTO.		(MO-B-)	(—)
	TEKEZA.	mu-	n-(MU-L-)	
MOSAMBIQUE GENUS.	TETTE.	mŭ-	mo-	
	SENA.	mu-	m-	(—)
	MAKUA.			
	KIHIAU.			
ZANGIAN GENUS.	KIKAMBA.			
	KINIKA.			
	SUAHELI.			
	KISAMBALA.*			
INT.	DATEIYE.	mo-		
HUNDA GENUS.	OTYIHERERÓ.		m-	
	SINDONGA.	mu-		(—)
	NANO.		u-	
	ANGOLA.	mŭ-	mo-	
KONGO G.	KONGO.	mu-	m-	u-
	MPONGWE.	om-	o-	
NORTH-WESTERN BRANCH.	DIKELE.	mu-, mi-, n-		(—)
	BENGA.	mw-		
	DUALLA.	mu-	mo-	m-
	ISUBU.	mw-		
	FERNANDIAN.	bu-, bw-, bo-, mo-, o-, (—)		

* Ki-*sambala* (Dr. Steere's letter, § 484) or Ki-*sambara* (Dr. Krapf) 7. is called by the Swaheli Mɐ-*semo* y-a Ki-*sambaɑs* 6.; and by the people themselves (the Wɐ-*shambala* 2., sing. M-*shambala* 1.) M-*buli* z-a Ki-*shambala* 10. Vide Dr. Steere's "Collections for a Hand-book of the Shambala Language, Zanzibar 1867," which I have received while this page is going through the press. The following tables of the forms of the prefixes will receive a few slight additions from this book.

Review of the First Derivative Prefix of Nouns. 253

FORMS. **mu-** in all these languages, *excepting* Kafir, Sesuto, Bayeiye, Mpongwe, Benga, Isubu, and Fernandian. N.B. Marked as short (**mŭ-**) in Tette and Angola.

mw- in *Benga* and *Isubu* before vowels.

mo- regularly in *Setshuâna* '(Seχlapi and Sesuto), *Benga, Dualla,* and *Isubu;* occasionally in *Tette* and *Angola* (besides the more usual form **mŭ-**), and in at least one noun in *Fernandian.* N.B. Marked as long (**mō-**) in Seχlapi. The form **mo-** met with in Bayeiye and Balojazi, according to Livingstone's Vocabulary, may be due to Setshuâna orthography.

mi- frequently in *Dikele.*

m- the only form met with in the *Kafir* language, and occurring, with other forms, in *Zulu, Makua, Kihiau, Kikámba, Kiníka, Suáheli, Kisambala, Otyihereró, Sindonga, Kongo, Dikele, Benga, Dualla,* and *Isubu.* N.B. Setshuâna **m-** = **MO-B-.**

om- in *Mpongwe.*

n- in *Dikele.* N.B. Tekeza **n-** = **MU-L-.**

bu-, bw-, bo- in *Fernandian.*

u- in *Nano* and *Kongo.*

o- in *Mpongwe* and *Fernandian.*

(**—**) The prefix is probably omitted in all the known South African *Bántu* languages,—although instances of such omission have not as yet been proved in Makua, Bayeiye, Mpongwe, Dualla, and Isubu.

RANGE OF MEANING. This prefix indicates persons in the singular number, and is sometimes (particularly in the Middle and North-western Branch languages) extended to animals. Other things, when treated as persons, may also belong to this class.

CORRESPONDENCE. THIS CLASS CORRESPONDS AS SINGULAR TO THE **2nd (BA-)** class throughout the *Bántu* languages. N.B. When the prefix of the 2nd class has the form **bo-** in the Kafir and Setshuâna dialects, it either corresponds to a singular of the 1st class in which the prefix has been omitted, or **bo-** is prefixed to the form with **mo-,**—thus, **bo-*mo-*.**

,, ,, **6th (MA-)** class in some especial cases in *Kafir, Zulu, Sesuto Sena,* (perhaps *Kikámba,*) and *Kongo.*

,, ,, **10th (TIN-)** class in a few nouns in *Angola,* transferred from the 9th (**N-**) class.

,, ,, **4th (MI-)** class in one noun in *Dualla* and another in *Isubu,* which have probably been transferred from the 3rd (**MŪ-**) class.

2. SECOND PREFIX: **BA-**.

517. The second prefix (**BA-**) is common to all South African *Bántu* languages.

FORMS OF THE SECOND (**BA-**) PREFIX.

Branch	Language				
SOUTH-EASTERN BR.	KAFIR SPECIES.	ba-	b-	be-	bo-
	SEXLAPI.				
	SESUTO.				
	TEKEZA.				
MOZAMBIQUE GENUS.	TETTE.	va-	wa-	a-	
	SENA.				
	MAKUA.				
	KIHIAU.	va-	wa-		
ZANGIAN GENUS.	KIKAMBA.			a-	(—
	KINIKA.				
	SUAHELI.	wa-	w-		
	KISAMBALA.				
INT.	DAYEIYE.	ba-			
BUYDA GENUS.	OTYIHEREBÓ.	va-	v-		o-
	SINDONGA.	a-			
	NANO.	va-	ma-		
	ANGOLA.			a-	
KONGO G.	KONGO.				
	MPONGWE.				(—)
NORTH-WESTERN BRANCH.	DIKELE.	ba-	b-		bo-
	BENGA.				
	DUALLA.				
	ISUBU.				
	FERNANDIAN.			be- (bu-), (?) bi-	

The following are among the Nouns of the First (**MŬ-**) and Second (**BA-**) Classes in the Original Bántu Language:
MU-NTU 1. "person, human being," pl. **BA-**NTU 2. (p. 208, §§ 140, 141, 412, and 426);
MU-KATHI 1. "wife, woman," pl. **BA-**KATHI 2. (pp. 208—211);
MU-NTU-ANA 1. "child," pl. **BA-**NTU-ANA 2. (pp. 208 and 209).

FORMS. **ba-** in the *North-western* Branch languages, and in the *Kafir* and *Setshuána* dialects. N.B. The **ba-** in *Bayeiye* may be due to Setshuána orthography.
be- in a few cases, in *Kafir*, *Zulu*, *Sex̌lapi*, and *Fernandian*.
bu- and **bi-** doubtful in *Fernandian*.
b- (before vowel stems) in the *North-western* Branch languages, and also in the *Kafir* and *Setshuána* dialects.
va- regularly in *Tekeza*, *Otyihereró*, and *Nano*.
v- (before vowels) in *Otyihereró*.
va- or **wa-** in *Tette*, *Sena*, and *Kihiau*.
wa- in *Suaheli* and *Kisambalu*.
w- (before vowels) in *Suaheli*.
ma-, by assimilation, in one case in *Nano*.
a- (the only form of the prefix) in *Makua*, *Kikamba*, *Kinika*, *Sindonga*, *Angola*, and the *Kongo* Genus (Kongo and Mpongwe),—and (with other forms) in *Tette* and *Sena*.
bo- (a mere phonetic modification of **ba-**) in one *Dikele* noun.
bo- (probably = **BA-**MU**-**) in the *Kafir* and *Setshuána* dialects, with certain classes of nouns.
o- in *Otyihereró* = Kafir and Setshuána **bo-**.
(—) The prefix omitted in the *Zangian* and *Kongo* Genera.
ETYMOLOGY. *Vide* § 443.
RANGE OF MEANING. Restricted to personal nouns in the plural,—the meaning chiefly defined by the correspondence of this class to the first.
CORRESPONDENCE. THIS CLASS CORRESPONDS AS PLURAL TO THE 1st (**MU-**) class in all South African *Bántu* languages. N.B. In the form **bo-** or **bo-**mo- (= **BA-**MU**-**) in certain cases in the Kafir and Setshuána dialects. (*Vide* p. 253.)
„ „ 9th (**N-**) class in a few personal nouns (which can also be transferred to the 1st class) in *Kongo*, *Dualla*, and *Isubu*. N.B. In these cases the 2nd prefix is prefixed to the 9th, as **ba-**n-, **a-**n-, &c.
„ „ 5th (**DI-**) class in one noun in *Kongo*.
„ „ 3rd (**MŪ-**) class in a few *Dualla* and *Isubu* nouns which indicate persons.

3. THIRD PREFIX: **MŪ-**.

518. The third prefix (**MŪ-**) is common to all South African *Bántu* languages.

FORMS OF THE THIRD (MŪ-) PREFIX.

Branch	Language				
SOUTH-EASTERN BRANCH.	KAFIR.		m-	—	(—)
	ZULU.	mu-			
	SEXLAPI.		mō-, m-		
	SESUTO.		(MO-B-)		
	TEKEZA.	mu-	m-	n-(MU-L-)	
MOSAMBIQUI GENUS.	TETTE.	mū-			
	SENA.	mu-	m-		
	MAKUA.				
	KIHIAU.				
ZANGIAN GENUS.	KIKAMBA.				
	KINIKA.				
	SUAHELI.				
	KISAMBALA.				
INT.	BAYEIYE.		mo-, om-, m(b)-		
BUNDA GENUS.	OTYIHERERÓ.				
	SINDONGA.		m-		
	NANO.		u-		
	ANGOLA.	mū-			
KONGO G.	KONGO.	mu-	m-		
	MPONGWE.		om-	o-	
NORTH-WESTERN BRANCH.	DIKELE.	mi-	n-		(—)
	BENGA.	mw-		m-	u-
	DUALLA.	mu-	mo-		
	ISUBU.				mw-
	FERNANDIAN.	bu-	bo-	b-	o- (—)

Original Bántu Nouns of the Third (MŪ-) and Fourth (MI-) Classes.

MU-TI 3. "tree, plant," pl. **MI-TI** 4. (§§ 428, 519 note);
MU-TIMA 3. "heart," pl. **MI-TIMA** 4. (p. 204);
MU-NUE 3. "finger," pl. **MI-NUE** 4. (pp. 204 and 205);
MU-LUM-(B)O 3. "mouth, lip," pl. **MI-LUM-(B)O** 4. (§ 439 note, pp. 238 and 243).

FORMS. **mu-** in all these languages, *excepting* Kafir, Sesuto, Mpongwe, Dikele, Benga, and Fernandian. N.B. The only form met with in Tette, Sena, Otyihereró, and Angola; in Tette and Angola noted as long (**mū-**).

mw- in *Benga* and *Isubu* before vowels.

mo- regularly in *Setshuána* (Seχlapi and Sesuto), *Dualla*, and *Isubu*. N.B. The vowel noted as long in Seχlapi (**mō-**). The **mo-** in Bayeiye may be due to Setshuána orthography.

mi- occasionally in *Dikele*.

m- the only form met with in the *Kafir* language,—with other forms in *Zulu, Tekeza, Makua, Kihiau, Kikamba, Kinika, Suaheli, Kisambala, Bayeiye, Sindonga, Kongo, Dikele, Benga, Dualla*, and *Isubu*. N.B. Setshuána **m-** = **MO-B-**.

(o)**m-** in Seχlapi and *Bayeiye*.

om- in *Mpongwe*.

n- before certain consonants in *Dikele*. N.B. Tekeza **n-** = **MU-L-**.

bu-, bo-, b- in *Fernandian*.

u- (with other forms) in *Nano* and *Benga*.

o- in *Mpongwe* and *Fernandian*.

(—) The prefix falls off in very few cases, noted, as yet, only in *Kafir, Zulu, Seχlapi, Dikele*, and *Fernandian*.

ETYMOLOGY. Probably originally identical with the preposition *mu-* "In," of Kongo, and *mo-* of the Bunda Genus and of Setshuána. (§§ 437—440.)

RANGE OF MEANING. The original local meaning is not always clearly visible in nouns of this class, which includes particularly many names of trees, and, in the South-eastern Branch, names of rivers. Although the personal nouns which originally belonged to this class, have as a general rule been drawn over to the 1st (**MŬ-**) class,—a few such are still to be found in the 3rd class in most of the South African Bântu languages.*

CORRESPONDENCE. THIS CLASS CORRESPONDS AS SINGULAR TO THE 4th (**MI-**) class universally;

---

* For personal nouns of the 3rd (**MŬ-**) class in Kafir, *vide* p. 160 (note), to which the Rev. J. W. Appleyard adds the following remarks: "There are a few more personal nouns in the 3rd class than those you mention. Thus u-**ma**-*duna* 3. 'a person of eminence or rank,' pl. i-**mi**-*duna* 4.; u-**ma**-*ginwa* 3. 'a profane person,' pl. i-**mi**-*ginwa* 4. Tribal names are also found in the same class, as the I-**mi**-*dushune* 4."

TO THE 6th (**MA-**) class, in a few cases, with a special plural meaning, in *Seḱlapi*, (perhaps in *Mpongwe*,) and in *Dikele*.

" " 10th (**TIN-**) class, only in nouns which have been transferred from the 11th (**LU-**) class, in *Mpongwe*.

" " 2nd (**BA-**) class in a few nouns (of persons) in *Dualla* and *Isubu*.

4. FOURTH PREFIX: **MI-**.

519. The fourth prefix (**MI-**) is met with in all South African *Bântu* languages.

THE FOURTH (**MI-**) PREFIX.

SOUTH-EAST. BR.	KAFIR SPECIES.	mi-	
	SETSHUANA.	me-	
	TEKEZA.	mi-	
	MOSAMBIQUE GEN.		
	ZANGIAN GENUS.		
INT.	BAYEIYE.	me-	
BUNDA GENUS.	OTYIHERERÓ.	mi-	vi-
	SINDONGA.		
	NANO.		
	ANGOLA.		
KONGO G.	KONGO.		
	MPONGWE.	in-	i-
NORTH-WESTERN BRANCH.	DIKELE.	mi-	
	BENGA.		
	DUALLA.		me-
	ISUBU.		m-
	FERNANDIAN.	bi(i)- be-	

FORMS. **mi-** in all South African *Bântu* languages, *excepting* the Setshuâna dialects, (Bayeiye,) Mpongwe, and Fernandian. N.B. With other forms in Nano, Benga, Dualla, and Isubu.

me- the only form in *Setshuâna*,— with other forms in *Benga, Dualla*, and *Isubu*. N.B. Bayeiye **me-** may be due to Setshuâna orthography.

m- in *Isubu*.

in- and **i-** in *Mpongwe*.

vi- in *Nano*.

bi- and **be-** in *Fernandian*.

RANGE OF MEANING. Apparently entirely dependent upon its correspondence to the 3rd (**MŪ-**) class.

CORRESPONDENCE. THIS CLASS CORRESPONDS AS PLURAL
TO THE 3rd (**MU**-) class universally.
" " **14**th (**BU**-) class regularly in *Kinika, Benga, Dualla,* and *Isubu.**
" " **1**st (**MU**-) class in one noun in *Dualla,* and another in *Isubu,* which probably belonged originally to the 3rd (**MU**-) class.
" " **7**th (**KI**-) class in one *Dikele* noun, which is probably a sort of diminutive of a noun belonging to the 3rd (**MU**-) class.
" " **6**th (**MA**-) class in one *Dikele* noun, doubtful.

5. FIFTH PREFIX : **DI-** OR **LI-**.

520. Nouns of the fifth (**DI**-) class are met with in all South African *Bântu* languages.

FORMS. **di-** in the languages of the *North-western* Branch.
    d- (before certain vowels) in the languages of the *North-western* Branch.
    dy- in *Benga.*
    dsh- in *Dualla.*
    (**d**)**zi-** in *Sena,* besides the more usual **ri-**.
    zi- in *Tette.*
    li- regularly in *Kafir* and *Zulu,*—with other forms in *Kihiau* and *Bayeiye.*
    le- in the *Setshuâna* dialects (Sesuto and Sexlapi). N.B. Bayeiye **le-** may be Setshuâna orthography.
    ri- in *Tekeza, Sena, Kihiau, Angola,* and *Kongo.*
    r- a doubtful form in *Fernandian.*
    e- (= *o*-**RI**-) regularly in *Otyihererú* and *Sindonga,*—with other forms in *Nano* and *Kongo.*
    ni- and (**i**)**n-** regularly in *Makua.*
    i- regularly in *Mpongwe,*—with other forms in *Kikámba, Nano, Benga, Dualla, Isubu,* and *Fernandian.*
    y- in *Kikámba* and *Isubu.* N.B. Modified from **i-**.
    (—) The prefix elided in the languages of the *South-eastern* Branch, in *Tette, Sena,* and *Kihiau,* in the *Zangian* Genus (being altogether omitted in Kinika, Kisuáheli, and Kisambala), and in *Angola.*

---

* The case of Dualla **bo**-*eli* (Isubu **bw**-*eli*) 14. " tree " pl. **mi**-*eli* 4., when compared with Zulu n-**mu**-*ti* 3. pl. i-**mi**-*ti* 4. (§ 428, note), seems to suggest that this correspondence of nouns of the 14th (**BU**-) class to those of the 4th (**MI**-) may have arisen from the circumstance that a noun of the 3rd (**MU**-) class (by a change of the consonant of the prefix) had acquired the form of the 14th (**BU**-)

THE FIFTH (**LI-**) AND SIXTH (**MA-**) PREFIXES.

SOUTH-EAST. BR.	KAFIR SPECIES.	li-	}	}	m-
	SETSHUANA.	le-			
	TEKEZA.	ri-	} (—)		
MOSAMBIQUE GENUS.	TETTE.	zi-			
	SENA.	ri- (d)zi-			
	MAKUA.	ni- (i)n-		ma-	
	KIHIAU.	li- ri-	}		
ZANGIAN GENUS.	KIKAMBA.	i- y-			m-
	KINIKA.		} (—)		
	SUAHELI.				
	KISAMBALA.				me-
INT.	BAYEIYE.	li- le-			ama-
BUNDA GENUS.	OTYIHERERÓ.	} e- (= O-RI-) {			me-
	SINDONGA.				
	NANO.		i-	va-	v-
KONGO G.	ANGOLA.	} ri-		} ma-	m-
	KONGO.				
	MPONGWE.	i-		am- ∴	a-
NORTH-WESTERN BRANCH.	DIKELE.	} di-, d- {		} ma-	m-
	BENGA.		dy-		
	DUALLA.		i- { dsh-		
	ISUBU.		y-		
	FERNANDIAN.		r-	ba-	b-

class. It would then either retain its old plural form with the 4th (**MI-**) prefix, or gain, by analogy, a new plural with the 6th (**MA-**) prefix, as Isubu **ma**-*li* 6. " trees."

Review of the Fifth Derivative Prefix of Nouns. 261

ETYMOLOGY. *Vide* § 441.
RANGE OF MEANING. In Kisambala "if anything is to be spoken of as remarkably large, it is brought into this class." (Dr. Steere's Collection for a Handbook of the Shambala Language, p. 6.) In Otyihereró, also, Hahn observes ("Grammatik" § 38) that the nouns of this class particularly indicate subjects in which there is something remarkable, prominent, especial, &c. We seem to observe this in e-*kaꜱ'e-ndu* 5. "very tall woman," pl. o-**ma**-*kaꜱ'e-ndu* 6., when compared with o-**mu**-*kaꜱ'e-ndu* 1. "woman," pl. o-**va**-*kaꜱ'e-ndu* 2. (§ 494 and note.) *Vide*, however, also e-*kaꜱ'e* 5. "tendency to produce none but female offspring," &c., p. 208, note. Rath's observation, that this prefix is mainly used when one of two things which constantly occur in pairs, is to be indicated (p. 200), is liable to many exceptions.

CORRESPONDENCE. THIS CLASS CORRESPONDS AS SINGULAR TO THE 6th (**MA-**) class in all South African *Bántu* languages.

„ „ 2nd (**BA-**) class in one *Kongo* noun.
„ „ 12th (**TU-**) class in a few exceptional cases in *Dualla* and *Isubu*,—probably in consequence of homophony with the 7th prefix.
„ „ 8th (**PI-**) class, doubtful, in *Fernandian*.

6. SIXTH PREFIX: MA-.

521. The sixth prefix (**MA-**) is common to all South African *Bántu* languages.

FORMS. **ma-** in all these languages, *excepting* Nano, Mpongwe, and Fernandian.
me- in a few cases in *Kikámba, Kisambala, Otyihereró*, &c.
m- before vowels, in *Kafir, Zulu, Setshuána, Makua, Kihiau, Kinika, Suáheli, Angola, Kongo, Dikele, Benga, Dualla,* and *Isubu*. N.B. Although **m-** is only found before vowels, yet **ma-** before vowels is not always shortened to **m-**.
va- and **v-** in *Nano*.
ba- and **b-** in *Fernandian*.
am- ∴ (with the initial consonant of the stem strengthened) and **a-** in *Mpongwe*.
(—) Prefix omitted perhaps in *Kikámba*.

RANGE OF MEANING. Plural (in Setshuána sometimes indicating a very great number), collective (particularly applied to liquids), sometimes abstract. (§ 452.) The liquid meaning, which may be after all a secondary one like that of tree or river in the 3rd prefix, appears, however, to have stamped this class early with the character of a liquid class (or gender). Evidences of this ancient structural peculiarity of the South African Bântu languages, are also visible in some West African Bântu languages, as in TIMNEH (Schlenker's "Grammar" p. 89) and BULLOM (Nyländer's "Grammar" p. 18),—and in at least one of the Oceanic Prefix-pronominal languages, viz., in FIJI (Hazlewood's "Grammar" p. 19).

CORRESPONDENCE. THIS CLASS CORRESPONDS AS PLURAL TO THE 5th (DI-) class regularly in all South African *Bântu* languages.

" " 14th (BU-) class regularly in *Setshuána, Makua, Kihiau, Kikámba, Otyiherero, Angola,* in the *Kongo* Genus (Kongo and Mpongwe), in *Dikele, Isubu,* and *Fernandian.* N.B. In Kikamba, Otyiherero, Angola, and Dikele, cases occur in which the 6th prefix is prefixed to the 14th, instead of taking its place.

" " 11th (LU-) class occasionally in the *Kafir* and *Setshuána* dialects, in *Tshiyao, Suáheli, Angola, Dikele, Dualla,* and *Isubu.* N.B. In some cases in Angola and Isubu the 6th prefix is prefixed to the 11th (as **ma-lu-**), instead of replacing it.

" " 9th (N-) class frequently in the *North-western* Branch languages (Benga and Fernandian excepted),—in a few cases in the *Kafir* and *Setshuána* dialects, and in *Tette.* N.B. Prefixed to the 9th (as **ma-n-**) in Tette, Dikele, Dualla, and Isubu.

" " 15th (KU-) class in *Seχlapi, Kikamba, Otyiherero, Sindonga,* and in the *Kongo* Genus (Kongo and Mpongwe). N.B. Prefixed to the 15th prefix (as **ma-ku-**), in some cases, in Otyiherero and Sindonga.

" " 1st (MŬ-) class in a few special cases in *Kafir, Zulu, Sesuto, Sena,* (perhaps *Kikamba,*) and *Kongo.*

" " 3rd (MŪ-) class in *Seχlapi* (in which correspondence the 6th prefix has, however, more of a collective meaning), in *Dikele,* and perhaps in *Mpongwe.*

" " 13th (KA-) class in *Nano* and *Dikele.*

" " 7th (KI-) class, very doubtful, in one *Sindonga* noun.

THIS (SIXTH) CLASS IS SAID ALSO TO CORRESPOND AS SINGULAR TO THE 4th (MI-) class in one case in *Dikele,* which is, however, very doubtful.

7. SEVENTH PREFIX: KI-.

522. With this modification, that the identity of the forms (vi- and i-) in the North-western Branch with

this prefix is not perfectly certain (§§ 503 and 507), we may state that the seventh prefix (**KI-**) is met with in all South African *Bántu* languages.

FORMS. **ki-** in the *Zangian* Genus, in *Kihiau*, *Angola*, and *Kongo*;
—in the two latter languages written in Portuguese orthography **qui-**.
ke- once or twice in *Kongo*.
iki- or **ik-** in *Makua*.
tyi- in *Otyihereró* and *Nano*.
ty- (before vowels) in *Otyihereró*.
tshi- in *Tekeza, Tette, Sena*, and perhaps *Kihiau*.
tshe- occasionally in *Tekeza*.
tsh- (before vowels) in *Sena* and *Kisambala*.
dshi- in *Kihiáu* and *Kinika*.
dsh- (before vowels) in *Sena, Kikamba, Kinika, Kisuáheli,* and *Isubu*.
shi- in *Tette* and *Sindonga*.
sh- (before vowels) in *Sindonga*.
si- and **s-** in *Kafir, Zulu*, and *Fernandian*.
se- in *Setshuâna*. N.B. Bayeiye **se-** may be due to Setshuâna orthography.
ez- (before vowels) in *Mpongwe*.
vi- and **v-** in *Dikele* and *Benga*.
i- in *Benga, Dualla*, and *Isubu*. N.B. Makua i- is probably merely the article, while the derivative prefix of the noun has been omitted.
e- regularly in *Mpongwe*.
y- (before some vowels) in *Dualla* and *Isubu*.
(**—**) The prefix omitted, as far as we know, only in *Sekĺapi* and *Makua*.

ETYMOLOGY. *Vide* § 441.

RANGE OF MEANING. Various,—chiefly either instrumental, or neutral,—in *Tette* and *Sena* indicating largeness, in *Kongo* and *Fernandian* used for the formation of diminutives. (§§ 430, 503, and 514.)

CORRESPONDENCE. THIS CLASS CORRESPONDS AS SINGULAR
TO THE **8**th (**PI-**) class in the *South-eastern* Branch and *Middle* Branch languages, and in *Dualla*. N.B. Although this correspondence has not yet been proved in Tekeza, Makua, and Bayeiye, we do not doubt that it also takes place in these languages.

„ „ **12**th (**TU-**) class in the *North-western* Branch languages.
„ „ **4**th (**MI-**) class in one noun in *Dikele*, doubtful.
„ „ **6**th (**MA-**) class, very doubtful, in one *Sindonga* noun.

THE SEVENTH (KI-) & EIGHTH (PI-) PREFIXES.

		7th (KI-)		8th (PI-)	
SOUTH-EASTERN BR.	KAFIR SPECIES.	si-	s-	zi-	z-
	SEX̱LAPI.	se-	(—)	li-	(fi-) (—)
	SESUTO.				
MOZAMBIQUE GENUS	TEKEZA.	tshi-	tshe-	psi-	
	TETTE.		shi-		
	SENA.		tsh- dsh-	pi-	
	MAKUA.	iki-	ik- i-		
	KIHIAU.		dshi- (tshi-)	vi- (wi-) hi- (i-)	
ZANGIAN GENUS	KIKAMBA.	ki-			i-
	KINIKA.		dshi- dsh-	vi-	(wi-)
	SUAHELI.				
	KISAMBALA.		tsh-	vy-	
INT.	BAYEIYE.	se-			
BUNDA GENUS	OTYIHEREBÓ.	tyi-	ty-		
	SINDONGA.	shi-	sh-	vi-	i-
	NANO.	tyi-			
KONGO S.	ANGOLA.	ki-			hi-
	KONGO.		ke-	y-	i-
	MPONGWE.		ez- e-		(—)
NORTH-WESTERN BRANCH.	DIKELE.	vi-	v-		
	BENGA.			bi-	be-
	DUALLA.	y-	i-		
	ISUBU.		dsh-		
	FERNANDIAN.	si-	s-		i-

8. EIGHTH PREFIX: PI-.

523. The eighth prefix (PI-) probably occurs in all South African *Bântu* languages,—although, as yet in

Tekeza, Makua, and Bayeiye, the forms of this prefix have not been ascertained.

FORMS. **pi-** in *Sena*. N.B. **psi-**, on p. 174, is a misprint.
    bi- in the *North-western* Branch languages.
    be- (a variety of **bi-**) in *Benga, Dualla,* and *Isubu*.
    vi- in *Otyihereró, Sindonga, Nano,* and *Kisambala*.
    vy- (before vowels) in *Kisambala*.
    vi- or **wi-** in *Kihiau, Kinika,* and *Kisuáheli*.
    psi- in *Tette*.
    zi- and **z-** in *Kafir* and *Zulu*.
    li- or **ŕi-** in *Setshuâna*.
    hi- (**ĭ-**) in *Kihiau* and *Angola*.
    i- in *Kikamba, Sindonga, Angola, Kongo, Mpongwe,* and *Fernandian*.
    y- in *Angola, Kongo,* and *Mpongwe*.
    (—) The prefix may be elided in *Sex̌lapi* and *Mpongwe*.

CORRESPONDENCE. THIS CLASS CORRESPONDS AS PLURAL TO THE 7th (**KI-**) class regularly in the *South-eastern* Branch and *Middle* Branch languages,—and occasionally in *Dualla*.
  ,, ,, 13th (**KA-**) class regularly in the *North-western* Branch languages and in *Kisambala*.
  ,, ,, 14th (**BU-**) class regularly in *Nano*.
  ,, ,, 5th (**DI-**) class in one doubtful case in *Fernandian*.

9. NINTH PREFIX: N-.

524. The ninth prefix (**N-**) occurs in all South African *Bântu* languages.

FORMS. **n-** in all *Bântu* languages. N.B. Sometimes a short vowel precedes the nasal, as **in-** in Tekeza, Sena, Tette, and Makua,—**en-** in Tekeza, Kinika, and Bayeiye,—**un-** in Kinika and Kisuaheli.
    n-ʼ.ʼ (with the initial consonant of the stem strengthened) in the *Kafir* and *Setshuâna* dialects, and in the *Kongo* Genus. N.B. The only form in the Kongo language.
    m- before labials, in all South African *Bântu* languages, *excepting* Kongo. N.B. Sometimes a short vowel precedes this nasal, as **im-** in Tekeza and Angola,—**em-** in Tekeza and Kinika.
    m-ʼ.ʼ (with the initial consonant of the stem strengthened) in the *Kafir* and *Setshuâna* dialects, and in *Mpongwe*.
    ń- before gutturals, in *Otyihereró, Sindonga, Nano,* and *Isubu*.

FORMS OF THE NINTH (N-) PREFIX.

Branch	Language			
SOUTH-EASTERN BRANCH	KAFIR.	n-∵	m-∵	(—)
	ZULU.			
	SEḰLAPI.			ń-∵ (—)∵
	SESUTO.			
	TEKEZA.	in-	im-	
MOZAMBIQUE GENUS	TETTE.	n-	m-	(—)
	SENA.	(l)n-		
	MAKUA.			
	KIHIAU.	n-		
SANGIAN GENUS	KIKAMBA.			
	KINIKA.	(u)n-	en-	em-
	SUAHELI.		m-	
	KISAMBALA.			
INT.	BAYEIYE.			
BUNDA GENUS	OTYIHERERÓ.	n-	m-	
	SINDONGA.			ń- (—)
	NANO.			
	ANGOLA.		im-	
KONGO S.	KONGO.	n-∵		
	MPONGWE.		m-∵	(—)∵
NORTH-WESTERN BRANCH	DIKELE.	n-	m-	(—)
	BENGA.			
	DUALLA.			
	ISUBU.			ń-
	FERNANDIAN.			

Approximate Forms of some Original Bántu Nouns of the Ninth (N-) Class.

N-*GUA* (**M**-*BUA*) 9. "dog," pl. **TIN**-*GUA* 10. (§§ 235 and 277, p. 247);
N-*DAGU* 9. "house, hut," pl. **MA**-*N*-*DAGU* 6. (pp. 195, 231, and 240).

N-*KUBO* 9. "hippopotamus," pl. **TIN**-*KUBO* 10. (p. 206);
N-*BUTI* 9. "goat," pl. **TIN**-*BUTI* 10. (p. 230);
N-*GILA* 9. "way, road," pl. **TIN**-*GILA* 10. (p. 201 note);
N-*BULA* 9. "rain," pl. **TIN**-*BULA* 10. (§ 118, pp. 195 & 240);

Review of the Ninth Derivative Prefix of Nouns. 267

ń-∵ (with the initial consonant of the stem strengthened) in *Seχlapi*.

(—) The prefix very frequently elided or omitted in all South African *Bântu* languages, Zulu and Kongo *excepted*. N.B. Cases of such omission have not yet been proved in Bayeiye and Fernandian; but we cannot doubt that they also occur in these languages.

(—) ∵ (with strengthened initial of the stem) in *Setshuâna* and *Mpongwe*.

CORRESPONDENCE. THIS CLASS CORRESPONDS AS SINGULAR TO THE 10th (**TIN-**) class in all South African *Bântu* languages, *excepting* Dikele.

" " 6th (**MA-**) class (by preference) in the *North-western* Branch languages, Benga and Fernandian *excepted*;—rarely in the *Kafir* and *Setshuâna* dialects, and *Tette*. N.B. The 6th (**ma-**) prefix is frequently prefixed to the 9th (as **ma-n-**, **ma-**m-) in Tette, Dikele, Dualla, and Isubu.

" " 12th (**TU-**) class, in one doubtful case in *Kikámba*.

" " 2nd (**BA-**) class in *Kongo*, *Dualla*, and *Isubu* (personal nouns). N.B. The 2nd prefix is, however, prefixed to the 9th (as **ba-n-**, **a-n-∵**, **a-∵**, &c.).

10. TENTH PREFIX: **TIN-**.

525. The tenth prefix (**TIN-** or **THIN-**) is met with in all South African *Bântu* languages. The Makua form of this prefix has, however, not yet been ascertained.

FORMS. **thin-**, **tin-** (**ti-***in*-), **tim-**, **thi-**, and **the-** in *Tekeza*.

zin- in *Kafir*, *Zulu*, *Tette*, *Sena*, *Bayeiye*, and *Kongo*. N.B. With strengthened initial of the stem (**zin-∵**) in Kafir, Zulu, and Kongo.

zim- (before labials) in *Kafir*, *Zulu*, and *Tette*. N.B. With strengthened initial of the stem (**zim-∵**) in Kafir and Zulu.

zi- in *Kafir*, *Zulu*, and *Tette*.

lin-∵, **lim-∵**, **liń-∵**, and **li-∵** (with strengthened initial of the stem) in *Setshuâna*. N.B. In Moffat's last edition of the New Testament in Seχlapi, *r* takes the place of *l* in this prefix, as well as in the eighth.

sin-∵, **si-∵**, and **shi-∵** (with strengthened initial of the stem) rarely in *Mpongwe*.

shin- (**gin-**), **shim-**, and **shi-** in *Angola*.

shon- (**jon-**), **shom-**, and **sho-** in *Angola*.

FORMS OF THE TENTH (TIN-) PREFIX.

SOUTH-EASTERN BRANCH.	KAFIR.	} zin-∴, n-∴, zim-∴, m-, zi- {	(—)
	ZULU.		
	SEⱩLAPI.	tin-∴ tim-∴ tin-∴ ti-∴	(—) ∴
	SESUTO.	lin-∴ lim-∴ li-∴	
	TEKEZA.	thin- thim- thi- the-	
MOZAMBIQUE GENUS.	TETTE.	} zin- zim- { zi- / n- m- }	(—)
	SENA.		
	MAKUA.		
ZANGIAN GENUS.	KIHIAU.	} ————— } n- m-	
	KIKAMBA.		
	KINIKA.	} (u)n- ni- en- em- mi- }	(—)
	SUAHELI.	————— m-	
	KISAMBALA.	n- ny-	
INT.	BAYEIYE.	zin-	
BUNDA GENUS.	OTYIHERERÓ.	ɘ'on- ɘ'om- ɘ'oṅ-	
	SINDONGA.	n- m- ṅ-	ɘ'o-
	NANO.	ɘ'on- ɘ'om- ɘ'oṅ-	
	ANGOLA.	shin-,shon-,shim-,shom-,shi-,sho-,(—)	
KONGO G.	KONGO.	zin-∴ n-∴	
	MPONGWE.	sin-∴ in-∴ im-∴ s(h)i-∴ i-∴	
NORTH-WESTERN BRANCH.	DIKELE.	} } ——— {	
	BENGA.		(—)
	DUALLA.	n- m- { ———	
	ISUBU.	ṅ-	
	FERNANDIAN.	i-	

ȝ'on-, ȝ'om-, and ȝ'oñ- in *Otyihereró* and *Nano*.
ȝ'o in *Otyihereró*, *Sindonga*, and *Nano*.
n- in *Kafir*, *Zulu*, *Sena*, *Kihiau*, the *Zangian* Genus, *Sindonga*, *Kongo*, *Benga*, *Dualla*, *Isubu*, and *Fernandian*. N.B. With strengthened initial of the stem (n-ˑ.ˑ) in Kafir, Zulu, and Kongo.—A short vowel sometimes precedes the nasal, as— un- in Kisuaheli and Kinika,—and en- in Kinika.
m- (before labials) in *Kafir*, *Zulu*, *Sena*, *Kihiau*, the *Zangian* Genus, *Sindonga*, *Benga*, *Dualla*, *Isubu*, and *Fernandian*. N.B. With strengthened initial of the stem (m-ˑ.ˑ) in Kafir and Zulu.—A short vowel sometimes precedes the nasal, as em- in Kinika.
in- ˑ.ˑ and im- ˑ.ˑ (with strengthened initial of the stem) in *Mpongwe*.
ni- (before the 11th prefix, as ni-u-) sometimes in *Kinika* and *Kisuáheli*.
ny- sometimes in *Kisambala*.
mi- (in certain combinations) in *Kinika*.
i- in *Fernandian*, and (with strengthened initial of the stem, as i-ˑ.ˑ) in *Mpongwe*.
(—) The prefix elided in the *Kafir* language, in *Seχlapi*, *Tette*, *Sena*, *Kihiau*, the *Zangian* Genus, *Angola*, *Dikele*, *Benga*, *Dualla*, and *Isubu*. N.B. The strengthened initial of the stem is, however, retained (— ˑ.ˑ) in Seχlapi.

CORRESPONDENCE. THIS CLASS CORRESPONDS AS PLURAL TO THE **9**th (**N-**) class in all *Bántu* languages, *excepting* Dikele.
 ,,   ,,   **11**th (**LU-**) class in the *South-eastern* Branch languages, in *Kihiau*, in the *Zangian* Genus, in *Otyihereró*, *Sindonga*, *Nano*, *Kongo*, (perhaps in *Mpongwe*,) in *Dikele* and *Fernandian*.
 ,,   ,,   **13**th (**KA-**) class in *Bayeiye* and *Nano*.
 ,,   ,,   **14**th (**BU-**) class in *Kisambala* and *Benga*.
 ,,   **1**st (**MŬ-**) class in *Angola*, in nouns transferred from the 9th (**N-**) to the 1st class.

11. ELEVENTH PREFIX: LU-.

526. The eleventh (**LU-**) class has *not* yet been found in Tette, Sena, Makua, or Benga,—although it may exist in these languages. It has amalgamated with the 5th (**le-**) class in Sesuto, with the 14th (**u-**) in Kisuáheli, and with the 3rd (**o-**) in Mpongwe. In the *remaining* South African Bántu languages the 11th exists as a separate class.

FORMS OF THE ELEVENTH (LU-), TWELFTH (TU-), AND THIRTEENTH (KA-) PREFIXES.

SOUTH-EASTERN BR.	KAFIR SPEC.	lu- ⎫		(KA-)
	SEᶜLAPI.	lo- ⎬ (—)		(XA-)
	SESUTO.	(le-) ⎭		(H'A-)
	TEKEZA.	li-		
MOZAMBIQUE GENUS.	TETTE.		⎫	⎫
	SENA.		⎬ tu-	⎬ ka-
	MAKUA.		⎭	⎭
	KIHIAU.	lu-		
SUNDA GENUS KIDANZI	KIKAMBA.	u-	tu-	⎫ ka- ⎧ k-
	KINIKA.	lu-		
	SUAHELI.	u- w-		
	KISAMBALA.	lu-		
INT.	BAYEIYE.	lo- ro-		
BUNDA GENUS.	OTYIHERERÓ.	⎫ ru-	⎫ tu-	⎫
	SINDONGA.	⎬	⎬	⎬ ka-
	NANO.	⎬ lu- (—)		⎬ ga-
	ANGOLA.	⎭	⎫ tu-	
KONGO G.	KONGO.	l- u-	⎭	
	MPONGWE.	(o-)		
NORTH-WESTERN BRANCH.	DIKELE.	la- g'a-	la- ⎫	a- dsh-
	BENGA.		⎬ l-	⎫
	DUALLA.	⎫	lo- ⎬	e- ⎬ y-
	ISUBU.	⎬ l-	l- ⎭	⎭
	FERNANDIAN.	lu- lo-	to-, tw-, t-	

FORMS. **lu-** in *Kafir, Zulu, Kihiáu, Kinika, Kisambala, Sindonga, Nano, Angola, Kongo,* and *Fernandian.*
lo- in *Seĉlapi* and *Fernandian.* N.B. Bayeiye **lo-** may be Setshuâna orthography.
li- in *Tekeza* (Lourenzo Marques).
le- in *Sesuto,* homophonous with the 5th prefix.
la- and **9'a-** in *Dikele.*
l- in *Kongo, Dualla, Isubu,* and *Fernandian.*
ru- in *Otyihereró* and *Sindonga.*
ro- in *Bayeiye.*
u- in *Kikámba, Kisuáheli,* and *Kongo.* N.B. In Kisuáheli homophonous with the 14th prefix.
w- (before vowels) in *Kisuáheli,* homophonous with the 14th prefix.
o- in *Mpongwe,* homophonous with the 3rd prefix.
(—) The prefix elided in *Kafir, Zulu, Seĉlapi,* and *Nano.*

ETYMOLOGY. *Vide* § 441.

RANGE OF MEANING. In Otyiheteró the missionaries believe that they have observed in this prefix the idea of length, extension, &c. It tallies curiously with this, that in *Timneh* (a Bântu language spoken near Sierra Leone) "rope-like or creeping plants have commonly the prefix **ra-** in the singular." (Schlenker's Grammar of the Temne language, p. 38.)

CORRESPONDENCE. THIS CLASS CORRESPONDS AS SINGULAR TO THE **10**th (**TIN-**) class in the *South-eastern* Branch languages, in *Kihiau,* in the *Zangian* Genus, in *Otyiheretó, Sindonga,* (perhaps in *Nano,*) in the *Kongo* Genus (Kongo and Mpongwe), in *Dikele,* and *Fernandian.* N.B. The 11th prefix may have the 10th prefixed (as **ni-u-**) in Kinika and Kisuáheli.

  „ „ **6**th (**MA-**) class in the *Kafir* and *Setshuâna* dialects, in *Tshiyao* (p. 178, note), *Suaheli, Angola, Dikele, Dualla,* and *Isubu.* N.B. The 6th prefix is regularly prefixed to the 11th in Angola (as **ma-**lu-), and sometimes in Isubu (as **ma-**l-).

  „ „ **12**th (**TU-**) class regularly in *Otyiheretó, Sindonga,* and *Kongo.*

12. TWELFTH PREFIX: **TU-**.

527. The twelfth prefix (**TU-**) occurs in all the *North-western* Branch languages, in *Tette, Sena, Kikamba, Otyiheretó, Sindonga, Angola,* and *Kongo,*—but is *extinct* in the South-eastern Branch, and in Kinika, Kisuáheli, and

Mpongwe. It has not yet been met with in Makua, Kihiau, Kisambala, Bayciye, and Nano, although it may possibly occur in one or more of these languages.

FORMS. **tu-** in all *Middle* Branch languages which possess this prefix, *viz.*, in Tette, Sena, Kikámba, Otyihereró, Sindonga, Angola, and Kongo.

to-, tw-, and **t-** in *Fernandian.*
lo- in *Benga, Dualla,* and *Isubu.*
la- in *Dikele.*
l- in *Dikele, Benga,* and *Isubu.*

RANGE OF MEANING. Diminutive Plural in Tette, Sena, Kikámba, Angola, and Fernandian; in other languages it has a different meaning.

CORRESPONDENCE. THIS CLASS CORRESPONDS AS PLURAL TO THE **13**th (**KA-**) class regularly in *Tette, Sena, Kikámba,* and *Angola.*

" " **11**th (**LU-**) class regularly in *Otyihereró, Sindonga,* and *Kongo.*

" " **7**th (**KI-**) class regularly in the *North-western* Branch languages.

" " **5**th (**DI-**) class, in a few cases (probably mistaken for the 7th), in *Dualla* and *Isubu.*

" " **9**th (**N-**) class, in one doubtful case, in *Kikámba.*

13. THIRTEENTH PREFIX: **KA-**.

528. Provided that our identification of the forms of the 13th prefix (**KA-**) be correct, we may say that it is found in all the *North-western* Branch languages, and also in all the *Middle* Branch languages, *excepting* Suáheli and Mpongwe.* In the two latter languages, as well as in those of the South-eastern Branch, it is now *obsolete.*

FORMS. **ka-** in all those *Middle* Branch languages in which it occurs. N.B. This was also the old Kafir form, as in *pa-***ka-***ti.* (*Vide* § 436.)

k- (before vowels) in *Kikámba.*
ga- in *Nano,* besides **ka-**.
χ**A-** in Seχlapi, and **H'A-** in *Sesuto,* obsolete forms, = Kafir **KA-**. (§§ 87 and 436.)

* Notwithstanding that the 13th prefix has *not* yet been met with in the Kihián vocabularies, it is not impossible that it may occur in this language.

dsh- (before vowels) and **a-** (before consonants) in *Dikele*.
y- (before some vowels) in *Benga, Dualla,* and *Isubu*.
e- regularly in *Benga, Dualla, Isubu,* and *Fernandian*.

ETYMOLOGY. Perhaps related to the Kafir genitive particle *ka-* (Setshuâna *χa*) "of." Vide § 441.

RANGE OF MEANING. Diminutive Singular in the Middle Branch languages, excepting in Kongo. It has, however, no diminutive meaning in the North-western Branch languages.

CORRESPONDENCE. THIS CLASS CORRESPONDS AS SINGULAR TO THE **12th (TU-)** class regularly in *Tette, Sena, Kikamba,* and *Angola.*

„ „ **8th (PI-)** class regularly in the *North-western* Branch languages, and in *Kisambala.*

„ „ **14th (BU-)** class regularly in *Otyihereró.*

„ „ **6th (MA-)** class frequently in *Nano,* and at least once in *Dikele.*

„ „ **10th (TIN-)** class in *Bayeiye* and *Nano.*

14. FOURTEENTH PREFIX: BU-.

529. The fourteenth prefix (**BU-**) is common to all South African *Bântu* languages,—although, in some of them, it appears to have almost amalgamated with other classes.

FORMS. **bu-** in *Kafir, Zulu, Tekeza, Benga, Isubu,* and *Fernandian.*
bo- in *Setshuâna,* and in the *North-western* Branch languages.
bw- (before vowels) sometimes in *Benga, Dualla,* and *Isubu.*
bi- usually in *Dikele.*
be- in *Tekeza,* doubtful.
b- (before some vowels) in *Kafir, Zulu, Dikele, Benga, Dualla,* and *Isubu.*
u- in all *Middle* Branch languages here described,—*excepting* Mpongwe, and perhaps Bayeiye.
w- (before vowels) in *Makua, Suâheli,* and *Angola.*
ow- (before vowels) in *Mpongwe.*
o- in *Bayeiye, Kongo,* and *Mpongwe.*
(—) The prefix sometimes elided in the *Kafir* and *Setshuâna* dialects, in *Kihiáu* and *Kinika.*

RANGE OF MEANING. This prefix implies very generally an abstract meaning, and in a few nouns in Seẋlapi it has a local one. In Otyihereró, besides the abstract meaning in the singular, it is also used in a plural sense with reference to diminutives.

FOURTEENTH (BU-) AND FIFTEENTH (KU-) PREFIXES.

SOUTH-EASTERN BRANCH.	KAFIR.	} bu-	b-		} ku- kw-	{
	ZULU.			(—)		{ k-
	SExLAPI.	} bo-			xo- (go-)	(—)
	SESUTO.				h'o- (go-)	
	TEKEZA.	bu-	be-		{ ko-	
MOZAMBIQUE GENUS.	TETTE.	} u- {			} ku- {	
	SENA.					
	MAKUA.		w-		u- w-	
ZANZIAN GENUS.	KIHIAU.		(—)			
	KIKAMBA.				} ku- {	
	KINIKA.		(—)			
	SUAHELI.		w-		kw-	
	KISAMBALA.					
INT.	BAYEIYE.	o-			ko-	
BUNDA GENUS.	OTYIHERERÓ.	} u- {			} ku- {	k-
	SINDONGA.					ko-
	NANO.				gu-	
	ANGOLA.		w-		} ku- {	
KONGO G.	KONGO.	} o-				
	MPONGWE.	ow-			(ow-, o-)	
NORTH-WESTERN BRANCH.	DIKELE.	bi-				
	BENGA.	bu-	} b- } bw-			
	DUALLA.	} bo-				
	ISUBU.	} bu-				
	FERNANDIAN.					

Review of the Fourteenth Derivative Prefix of Nouns. 275

CORRESPONDENCE. THIS CLASS CORRESPONDS AS SINGULAR
TO THE 6th (MA-) class in *Setshuâna, Sena, Makua, Kihiáu, Kikámba, Otyihereró, Angola, Kongo, Mpongwe, Dikele, Isubu,* and *Fernandian.* N.B. The **ma**- may be prefixed (as **MA**-*BU*-) in Kikámba, Otyihereró, Angola, and Dikele.

„ „ 4th (MI-) class in *Kinika, Benga, Dualla,* and *Isubu.* N.B. The fourth prefix may be prefixed (as **mi**-*o*-) in Benga and Dualla.

„ „ 8th (PI-) class in *Nano,* the 4th (**mi**-) prefix being probably softened here (as it sometimes is) to the form of the 8th (**vi**-).

„ „ 10th (THIN-) class in *Kisuáheli* and *Kisambala,* and in one case in *Benga.* N.B. The 10th may be prefixed to the 14th prefix (as **ni**-*u*-) in Kisuaheli. This correspondence probably originates in the fourteenth prefix having been confounded by homophony with the eleventh.

THIS CLASS ALSO CORRESPONDS AS PLURAL
TO THE 13th (KA-) class regularly in *Otyihereró.*

15. FIFTEENTH PREFIX: KU-.

530. The fifteenth prefix (KU-) is met with in all the *South-eastern* Branch and *Middle* Branch languages, *excepting* Mpongwe, where it has apparently amalgamated with the 3rd prefix (OW-). The fifteenth class does *not* occur in the North-western Branch languages, excepting a faint trace of it in Isubu.

FORMS. **ku**- in *Kafir, Zulu, Tekeza, Tette, Sena, Kihiáu,* in the Zangian Genus, in *Otyihereró, Sindonga, Angola,* and *Kongo.*
kw- (before vowels) in *Kafir, Zulu,* and *Sudheli.*
ko- in *Tekeza, Bayeiye,* and *Sindonga.*
k- (before certain vowels) in *Zulu,* and *Otyihereró.*
gu- in *Nano.*
χo- (**go**-) in *Seχlapi.*
h'o- (**go**-) in *Sesuto.*
u- and **w**- in *Makua.*
ow- and **o**- in *Mpongwe,* homophonous with the third prefix, and apparently amalgamated with the 3rd class.
(—) The prefix does not appear in one *Seχlapi* noun, which has, however, probably been transferred to the 15th from the 16th class. (§ 435.) N.B. The omission of this (or the kindred 17th) prefix in the Zangian Genus has occasioned the curious construction of the Zangian locative cases. (§§ 478—480.)

ETYMOLOGY. Originally identical with the preposition *ku*- " to."
(§§ 433 and 434.)
RANGE OF MEANING. Infinitive and local.
CORRESPONDENCE. THIS CLASS CORRESPONDS AS SINGULAR
TO THE 6th (**MA**-) class in *Sex̌lapi*, *Kikámba*, *Otyihereró*, *Sindonga*,
Kongo, and *Mpongwe*. N.B. The 6th prefix may be prefixed (as **ma**-*ku*-) in Otyihereró and Sindonga.

SIXTEENTH (**PA**-), SEVENTEENTH, AND EIGHTEENTH PREFIXES.

16. SIXTEENTH PREFIX: **PA-**.

MOSAMBIQUE GENUS	TETTE.	} pa-			
	SENA.				
	MAKUA.				
	KIHIAU.	pa-			
ZANGIAN GENUS	KIKAMBA.	wa-			
	KINIKA.	va-	} (—)	(—)	
	SUAHELI.	pa- ma-			
	KISAMBALA.	ha-			
INT.	BAYEIYE.				
BUNDA GENUS	OTYIHERERÓ.	po-		ko-	mo-
	SINDONGA.				
	NANO.				
	ANGOLA.				
KONGO G.	KONGO.				
	MPONGWE.				
NORTH-WESTERN BRANCH	DIKELE.				
	BENGA.				
	DUALLA.				
	ISUBU.	o-			
	FERNANDIAN.				

531. The sixteenth (**PA**-) class includes very few nouns, and in most languages in which it occurs, only once. This prefix has been met with in *Tette*, *Sena*, *Kihiáu*, in the *Zangian* Genus, in *Otyihereró*, and probably in *Isubu*. It has *not* been found in any of the languages of the South-eastern Branch, nor in those of the North-western (excepting perhaps in one case in Isubu), nor in the Kongo Genus. Whether it occurs

in Makua, Bayeiye, Sindonga, Nano, and Angola, is uncertain.

FORMS. **pa-** in *Tette*, *Sena*, *Kihiáu*, and *Kisuáheli*.
    va- in *Kinika*.
    wa- in *Kikámba*.
    ma- (besides **pa-**) in *Kisuáheli*.
    ha- in *Kisambala*.
    po- in *Otyihereró*.
    o- in *Isubu*.

ETYMOLOGY. Identical with the preposition *pa-* "at, near." (§§ 435 and 436.)

RANGE OF MEANING. Near locality; without correspondence to any other prefix as singular or plural.

17. SEVENTEENTH PREFIX: **KO-**.

532. The seventeenth prefix (**KO-**) occurs only in *Otyihereró*, and perhaps in the *Zangian* Genus.

FORMS. **ko-** in *Otyihereró*.
    (—) The prefix elided (with *-ni* suffixed to the stem) in the *Zangian* Genus (Kikámba, Kinika, Kisuáheli, &c.).

ETYMOLOGY. Related either to the Kafir preposition *kwa-* (Setshuâna *kuâ-*) "from," or to *ku-* "to, from." In the latter case, this class has merely branched off from the 15th (**ku-**) class.

RANGE OF MEANING. Distant locality; without correspondence to any other prefix as singular or plural.

18. EIGHTEENTH PREFIX: **MO-**.

533. The eighteenth prefix (**MO-**) is only met with in *Otyihereró*, and probably in the *Zangian* Genus (Kikámba, Kinika, Kisuáheli, &c.).

FORMS. **mo-** in *Otyihereró*.
    (—) The prefix elided (with *-ni* suffixed to the stem) in the *Zangian* Genus.

ETYMOLOGY. The meaning of the Zangian preposition *mua-* "from" appears to be too different from that of the 18th prefix to admit of a comparison. It is more probable that the preposition *mu-* "in" is to be looked for in this prefix; and that the 18th class has branched off from the 3rd (**mu-**)

RANGE OF MEANING. Present locality; without correspondence to any other prefix as singular or plural.

SYNOPTICAL Table of the Systems adopted by different

DATE.	1834.	1850.	1850. 1862. 1859.	1855. 1859.	1837.	MSS.	1865.	1867.	1851.
NOMEN-CLATURE.	Declensions.	"Begyndelser."	Species. "Classen." Classes.	Species. Classes.	Declensions.	Concords.	Classes.	Classes.	"Genera."
AUTHORS. (Languages.)	BOYCE.*	SCHREUDER.	APPLEYARD. BONATZ. (K.) GROUT. (Z.)	COLENSO. (Zulu.)	ARCHBELL. (Setshuána.)	HUGHES.	STEERE. (Swahili)	STEERE. (Shambala.)	BLEEK.
MU-	1.	1.	} 1.	} 1.	1.	1.	} 1. & 2.	1. & 2. {	1.
BA-	9.	9.			6.	2.			2.
MU-	6.	6.	} 6.	} 5.	2.	3.	} 3.	3. {	3.
MI-	12.	13.			7.	4.			4.
DI-	2.	2.	} 2.	} 2.	(3. ?)	7.	} 6.	7. {	5.
MA-	10.	10.			9.	8.			6.
KI-	4.	4	} 4.	} 4.	4.	10.	} 5.	5. {	7.
PI-	11.	12.			8.	12.			8.
N-	3.	3.	3.	3.	3.	11.	4.	4.	9.
TIN-	11.	11.	3. & 5.	3. & 6.	8.	12.	4., 7., & 8.	4. & 6.	10.
LU-	5.	5.	5.	6.	10.	9.	7.	6.	11.
TU-									12.
KA-								5.	14.
BU-	7.	7.	7.	7.	5.	5.	8.	6.	13.
KU-	8.	8.	8.	8.		6.	10.	9.	15.
PA-							9.	8.	16.
KO-							11.		
MO-							12.		

* Also in the later editions of BOYCE'S Grammar of the Kafir Language, 1844 and 1863.

The different Systems of Classifying the Bântu Nouns.

Authors for the Classification of Nouns in the Bântu Languages.

BLEEK* (1856) Classes.	VETRALLA (Kongo) 1659 "Principiationes."	WILSON (Mpongwe) 1847 Declensions.	PRESTON AND BEST (Dikele) 1854 Declensions.	MACKEY (Benga) 1855 Classes.	SAKER (Dualla) 1855 Classes.	MERRICK (Isubu) 1854 Classes.	NUMBERS (Singular or Plural)
1.	2.	} 4. {	} 4. {	5.	1.	2.	Sng.
2.	1. & 2.						Pl.
3.	} 2. {		} 3. {	3.	} 2. {	3.	Sng.
4.				3. & 4.			Pl.
5.	1.	} 3. {	2.	} 2. {	3.	6.	Sng.
6.	1. & 2.		2., 5., 7., & 9.		3., 5., & 6.	5., 6., 7., 8.	Pl.
7.	} 3. {	} 2. {	8.	6.	7.	4.	Sng.
8.			1.	1.	4.	1.	Pl.
9.	} 4. {	1.	7.	} 7. {	6. & 8.	7. & 9.	Sng.
10.		1. & 4.	6.		8.	9.	Pl.
11.	7.	4.	5. & 6.		5.	6.	Sng.
12.	7. & 8.		8.	6.	7.	4.	Pl.
13.	6.		. 1.	1.	4.	1.	Sng.
14.	2.	} 4. {	9.	4.	2.	5.	Sng.
15.	5.						Sng.
16.							Local.
17.							
18.							

* Also in HAHN'S "Gramm. des Hereró" 1857, FREDOUX'S "Sechuana Gramm." 1864, &c.

f. THE DIFFERENT SYSTEMS OF CLASSIFICATION.

534. In order to guide the student in the perusal of other South African grammars, and to facilitate the comparison of our nomenclature with that of other grammarians, the Synoptical Table on pp. 278 and 279 has been constructed. From this, it will be seen that every one of the various modes of classification is mainly founded upon one of two principles. The majority of these systems combine the singular and plural forms corresponding to each other into one class. The objections to this method have been already stated, §459. Although APPLEYARD theoretically agrees with us on this point, he still thinks that "in particular grammars" "it may be as well to include such corresponding prefixes under one class," "as bringing the matter into more convenient shape." In this, I cannot agree with this excellent grammarian. The plan might answer sufficiently well, if it concerned the forms of the nouns alone; but in giving the other forms of concord, it is surely superfluous and encumbering to have, for instance, to give doubly the forms of our 10th (zin-) class in Kafir, because it corresponds as plural to the 9th (n-), and also to the 11th (lu-) class,—or is by Appleyard included with them under his 3rd and 5th "species" respectively. A few of the systems of classification agree with ours in assigning each distinct concord-indicating derivative prefix to a separate class. Here, some give in one row all the classes of the singular number, and let the plural classes follow in another. Among these grammarians is BOYCE, the compiler of the first Kafir Grammar; he has, however, wrongly placed our 8th and 10th classes together in his 11th "declension."[*] The Zulu grammarian SCHREUDER has corrected this error,

---

[*] In this he is followed by the Zulu grammarian BRYANT, whose system has not been incorporated into our table, as it is only given in an essay published in a periodical. It is identical with Boyce's, with the exception that Boyce's 2nd Declension (our 5th class) is Bryant's 3rd Class, and Boyce's 3rd Declension (our 9th class) is Bryant's 2nd Class.

and thus enumerates thirteen " beginnings;" the first ten of which are identical in numbers with Boyce's declensions. The Setshuâna grammarian HUGHES agrees with us in our numeration of the " classes " as far as the 4th of his " concords ;" but in the numbering of his remaining " concords" no clear principle can be discovered. In our own classification (the numbers of which, as now fixed, date from about the year 1853) the principle upon which the houses in streets are so frequently numbered, has been (as far as possible) adopted. One side of the street may be supposed to contain all the singular classes and odd numbers, while the other side contains the plural classes, which are indicated by the even numbers. The practical convenience of this method will, we trust, soon lead to its general adoption, and thus obviate the interminable confusion which the practice of employing a different nomenclature for each language inevitably causes. It will be seen that the only other system of classification, which has been adopted by more than one author, is APPLEYARD's. This, besides being based upon an arrangement of which we cannot approve, does not, of course, provide for the enumeration of those classes which are not to be found in Kafir; nor is its principle apparently favorable to extension.

g. THE ANCIENT FORMS OF THE DERIVATIVE PREFIXES OF THE NOUNS.

535. The forms possessed by the derivative prefixes of the nouns in that language from which the present South African Bântu languages have descended, can be arrived at by a comparison of the most primitive existing forms in the different dialects. (*Vide* Table on pp. 282—284.) The primitive forms of the prefixes are tolerably constant, while most of the secondary ones bear internal evidence of a more recent origin, dating since the division of the one language of the original Bântu nation into different branches, genera, and species. It is only in one or two instances that we cannot be quite sure as to the form

THE FULLEST FORMS OF THE DERIVATIVE PREFIXES

Class of Prefix.	1.	2.	3.	4.	5.
SOUTH-EASTERN BRANCH					
KAFIR.	m-	} ba-	m-	} mi-	li-
ZULU.	mu-		mu-		li-
SEĊLAPI.	} mo-		} mō-	} me-	le-
SESUTO.					le-
MOAMBIQUE GENUS					
TEKEZA.	mu-	} va-	mu-	} mi-	ri-
TETTE.	mŭ-		mŭ-		zi-
SENA.	} mu-		} mu-		ri-
MAKUA.		a-			ni-
KIHIAU.		va-			li-
NYIGAN GENUS					
KIKAMBA.	} mu-	} a-	} mu-		i-
KINIKA.					} (—)
SUAHELI.		} wa-			
KISAMBALA.					
BUNDA GENUS					
DAYEIYE.	mo-	ba-		me-	li-
OTYIHERERÓ.	} mu-	va-		} mi-	} e·(o-RI-)
SINDONGA.		a-			
NANO.		va-			
KONGO G.					
ANGOLA.	mŭ-	} a-	mū-		} ri-
KONGO.	mu-		mu-		
MPONGWE.	om-		om-	in-	i-
NORTH-WESTERN BRANCH					
DIKELE.	mu-	} ba-	mi-	} mi-	} di-
BENGA.	mo-		mw-		
DUALLA.	mu-		mo-		
ISUBU.	mo-		mu-		
FERNANDIAN.	bu-		bu-	bi-	
ANCIENT BANTU.	**MÚ-**	**BA-**	**MŪ-**	**MI-**	**DI- (LI-)**

Ancient Forms of the Derivative Prefixes of Nouns.
OF THE NOUNS IN THE BANTU LANGUAGES.

6.	7.	8.	9.	10.	11.
ma-	si-	zi-	n-	zin-∴	lu-
	se-	fi-		fin-∴	lo-
		li-		lin-∴	(le-)
				thin-	li-
	tshi-	psi-		zin-	
		pi-			
	ki-	vi-		n-	lu-
		i-			u-
					lu-
		vi-			u-
					lu-
	se-			zin-	lo-
	tyi-			ɣ'on-	ru-
	shi-	vi-		ɣ'o-, n-	lu-
va-	tyi-			ɣ'on-	
ma-	ki-	i-		shin-	
				zin-∴	
am-∴	ez-			sin-∴	(o-)
ma-	vi-	bi-		(—)	la- (ɣ'a-)
	i-			n-	l-
	dsh-				
ba-	si-			n- i-	lu-
MA-	**KI-**	**PI-**	**N-**	**THIN-**	**LU-**

THE FULLEST FORMS OF THE **BANTU** PREFIXES. (*Cont.*)

	Class of Prefix.	12.	13.	14.	15.	16.
SOUTH-EASTERN BRANCH.	KAFIR.		(KA-)	bu-	ku-	
	ZULU.					
	SEXLAPI.		(χA-)	bo-	χo-	
	SESUTO.		(H'A-)		h'o-	
	TEKEZA.			bu-		
MOSAMBIQUE GENUS.	TETTE.	tu-	ka-		ku-	pa-
	SENA.			u-		
	MAKUA.				u-	
ZANGIAN GENUS.	KIHIAU.			u-	ku-	pa-
	KIKAMBA.	tu-	ka-			wa-
	KINIKA.					va-
	SUAHELI.					pa-
	KISAMBALA.					ha-
INT.	BAYEIYE.			o-	ko-	
MUNDA GENUS.	OTYIHERERÓ.	tu-	ka-	u-	ku-	po-
	SINDONGA.					
	NANO.				gu-	
KONGO G.	ANGOLA.	tu-			ku-	
	KONGO.					
	MPONGWE.			(ow-)	(o-)	
NORTH-WESTERN BRANCH.	DIKELE.	la-	dsh-, a-			
	BENGA.	lo-	e-	bo-		
	DUALLA.					
	ISUBU.					o-
	FERNANDIAN.	to-				
	ANCIENT BANTU.	**TU-**	**KA-**	**BU-**	**KU-**	**PA-**

possessed by the derivative prefixes of the nouns in the original Bântu language. The form of the 5th prefix must have been either **DI-** or **LI-**, and that of the 10th prefix was probably **THIN-**. But there can be no doubt that, in the original Bântu language, **MU-** was the derivative prefix of the nouns of the 1st class, **BA-** of those of the 2nd, **MU-** of the 3rd, **MI-** of the 4th, **MA-** of the 6th, **KI-** of the 7th, **PI-** of the 8th, **N-** of the 9th, **LU-** of the 11th, **TU-** of the 12th, **KA-** of the 13th, **BU-** of the 14th, **KU-** of the 15th, and **PA-** of the 16th class.

536. Although comparison clearly shews that the forms given above must have been those of the derivative prefixes of the nouns at that period which immediately preceded the dismemberment of the original Bântu language,—there are, in some instances, forms yet older, at which we can still arrive. To ascertain these, we have to consult, besides the derivative prefixes of the nouns, also the pronominal elements,—which were originally identical with the prefixes, and which constitute the different forms of concord referring to them. Thus it will appear (for example) that **MU-** was not the most ancient form of the first prefix, but merely a phonetic adaptation of a still older form, which appears to have been something like **NGUA-**. The forms of particles as short as were these derivative prefixes of the nouns, must have been early affected, by their peculiar prefixed position, in a different manner from that in which the same elements would be moulded, when occurring in their pronominal capacity as marks of concord. The crushing weight of the stem must always have had the tendency to grind the prefixes into the most easily articulated forms. The influence of the stem can be clearly seen in the Zulu prefixes of the 1st and 3rd classes; which usually retain the form **mu-** before monosyllabic stems only, and before longer stems are contracted to **m-**. In Setshuâna the 9th prefix is entirely absorbed before almost all stems which are not monosyllabic,—as *kuana* 9. "lamb,"

from ṅ-*ku* 9. "sheep," &c. In positions, therefore, where the weight of the stem was not pressing upon the forms of concord (with which the derivative prefixes of the nouns were originally identical), and where they stood either unencumbered, or else combined with such elements as affected them differently, we may expect that they would sometimes better preserve their original form. The tendency towards the use of such sounds as are most easily pronounced in the prefixual position, explains the fewness of the phonetic elements now to be met with in the whole number of the prefixes of the nouns. We shall see this more clearly by arranging the prefixes of the nouns, according to their phonetical relations, in the forms which they probably had in the original Bântu language.

	A	I	U
M	**MA**- (6.)	**MI**- (4.)	**MU**- (1., 3., & 18.)
K	**KA**- (13.)	**KI**- (7.)	**KU**- (15. & 17.)
P	**PA**- (16.)	**PI**- (8.)	
B	**BA**- (2.)		**BU**- (14.)
L		**LI**- or **DI**- (5.)	**LU**- (11.)
T		**TIM**- or **THIN**- (10.)	**TU**- (12.)
N		**N**- (9.)	

It will be seen from this that **m** and **k** are favorite letters as consonants of these prefixes.

In the course of the second section of this part, it will be our business to ascertain (by analysis of the different forms of concord belonging to each class) the original form of each derivative prefix, as indicated by the various pronominal elements which must once have been identical with it. It is necessary thus to elucidate the most ancient ascertainable forms of the prefixes, if we desire to extend this comparison to those members of the Bântu family which are found *out of* South Africa (as Timneh,

Bullom, &c.), and still more to other Prefix-pronominal languages (such as the Gôr family, &c.). Those comparisons which already offer themselves will, therefore, be deferred until the end of this part of our Grammar.

h. THE MUTUAL CORRESPONDENCE OF THE CLASSES OF NOUNS AS SINGULAR AND PLURAL.

537. As some of the correspondences between those prefixes which answer to each other as singular and plural, occur regularly in all Bântu languages, while others are only met with in some, or even one, of these languages,—the following table has been constructed, in order to shew the distribution of the correspondences of the different classes (or genders), throughout the South African Bântu languages. In this table, the ten prefixes of the singular number are arranged from the top to the bottom of the table, and the seven plural prefixes from left to right. The table contains seventy squares, and all of these in which such singular and plural prefixes meet as do not correspond to each other, have been left blank. Those squares which indicate correspondences met with in all SOUTH AFRICAN BÂNTU languages, have these words printed so as almost to fill the square. Those correspondences again, which are only met with in some of these languages, are indicated (in the squares) by the names of the Branches, Genera, Species, or single languages in which they occur. The names of the different languages have been so placed in each square, as to indicate to some degree their geographical position; thus the Western languages are to the left, the Eastern to the right, the Northern in the upper, and the Southern in the lower part of the square. The North-western Branch (N.W. Br.) has always been placed in the left hand corner at the top, the South-eastern Branch (S.E. Br.) in the right hand corner at the bottom; the Bunda Genus occupies the opposite lower left hand corner, and the Zangian Genus is opposite to the North-western Branch

288   The Concord.

A TABLE shewing the Distribution of the Correspondences between the SINGULAR and PLURAL Derivative Prefixes (and Classes) of Nouns in the South African Bântu Languages.

PLURAL. / SINGULAR.	2. BA-	4. MI-	6. MA-	8. PI-	10. THIN-	12. TU-	14. BU-
1. MU-	SOUTH AFRICAN BANTU	Imbu 1 Dualla 1	(? Kikumba) Kongo Sena Sesuto Kafir Sp.				
3. MU-	Imbu Dualla	SOUTH AFRICAN BANTU	Ditele (Mponqwe) Setshuana		Angola (Mponqwe)		
5. DI-	Kongo 1		SOUTH AFRICAN BANTU	(? Fernandian 1)		Imbu Dualla	
6. MA-		Ditele 1		Dualla MIDDLE BRANCH S.E. BR.			
7. KI-		Ditele 1	(? Bindongo 1)			N.W. BR.	

Mutual Correspondences of the Classes of Nouns. 289

SINGULAR \ PLURAL	2. BA-	4. MI-	6. MA-	8. PI-	10. THIN-	12. TU-	14. BU-
9. N-	Imbu Dualla Kongo						
11. LU-			N.W. Bа. (excepting Benga) Tette Setshuána Káfir Sp.		SOUTH AFRICAN BANTU (excepting Dikele)	Kisamba	
13. KA-			N.W. Bа. (excepting Benga) Angola Setshuána Sukell Taki-yo Káfir Sp.		Fernandian Zangian Dikele Genus (Mpongwe) Kisiau Nano S.E. Sindonga Bа. Otyiherero	Kongo Sindonga Otyiherero	
14. BU-			Dikele Nano	N.W. Bа. Kisambala	Nano Bayeiye	Kisamba Tette Sena Angola	Otyiherero
15. KU-		Imbu Dualla Benga Kinika	Fernandian Kikamba Kisiau Imbu Makua Dikele Kongo G. Angola Setshuána Otyiherero	Nano	Benga : Kisambala		
			Kongo G. Kikamba Sindonga SeXlapi Otyiherero				

in the right hand top corner. As some of the correspondences between the classes of nouns (as singular and plural) are so exceptional as to occur in one language only, and occasionally in only one instance, the cipher "1" has been added to indicate the latter anomalous cases.

538. It must, however, be borne in mind, that in some instances the plural prefixes do not replace those of the singular, but are prefixed to them. Thus we find:

BA-*MU*-, the 2nd prefix (**BA**-) prefixed to the 1st (**MU**-), in the *Kafir* and *Setshuána* dialects, and in *Otyiereró*. In Seĥlapi these combined prefixes have still sometimes the form **bo**-*mo*-, but they are generally now contracted to **bo**- in the Kafir and Setshuána dialects, and in Otyiereró to **o**-.

BA-*N*-, the 2nd prefix (**BA**-) preceding the 9th (**N**-), in *Kongo* (**a**-**n**-) and *Isubu* (**ba**-**n**-).

MA-*N*-, the 6th prefix (**MA**-) preceding the 9th (**N**-), in *Dikele*, *Dualla*, and *Isubu*.

MA-*LU*-, the 6th prefix (**MA**-) preceding the 11th (**LU**-), in *Angola* and *Isubu*.

MA-*BU*-, the 6th prefix (**MA**-) preceding the 14th (**BU**-), in *Kikámba*, *Otyiereró*, *Angola*, *Dikele*, and *Dualla*.

MA-*KU*-, the 6th prefix (**MA**-) preceding the 15th (**KU**-), in *Otyiereró* and *Sindonga*.

THIN-*LU*-, the 10th prefix (**THIN**-) preceding the 11th (**LU**-), in *Kinika* and *Kisuáheli* (**ni**-**u**-, **mi**-**u**-, &c.).

MI-*LU*-, the 4th prefix (**MI**-) preceding the 11th (**LU**-), in *Benga* and *Dualla*.

539. There is, of course, no doubt that the correspondences which are common to all South African Bântu languages, already existed in the mother tongue whence all these spring. Nor can we doubt that the same is the case with regard to correspondences which, although not present in every Bântu language, are yet of more or less frequent occurrence in each of the three Branches. Concerning correspondences which are met with in one Branch[*] only, or merely in one language,[†] it is more difficult to

---

[*] Such as the correspondence of the 12th (**TU**-) class as plural to the 7th (**KI**-) in the *North-western* Branch.

[†] *E.g.* the 14th (**BU**-) class as plural to the 13th (**KA**-) in *Otyiereró*.

decide whether they are ancient arrangements which have been retained, or special acquisitions of the language or group of languages in which they occur. But with regard to many of the correspondences, which appear in a few languages, sometimes only in one,—there is no doubt that the surrounding circumstances are such as to render it highly probable that they only owe their existence to the power of analogy or of logical inference. Few of these latter can, with any degree of probability, be supposed to be more than modern innovations. As far as we can see, the mother tongue, whence the present South African Bântu languages are derived, may have possessed a system of prefixual correspondence approximate to that laid down in the following table. Those correspondences, regarding the originality of which we are not perfectly certain, have been marked "(?)." More doubtful cases have been entirely omitted.

The Probable **Ancient** Correspondences of the Derivative Prefixes of the Nouns in the South African **Bântu** Languages.

SINGULAR PREFIXES.	PLURAL PREFIXES OF THE NOUNS.						
	2.	4.	6.	8.	10.	12.	14.
1. MŬ-	BA-		MA-				
3. MŬ-		MI-	MA-				
5. DI-			MA-				
7. KI-				PI-		(?)TU-	
9. N-			MA-N-		THIN-		
11. LU-			MA-LU-		THIN-	TU-	
13. KA-			(?) MA-	PI-	(?)THIN-	TU-	(?)BU-
14. BU-			MA-BU-				
15. KU-			MA-KU-				

540. A comparison of the tables which illustrate the present and ancient correspondence of the prefixes, will

shew that not even the fullest of the present South African Bântu languages has retained all the correspondences which certainly existed at the period preceding their separation from the parent stock. Upon the whole, there is an evident tendency in these languages to restrict each singular prefix to the use of one especial plural; and thus to introduce a greater regularity into the method of correspondence. But, in some languages, this tendency is counteracted; chiefly because certain prefixes of nouns have been confounded with others (on account of their similarity of form), and the correspondence belonging to the one class thus applied to the other. The extensive domain of correspondence, which seems to have been the original property of the 6th (**MA**-) class, suggests the facility with which this prefix might either have superseded all other plural prefixes, becoming itself the exclusive indicator of the plural; or have acquired (by the side of the different plural correspondences) the force of a dual prefix,—a meaning which, in a certain very restricted sense, it even now possesses. (*Vide* p. 200.) The contemplation of such possibilities is by no means futile, for we generally find that wherever peculiar facilities exist for a different grammatical arrangement in a given language (or group of languages),—it will be observed as an achieved fact, in some kindred language or family of languages.

2. THE GENDERS AND NUMBERS OF NOUNS IN THE HOTTENTOT LANGUAGE.

541. In comparing the different forms of the derivative particles (prefixes) of nouns in the South African Bântu languages, we perceive that they evince a tendency to reduce the derivative particle (prefix) to a single letter (either vowel or nasal),—or even to elide it altogether. In the latter case, the class of the noun is no longer indicated by any formal element in the noun itself; and in the former, many instances of homophony of the prefixes are

produced, which render the derivative particle itself an uncertain guide to the class of the noun of which it forms a part. And while derivative particles, originally different, have thus become identical in form, the same phonetic changes may have taken place in the signs of concord (derived from the prefixes) rendering these also throughout identical. In this case, two originally distinct classes of nouns, by mere homophony, become one, as has been the case with regard to the 5th and 11th (le-) classes of nouns in Sesuto. (§ 456.) On the other hand, although the forms of different derivative particles may become identical, the forms of concord referring to them may yet remain either partly or wholly distinct; in which case the two classes continue to be kept separate; not, however, on account of the forms of their derivative particles, which have become homophonous, but because some of their forms of concord have remained distinct. In this manner, the 1st and 3rd (**MU-**) classes (which in most Bântu languages have the same forms for their derivative prefixes) still exist as perfectly distinct classes in all known South African Bântu languages, because they differ in some of their forms of concord,—as -mu- Zulu objective pronoun of the 1st, and -wu- the same of the 3rd class,— -ke possessive pronoun suffix of the 1st, and -w-*o* of the 3rd class. The natural inclination to maintain logical distinctions in the grammatical classification of the nouns may have assisted in keeping these classes asunder, notwithstanding the homophony of their derivative prefixes. This tendency may also, on the other hand, lead to the combination of two originally distinct classes, on account of their similarity of meaning. The two local classes, the 15th (**KU-**) and 16th (**PA-**) appear in the South-eastern Branch languages to have been thus thrown into one. Classes may also disappear, because the derivative particles, which in the first instance constituted them, cease to be employed. In this manner the 13th (**KA-**) class is unknown in the South-eastern Branch languages,—diminutives being formed here exclusively by suffixes (-*ana*, -*anyana*, &c.), and not by the prefix **KA-**, so commonly used for the same purpose in the Middle Branch. Lastly, a class which only contains one or a few nouns must disappear, when the noun or nouns which constitute it, become obsolete.

542. We must also particularly bear in mind that, although the form of the derivative particle was, in the first instance, the determining element of the concord, and indicative of the class (or gender) to which a noun belonged,—yet the more a language has subsequently undergone phonetic changes, the less we shall find this to be the case. This goes frequently so far that a noun may belong to a class without bearing any visible mark of the derivative particle which, in the first instance, constituted the class (or gender), and was its sign. These general rules (deduced from the comparative study of the concord-indicating derivative particles of the nouns in the South African Bântu languages) are also borne out by a comparison of the forms of the derivative particles of the nouns in the different Hottentot dialects,—and still further by a comparison of the latter with those met with in the kindred Sex-denoting languages.

543. Firstly, the comparatively small number of eight classes (or genders) to be found in the fullest HOTTENTOT dialect, leads us to suppose that an originally larger number has been reduced to this by means of the processes indicated in § 541.* In Mpongwe, one of the most

---

* Although we do not assert that it is either right or advisable to compare, in detail, the Hottentot derivative suffixes of the nouns with the Bântu prefixes, it is not wholly impossible that such a comparison may be justified at a future stage of our researches. One inclined to hypothesis would at once suggest that in the Hottentot masculine singular gender (-**p** or -**bi**, -**mi**, &c.) we may be supposed to see a combination of the Bântu 1st (**MŬ**-), 3rd (**MŪ**-), 14th (**BU**-), 15th (**KU**-), and 16th (**PA**-) classes, with their personal, local, and abstract meanings;—that the 2nd (**BA**-) class has assumed the dual meaning so consonant with its supposed etymology in the Bântu languages, and is to be discerned in the Hottentot masculine dual (-**kha**) gender. The masculine plural (-**ku**) gender might then (by the same power of forcible hypothesis) be

modernized of the South African Bântu languages, we have seen that the number of the classes of nouns has been reduced from sixteen to ten. The Hottentot language is, however, not merely remarkable for a yet greater reduction in the number of the classes,—its distinctive characteristic among the South African languages being that the division of the nouns into classes has been brought throughout into some reference to certain logical distinctions. Every class (or gender) in Hottentot possesses a distinct numerical value, and five out of the eight classes (or genders) contain a clear reference to sex; while the remaining three classes (or genders) are also logically distinct, as leaving the sex undetermined. We thus have, with easy nomenclature, three *masculine* genders or classes (masc. singular, masc. plural, and masc. dual), two *feminine* ones (fem. singular and fem. plural), and three *common* genders or classes (common singular, common plural, and common dual). The numerical correspondence of these classes appears upon the whole to be very strictly carried through in the Hottentot language; but the reference to sex really extends only to such nouns as indicate beings in which the sex can be distinguished. Other nouns belong respectively to masculine, feminine, or common classes (or genders), merely on account of the suffix with which they are formed. It must, however, be remarked that there are a good number of nouns of

identified with the 12th (**TU**-) class, the feminine singular (-**s** or -**si**) with the 7th (**KI**-, Kafir **si**-) class, and the feminine plural (-**ti**) with the corresponding plural 8th (**PI**-) class. The common singular (-**i**) and plural (-**n**) classes might then appropriate the 9th (**N**-) and 10th (**THIN**-) classes to themselves, whilst for the common dual (-**ra**) gender would only remain the 6th (**MA**-) class with its inclination to a dual meaning. Such an explanation would only allow three classes (the 4th **MI**-, 11th **LU**-, and 13th **KA**-) to have become quite extinct. But, well as it provides for the other classes, it does so merely upon wild assumptions which are without a shadow of scientific proof. But, as mere hypotheses, shewing the possibility of a system of classification so extensive as that of the Bântu languages, being compressed within as narrow a sphere as that of the Hottentot classes (or genders) of nouns, these suppositions are perhaps not wholly out of order.

this impersonal character which are, with slight changes of meaning, used either with masculine, feminine, or common suffixes. Thus many nouns belong, in one dialect, to one gender (or class), and in another to a different gender, and even in the same dialect some authors give a noun with a masculine suffix, which others appear to know only as feminine, or common, and *vice versa.* The lists of nouns given below afford many examples of this plurality in the genders belonging to one and the same noun, and the frequent recurrence of such instances renders it probable that many nouns exist in different genders with variations of meaning which are so slight as to be barely perceptible to a foreigner.* To discern the delicate meanings implied by these changes in the forms of the nouns, and to interpret them aright is one of the most difficult tasks in the *synonymique* of the Hottentot language; and the different authorities are very frequently at variance on these almost intangible points. According to the Rhenish missionaries, Krönlein (p. 121) and Vollmer, the masculine gender in Hottentot implies something large and prominent. This seems also in some way to be the case in the ILOIGOB language (Ukuafi and Masai) which, geographically speaking, is in East Africa the nearest sex-denoting language to the Hottentot. (Erhardt's "Vocabulary of the Enguduk Iloigob," 1857.) It is clear that the presence of nouns representing impersonal objects in classes (or genders) to which a sex-denoting character had become attached, must naturally have favoured their personification, thereby frequently leading the mind to ascribe to these objects the most obvious attributes of the

---

* In this respect we may study with particular advantage such pieces of Hottentot traditional literature as have been taken down from the lips of natives. The first translation of the Gospels into the Nama dialect appears to me for this very reason also particularly worthy of attention, as being chiefly the work of a native (the excellent Mrs. Schmelen) and, therefore, probably in some ways more idiomatic than any of the later translations. However, as it was the first attempt at translation into this difficult language, we must not expect too much from it as a source of knowledge of the language.

respective sexes. But this does not prove that the suffix, which now indicates the gender, had not originally quite a different meaning. In fact, in many masculine nouns in Hottentot there is no doubt that the suffix of the masculine singular has a sort of local meaning, and this meaning seems also to influence the character of this gender, even in some of the most advanced Sex-denoting languages. For example, in Latin, *diē-s* (French "jour") m. s., and *diē-s* (French "journée") f. s. differ from each other almost in the same manner as the corresponding Hottentot nouns *tsē*-p m. s. "day as date," and *tsē*-s f. s. "day as a period."

544. The division of the nouns into classes in Hottentot is radically based upon the same principle as in the Bântu languages; but the present state of the Hottentot language shews that the power of analogy has been far more actively exercised in it. This power of analogy has been chiefly brought to bear upon the correspondences of singular, plural, and dual classes. It is not impossible that one or two of the derivative suffixes of the nouns in Hottentot may originally have had a sex-denoting meaning, or a meaning which at least predisposed them to indicate difference of sex,—yet it would be absurd to suppose that all of the eight concord-indicating derivative suffixes of nouns in the Hottentot language (or even the majority of them) can have originally denoted those distinctions of sex which they now impart to nouns indicating beings in which this distinction can be naturally observed. When the idea of so profound a natural distinction as that of sex (with its soul-stirring associations) was once clearly imparted to the grammatical division of the nouns into classes, it must have had the tendency of bringing this classification more and more into harmony with itself. It must have developed the power of analogy, thereby placing the correspondences between singular, plural, and dual classes upon a more regular footing, and attaching to every one of the classes a distinct logical meaning. This same tendency, in the English language, has expelled

from the two sex-denoting genders (or classes) almost all nouns representing things or ideas in which sex cannot be distinguished, and has thus obliterated in English those perplexing features of the Sex-denoting languages, which are still so clearly visible in its German cousins. It is this same tendency towards a coincidence of logical and grammatical classification, which, in the first instance, after the distinction of sex had been introduced, made the whole world appear as if divided by sexual distinctions.

545. But it is not necessary, nor even probable, that the original meaning of any of the concord-indicating derivative suffixes of nouns in the Hottentot language implied a distinction of sex. To assume, for example, that the suffix of the masculine singular (-p) had originally the meaning of "man," or the feminine singular (-s) that of "woman," would in no way explain the peculiar division of the nouns into classes, as we find it in Hottentot, and would be opposed to all that is probable regarding the etymology of these suffixes, and also to the fact that so many nouns are included in the sex-denoting classes to which the distinction of sex can only by great force be applied. On the contrary, it is probable that the idea of sex was at first as little implied in any of the Hottentot derivative suffixes, as the idea of "tree" or "river" in the 3rd Bântu prefix, although the latter prefix now appears to impart to many nouns one of these two ideas. (§§ 427 & 428.) As the idea of "tree" or "plant" was probably grafted upon this prefix by the process of forming nouns in analogy with MU-*TI* 3., in like manner the idea of masculine or feminine gender may have been imparted to Hottentot suffixes which had no such meaning originally. If the word for "man" were formed with one suffix (-p), and the word indicating "woman" (be it accidentally or not) by another (-s), then other nouns would be formed with the same suffixes, in analogy with these, until the majority of the nouns of each sex were formed with certain suffixes which would thus assume a sex-denoting character.

This has been carried so far in Hottentot, by the power of analogy, that (as far as we know) no noun indicating a female being now belongs to the masculine class or gender, —an apparent anomaly which is still to be met with in GAELIC,* if I may trust to A. Stewart's "Elements of Galic Grammar," 1801, p. 46. But a neuter gender (*i.e.* a class which comprehends nouns to which the distinctions of sex do not apply) had not yet been brought into existence; and the neuter nouns were still in the same classes with those in which sex could be naturally distinguished. The classes of the nouns in Hottentot thus possessed no naturally inherent sex-denoting character, but were (so to speak) merely coloured by a sex-denoting dye, which has only thoroughly pervaded the nature of the classes in the most advanced of our Sex-denoting languages.

THE NAMA DIALECT.

546. The NAMA dialect possesses the best preserved forms of the concord-indicating derivative suffixes of the nouns, and also contains a greater number of genders (or classes) of nouns than any other Hottentot dialect. The common singular (-i) gender (or class) is only met with in Nama, or, at least, has only been proved to exist in this dialect. We frequently find some of the forms of the masculine singular suffix confounded with this common singular suffix (-i). The original form of the suffix of the masculine singular appears to have been -BI; but it is rarely met with in this form,† even in Nama, excepting as

* We must remember that in German student slang the most usual term by which a woman is indicated is also a masculine word.

† In the sentences *o-p ge |gīri-*bi *ge tē-he* "then he was questioned by the jackal," and *ani-*p *ge goma |gīri-*bi *ge |kuri-he* " the cock was once, it is said, overtaken by the jackal " (Krönlein's *M.S.* in the Grey Library, p. 29), the -bi of *|gīri-*bi "jackal" appears to be the full form of the suffix retained for the purpose of indicating the causal case. In like manner, the ancient form of the suffix of the feminine singular (-si) appears to be retained in the same circumstances. Thus we find, on the same page, *o-*p *ge ≠hira-*si *ge |ana!gā-he* " then he was accused by the

an objective pronoun (-bi) after the verb. After vowel stems the suffix always loses its own vowel, but retains, in Nama, the labial explosive consonant,—which is either -b or -p, according to its position at the beginning or end of a syllable. This derivative suffix is -b when ("anlautend") it combines with a following vowel (-*a*, in the so-called objective case), and thus begins a separate syllable; but it is -p when the suffix ("auslautend") terminates a syllable.*
If, however, the stem ends in a consonant (nasal *m* or *n*, or liquid *r*) the vowel of the masculine singular suffix remains, whilst the consonant of the suffix is either assimilated to the ending consonant of the stem, or elided after it.†
Thus -mi, -ni, and -i are only modified forms of the masculine singular suffix -BI,—and, in their peculiar positions, equivalent to, and etymologically identical with, the forms -b or -p. (§ 423.) No other concord-indicating suffix in Nama undergoes any change through the influence of the stem, excepting that the suffix of the common plural (-n) may adopt a vowel before the nasal (as -in) when following a stem which ends with a consonant. The suffix of the masculine plural which is -ku, according to Schmelen, Knudsen, and Tindall, is by Vollmer and Krönlein written -gu. I am inclined to consider the

hyena." It may, however, be that the *i*, in which in these cases the suffixes end, is not part of the original derivative suffix, but identical with the substantive particle, which we observe in the !Kora forms *kuee*-b-*i* m. s. "he is a man," *kuee*-ku-*i* m. pl. "they are men," *kuee*-m-*a*-*i* com. pl. obj. "they are people." (Appleyard, pp. 21 and 22.) The use of the substantive particle for the formation of a sort of causal case would be analogous to the way in which the Setshuána particle *ki* (and the corresponding so-called causal form in Kafir, § 462) is employed after passive verbs.

* This is Schmelen's and Tindall's orthography, which we believe to be the correct one upon this point. The Rhenish missionaries write -b in both cases. Schmelen frequently gives -pb-*a* as the objective form of the masculine singular.

† Schmelen and Knudsen assimilate the consonant of this suffix to an *m* ending the stem, while more modern authors appear to elide it.

former orthography as the better one, although in the examples given in §§ 421—424 and § 444 I have followed the other.

547. Besides the simple forms of the suffixes, we have those with the suffixed particle -a, which, in Nama, always coalesces with the concord-indicating derivative suffix. When the vowel of the derivative suffix is an a, the suffixed -a combines with this and forms one vowel only. The same is the case with regard to the vowel i, in the suffix of the feminine plural (-ti) and in that of the common singular (-i). The i sound in these two suffixes is changed, by vowel harmony, through the influence of the a into an -e (the suffixed -a being itself absorbed by the vowel -e),—and -te and -e are thus the modified forms of these suffixes. The vowel u of the suffix of the masculine plural (-ku) and the i of some forms of the masculine singular (-mi, -ni, and -i) are not treated in this manner, but are simply elided before the suffixed -a (as -k-a masc. plur., -m-a, -n-a, and -a masc. sing.).

548. In this form with the suffixed -a two principal meanings are to be discerned. Firstly, it is always used whenever a noun is in the accusative or objective case; and on this account we call it the *objective form*, although the title refers only to one portion of its meaning. Secondly, the -a appears also to possess the value of a relative particle, which refers the noun or adjective to an antecedent pronoun or noun, and thus gives it the character of an apposition.

*Inû-p-ei-*p ge |giri-ǂ-*a* ge /awa " then he, the jackal, ascended;"
*o-*p ge χam-m-*a* ge mī " then he, the lion, said;"
*o-*s ge khoi-ǂ-*a* ge ǁnā " then she, the woman, fell."

Whether the objective and also the appositional or relative value are to be derived from one original meaning, or whether two primarily different suffixes have by homophony been thrown into one, is, as yet, uncertain. As it now stands, the twofold meaning of this form is frequently perplexing and confusing, where identity of class (or gender) exists between a subjective pronoun and an objective noun following it. In the sentence

> o-p-ge /au-b-a /hu-b-a ra nã //ga "then he, the serpent, the white man did bite want" (then the serpent wanted to bite the white man),

both nouns are formed with this suffixed -a, although the one only as the object of the verb, and the other as in apposition to the subjective pronoun ; but if either /au-b-a or /hu-b-a were omitted, the context alone could shew in what sense (as objective, or in apposition) the remaining form with -a was used.

549. The form with the suffixed -a, besides indicating either the object or an apposition, is also used merely as a variation of the form without -a, before certain suffixed directives (or postpositions). Euphony alone appears to decide that, for example, the postposition -χu "from" is generally preceded by the form with the suffixed -a,— whilst -χa " by," -!na "in," and most other postpositions usually accompany the form of the noun without the suffixed -a. The employment of this suffixed -a is thus similar to that of the Kafir article, which is now more dependent upon usage and euphony than on any logical requirement. (§§ 463 and 464.) On this account I once named the form with -a the "definite form" of Hottentot nouns. (De Nominum Generibus, p. 40.) But the fact that the objective or accusative case of nouns in Hottentot is never found without this suffixed -a, renders the term "objective" the most convenient name for this form, although it does not convey its whole force and meaning. A comparison of this Hottentot objective form with the Ethiopic and Arabic termination -a, for the accusative of nouns, naturally suggests itself,—always supposing that these languages stand sufficiently near, grammatically speaking, to the Hottentot, to admit of such a comparison. In some ways, we are also reminded of the termination -a of the so-called "status emphaticus" of Aramaic nouns,

which is also said to be met with in the Assyrian language,—and may, or may not, be identical in origin with the accusative termination in Arabic and Ethiopic.

550. With regard to the Hottentot objective form in -*a*, it is, however, to be remarked that the -*a* is by no means inseparably connected with the derivative suffix of the noun, but, on the contrary, always stands after whatever may follow the noun to define it. *E.g.*, when a so-called possessive pronoun is suffixed to the noun, the -*a* stands after the pronoun, combining with it in the same manner as in other positions with the derivative suffix of the noun.

tara-s f. s. "wife," obj. *tara*-s-*a*,—*tara*-s ā-p "his wife," obj. *tara*-s ā-b-*a*;

tara-ti f. pl. "wives," obj. *tara*-te,—*tara*-ti ā-p "his wives," obj. *tara*-ti ā-b-*a*;

goma-n comm. pl. "cattle," obj. *goma*-n-*a*,—*goma*-n ā-ti "their (the women's) cattle," obj. *goma*-n ā-te;

tana-ti f. pl. "heads," obj. *tana*-te,—*tana*-ti ā-ku "their (the men's) heads," obj. *tana*-ti ā-k-*a*, &c.

Or, when two or more nouns, very closely connected by the conjunction *tsī* "and," are in syntactical positions requiring the -*a* form, the various terminations of the nouns do not themselves adopt the particle -*a*, but it is affixed to the pronoun which, following the conjunction *tsī*, represents all the preceding nouns. In the sentence *tsī |gui gama*-s *tsī |gui gu*-s *tsī |gui bǧri*-s *tsī*-n-*a χú-ba*-bi "and (she, the woman) one cow and one sheep and one goat and-them left-for-him" (and she left one cow, one sheep, and one goat for him), *gama*-s "cow," *gu*-s "sheep," and *bǧri*-s "goat," are not given in the objective form, although used in an objective sense, and the common singular pronoun -n (employed here instead of the feminine plural, because the sex is a matter of indifference) is followed by the objective particle -*a*, instead of the latter being suffixed to each of the different nouns to which the pronoun refers.

551. The non-existence of a feminine dual suffix in Nama causes the suffix of the common dual (-ra) to be used wherever a feminine dual is required. Upon the whole, the common genders (or classes) are not unfrequently used in place of the sex-indicating ones, in cases where the sex of the noun is a matter of indifference. Thus the common plural suffix (-n), especially, is frequently used in correspondence with the masculine singular (-p), or the feminine singular (-s) suffix. For example, nouns indicating animals which (like our "dog" and "cat") generally belong in the singular to one of the sex-indicating genders (masculine or feminine) even when used without any reference to sex, have often a corresponding plural suffix of the common gender. Also names of other things, in which no distinction of sex is naturally present, sometimes have the common plural corresponding to a masculine or feminine singular. That the masculine singular (-p) gender is particularly inclined to this correspondence with the common plural (-n) deserves to be noticed; for, the same correspondence will also be found in some kindred languages. For the same reason, it is important to remark that the feminine singular suffix in Nama may also have a collective meaning. For instance, *gu-s* f. s. may simply mean "ewe," or, as collective, "flock of sheep" = *gu-lhau-s* f. s.

552. The following tables will illustrate two ways in which the correspondence of the Nama derivative suffixes (and genders or classes) of nouns may be viewed. The Nama nouns have generally been transcribed according to the System of Lepsius; but the pronunciation of most of the nouns in the other Hottentot dialects is too imperfectly indicated to render such a transcription feasible. The !Kora, Cape, and Eastern nouns in the following lists, are, therefore, spelt as they appear in the vocabularies or texts furnished by the respective authorities, whose names are always appended.

NAMA DERIVATIVE SUFFIXES OF NOUNS.

Nama Suffixes.	Without suffixed -*a*.		With suffixed -*a*. (Objective, &c.)	
	Masculine.	Feminine.	Masculine.	Feminine.
Singular.	-p (-b) -mi -ni -i	-s	-b-*a* -m-*a* -n-*a* -*a*	-s-*a*
Indefinite.	-i		-e	
Plural.	-ku (-gu)	-ti	-k-*a*	-te
Indefinite.	-n -in		-n-*a* -in-*a*	
Dual.	-kha		-kha	
Indefinite.	-ra		-ra	

Abbreviations of the Names of Authorities in the Lists of Hottentot Nouns.

FOR THE NAMA DIALECT.

Schm. Schmelen. (Gospels 1831, &c.)
Kn.   Knudsen. (Luke 1846, MS. Grammar in Sir G. Grey's Libr., &c.)
Tind. Tindall. (Gramm. and Voc. 1857, MS. Matthew in Sir G. Grey's Libr., &c.)
Kr.   Krönlein. (MSS. in Sir G. Grey's Libr., New Testament 1866, &c.)

FOR THE !KORA DIALECT.

Licht. Lichtenstein. (Vocabularies in "Travels," &c.)
Borch. Borcherds. (MS. Vocab. 1801, in Sir G. Grey's Libr.)
Burch. Burchell. (Vocabulary in "Travels," 1824.)
W.   Wuras. (Grammar in Appleyard 1850, MS. Catechism in Sir. G. Grey's Libr., &c.)

FOR THE EASTERN DIALECT.

Sparrm. Sparrmann. (Vocabulary in "Travels," 1782.)
Thunb. Thunberg. (,, ,, ,, 1789.)
Barr. Barrow. (,, ,, ,, 1806.)
Van d. K. Van der Kemp. (Title of lost Catechism, 1806.)

FOR THE CAPE DIALECT.

Herb. Herbert. (Vocabulary in "Travels," 1638.)
Ten Rh. Ten Rhyne. (Voc. in Latin description of the Cape, 1668.)
Lud. a Ludolf. (First Vocabul., received from N. Witsen, 1710.)
Lud. b ,, (Second ,, ,, ,, ,, ,, ,,)
Leibn. Leibnitz. (Texts received from N. Witsen, 1717.)

NAMA SUFFIXES.	WITHOUT AND WITH SUFFIXED -a.				
	Singular.		Plural.		Dual.
Masculine.	-p (-b) -mi -ni -i	-b-a -m-a -n-a -a	-ku (-gu)	-k-a (-g-a)	-kha
Feminine.	-s	-s-a	-ti	-te	
Common.	-i	-e	-n -in	-n-a -in-a	-ra

NAMA HOTTENTOT NOUNS.

ǁkhōī-**p** Tindall (*kooi*-**p** Schmelen, *koi*-**b** Knudsen, ǁ*khoi*-**b** Krönlein, !Kora *köu*-**b** or *keu*-**b** Lichtenstein or *hwee*-**p** Borcherds or *kuee*-**b** Wuras, Eastern *kui*-**p** Thunberg, Cape *que* Ludolf b) masc. sing. "man," *khoi*-**b**-*a* m. s. obj., *khoi*-**ku** (!Kora *kuee*-**ku** Wuras) m. pl., *khoi*-**k**-*a* m. pl. obj., *khoi*-**kha** (!Kora *kuee*-**ka** Wuras) m. dual,—*khoi*-**s** (!Kora *kuee*-**s**, Eastern *ku*-**s** Thunberg, Cape *quie*-**s** Leibnitz or *qui*-**s** Ludolf b) fem. sing. "woman, female, girl," *khoi*-**s**-*a* (Eastern *quai*-**sh**-*a* Barrow) f. s. obj., *khoi*-**ti** (!Kora *kuee*-**tee** Wuras) f. pl., *khoi*-**te** f. pl. obj.,— *khoi*-**i** com. sing. "man, person," *khoi*-**e** c. s. obj., *khoi*-**n** (!Kora *köh*-**n** Lichtenstein or *kuee*-**n** Wuras) c. pl., *khoi*-**n**-*a* (!Kora *kuee*-**n**-*a* Wuras, Eastern *keu*-**n**-*a* Thunberg or *quai*-**n**-*a* Barrow, Cape *quee*-**n**-*a* Leibnitz) com. pl. obj., *khoi*-**ra** com. dual;

au-p (*ao*-b Krönl., !Kora *au*-b Wuras) m. s. "man, husband, aged man," *au*-b-*a* m. s. obj., *au*-ku m. pl., *au*-k-*a* m. pl. obj., *au*-kha m. dual,—*au*-s f. s. "a woman, an aged female," —*au*-ï c. s. "any aged person," *au*-ö c. s. obj.;

aχa-p m. s. "a lad, youth," *aχa*-ku m. pl.,—*aχa*-ro-p m. s. (dimin.) "little boy," *aχa*-ro-n c. pl. "little children,"—*aχa*-s f. s. "a girl," *aχa*-ti f. pl.;

* *ōā*-p (!Kora *oaam* Wuras) m. s. "son," *ōa*-b-*a* m. s. obj., *ōa*-ku m. pl., *ōa*-k-*a* m. pl. obj., *ōa*-kha m. dual,—*ōa*-s f. s. "daughter," *ōa*-s-*a* f. s. obj., *ōa*-ti f. pl., *ōa*-te f. pl. obj.,—*ōa*-n c. pl. "children," *ōa*-n-*a* c. pl. obj.;

* /*kōa*-p (/*kuā*-p Tindall, /*gōa*-b Knudsen, Krönlein, and Vollmer) m. s. "boy, son," /*kōa*-b-*a* m. s. obj., /*kōa*-ku m. pl., /*kōa*-k-*a* m. pl. obj., /*kōa*-kha m. dual,—/*kōa*-s f. s. "girl, daughter," /*kōa*-s-*a* f. s. obj., /*kōa*-ti f. pl., /*kōa*-te f. pl. obj.,—/*kōa*-ï c. s. "any child," /*kōa*-ö c. s. obj., /*kōa*-n c. pl. "children," /*kōa*-n-*a* c. pl. obj.,—/*kōa*-ro-p m. s. "little boy, little son," &c.;

/*gā*-p (!Kora *ǁgaa*-b Lichtenstein) m. s. "servant," /*gā*-b-*a* m. s. obj., /*gā*-ku m. pl., /*gā*-k-*a* m. pl. obj., /*gā*-kha m. dual,—/*gā*-s f. s. "maid-servant," /*gā*-s-*a* f. s. obj., /*gā*-ti f. pl., /*gā*-te f. pl. obj.,—/*gā*-ï com. s. "any servant," /*gā*-ö c. s. obj., /*gā*-n c. pl., /*gā*-n-*a* c. pl. obj.;

!*kāsa*-p or !*kā*-p Tindall (/*gāsa*-b or /*gā*-b Knudsen, Krönlein, and Vollmer) m. s. "brother," !*kāsa*-b-*a* or !*kā*-b-*a* m. s. obj., !*kāsa*-ku or !*kā*-ku m. pl., !*kāsa*-k-*a* or !*kā*-k-*a* m. pl. obj., !*kāsa*-kha or !*kā*-ku-kha m. dual,—!*kāsa*-s or !*kā*-s f. s. "sister," !*kāsa*-s-*a* or !*kā*-s-*a* f. s. obj., !*kāsa*-ti or !*kā*-ti f. pl., —!*kā*-ï c. s. "brother or sister," !*kā*-n c. pl. (German "Geschwister");

≠*gui*-p (!Kora *t'geu*-b Licht., Eastern *t'koi* Sparrmann or *koy*-p Thunberg, Cape *qui* Ludolf b) m. s. "nose,"—≠*gui*-s Krönl. (Western ≠*deu*-s) f. s.;

ǁ*khai*-p m. s. "breast, chest," ǁ*khai*-ku m. pl.,—ǁ*khai*-s (Kr.) f. s.;

/*nā*-p m. s. "belly, stomach" ("inside," from /*na* "in"), /*nā*-b-*a* m. s. o., /*nā*-ku m. pl.;

sō-p (or *sōi*-p Tind., Western *soe*-p) m. s. "lung," *so*-kha m. dual,—*sō*-n c. pl., *sō*-n-*a* c. pl. o.;

---

* The noun *ōa*-p usually, if not always, follows another noun (or pronoun) which is in the possessive case, in the manner of a suffix, and there can be hardly any doubt that it is a mere variety of the fuller noun /*kōa*-p, which, when thus following a noun or pronoun, loses its initial consonant and click. It appears to be an abbreviation similar in its nature to that of the Zulu noun u-mnu-*ntw-ana*, which, when standing before another noun, is frequently contracted to u-m-*la*, as u-m-*la ka baba* "child of my father," &c.

//ai-p m. s. "time," //ai-b-a m. s. o., //ai-ku m. pl., //ai-ï c. s., —//ai-s f. s. "nation," //ai-s-a f. s. o., //ai-ti f. pl., //ai-te f. pl. o.;

/ai-p (!Kora ſˤai-b Licht. or 'kāi-p Burchell, or ʌei-b Wuras, Eastern ſei Sparrm. &c., "fire") m. s. "piece of firewood, large fire" (Vollmer), "fuel, firewood" (Tindall),—/ai-s (!Kora ſgey-s Borcherds) f. s. "fire,"—/ai-n-a c. pl. o. "firewood" Vollmer (/ai-χa "fiery, hot," &c.);

hei-p (!Kora heyie-p Borcherds or hei-b Wuras, Cape ay Ludolf a) m. s. "log of wood, pole, beam," hei-ku m. pl., hei-k-a (!Kora hei-kŏ-a Licht., Cape e-qu-a Lud. b and Ten Rhyne) m. s. o., hei-kha m. dual,—hei-s f. s. "tree (growing)," hei-ti f. pl., hei-te f. pl. o.,—hei-i c. s. "stick," hei-n c. pl., hei-ra c. dual;

/hau-p m. s. "a rock,"—/hau-s f. s. "rocky ground," /hau-s-a f. s. o., /hau-ti f. pl., /hau-te f. pl. o.;

≠ara-p m. s. "kernel," ≠ara-ku m. pl., ≠ara-n c. pl.;

ari-p (!Kora arri-b Licht.) m s. "dog," ari-ku m. pl.,—ari-s (!Kora arrie-s Licht.) f. s.,—ari-n (alii-n Schm.) c. pl., ari-n-a (!Kora ali-n-a Borch.) c. pl. o.;

/ari-p m. s. "a red wild edible root, with small fine leaves,"—/ari-s f. s. "a yellow root," /ari-ti f. pl.;

!aita-p m. s. "a flea,"—!aita-s f. s.;

ani-p m. s. "bird," ani-n c. pl.,—ani-s f. s., ani-ti f. pl.,—ani-ro-i c. s. (dim.) "little bird" (vide Cape k'anni-qu-a, § 557);

!khei-p Tind. (kayi-p Schm., /hai-b Kn., !Kora ˀgei-b) m. s. "pockethandkerchief," /khei-b-a m. s. o., /khei-ku m. pl.,—/khei-s (/kay-s Schm.) f. s., /khei-s-a f. s. o.,—/khei-i c. s., /khei-n c. pl., /khei-n-a c. pl. o.;

//ku-p (!Kora ſˤkuhm Licht., &c.) Tind. (//gŭ-b Kn. and Kr.) m. s. "tooth," //ku-b-a m. s. o., //ku-ku m. pl, ('koe-s Schm. f. s.);

/hā-p (/gŭ-b Kr. and V.) m. s. "back;"

//ā-p (Kr.) m. s. "back,"—//ā-s (Vollm.) f. s. "piece from the back," //ā-i c. s.;

//kan-ni m. s. "flesh," //kan-n-a (Schm. John xi. 51.) m. s. o., —//kan-s f. s., //kan-s-a f. s. o., //kan-ti f. pl.,—//kan-i (Krönl.) c. s., //kan-in c. pl.;

//kam-mi Schm. (//gam-mi Kn. and Vollm.) m. s. "water," //kam-n-a (!Kora, Cape, and Eastern) m. s. o., //kam-ku m. pl., //kam-k-a m. pl. o.,—//kam-s Tind. (//gam-s Kr.) f. s. //kam-s-a f. s. o. (//kam-ö "without water, waterless," //kam-ro-p m. s. (diminut.) "a tear," //kam-a "to fetch water," //kam-soa-s f. s. "watercask");

am-mi m. s. "shore,"—am-s f. s. "mouth, lip, door,"* am-ti f. pl. "songs" (am "front");

---

* In the other dialects we find masculine suffixes for the word "mouth." Vide Cape kam-qu-a, § 557.

Nama Hottentot Derivative Suffixes of Nouns.

om-**mi** or *um*-**mi** (Cape *kǃom-me* Leibnitz) m. s. "house as a place," *om*-**m**-*a* (!Kora *tǃkchom*-**m**-*a* Licht. or *kgom*-*a* Borcherds, Eastern *kom*-**m**-*a* or *om*-**m**-*a* Thunberg) m. s. o., *om*-**ku** m. pl., *om*-**k**-*a* m. pl. o., *om*-**kha** m. dual, —*om*-**s** or *um*-**s** f. s. "habitation, dwelling," *om*-**ti** f. pl., —*om*-**ī** c. s. "store-room," *om*-**ē** c. s. o. ;

!hom-**mi** m. s. "mountain," *!hom*-**m**-*a* (!Kora *tǃkoem*-*a* Borch.) m. s. o., *!hom*-**ku** m. pl. "mountains,"—*!hom*-**n** c. pl. "hills, mountains as elevations;"

dom-**mi** (*toem*-**mi** Schm.) m. s. "throat, voice, manner," *dom*-**m**-*a* (Cape *dom*-**m**-*a* Lud. b) m. s. o., —*dom*-**s** (*dum*-**s** Tind.) f. s. ;

tara-**s** f. s. "a woman, wife," *tara*-**s**-*a* f. s. obj., *tara*-**ti** f. pl., *tara*-**te** f. pl. obj. ;

sorō-**s** f. s. "body," *sorō*-**s**-*a* f. s. obj., *soro*-**ti** f. pl., *soro*-**te** f. pl. obj. (*tsooroo*-**p** Schmelen m. s., *tsooroo*-**b**-*a* m. s. obj.) ;

tana-**s** (*tanna*-**ss** Schmelen, *dana*-**s** Tindall) f. s. "head," *tana*-**s**-*a* f. s. obj., *tana*-**ti** f. pl., *tana*-**te** f. pl. obj. (also *tanna*-**p** Schmelen m. s.) ;

gaka-**s** Tind. (*kaga*-**s** Kn., *gaga*-**s** Kr. and Vollm.) f. s. "spirit, ghost," *gaka*-**s**-*a* (*kaka*-**ss**-*a* Schm.) f. s. o. (*gaga*-**b** Vollm. m. s.) ;

!kan-**s** Tind. (*!gan*-**s** Kn., *!gān*-**s** Vollm.) f. s. "chin" (Cape *gan*-**n**-*a* Lud. b, Western *gan*-**n**-*a* m. s. o.);

≠*kai*-**s** (≠*gai*-**s** Knud. and Kr.) f. s. "ear," ≠*kai*-**s**-*a* f. s. obj., ≠*kai*-**ti** f. pl., ≠*kai*-**te** f. pl. obj., ≠*kai*-**ra** c. dual,—≠*kai*-**p** Schmelen m. s., ≠*kai*-**b**-*a* Schm. m. s. obj., ≠*kai*-**ku** Schm. and Kn. m. pl., ≠*kai*-**kha** Schm. m. dual,—≠*kai*-**n**-*a* Schm. com. pl. obj.;

kamana-**s** Tind. (*gamana*-**s** Kr.) f. s. "loin," *kamana*-**ti** Kn. f. pl.,—*kamana*-**p** (*ga*-*mana*-**b** V.) m. s.;

/*ani*-**s** f. s. "pit of the stomach," —/*ani*-**ku** m. pl. "lower part of chest;"

kŏa-**s** Tind. (*gŏa*-**s** Kr.) f. s. "knife,"—*kŏa*-**p** Schm. (*gŏa*-**p** Kn., Cape *droa*-**f** Herbert) m. s., *kŏa*-**b**-*a* m. s. o., *kŏa*-**ku** m. pl, *kŏa*-**kha** m. dual;

/*guru*-**s** Tind. (!Kora *guruh*-**s** Licht.) f. s. "quiver,"—/*guru*-**p** (!Kora *tǃguruh* Licht. or "*gurū*-**p** Burchell or *kurru*-**b** Wuras, Eastern *tǃgulu* Sparrm. &c.) m. s. "thunder;"

χ*u*-**s** f. s. "a vessel" (ā-χū-**s** f. s. "a vessel to drink out of"), χ*u*-**ti** f. pl.,—χ*u*-**ī** c. s. "a thing," χ*u*-**n** c. pl. "goods," χ*u*-**n**-*a* c. pl. o. (-χ*u* "from," χú "to leave," !Kora *chuh*-**b** Licht. or *gu*-**b** Wur. m. s., *chú*-**kŏ**-*a* Licht. or *gu*-**ku**-*a* W. m. pl. o. "goods, things") ;

≠*u*-**i** c. s. "food," ≠*u*-**e** c. s. o., —≠*ū*-**n** c. pl., ≠*u*-**n**-*a* c. pl. o. (Cape *oun*-**qv**-*a* Kolb, !Kora *tǃuhn*-**kŏ**-*a* Licht. m. pl. o.).

1 s

THE !KORA DIALECT.

553. The forms of the concord-indicating suffixes of the nouns in the !KORA dialect are essentially the same as in Nama. The suffix of the !Kora masculine dual (Nama -**kha**) is written -**ka** by Wuras; but as Schmelen has the same spelling for it in Nama, it is possible that the !Kora and Nama pronunciations of this suffix do not materially differ. The vowel termination of the !Kora feminine plural suffix -**tē** (or -**dē**) agrees more nearly with the objective form of this suffix in Nama (-**te**), than with the Nama form without the -a (-**ti**). No double form of this suffix is given by the !Kora grammarian Wuras; but as the Nama grammarian Tindall has also not noticed the fine distinction between the vowel sounds of these two forms (so clearly laid down by the Rhenish Missionaries Knudsen and Krönlein), it is not impossible that the !Kora dialect may also possess such double forms with their different shades of meaning. The other objective forms of the suffixes are exactly the same as in Nama, with this exception, that the masculine plural suffix -**ku** retains its *u* before the objective particle (-*a*) in !Kora as well as in the Cape and Eastern dialects. The common singular (-**i**) gender or class of nouns has, as yet, been found in the Nama dialect only; and appears, at all events, to be unknown in !Kora. The common dual suffix -**ra** is given by Wuras as suffixed to the objective form of the feminine singular, as *kuee-s-a-*ra "two women." (Appleyard, p. 18.) As yet, we have met with no precisely analogous formation in Nama; but, in one instance, the masculine dual suffix (-**kha**) appears to be affixed to the form of the masculine plural (-**ku**), viz. Nama /*kā-ku-***kha** m. dual, "two brothers."

554. The derivative suffix of the masculine singular is the same in the !Kora dialect as in Nama, viz. -**p** or -**b**, with its variety -**mi** after stems ending in *m* (as !Kora '*hum-***mi** Wur. = Nama /*hom-***mi** m. s. "heaven"), &c.

We must, however, except those cases in which the *m* ending the stem appears not to be a full nasal consonant, but merely an indication of that nasal pronunciation of the syllable which we have marked in Nama, according to the system of Lepsius, by a Greek circumflex ͂ over the vowel. In !Kora this nasalization appears, in the masculine singular and in the feminine singular, in the substantial shape of a nasal preceding the consonant in which the syllable terminates. The ending nasal adapts itself in these cases to the nature of the consonant of the suffix, being *n* or *ṅ* before the -s of the feminine singular, and *m* before the -p of the masculine singular. But the -p of the latter suffix is most generally elided after this *m* (which represents the nasalization of the syllable which it terminates), and the nouns thus frequently appear without derivative suffix; for example,

t'kaam Licht. (= Nama *!kā̃-p*) m. s. "brother,"
t'kaan-s Licht. (= Nama *!kā̃-s*) f. s. "sister."

In the plural and dual forms of these nouns, the nasalization has not been marked at all by Wuras in the only examples of them which he has given:

mum-p (*muhm* Licht. = Nama *mũ-p*) m. s. "eye,"
mu-ku (Nama *mũ-ku*) m. pl. "eyes,"
mu-ka (Nama *mu-kha*) m. dual "two eyes."

555. The scantiness of our materials for a knowledge of the !Kora dialect, obliges us to make use of all that is accessible to us, and to place nouns supplied by BORCHERDS, BURCHELL, and LICHTENSTEIN, side by side with the very few that are given by WURAS, in his grammatical sketch (Appleyard pp. 17—26) and in his short Catechism, a manuscript revision of which is in Sir George Grey's Library. (No. 21d.) We should be in a very different position, if Wuras' "Vocabulary of the ⁀Korana language" (a manuscript of 32 pages, with double columns, containing an English-!Kora vocabulary of more than 1700 words), presented by the author to Sir George Grey, had been accessible to us. Probably

in that case it would also have been feasible to adopt one uniform orthography* for !Kora; but it has now been deemed safer to allow the different authorities to spell their nouns in their own fashion, and we have not even tried to reconcile the Wuras of the Grammar, who uses the letters ƒ (/), y (//), q (!), and v (≠) to designate the clicks, with the Wuras of the Catechism, who expresses them by the signs ∧ (/), ⊓ (//), ∩ (!) and ⌐ (≠).

!KORA DERIVATIVE SUFFIXES OF NOUNS.	WITHOUT AND WITH SUFFIXED -a.			
	Singular.		Plural.	Dual.
Masculine.	-p, -b -mi (—)	-b-a -m-a	-ku	-ku-a (-kŏ-a)	-ka
Feminine.	-s	-ss-a	-tē (-tee) -dē (-dee)		-s-a-ra
Common.			-n	-n-a	

!KORA HOTTENTOT NOUNS.

*kuee-*b Wuras or *kŏu-*b or *keu-*b Lichtenstein or *kwee-*p Borcherds (Nama *khoi-*p) m. s. "man," *kuee-*ku W. (Nama *khoi-*ku) m. pl., *kuee-*ka W. (Nama *khoi-*kha) m. dual,— *kuee-*s W. (Nama *khoi-*s) f. s., *kuee-*tee W. (Nama *khoi-*ti) f. pl., *kuee-*s-a-ra W. f. dual, —*kuee-*n W. or *kŏh-*n Licht. (Nama *khoi-*n) com. pl., *kuee-*n-*a* W. (Nama *khoi-*n-*a*) c. pl. obj.;

ǀ'*ko-*b Licht. or *ǀ'koo-*b Borch. or *ƒkoo-*p Wuras (Nama /*ko-*p, Eastern *ǀ'go* Sparrm., Cape *koo*,

---

* In this Manuscript Vocabulary, which begins with remarks on *Pronunciation*, Wuras distinguishes eight different clicks, *viz.*

the palatal or very broad click ⊓ (//), the semi-palatal or half broad click ⊔;

the second palatal or round click ∩ (!), the semi-second palatal or half round click ∪;

the third palatal click ⌈ (≠), the semi-third palatal click ⌐;

the dental click ∧ (/), the semi-dental click V.

Lud. b) m. s. "child, boy,"—ǃʹkŏ-s Licht. or ſkŏo-s W. (Nama ǀkŏ-s, Eastern ǃgŏ-s Sparrm., Cape goi-s Lud. a or kŏ-s Lud. b or kǃŏ-s Leibn.) f. s. "girl,"—ſkŏ-n-a (Cape go-n-a Lud. a) com. pl. obj. "children;"

ǃʹgaa-b Licht. (Nama ǃgã-p) m. s. "servant;"

ʹgoe-b or ˚gu-b Wuras (Nama ǃkhu-p) m. s. "lord, master," ˚gu-ku ˙(Nama ǃkhu-ku) m. pl., ˚gu-ku-a (Nama ǃkhu-k-a) m. pl. o.;

Saa-b (Nama Sã-p) m. s. "Bushman" (Cape Soa-qu-a, Soan-qu-a or Sou-qu-a Records m. pl. o.);

Cy ⟘ kŏa-b or Tʃhuʹkŏa-b Wuras (Nama Tsui-ǁkwa-p Tind. or Tsoei-kwa-p Schm. or Tsui-ǁgoa-b Krönlein, Cape Tikḡuoá Kolb, Eastern Thuickwe Van der Kemp, Western Theu-ǁkwa-p) m. s. "God," Cy ⟘ kŏa-b-a (Nama Tsui-ǁkwa-b-a) m. s. obj. (§ 397);

haa-b W. (Nama hã-p) m. s. "horse," ha-oqu-a Licht. m. pl. obj.,—haa-s W. (Nama hã-s) f. s.,—ha-n-a W. com. pl. obj.;

dau-b Licht. (Eastern dʹau Sparrm.) m. s. "zebra,"—dau-s Licht. f. s. (Cape dou-qu-a Records m. pl. o.);

ǃʹhai-b Licht. or ǃʹkei-p Borch. (Nama ǃnai-p) m. s. "giraffe;"

ǃʹnaitaa-b Licht. (Nama ǀnira-p) m. s. "baboon;"

arri-b Licht. (Nama ari-p) m. s. "dog,"—arrie-s Licht. (Nama ari-s) f. s. "bitch," ali-n-a Borch. (Nama alii-nn-a Schm. or ari-n-a Vollmer) c. pl. o. "dogs;"

ǃʹgeuee-b (Nama ǀgīri-b or ǀgeira-p p. 112 note, Cape kenlèe Lud. b)* m. s. "jackal;"

chai-b Licht. or gei-p Borch. (Nama χei-p) m. s. "koodoo," —chai-s f. s. (Nama χei-ǃ c. s.);

gau-b Licht. or ghow Borch. (Nama gau-p) m. s. "gnu, wildebeest;"

ʹkarra-b Burchell (Nama ≠khara-p, Cape ʹt ʹchaka Lud. b) m. s. "whale;"

ǃʹhaa-p Licht. (Nama kãã-p Schmelen, ǀkha-p Tind.) m. s. "body;"

ǃʹgneu-b Licht. (Nama ǁnui-p) m. s. "fat;"

ǃʹkoo-b Licht. (Eastern ǃgo Sparrm., kŏ-p Thunb.) m. s. "meat, flesh;"

ǃʹkei-b Licht. (Nama ≠ei-p, Cape y Lud. b) m. s. "foot" (Cape i-qu-a = Nama ≠ei-k-a m. s. o.);

iim W. (Nama ĩ-p) m. s. "father;"

ǃʹkaam Licht. (Nama ǃkã-p) m. s. "brother,"—ǃʹkann-s Licht. (Nama ǃkã-s, Eastern ǃʹkang-s Sparrm. or kan-s Thunb.) f. s. "sister;"

oaam Wur. (Nama õa-p) m. s. "son;"

gomaa-p Borch. or ʹkomdam-p Burchell (Nama koma-p Schm.

---

* From this word, which I have also heard pronounced ǀgie-b by some Western Hottentots, the Kafir i-n-ǀi 9. is probably derived.

or *goma*-p Vollm. or *guma*-p Tind. or *kama*-b Knuds. or *gama*-p Krönl., Eastern *kuma*-p Thunb., Western *guma*-p) m. s. "ox,"—*gomaa*-s Borch. or *gumang*-s Licht. (Nama *goma*-s, &c.) f. s. "cow," *guman*-de Licht. (Nama *goma*-ti, &c.) f. pl.,—*guma*-n Licht. (Nama *goma*-n, &c.) c. pl. "cattle" (§ 226, note);

t'*juhnkam* Licht. or t'*kchaam* Borch. (Cape *thouqua* Lud. a or *ouck'ha* Lud. b, Eastern *guka* or *nuka* Sparrm. or *koka* Thunb.)† m. s. "hyena;"

t'¹*nom* Licht. (Nama *tsaū*-p) m. s. "calf,"—t'¹*noun*-s Licht. f. s. (Cape t'*nona* Lud. a or *nona* Lud. b);

t'¹*kaum*-p Licht. (Cape *K'on* Lud. b) m. s. "hyrax capensis,"—t'²*kaung*-s Licht. f. s.;

t'¹*naum* Licht. (Cape *nouw* Lud. a) m. s. "ear," (Eastern t'*nun*-qu-a Sparrm. m. pl. o.,—!Kora *qnau* or ⌐*nau* W., Nama ǁ*nŏu* Tind. or ǁ*nŏu* Krönl., Cape *k'nom* Lud. b "to hear");

t'¹*kuhm* Licht. (Nama ǁ*kŭ*-p, Cape *kon* Lud. a, Eastern *kom* Thunb.) m. s. "tooth;"

t'²*kam* Licht. (Nama !*kŭ*-p) m. s. "back;"

muhm Licht. or *mum*-p Wur. (Nama *mŭ*-p, Cape *moe* Lud. a or *mon* Lud. b) m. s. "eye," *mu*-ku (Nama *mū*-ku) m. pl, *mu*-ka (Nama *mū*-kha) m. dual (*mu* W., Nama *mŭ*, Cape *k'mon* Lud. b "to see");

t'¹*kŏăm* Licht. or '*oam* or '*oam* Wuras (Nama ǁ*ŏa*-p, Cape *ŏá* Lud. b. or *kŏá* Leibn.) m. s. "arm;"

tiim Licht. m. s. "thigh" (Nama *ñ*-s f. s.);

koem-b-a Wuras (Nama *ui*-b-a) m. s. obj. "life" (Cape *k!öin* Leibn.);

'*hum*-mi or '*hoem*-mi or '*hum*-i Wuras (Nama /*hom*-mi Knudsen or /*hum*-i Tind., Cape t'¹*hom*-mi or t'¹*hom*-me Leibn.) m. s. "heaven;"

t'²*hom*-m-a Licht. (Cape *gom*-m-a Lud. a or *chom*-m-a Lud. b) m. s. o. "belly;"

t'*on*-kŏ-a Licht. (Nama /*ŭ*-k-a, Cape *nuc*-qu-a Lud. b) m. pl. o. "hair;"

t'²*koro*-ko-a Licht. (Nama ǁ*koro*-ka, East. t'*kolo*-qu-a Sparrm.) m. s o. "nails" (Cape *clo* Lud. b = Nama ǁ*horo*-p m. s.);

t'¹*un*-ko-a Licht. (Nama /*kunu*-k-a, Cape *ou*-cqu-a Lud. b) m. pl. o. "fingers;"

oa-gei-s W. (Nama *oa*-xai-s) f. s. "virgin;"

t'²*kaau*-s Licht. or t'*koe*-s Borch. (Nama !*kkau*-s) f. s. "hippopotamus" (Cape *t kou*-w Ludolf a or *chă au* Lud. b, Eastern t'*gao* Sparrm. or *kou* Thunb. m. s.);

t'*kabaa*-s Borcherds (Nama !*naba*-s) f. s. "rhinoceros" (Cape *tnabba* Lud. a or *nabba* Lud. b);

saan-s f. s. "rheebok, redunca capreolus" (Cape *sää* Lud. b = Nama *yă*-p m. s.);

† Thence Kafir i-m n/*uha* 9. (= Zulu i-m-*pisi*, Man/olosi m-*isi*, Maxloenga m-*ise*, Sesuto *pīre*, Sečlapi *phiri*).

ǂhunn-s Licht. or ǂkoo-s Borch. f. s. "springbok" (Nama ǁkû-p m. s.);

dariing-s Licht. (Nama dani-s Tindall or taani-ss, Schmelen) f. s. "honey" (Nama taani-p Schm. m. s.).

THE CAPE DIALECT.

556. The forms of the derivative suffixes of nouns in the Hottentot dialect spoken at the Cape of Good Hope nearly two hundred years ago, agree, as far as we can ascertain them, almost entirely with those in the !Kora dialect. The masculine plural, especially, has the same uncontracted objective form -kw-*a* (spelt -qu-*a* in the vocabularies) as in !Kora. The feminine plural suffix -die stands nearest to the -dee (*i.e.* -dē) which we occasionally find in !Kora. The masculine singular also, after stems which end in *m*, has the same form (-mi) as in Nama and !Kora (with an occasional slight variation -me in the Cape dialect only) and -m-*a* in the objective. This is the only instance in which we have been able to ascertain the existence of double forms (with and without suffixed -*a*) in the Cape dialect; and, generally speaking, the materials for this dialect are so scanty that it is much if we succeed in ascertaining even one form of each suffix. No dual suffixes have as yet been discovered in our specimens of this dialect, but this is, of course, no proof of their non-existence.

557. The only remarkable exception to the similarity of the suffixes in the Cape and !Kora dialects is that the suffix of the masculine singular, when following a vowel, has fallen off in the Cape dialect, in all but a few cases. In the first instance, the original -b of this suffix appears to have been pronounced softly, like *v*, or German *w* (as it so frequently is in Nama, especially by the Orlams), and in the rare cases above alluded to in the Cape dialect the nouns of the masculine singular have still retained their derivative suffix in this softened form, as -w or -ƀƀ.*

---

* What the latter curious letter is really intended to indicate is not quite clear to us, but it may have been merely meant for a double *v* (-vv), the old sign for *w*.

t kau-ŵ (Lud. a) m. s. "hippopotamus;"

choassou-ŵ Lud. b or *t gwassou* Lud. a (!Kora *choas-au-*ƀ Licht.) m. s. "leopard, tiger;"

ǂAu-ƀƀ Lud. b (Nama and !Kora |*kau-*p or |*kau-*ƀ) m. s. "buffalo;"

k'ou-ƀƀ (Lud. b) m. s. "musk cat."

But all other masculine singular nouns with vowel stems, that occur in the vocabularies and texts which constitute the material for our knowledge of the Cape dialect, are destitute of any vestige of the derivative suffix. A more partial apocope of this suffix has been observed in !Kora, where it generally disappears after nasalized syllables. There are some other instances in Nama and !Kora, in which the suffixes of nouns of the masculine singular appear to be missing,* but as they are not certain, these cases have not been noticed in the tables. In Sparrmann's vocabulary, no masculine singular noun with a vowel stem retains any trace of the suffix, while Thunberg generally gives the suffix -p. The labial nature of the masculine singular suffix in Hottentot has evidently given it a

CAPE HOTTENTOT SUFFIXES.	WITHOUT OR WITH SUFFIXED -*a*.		
	Singular.		Plural.
Masculine.	-ƀƀ -ŵ -mi, -me (—)	-m-*a* -n-*a*	-kw-*a* (-qu-*a*)
Feminine.	-s		-die
Common.			-n-*a*

* Nama ǂẽn (Vollmer) "hollow of the hand" (ǂẽn-**khs** m. dual) and |ua (Cape *tga* Lud. a) are probably nouns of the masculine singular. Lichtenstein ends several !Kora nouns with *h*,—which may, or may not, be a misprint for *b*.

Cape Hottentot Derivative Suffixes of Nouns. 317

natural tendency to disappear,—and, therefore, we must not wonder that, in comparing the more developed Sex-denoting languages, we find that they have very frequently entirely thrown off this concord-indicating derivative suffix, whilst retaining the more tenacious one of the feminine singular.

CAPE HOTTENTOT NOUNS.

t'au-ɓɓ Ludolf b (Nama |*kau*-p, !Kora *t'ᵇkaau*-b Lichtenstein) m. s. "buffalo" (!Kora *t'kou*-s Borcherds f. s.);

choassou-w Ludolf b or *tgwassou* Lud. a (!Kora *chóasau*-b Licht., Eastern *koessau* Sparrmann or *gvassu*-p Thunb., Western *χuazau*-p) m. s. "leopard, tiger;"

qu'aü Lud. b (Nama /*au*-p, !Kora *t'au*-b Licht.) m. s. "neck;"

qu'au Lud. b (Nama ≠*hau*-p Tindall or ≠*gau*-b Krönlein) m. s. "heart;"

k'chou Leibnitz (Nama /*hu*-p, !Kora '*hoe*-b or ˄*hu*-b Wuras) m. s. "earth, land;"

thoughou Lud. a (Nama *truχu*-p) m. s. "night" (Bantu **BU-TUKU** 14. § 453, notes);

hacquou Lud. b or *haghgou* Lud. a (Nama *hagu*-p, Eastern *hango** Sparrm.) m. s. "hog" (Nama *hagu*-ku m. pl., *hagu*-k-a m. pl. obj.,—*hagû*-n c. pl., *hagu*-n-a c. pl. o.);

ceregou Lud. b (?Nama /*huro*-b) m. s. "land-tortoise,"—*sirigoe*-s Ten Rhyne f. s.;

bú Leibnitz (Nama *abo*-p, !Kora *aboo*-b Licht.) m. s. "father;"

koo Lud. a or *k?oó* Leibn. (Nama //*ŏ*-p, !Kora '*oo*-b or ⌐*oo*-b Wuras) m. s. "death;"

to Leibn. or *koo* Lud. b (Nama /*ko*-p Tind. or /*gō*-p Krönl., !Kora *fkoo*-p Wuras, Eastern *t'go* Sparrm.) m. s. "boy, son;"

k'öá Lud. b or *toa* Lud. a (Nama !*oã*-p Knudsen, !Kora *t'ᵇkoam*-p Licht.) m. s. "hare" (Nama /*uã*-s Tind. or /*ōa*-s Krönl., !Kora *t'ᵇkoang*-s Licht. f. s.);

chüa Lud. b or *twoha* Lud. a (Nama ≠*khua*-p Tind. or ≠*χoa*-b Knuds., !Kora *t'ᵇkoaa*-b Licht.) m. s. "elephant" (!Kora *t'ᵇkoaa*-s Licht. f. s.);

öd Lud. b or *köd* Leibn. or *Ouá* Kolb (Nama //*ɐa*-p or //*oã*-p, !Kora *t'ᵇkŏam* Licht. or '*oam* Wur.) m. s. "arm," *one*-qu-a Lud. a (Nama //*oã*-k-a) m. pl. o. (Nama //*oã*-kha m. dual);

choaa Lud. b (Nama ≠*hoa*-p, !Kora *t'goaa*-p Borch.) m. s. "cat;"

toya Lud. a (Nama ≠*oa*-p, !Kora *t'ᵇkoaa*-b Licht. or '*kŭã*-p Burchell, Eastern *qũa* Barrow) m. s. "wind;"

tGa Lud. a or *k'chá* Lud. b (Nama //*khã*-p, &c., § 472 note) m. s. "moon;"

---

* Kafir i-*hangu* 9., p. 160.

Thá Lud. a (Nama /ká-**p**) m. s. "grass;"

k'á (Nama /á-**p**, !Kora t'¹*kah*-**p** Licht.) m. s. "river;"

k'gcá Lud. b (Nama *gá*-**p**) m. s. "gander, goose" (Nama *gá*-**s** f. s., Dutch *gans*);

chá Lud. b (Nama χá-**p**, Eastern t'*ka* Sparrm.) m. s.;

chra Lud. b or *kearra* Lud. a (Nama ≠*khara*-**p**) m. s.;

'*t'chaka* Lud. b (Nama ≠*khara*-**p** Tind., !Kora '*karra*-**b** Burch.) m. s. "whale;"

qua Lud. b (Nama //*kwá*-**p**) m. s. "knee;"

qua Leibn. m. s. "day," *qua*-**qu**-*a* m. pl. o. (*Qua-nti* "Daghkloof" Records p. 435, Nama //*kua* "to dawn");

sáá Lud. b (Nama *yá*-**p**) m. s. "rheebok" (!Kora *saan*-**s** Licht. f. s.);

K'kamma Lud. b (Nama //*khama*-**p**, !Kora t'*kamkam* Borch., Eastern *kamma*-**p** Thunb.) m. s. "hartebeest,"—*t hammma*-**s** Lud. a (!Kora *k'hámaa*-**s** Licht.) f. s.;

bree Lud. a (Nama *bere*-**p**, !Kora *barii*-**p** Burchell, Eastern *bræ* Sparrm. or *brè* Thunb.) m. s. "bread;"

houry Lud. b or *houri* Leibn. (Nama *huri*-**p**) m. s. "sea;"

qui Lud. b (Nama ≠*gui*-**p**, !Kora t'*geu*-**b** Licht., Eastern t'*koi* Sparrm. or *koy*-**p** Thunb.) m. s. "nose;"

k'qui que Lud. b (Nama /*kui khoi*-**p**) m. s. "one man," *quee*-**n**-*a* Leibn. (Nama *khoi*-**n**-*a* or *koi*-**n**-*a*, !Kora *kuee*-**n**-*a* Wuras, Eastern *keu*-**n**-*a* Thunb.) com.

pl. obj. "men, people, Hottentots" (= Nama *Khoi-khoi*-**n**-*a*, Gona Hottentot *Khwe-khwe*-**n**-*a* Van der Kemp, com. pl. obj.);

únwie Lud. a or *Oũnwie* Kolb (Nama //*nui*-1 c. s. or //*nui*-**p** m. s.) "butter, fat;"

sorrie Lud. a or *soré* Lud. b (!Kora *soroᶜh*-**b** Licht. or *sŏrrei*-**p** Burchell, Eastern *surrie* Barrow) m. s. "sun" (Nama *sori*-**s**, !Kora *solee*-**s** Borcherds or *sorree*-**s** Wuras f. s.);

ammy Lud. b (Nama /*ami*-**p**, !Kora t'*kammie*-**p** Borcherds) m. s. "ostrich" (Nama /*ami*-**s** f. s.);

sem-**me** Lud. a or *sam*-**me** Kolb m. s. "female breast" (Eastern *sam*-**m**-*a* Thunb. m. s. o., Nama *tsam*-**koe** Schmelen or *sam*-**ku** Tind. m. pl., *tsam*-**ka** Schm. m. dual,—Western *sam*-**s** f. s., Nama *sam*-**ra** Kn. com. dual);

t?hom-**mi** or *t?hom*-**me** Leibn. (Nama /*hom*-**mi**, !Kora '*hoem*-**mi** or '*hum*-**mi** Wuras, Eastern *kōm* Barr. "air, light") m. s. "heaven, sky;"

t?am-**mi** Leibn. or *kam*-**me** Lud. a or *chtam*-**mey** Herbert (Nama //*kam*-**mi**) m. s. "water," *kam*-**m**-*a* Lud. b (Nama //*kam*-**m**-*a*, !Kora t'¹*kam*-**m**-*a* Licht. and Borch., Eastern t'*kam*-**m**-*a* Sparrm. or *kam*-**m**-*a* Thunb.) m. s. o.;

k?om-**me** Leibn. (Nama *om*-**mi** or *um*-**mi**) m. s. "house," *k?om*-**m**-*a* Lud. b (Nama *om*-**m**-*a*, !Kora t'³*kchom*-**m**-*a* Licht. or *kgom*-*a* Borch., Eastern *kom*-**m**-*a* or *om*-**m**-*a* Thunb.) m. s. o.;

om-**m**-*a* Lud. b (Nama !*om*-**m**-*a* or !*um*-**m**-*a*) m. s. o. "hand;" *TGam*-**m**-*a* (Lud. a) or *Cham*-**m**-*a* (Lud. b) or *gam*-**m**-*a* Ten Rhyne (Nama χ*am*-**m**-*a*, !Kora *cham*-**m**-*a* Licht. or *gam*-**m**-*a* Borch., Eastern *t̕Gam*-**m**-*a* Sparrm. or *Kám*-*a* Thunb.) m. s. o. "lion;"

tam-**m**-*a* Lud. a (!Kora *tam*-**m**-*a* Licht.) m. s. o. "tongue" (Nama *nam*-**s**, Western *tam*-**s**, f. s.);

dom-**m**-*a* Lud. a (Nama *toem*-**m**-*a* Schmelen or *dom*-**m**-*a* Knudsen) m. s. o. "throat;"

k̕aum Lud. b (Nama //*ou*-**p**, !Kora *t̕ᶻkchau*-**b** Licht., Eastern *t̕gau* Sparrm.) m. s. "fish;"

qu̕ein Lud. b or *Qu̕ein* Kolb (Nama *eī*-**p**) m. s. "liver;"

y Lud. b (Nama ≠*ei*-**p**, !Kora *t̕¹kei*-**b** Licht.) m. s. "foot,"

i-**qu**-*a* Lud. a (Nama ≠*ei*-**k**-*a*) m. pl. o. "feet;"

y-**qu**-*a* Lud. b (Nama /*ui*-**k**-*a*) m. pl. o. "stones" (Nama /*ui*-**p**, !Kora *t̕ᶻeu*-**b** Licht., Eastern *Oi*-**p** Thunb. m. s. "stone");

ou-**oqu**-*a* Lud. b (!Kora *t̕ᶻun*-**kō**-*a* Licht., Eastern *t̕nani*-**qu**-*a* Sparrm., Nama /*kunu*-**k**-*a*) m. pl. o.,—or *ou*-**n**-*a* (Lud. a)* c. p. o. "fingers;"

ha-**okw**-*a* Lud. a or *ha*-**oqu**-*a* Lud. b and Leibn. or *ha*-**qu**-*a* Records (!Kora *ha*-**oqu**-*a* Licht., Nama *ha*-**k**-*a*, Eastern *han*-**qu**-*a* Sparrm. or *ha*-**kv**-*a* Thunb.) m. pl. o. "horses" (Nama and !Kora *hā*-**p**. Eastern *haa*-**p** Thunb. m. s.,—Nama and !Kora *hā*-**s**, Eastern *ha*-**ss** Thunb. f. s. = Kafir *i*-*hashi* 5. "horse,"—Nama *ha*-**n** c. pl.);

k̕anni-**qu**-*a* (Lud. b) m. pl. o. "birds" (Nama *ani*-**p** m. s.,—*ani*-**s**, !Kora *zannii*-**s** Wuras, f. s. "bird,"—Nama *ani*-**n** c. pl.);

ham-**qu**-*a* (Lud. a) or *quam*-**qu**-*a* (Lud. b) m. pl. o. "mouths,"—//*am*-*a* Krönl.† (!Kora *t̕ᶻkcham*-**m**-*a* Licht., Eastern *t̕gam*-**m**-*a* Sparrm.) m. s. o. "mouth," (Nama *am*-**s** f. s., *am*-**ti** f. pl.);

quin-**qu**-*a* Lud. b (!Kora *t̕¹geun*-**ko**-*a* Licht.) m. pl. o. "entrails" (Nama /*gūi*-**ti** f. pl. or /*gūi*-**n** c. pl.);

k!o-**s** Leibn. or *ko*-**s** Lud. b (Nama /*kō*-**s** Tind. or /*gō*-**s** Krönl., !Kora *t̕ho*-**s** Licht. or *fhoo*-**s** Wuras, Eastern *t̕go*-**s** Sparrm.) f. s. "girl, daughter;"

kobo-**s** Leibn. (Nama *khobo*-**s**) f. s. "maid-servant;"

quie-**s** Leibn. (Nama *khoi*-**s** or *koi*-**s**, !Kora *kuee*-**s** Wur.) f. s. "woman, wife,"—*k̕qui qui*-**s** Lud. b (Nama /*kui khoi*-**s**) f. s. "one woman;"

traqueo-**sh** Herbert or *drako*-**s** Krönlein† (!Kora *kalakwee*-**s** Borch., Hill Damara *tara*-*khoi*-**s**) f. s. "woman" (Eastern *trakūsi* [?] Sparrm. "young girl);"

---

* This form may, however, be masc. sing. obj., *oun*-*a* = Nama /*kunu*-**b**-*a*.

† Words given to the Revd. G. Krönlein by an old Hottentot man at Genadendal, in November 1864. He died the following day.

goie-**s** Lud. a or *hoo*-**s** Lud. b (Eastern *ǀgoö*-**s** Sparrm. or *Gó*-**s** Thunb.) f. s. "cow" (Nama ǁgö-p m. s. "bull"); *gou*-**die** Lud. a or *hoe*-**die** Lud. b (Nama *gu*-**ti**) f. pl. "sheep" (ǃKora *ku*-**s** W., Nama *gu*-**s**, Eastern *ǀgu*-**s** Sparrm. f. s.,— ǃKora *ǀ'guh*-**b** Licht. or *ku*-**p** Wuras = Nama *gu*-**p** m. s., Eastern *ǀ'gu*-**ku** Sparrm. = Nama *gu*-**ku** m. pl.,—ǃKora *ku*-**n**-*a* Wuras, Eastern *Go*-**n**-*a* Thunb. = Nama *gu*-**n**-*a* c. pl. o.); *chau*-**n**-*a* Lud. b (Nama ǁ*khau*-**n**-*a*) com. pl. obj. "lambs" (Nama ǁ*khau*-**p** m. s., ǁ*khau*-**s** f. s.).

REVIEW OF THE DERIVATIVE SUFFIXES OF THE NOUNS.

558. The fewness of the concord-indicating derivative suffixes of nouns in Hottentot, and the close resemblance which their forms present in the different dialects, enables us to compress a review of the different forms into one page. What little we had to say regarding the etymology, force, and meaning of these suffixes, and their mutual correspondences, has been given in §§ 424, 444, 447, 543—545, 551 & 553, and it would, therefore, be needless to repeat it here. When the study of Hottentot has received that attention which the position of this language merits, this chapter of South African Comparative Grammar promises to be particularly rich in observations on nice distinctions which will be of great importance to general philology.

REVIEW OF THE CONCORD-INDICATING DERIVATIVE SUFFIXES OF HOTTENTOT NOUNS.

Hottentot Derivative Suffixes of Nouns.		NAMA DIALECT.		KORA DIALECT.		CAPE DIALECT.		OLD FORMS.
		Without suffixed -a.	With suffixed -a.	Without -a.	With -a.	Without -a.	With -a.	
MASCULINE. SINGULAR. {	after pure vowels	-p, -b (?-bi)	-b-a	-p, -b	-b-a	-bb, -w (-f)		} -BI
	" nasalization			(-), -p				
	" n	-mi	-m-a	-mi	-m-a	-mi, -me	-m-a	
	" n	-ni	-n-a				-n-a	
	" r	-ri	-r-a					
PLURAL.		-ku (-gu)	-k-a (-g-a)	-ku	-kn-a (-kδ-a)	-ku-a-(gu-a)-	-KU
DUAL.		...	-kha		-ks			-KHA
FEMININE.	SINGULAR.	-s (-si?)	-s-a	-s	-s-a (-ss-a)	-s (-sh)		-S(I)
	PLURAL.	-ti	-te	-tü	-tö (-dö)		-die	-TI
	DUAL.			-s-ra				
COMMON.	SINGULAR.	-i	-o	-n	-n-a			-I
	PLURAL.	-n, -in	-n-a, -in-a				-n-a	-IN
	DUAL.		-ra					-RA

It would, in some ways, have been convenient here, to give a comparison between the concord-indicating signs of gender in Hottentot, and those of the kindred Sex-denoting languages. But, in many of the latter languages, these signs of gender have either wholly or partly disappeared from their position as derivative suffixes, and can now only be recognised in the other forms of concord; and this comparison will, therefore, be more appropriately given at the end of the Second Part.

www.ingramcontent.com/pod-product-compliance
Lightning Source LLC
Chambersburg PA
CBHW032048220426
43664CB00008B/907